NEW WORDS AND THEIR MEANINGS

This edition produced for Parragon Books 1993.

A CIP record for this book is available from the British Library

Designed by Planet X
Typeset by Florencetype Ltd, Kewstoke, Avon
Printed by Cox and Wyman, Reading, Berkshire

NEW WORDS AND THEIR MEANINGS

introduction

Neologisms is a dictionary of nearly 2,700 new words and phrases that have entered the language since 1960.

I have tried within the dictionary to encompass as wide as pertinent a range of vocabulary, the sole proviso being that the word or usage has entered the language in the last thirty years. The bulk of that vocabulary is indeed neologisms (new words), although there is, inevitably, a substantial representation of old words in fresh usages. The basic qualification for inclusion has been that the language in question has entered the mainstream. I have also used British, rather than American English as the benchmark for inclusion. On the whole, as the two languages have moved increasingly close, the differences are marginal at best, but for my purposes it is a word's arrival on this side of the Atlantic that marks it as eligible or otherwise. I have, as far as possible, included citations (though not first uses) for many of the entries.

Of course, one person's mainstream is another's marginalia, but that said, my aim has been to concentrate on the essentials. Thus this is neither a dictionary of jargon nor of slang, although examples of both have been included, earning their place on the basis of having made the leap from specific to general use. Nor have I included the plethora of endlessly generated technical terms. At the same time I have attempted to exclude the vast range of nonce words, one-off coinages that when newly minted seemed apparently bound to enter the general vocabulary, but soon vanished, lost amid the linguistic ephemera. Instead, taking the thirty-year timescale, I have tried as far as possible to concentrate on the prime candidates, those that have lasted the course and achieved, at least for a reasonable period, the patina of regular use.

The isolation of the vocabulary of the thirty-year period is, at best, an inexact science. Like the human affairs it describes, language does not fit itself neatly into chronological limits, stopping dead at the end of one decade, primed for rebirth as the next begins. The lexicographer, having decided to make this essentially arbitrary cut-off point, ought therefore attempt to justify his or her stance. For my purposes it is based on the broadbrush assumption, felt (perhaps erroneously) by many people, that 'the Sixties' spelt out a new era in Western society. And to underpin that new era, the vocabulary went, as they said back then, through some changes. These, I hope, can be seen in the words that are listed below.

There are two basic problems, or areas of potential dispute, involved in compiling this dictionary. They are, one could say, of quantity and quality. Quantity, for my purposes, refers to the words one chooses to include and those which have been excluded; quality, being what falls outside the chronology and what is seen to fit.

To deal first with quantity. The obvious difficulty in setting down this arbitrary cut-off point, this way-station in linguistic development, is that of any dictionary that moves inside the all-embracing generality of such tomes as the *Oxford English Dictionary* or *Webster*, and aims to corral a specific area of speech. What goes in and what does not? Where, in a dictionary of slang, does slang blur into colloquialism, and thus lose its distinct and separate character? In one of jargon, where does the jargon, the 'professional slang' merge into technical terminology, off-limits to all but the expert?

In the simple graphic with which Sir James Murray attempted to depict English vocabulary, he demonstrated the way language spreads out like spokes from a common centre, then dividing into 'literary' and 'colloquial' hemispheres and thence to scientific, technical, slang, dialect and so on. It's also clear that nothing is so easily defined. 'The circle of the English language,' he pointed out, 'has a well-defined centre but no discernible circumference.' In the end, however all-embracing one wants to be, compiling a dictionary means one has to choose a circumference, however arbitrary it may be.

Neologisms is hardly another *OED*, but it deals with vocabulary and as such the compiler still faces the same problem. There are literally thousands of new coinages that I've chosen to ignore. Science, which, *inter alia*, can claim the longest word in the English language (the proper chemical name of 'tryptophan synthetase A protein' – a 1,913 letter enzyme with 267 amino acids) leads the field in such creativity. Its examples are not to be found here. Computing, another linguistic gusher, is similarly productive of new terms. Here I've tried to pick and choose between the vocabulary that is in general use – floppy disk, laptop, windows, workstation – and exclude the more technically arcane terms. Readers who wish to unravel a paragraph such as this – 'The I/O registers pertain predominantly to the XGA's display controller. The memory-mapped registers, however, refer primarily to the graphics co-processor. The XGA's power-on self-test routines set the base addresses for both registers.' – will have to look elsewhere. What I've tried to do, nonetheless, is second-guess the future. Thus there are terms like OOP (Object Orientated Processing) and GUI (Graphic User Interface) which while ostensibly 'difficult', are becoming increasingly well-known as more and more people use the machines.

Second-guessing is dangerous. The way language, long dormant, can suddenly pop up in the midst of the mainstream is unpredictable. Typical is the vocabulary of the Gulf War. While the six-week campaign produced little or no slang (the slang lexicographer Eric Partridge, a connoisseur of the coinages of two world wars, would have had little to chew on here) it thrust into the limelight a number of terms that had hitherto been military-issue only. 'Collateral damage', 'friendly fire', 'KIA' and the rest were all touted in the media as fascinating novelties. The fact is that most , if not all, had been around since the Vietnam War and even earlier. Only General Schwarzkopf's magnificent obfuscation 'scenario-dependent' (as in 'We don't know, but we'll see what happens') seemed truly original.

To return, once again, to computers, the first business machines appeared in the early 1950s and as they developed, they accrued much of the vocabulary that has become commonplace today. But these machines of the pre-personal computer age, that is before 1980, were very much the province of a priesthood, an exclusive brethren whose vocabulary was equally discrete. Not until the personal computer revolution of the 1980s did that vocabulary, and the many accretions that have followed, enter general use – and thus qualify for this dictionary.

This kind of linguistic 'late blooming' brings me to the second area of debate, that of quality, or whether words are chronologically eligible for inclusion here. Usually the choice is simple. Looking through the headwords listed below, a good deal of those I have chosen are, indisputably, neologisms that have emerged since 1960. These can be prosaic – **car coat, bottle bank, invisible earnings** – or somewhat more rarified – **blitter, cabbage patch kid, window of opportunity** – but their first use falls, to the best of my knowledge and that of the authorities I have consulted, within the prescribed period. So much for the simple part.

The debatable areas emerge when one considers that new vocabulary that springs from those topics that, while certainly in existence prior to 1960, are generally accepted as having entered the general public consciousness somewhat after that date. Typical are such concerns as nuclear warfare, 'recreational' drug use, the 'new' (post-Freudian) therapies, the world of personal computing, 'green' issues, and the increasing intrusion of the language of marketing, business and the media into everyday life.

All these are productive of large vocabularies, and while some undoubtedly predate my cut-off point, I would claim that their wider use – however well-known they may have been amongst the relevant specialists, be they drug-takers or nuclear strategists – postdates 1960. There are a number of such terms within the book. Two, **jet-set** and **détente** are good examples of the problem. Their definitions are simple enough, it is their dating that provides the difficulty.

The first jet to carry passengers was the Comet which made its first trip, to Johannesburg, in 1952. Transatlantic flights began soon afterwards, and in 1954 Boeing, with the 707, joined the party. The use of 'jet set' as a hi-tech synonym for what used to be called 'Cafe Society' or the 'smart set' began around 1963, when enough of the well-heeled had chosen to forsake the slower, if more luxurious ocean liners, for the cramped but speedy airways. However, to blur the issue, the term jet set, this time as a synonym for fast-living juvenile delinquents, was used in the USSR *c.*1957 to berate such youngsters, who looked to the West, epitomized by the jetplane, for their inspiration. Thus jet set, technically, predates 1960, but still, I would claim, sits, as far as its popular use goes, well within my period.

Détente, meaning the easing of strained relations within the world of politics, a situation in which rival powers or interests agree to disagree peacefully, dates back at least to 1908 when the current European balance of power was thus defined by *The Times*. But the use of détente in its contemporary sense, as a warmer period within the overriding Cold War, is very much a phenomenon of a specific period: 1971–2, when the US and USSR achieved a degree of amicability (epitomized in the Anti-Ballistic Missile Treaty of 1972) hitherto unknown. Once again, I would claim that détente, in this context and as used by a mass of people outside the diplomatic or political specialists, deserves inclusion here.

On lighter note there is a third example: the Filofax. The trademark Filofax was registered in 1941, and the word thus coined, but it took another forty years or more before the exemplar of what rivals, deprived of the trade name, were forced to call the 'personal organizer', became a vital accessory for the chic businessman or woman. Emblematic of the 1980s, it would seem foolhardy to exclude it.

There is also the question of whether any trend can be seen within the book as a whole. Technology, for example, appears to have entered the language in a way that it had previously not. The pure proliferation of the media, of computers, of the worlds of marketing and business (at least during their heyday in the 'yuppie 1980s') seems to have brought the vocabulary of such once-arcane areas into far greater prominence. Language obviously reflects the times in which one lives, but the insouciance with which non-professionals absorb these terms into their daily lives is surely something new.

Thus, hedging every bet, I offer this open-ended, imprecise (in its extent, but not, I trust, in its definitions), and, like any such compilation, essentially unfinished collection of words culled from the mainstream of our modern language. I hope that it will be of use, of interest, and, writing as one who compiles dictionaries far more from pleasure than from duty, of enjoyment.

Jonathon Green
March 1991

Time was, even in a compilation of new words, that the period between hard and paperback editions would demand few major changes. One would inevitably have missed a few state-of-the-art coinages – a new teenage craze, some new socio-economic acronym, that kind of thing – but the great pillars of the world, and thus the words to describe them, remained reasonably stable. Time was, but it certainly ain't no more. In the scant ten months between writing the above introduction and penning this note, those pillars have indeed been shaken. Notably Gorbachev – and thus **Gorbymania** – has been relegated to the footnotes, most of the jargon that accrued to the superpowers' standoff has become no more than a curiosity. The constraints of publishing prohibit me from making extensive textual corrections. However, Gorby's achievements should be read in the past tense; nuclear jargon should be seen in its historical context, and USSR should now, where appropriate, read CIS.

Jonathon Green
February 1992

ABM *abbrev.* [1972]
Anti-Ballistic Missile: a missile used to shoot down another missile, e.g. the Patriot missiles used against the Scuds during the Gulf War. Thus the **ABM Treaty** (Anti-Ballistic Missile Treaty): signed in 1972 by President Nixon and General Secretary Brezhnev, a treaty which severely limited both sides' deployment of anti-ballistic missiles and as such put a temporary but vital brake on the arms race; it remains the single most concrete achievement of every round of arms talks to date. It may be assumed that with the end of the Cold War this treaty, while important, has become less vital to world peace.

* *'Scientists recalled a similar optimism (which soon proved to be unfounded) about ABM defence in the 1960s, and strategists predicted a serious instability if one superpower appeared to be nearing invulnerability.'* (A. Wilson, *The Disarmer's Handbook*, 1983)
* *'The 1972 ABM Treaty severely limited the number of anti-ballistic missiles allowed each country.'* (R.C. Aldridge, *First Strike!*, 1983)

abort *v.* [1966]
to abandon, to bring to an abrupt halt; originally found in space terminology (e.g. 'abort a mission'), but currently used in a variety of technological situations, especially that of computing where one can 'abort' a ⇨program.

* *'There were capacities to abort the mission on the ground and in the air, by automation and by decision, by the crew and by Mission Control.'* (N. Mailer, *Of a Fire on the Moon*, 1970)

Absurd, theatre of the *n.* [1962]
a form of theatre that concentrates on the absurdity of the human condition, as epitomized by the work of Samuel Beckett, Eugene Ionesco, *et al.*

* *'This does not mean that the . . . more startling manifestations of the Theatre of the Absurd did not provoke hostile demonstrations.'* (M. Esslin, *The Theatre of the Absurd*, 1968)

AC/DC *adv., adj.* [1970]
bisexual, 'swinging both ways'; from the two forms of electrical current, in which the abbreviations stand for 'alternating current' and 'direct current'.

acapulco gold *n.* [1967]
a particularly potent variety of marijuana, allegedly grown in or around the area of Acapulco, Mexico. Like every 'recreational' drug, marijuana and hashish have gained a wide variety of nicknames, e.g.: Lebanese gold, Lebanese red, Afghani, Af, black Pak, Turkish pollen, Mexican green, Durban poison, Congo bush, and Acapulco red.

* *'Cheers go up in the dark. Acapulco Gold! oh shit we're esoteric heads and we know the creamiest of all the marijuana.'* (T. Wolfe, *The Electric Kool-Aid Acid Test*, 1969)

* *'Name your poison! Durban? Gold from Acapulco? Burnt Congo Brown? Red Lebanese suncakes? A touch of tincture?'* (N. Fury, *Agro*, 1971)

access *v., adj.* [1973]
to use, to understand and (for those who 'have access'), to influence; like ⇨interface and ⇨hands-on, access offers a technological edge to an otherwise pedestrian meaning. *also*: the concept of offering time on the state or independent TV networks to minority or special interest groups to promote their own opinions and cases, usually with some professional guidance; thus **access broadcasting**; **access programmes**.

* *'The working party is against "access courses", believing that if blacks were helped to the starting line, once they were in the force they would be seen as second-class citizens, and would struggle to keep up.'* (R. Chesshyre, *The Force*, 1989)

acid *n., adj.* [1966]
a slang term for ⇨LSD; the same term was used in the 1980s to describe ⇨Ecstasy. Other than ⇨acid head and ⇨acid rock, the 1960s used the word mainly as a noun; its use as an adj. in a variety of combinations (see below) came in the 1980s.

* *'The acid was in some orange juice in the refrigerator and you drank a paper cup full of it and you were zonked.'* (T. Wolfe, *The Electric Kool-Aid Acid Test*, 1969)
* *'Guru Josh. He's big, he's bad, he's mad, he's back. Acid noises plus. Get those pyjamas on.'* (*The Independent*, 24 May 1990)

acid head *n.* [1966]
see **head**.

acid house *n., adj.* [1988]
a style of music, with a frequency of 122–135 beats per minute, (plus the attendant clothes, parties, and allied paraphernalia), that blends ⇨house music with the drug ⇨Ecstasy, otherwise known as ⇨acid. Further developments (probably shortlived) included **acid ska** (a mix of West Indian ⇨ska music) and the music that supposedly accompanied the consumption of and was inspired by Ecstasy, the preferred combination of contemporary ⇨skinheads, whose parents liked unadorned ska.

acid house party *n.* [1988]
an illegal party, often held in a large building such as a warehouse, and often outside the big cities, where thousands of young people pay for their entertainment and, allegedly, consume ⇨acid and other illegal drugs. In the way of all such youthful pleasures, the parties caused a good deal of furore among MPs, policemen, tabloid journalists, and kindred upholders of the national morality.

* *'Two teenage girls had provided information that Rastafarians were selling tickets to Saturday night "acid house parties" at which drugs were being traded.'* (R. Chesshyre, *The Force*, 1989)

acid rain *n.* [1975]
rain that contains a high concentration of acidity, which is created by the release into the atmosphere of a variety of pollutants, primarily sulphur and nitrogen oxides. Similar forms of pollution include acid mist and acid precipitation.

* *'It is more realistic to talk of reducing the effects of acid rain than removing it altogether.'* (*Daily Telegraph*, Student Extra, 1989)

acid rock *n.* [1967]
a form of rock music that emerged in the late 1960s, pioneered by the ⇨psychedelic bands of America's West Coast and by the Beatles' album *Sergeant Pepper's Lonely Hearts Club Band.* The songs and music were infused with the ethos and philosophies of psychedelia, and when (as they all too often were) they were bad, the inflated pretensions that came from taking ⇨LSD or 'acid'.

* *'And it was that sound that the Beatles picked up on, after they started taking acid, to do a famous series of acid rock record albums,* Revolver, Rubber Soul, *and* Sergeant Pepper's Lonely Hearts Club Band.' (T. Wolfe, *The Electric Kool-Aid Acid Test,* 1969)

act, get one's – together *phrase* [1976]
also **get one's head together**: to calm down, to take stock; the image is of recovery from a disorientating drug experience.

* *'Looking for a proper place to sit down . . . and get my head together.'* (H.S. Thompson, *Fear and Loathing in Las Vegas,* 1971)
* *'I'm on a really heavy trip right now, you know? Like, I can't get my act together.'* (C. McFadden, *The Serial,* 1976)

actioner *n.* [1968]
industry and critical slang for an action movie, e.g. the Indiana Jones series; the term echoes the pattern of oater (western) or meller (melodrama). Actioners are the eternally popular species of escapist film plotting, containing a mix of thrills, spills, sex and violence.

action replay *n.* [1973]
see **instant replay.**

additive *n.* [1970]
any form of chemical adulterant – whether to enhance the flavour or preserve the commodity – that has been added to a foodstuff. While these additives can be natural, the usual assumption is that they are artificial, and thus assumed to be potentially harmful. The most frequent use of the term is in labelling, where supposedly ⇨green manufacturers cite their products as 'additive-free'.

adult *adj.* [1972]
1. *a euphemism for* pornographic; thus *adult bookstore, adult cinema,* etc.

* *'Buy and exchange the very best in Genuine Adult Videos from the USA and Continent with Galaxy Video Private Members Club.'* (*Cheap Thrills* magazine, August 1990)

2. reasonably sophisticated, by the standards of current television; in the UK this implies those programmes shown after 9pm, the cut-off point at which broadcasters optimistically assume that children are in bed.

advance (man) *n.* [1968]
the preparation in advance of a live audience, or the briefing of radio or TV stations to obtain the maximum vote-catching exposure for a political candidate. Such activities are performed by the 'advance man' whose job includes arranging 'spontaneous' banner-waving demonstrations ready for the cameras, writing 'local' inserts for the candidate's rote speech and generally geeing up the local party activists. Depending on their efforts there can be 'good advance' or 'bad advance'. Such promotions descend from carnival and circus hucksters who would always send someone on ahead of the show to whip up enthusiasm in the next town they were due to play.

The negative side of advance is known as **black advance**: the deliberate disruption of an opponent's campaign by a series of dirty tricks. An inverted version of traditional 'advance' that a candidate sends out ahead of his canvassing to promote his cause: both legal and illegal methods are used to harass and confuse the candidate's supporters and alienate potential voters.

advertorial *n.* [1986]
from **advertisement** + **editorial**: a newspaper feature which appears from its design to be a piece of editorial, but which is in fact a large advertisement, and has been paid for as such.

* *'The videos which accompany them have such flimsy storylines that they are nothing more than advertorials.'* (*The Independent*, 15 October 1990)

advocacy *n., adj.* [1967]
any form of media in which the writing, broadcasting or advertising is geared towards pushing forward a given point of view. Derivatives include **advocacy journalism, advocacy advertising**, etc.

aerobics *n., adj.* [1980]
a fashionable keep-fit exercise regime which depends on increasing oxygen intake in order to stimulate the activity of the heart and lungs.

* *'It all seemed to start off with a group who all seemed to know each other – they went to the same aerobics classes or coffee mornings.'* (*The Independent*, 16 October 1990)

aerobie *n.* (1986)
a plastic ring, the equivalent to a hollow ⇨frisbee, approximately the size of a record album, which can be thrown either over distance or from person to person. Its aerodynamic qualities have made it, according to the Guinness Book of Records, the man-made object thrown furthest, a distance of 1114.5 feet.

Af *n.* [1969]
see **Acapulco gold.**

affinity card *n.* [1989]
a form of credit card that automatically subtracts a tithe of any transaction and donates it to the charity of the user's choice – specified on the card.

affirmative action *n.* [1965]
the hiring of minority/⇨disadvantaged/poor individuals for jobs – or the enrolling of similar groups in college/university courses – that might require higher credentials than those they can offer, on the principle that their poverty, etc., has made it impossible for them to obtain such credentials. The problem for those who criticise such schemes, is that despite their basic worthiness, good intentions cannot replace necessary credentials and it may be that those so employed still cannot perform the job or academic work as required. From the other side, those who benefit have their own criticisms, seeing affirmative action as just a euphemism for the old 'quota systems'.
See also **positive discrimination; tokenism.**

* *'The contractor will take affirmative action to ensure that applicants are employed, and employees treated . . . without regard to their race, creed, colour or national origin.'* (US Government Executive Order 10925, March 1961)

afghan (coat) *n.* [1969]
a fur-lined sheepskin coat (worn with the skin side outside), first imported to the West in the late 1960s by early returnees from the ⇨hippie trail to Afghanistan, and soon registered as a badge of true hippiedom.

* *'His lean body engulfed in an off-white afghan coat.'* (N. Fury, *Agro*, 1971)

Afghani *n.* [1969]
see **Acapulco gold**.

Afro *n.* [1967]
a hairstyle which features extremely bushy hair; the style, which was supposed to reflect natural 'African' hair, rather than the artificially straightened styles of the despised 'Uncle Tom', was particularly popular among liberation-minded blacks in the late 1960s and 1970s and can be seen at its best on a variety of ⇨Black Panthers, rock stars such as Jimi Hendrix, etc. Some whites (e.g. Eric Clapton) also paraded the style.
See also **natural**.

* *'The tension had been too great. Debbie Reynolds was yukking across the stage in a silver Afro wig . . . to the tune of "Sergeant Pepper".'* (H.S. Thompson, *Fear and Loathing in Las Vegas*, 1971)

ageism *n.* [1970]
a bias against the old simply because they are old; emanating from the same spirit, and originating at around the same period as ⇨sexism. Pressure groups against ageism include the Grey Panthers (modelled on the ⇨Black Panthers of the 1960s).
– **ageist**, *adj.*

* *'We let her move in because we wanted to make a statement about ageism in America.'* (C. McFadden, *The Serial*, 1976)

agent orange *n., sometimes caps.* [1970]
also **agent blue/purple/white**: a variety of herbicides, the best known of which is agent orange, containing a deadly toxin, dioxin. Used in South-East Asia (notably Vietnam) by US forces for defoliation purposes, the poison affected not only plant life but, without their knowing it at the time, both the local civilian and the US military personnel. The short-term result was the destruction of much of Vietnam's agriculture; the long-term is still showing up in a mass of infant birth defects, both in Vietnam and in the US.

* *'So US soldiers absorbed Agent Orange through the skin, or in water they drank.'* (G. Emerson, *Winners and Losers*, 1976)

Age of Aquarius *n.* [1967]
an astrological term referring to a new age of peace, freedom, brotherhood and the conquest of space; it neatly coincided with the 1960s, at which point all such phenomena seemed feasible and for which, among the more starry-eyed, it became a synonym.

* *'I mean, who among us is ready to follow Spiro Agnew, torch in hand, into the Aquarian Age?'* (A. Hoffman, *Woodstock Nation*, 1969)

aggro/agro *n.* [1969]
an abbreviation for aggravation, with the implicit assumption of violence; now in more general use, but coined specifically for the ⇨skinhead gangs who emerged in 1969; a more recent version is **agg**, used as a verb or noun.

* *'When Hell's Angels and Skinheads meet there's*

only one outcome: Aggro!' (N. Fury, *Agro*, 1971)

* *'Inside one of the houses the search team has encountered a bit of aggro.'* (A.F.N. Clarke, *Contact*, 1983)

a-go-go *adv.* [1966]
fashionable, exciting, full of energy; the implication is of the frenetic action of a ⇨discotheque, among the earliest of which was the Whiskey A-Go-Go; thus **go-go dancer**: the exhibition dancer at a discotheque.

agony aunt/uncle *n.*
an advisor to the lovelorn or, more usually, sexually perturbed or otherwise unhappy and confused; such 'aunts' and 'uncles' appear in the newspapers and on radio and (less often) television; the term descends directly from the old 'agony columns' or personal columns, published in the daily press, most famously on the (pre-1966) front page of *The Times*, where anguished appeals rubbed shoulders with the more mundane advertisements, and notices of births, marriages, and deaths.

agri- *prefix.* [1976]
an abbreviation of agriculture and hence a prefix used in a variety of combinations to refer to farm-related topics. The best known is ⇨agribusiness, but other compounds include agricorporation, agricrime (the stealing of farm machinery), agripower, agriproletariat, etc.

* *'The deal is one of a series struck by BOCM in its drive to expand its UK agrifeeds operations.'* (*The Independent*, 6 April 1990)

agribusiness *n.* [1976]
those wide-ranging enterprises which produce, process, and distribute farm products, as well as their ancillary suppliers and allied businesses.

-aholic *suffix.*
a number of nonce words have appeared, some more durable than others, based on the pattern of alcoholic (for all that the real suffix is *-ic*); they include bookaholic (1977), golfaholic (1971), hashaholic (1972), and sweetaholic (1977).
See also **chocoholic**; **workaholic**.

AI *abbrev.* [1971]
Artificial Intelligence: the continuing research into creating computers that are less like machines and more like humans in their approach to problems and their solutions. The addition of human-type thought, intuition, speech and similar attributes will theoretically lead to the first real androids, the exemplars of AI in action.
See also **artificial intelligence**.

-Aid *suffix.* [1984]
the original 'Aid' was **Band Aid**, which began as a Christmas record in 1984, recorded by a wide range of stars as a means of raising money for famine relief in Africa; this developed into **Live Aid**, a pair of superstar charity concerts held on the same day – 7 July 1985 – in Wembley Stadium, London and JFK Stadium, Philadelphia. Since then Aid has been tacked onto a variety of similar projects, notably **Sport Aid** (run by sports stars) and (for smaller causes) **Mandarin Aid** and **Sheep Aid**. A similar project, created by British comedians, ran under the name Comic Relief.

* *'At the Live Aid benefit, Madonna shows her*

navel for a good cause.' (Chronicle of America, 1990)

AIDS *abbrev.* [1982]
an acronym for Acquired Immune Deficiency Syndrome: after much debate, this term was coined in July 1982 by researchers at the Centre for Disease Control in Washington, DC. A number of alternatives had been put forward, notably GRID: Gay-Related Immune Deficiency and ACIDS: Acquired Community Immune Deficiency Syndrome, both of which were intended to reflect what was seen as the uniqueness of the problem to the ➪gay community. These were rejected as intravenous drug users, haemophiliacs, and heterosexuals began to be diagnosed with similar symptoms. AIDS, with the grim ironies of 'help' for those who were initially seen as actually helpless, remains a compromise, but has stuck. Certainly HTLV and HIV, more technically accurate acronyms, surface far less often in general use.

* *'Twelve of the fifteen men there are HIV positive, and two have AIDS.'* (*The Independent*, 23 May 1990)

air breather *n.* [1960]
a jet engine that requires an intake of air for the combustion of its fuel.

* *'The final portion of the strategic triad is the air wing – or, as former Defense Secretary Brown called it, "the air breathing leg".'* (R.C. Aldridge, *First Strike!*, 1983)

air burst *n.* [1960]
a nuclear explosion that is detonated sufficiently far above the ground to ensure that none of the fireball actually touches the ground and thus none of the effect of the explosion is dissipated by local geographical factors. It ensures the maximum production and dissemination of radiation in the immediate area of the detonation, and is designed for use against any large-scale concentration – notably large cities or industrial areas.

* *'Low yield air bursts over cities or near forests will tend to produce massive fires.'* (P. Ehrlich, C. Sagan *et al.*, *The Nuclear Winter*, 1984)

airbus *n.* [1960]
a short-range passenger aircraft designed, like the 'bus' its name incorporates, to ferry passengers on regular journeys. The aircraft was built by a consortium of European firms.

* *'When the airline takes delivery of the 19 new European Airbuses it has ordered...'* (*Independent on Sunday*, 17 June 1990)

airhead *n., adj.* [1982]
a fool, an idiot, one whose head contains not brains but empty space.

* *'Redundant city whizz kid Thornton Streeter ... is cushioning downward mobility by letting out rooms to his airhead Sloane friends.'* (*The Independent*, 29 May 1990)

air miss *n.* [1970]
the official description of a narrow escape from collision by two aeroplanes flying excessively close to each other.

airplay *n.* [1973]
the broadcasting of a given record on the radio.
See also **needle time**.

ALCM *abbrev.* [1977]
Air-Launched Cruise Missile: a subsonic air-to-ground ➪cruise missile which is deployed on a variety of US strategic bombers in addition to

nuclear bombs and other missiles. Like all cruise missiles it is highly accurate and delivers its 200 kiloton warhead after a 2500 km flight to within 30m of a target. The Russians also deploy ALCMs, the most accurate and penetrative of which are the AS-4 (Kitchen) and AS-6 (Kingfish).

✱ *'The "high-low flight" scenario for an ALCM begins when the missile is released from the bomber at about 45,000 feet.'* (R.C. Aldridge, *First Strike!*, 1983)

al dente *adj.* [1970]
from Italian 'for the teeth', thus slightly resistant to the bite; originally used only for pasta, but now extended to vegetables.

✱ *'The real perils of 20th century designer living . . . are expresso coffeemaker's wrist and choking from eating al dente vegetables while wearing a brace.'* (*The Independent*, 22 June 1990)

Al Fatah *n.* [1966]
originally the Syrian wing of the Palestine Liberation Organization (*see* **PLO**), it was incorporated into the PLO under its leader Yasir Arafat (*b.* 1929) and came to dominate the organization. The word 'fatah' means 'fight' or 'resistance' in Arabic.

✱ *'From 1967 onwards [the PLO] was dominated by Al Fatah, the Syrian wing associated with Yasir Arafat.'* (A. Palmer, *Dictionary of 20th Century History*, 1981)

ALGOL *abbrev.* [1961]
an acronym for Algorithmic Language: a computer language intended for programming in higher mathematics and complex technology; designed by a committee of European academics and still more popular in Europe than in the US.

✱ *'ALGOL A programming language much loved by some European academics.'* (D. Jarrett, *The Good Computing Book for Beginners*, 1980)

all-in-one *n., adj.* [1960]
a garment such as a ➪body or ➪catsuit which covers the entire body, rather than being composed of a separate top and bottom.

all-nighter *n.* [1967]
anything that lasts all night, usually a party or, more recently, a ➪rock concert or similar event.

all singing, all dancing *phrase.* [1970]
particularly spectacular. Originally a military term, it has been adopted to civilian use, especially in marketing and business where it is often found describing a presentation or promotion.
See also **bells and whistles.**

all systems go *phrase.* [1962]
everything functioning correctly, all in working order; thus ready to proceed; coined in the US and referring to the checking out of a system, for example that of a spacecraft prior to launch, the 'go' can be traced back to the late 19th century when two parties agreeing on a successful deal would say, 'It's a go.'

all-terrain vehicle *n.* [1988]
a cross between a car and a motorbike, featuring four large low-pressure tyres which permit the vehicle to 'bounce' across difficult terrain.
See also **off-road.**

all-time *adj.* [1970]
unrivalled, one of a kind, record-breaking; often found as *all-time high; all-time low, all-time great,* etc.

* *'Capital FM: the all-time great radio station'* (advertisement for Capital Radio, 1991)

alpha test *n.* [1980]
see **alpha version**.

alpha version *n.* [1980]
the earliest usable version of a piece of computer software; thus **alpha test**: the tests that can be carried out on that version; alpha versions, of which there may be many, never leave the software development house and are strictly for internal assessment. The alpha version precedes the more developed ➪beta version, which is often that which is given out to magazine reviewers, professional testers, etc.

* *'Apple finally distributed an alpha version with the System 7.0 development kit.'* (*Byte*, July 1990)

alternative *adj.* [1967]
originally a back-formation from ➪alternative society, alternative was used initially in a number of compounds, all indicating a set of cultural values that ran contrary to the mainstream. Typical among these were ➪alternative medicine, alternative press, ➪alternative therapies (*see also* **New Age**). As the ➪hippie dream faded, alternative by itself came more and more to be used as a pejorative, which other than in compounds, notably ➪alternative comedy, is its primary use today.

* *'The Maginnises, who lived next door and whose kids went to the same alternative nursery school as hers.'* (C. McFadden, *The Serial*, 1976)
* *'Sitting on top of a former garage beside the canal in deepest alternative Camden Town.'* (J. Meades, *Peter Knows What Dick Likes*, 1989)

alternative comedy *n.* [1984]
a style of comedy that developed in the early 1980s, particularly at such venues as London's Comedy Store, and featured such performers as Rik Mayall, Robbie Coltrane, Dawn French and Jennifer Saunders, *et al.* At the time they did indeed offer an alternative to television's tired stereotypes, but increasing fame has gradually rendered them as mainstream as any predecessor.

* *'The "Keith Allen Show" . . . features the erstwhile alternative comedian interviewing famous "personalities".'* (*Private Eye*, 16 March 1990)

alternative medicine *n.* [1967]
any of a variety of medical methods – homoeopathy, Bach flower remedies, acupuncture – which are simply rejected, or at best grudgingly recognized by the medical establishment, but which are seen as viable alternatives by those who are similarly dismissive, in their turn, of the efficacy of mainstream cures. In many cases such methods reject the synthetic drugs prescribed by mainstream doctors, preferring to rely on natural cures.
See also **alternative therapies**.

* *'Who uses alternative medicine?'* (headline in *Independent on Sunday*, 25 March 1990)

alternative society *n.* [1967]
also known as the ➪counter-culture (to the academic) and the ➪underground (to the media), the alternative society was a coverall brand-name for the world the ➪hippies of the

1960s believed they could create. In many ways similar to conventional, ◇straight society, with newspapers, shops, restaurants and small businesses of many types, its enterprises still claimed a set of cultural values that ran contrary to the mainstream.

* *'They will try to crush any part of the alternative society that they cannot buy.'* (M. Farren, *Watch Out Kids*, 1972)

alternative therapy *n.* [1986]
any of a variety of therapies that are based on theories outside mainstream medicine or (Freudian) therapy. Thus the **alternative therapist**: one who practises such therapies.
See also **alternative medicine; new therapy**.

Amnesty International *n.* [1961]
an international organization formed in 1961 to campaign for human rights and to support articles 18 and 19 of the United Nations Universal Declaration of Human Rights, which deal with freedom of thought and conscience and freedom of expression. It was directly inspired by lawyer Peter Benenson, who had been appalled by the seven-year sentences meted out to a group of Portuguese students who were overheard toasting 'Freedom' in a restaurant. A major article, written by Benenson, called 'The Forgotten Prisoners' and published around the world in late May 1961, led to the year-long 'Appeal for Amnesty' and thence to the founding of Amnesty International.

* *'Amnesty International plays a specific role in the international protection of human rights.'* (Amnesty International, *Voices for Freedom*, 1986)

anabolic steroids *n.* [1961]
the bête-noire of modern sporting competition, anabolic steroids, which are used in medicine to accelerate the healing of wounds, are consumed by a variety of sportsmen and women (and racehorses and greyhounds) to increase their strength and stamina. Steroids, a term coined in 1936, is a generic term for a group of compounds which include the sterols, bile acids, heart poisons, saponids and sex hormones. Their use can lead to profound changes in growth; 'anabolic' (from Greek meaning 'throwing up') means that this growth process is accentuated.

* *'Larkey McBuffum was a crooked Chicago pharmacist who had been selling steroid pills to junior high school football players.'* (C. Hiaasen, *Skin Tight*, 1989)

anchor *n.* [1960]
an abbreviation of the slightly earlier 'anchorman': the compere (or commere) of a television programme, especially a news show. Such 'anchors' have graduated from simply reading the news, to becoming celebrities in their own right – as seen in the Gulf Crisis where such US anchors as Dan Rather or Ted Koppell appeared to be offering their own diplomatic interventions, rather than simply reporting on events.

* *'Anchorman Desmond Lynam – so smooth that it has been suggested that he wouldn't be ruffled by a mid-Grandstand announcement of nuclear war.'* (*Independent on Sunday*, 3 June 1990)

angel *n.* [1976]
used in the tabloid press as a synonym for 'nurse' and derived from the eponymous BBC television soap opera of the 1970s.

angel dust *n.* [1970]
a slang nickname for phencyclidine or ➪PCP. An animal tranquillizer (allegedly designed for pigs, thus earning its alternative nickname of 'hog') which gained some popularity among recreational drug users in the early 1970s; like marijuana it is consumed by mixing the drug – in powder form – with tobacco, and smoking the resulting cigarette.

* *'All the fine ladies are making a fuss/But I can't pay attention 'cos I'm on that dust.'* (Beastie Boys, 'No Sleep Till Brooklyn', 1985)

animal rights *n., adj.* [1978]
the concept of animals, as well as humans, having 'civil rights', and thus deserving fair treatment on both ethical and moral grounds; thus **animal rights protest/protestor**: a campaign or one who campaigns (with increasing violence of a sort that is more usually associated with guerrilla warfare) for such rights.

* *'Francis Kelly . . . was conditionally discharged . . . after admitting stealing 32 rabbits from a farm at Lymm, Cheshire, as part of an animal rights protest.'* (*The Independent*, 24 May 1990)

anorexia (nervosa) *n.* [1963]
a condition, most usually found in weight-conscious teenage girls, of serious emaciation, which is thought to be brought on by the denial of appetite due to some form of emotional disturbance. The term was coined as early as 1650, when it was usually written 'anorexy', and has been found in medical literature ever since, but its more general use has emerged only over the last thirty years.

* *'When Karen began to waste away from anorexia, they would whittle away the dolls with kitchen knives.'* (*Sunday Correspondent*, 17 June 1990)

anti-psychiatry *n.* [1967]
a movement in therapeutic practice, pioneered in the 1960s by R.D. Laing, David Cooper and other analysts, which rejects traditional concepts of psychiatry – especially such treatments as ECT, leucotomy, major tranquillizers and any form of authoritarian psychiatry – in favour of the properly self-directed resolution of personality disorders. Psychiatrists and mental hospitals were seen as socially repressive and ostensible 'madness' quite possibly as a healthy response to a sick world.

* *'[David] Cooper had already experimented with an "anti-psychiatry unit" at Shenley Mental Hospital.'* (R. Hewison, *Too Much*, 1986)

Anton Piller application *n.* [1976]
a legal application, e.g. for a search warrant for documents, of which the defendants are not notified, since the judge believes that were they to know of the application, they would tamper with the evidence in question. The name comes from the case of Anton Piller (a German firm) *v.* Manufacturing Processes and others. Piller wished to bring a copyright action against their London agents, for which they required certain documents; since they believed that it would be in the defendants' interests for those documents to vanish, their counsel was able to persuade the judge to make a secret order for a search.

* *'The requirement in an Anton Piller order that the defendant "forthwith" permit the plaintiff's representatives to enter the premises to be searched.'* (*The Independent*, 28 January 1991)

AOR *abbrev.* [1980]
an acronym for Adult Orientated Rock/Album Orientated Rock: music aimed at those who were teenagers in the 1960s and who are now assumed to have adopted 'mature' lifestyles, although still true to the idols of their youth. Such music lacks the gut appeal of rock 'n' roll, retaining only the banality of its lyrics.

✱ *'AOR is formulated to make any sort of comprehension on the part of the listener unnecessary by softening the subconscious.'* (T. Hibbert, *Rockspeak*, 1983)

APEX *abbrev.* [1971]
an acronym for Advance Purchase Excursion: cheap fares available for holiday-makers who purchase their tickets in advance; APEX fares cover holidays that are of a declared length, usually 22–45 days. Thus **backdated APEX**: cheap tickets issued on the APEX scheme but sold illegally through ⇨bucket shops and demanding neither any form of mandatory advance booking period nor minimum stay requirement.

✱ *'APEX tickets are not open; the scheme is designed for holiday-makers who are only interested in travelling between one or two places at set times.'* (*The Flier's Handbook*, 1978)

appearance money *n.* [1980]
a thinly disguised bribe – usually dignified by the euphemism 'fee' – that is paid to star athletes in the form of 'expenses money', but really to ensure their appearance at a given venue and thus bring in the paying customers to a stadium.
See also **boot money**.

APR *abbrev.* [1979]
annual percentage rate: the rate at which interest is assessed over a twelve-month period.

✱ *'Always find out the true rate of interest – the annual percentage rate (APR) – and what your monthly repayment will be.'* (*The Independent*, 31 March 1990)

Aqua Libra *n.* [1988]
a form of non-alcoholic soft drink, imbued with a variety of herbs, which was merchandised successfully to the health-conscious in the late 1980s.

architecture *n.* [1980]
the internal design of a computer, describing the way in which its components are sited and linked together, in the same way as are those of buildings. The architecture is a concept lying behind the construction of the machine, and does not refer to the actual chips, boards, wiring, etc.

✱ *'In computers, an architecture describes what a machine will look like to the people who are going to write software for it.'* (T. Kidder, *The Soul of a New Machine*, 1981)

arc light *n.* [1968]
a bomb strike delivered by a B-52 bomber; the flash and explosion of the massive bomb payload gives the bright light that earned this nickname.

✱ *'We can see an arc light reflect off the clouds, then hear the sound.'* (D. Bodey, *F.N.G.*, 1985)

Argy *n.* [1982]
a slang diminutive coined by the *Sun* newspaper to describe the Argentinians during the Falklands War of April–June 1982.

* *'Are you feeling shirty with the enemy? Want to give those damn Argies a lot of bargy? Course you do!'* (*Sun*, 30 April 1981)

Arica *n.* [1973]
a ⇨new therapy designed to raise one's consciousness and 'transform your ability to experience living' through an 'electric' set of mind/body training techniques. The name comes from a city in N Chile where the system was first used in the late 1960s by Oscar Ichazo.

* *'The dozens of consciousness crazes – EST, TM, Arica, Scientology, transpersonal psychology, yoga – that gave the Me Decade much of its zest.'* (J. Stevens, *Storming Heaven*, 1988)

aromatherapy *n.* [1973]
originally 'aromatotherapy': a ⇨new therapy which depends on the treatment of the skin with a variety of oils, essences, and similar substances extracted from natural products.

arrogance of power *phrase.* [1966]
a term coined in a lecture by Sen. J. William Fulbright in 1966, one of a series which criticized the involvement of the US abroad, particularly in Vietnam and the Dominican Republic. Fulbright's theory was that the US needed such involvements only to make sure that the world remembered just how powerful a nation it was, and how necessary it was to foist the American way of life on the world, wanted or not, rather than in pursuit of genuine support for the Third World peoples in question.

* *'For a lack of a clear and precise understanding of exactly what these motives are, I refer to them as the "arrogance of power" – as a psychological need that nations seem to have . . . to prove that they are bigger, better, or stronger than other nations.'* (Sen. J. William Fulbright, 1966)

art house *n., adj.* [1960]
a cinema that is dedicated to classic films, cult specialities and other pictures that have remained outside the mainstream Hollywood tradition. The snappier US term has replaced the British 'specialized hall'.

* *'The project was merely a remake of Peter Brook's 1963 art house black and white version.'* (*Independent on Sunday*, 24 June 1990)

artificial intelligence *n.* [1971]
the re-creation by machine technology of human intelligence; AI, as it is abbreviated, is the current goal of many computer programmers, although other than ⇨expert systems (which are created not by machine but by humans) and chess programs (which as compilations of possible moves rather than truly intuitive, spontaneous decision-making can still be outwitted by a talented grand-master) it has yet even to approach anything but a consuming fantasy. Machines can be made ever more powerful, but they remain humanity's creation, and do not think for themselves.

* *'An Artificial Intelligence program, which seeks to extend existing knowledge.'* (*PC World*, April 1990)

art rock *n.* [1972]
for its consumers, a variety of rock music which forsakes the essential simplicities of rock 'n' roll for the incorporation of traditional or classical music, employing orchestras, jazz orchestration, etc; for its detractors,

heavyweight, pretentious music far from the spirit of rock 'n' roll.

* *'They . . . started mixing all the musics stored in their well-educated little beans . . . and before we knew it we had art-rock.'* (L. Bangs, *Psychotic Reactions and Carburetor Dung*, 1988)

ASCII *abbrev.* [1963]
an acronym for American Standard Code for Information Interchange: a standard character encoding scheme that was introduced in 1963 and is now used on many machines; files written in ASCII can be read by most editing (word processing) programs, and are thus ideal for transferring data between different programs or users working on different machines.

* *'ASCII American Standard Code for Information Interchange. This was established by ANSI in 1963.'* (D. Jarrett, *The Good Computing Book for Beginners*, 1980)

ASEAN *abbrev.* [1967]
an acronym for the Association of South East Asian Nations, an association of non-communist SE Asian states founded in August 1967 after the signing of the Bangkok Declaration; members include Malaysia, Indonesia, the Philippines, Singapore, and Thailand.

* *'In foreign affairs, Malaysia joined ASEAN in 1967 and originally . . . adopted a pro-Western, anti-communist posture.'* (J.D. & I. Darbyshire, *Political Systems of the World*, 1989)

aspirational *n., adj.* [1988]
used as a noun as a synonym for a self-help manual – a book that gives advice on the best way in which to achieve one's aspirations. Used as an adjective when reflecting or symbolizing a lifestyle to which someone aspires.

assertiveness training *n.* [1975]
the training of otherwise submissive individuals to be confident, even aggressive in their social and professional life.
See also **Arica, est, new therapy, rolfing**

* *'Gestalt therapists, rolfers, assertiveness trainers, transactional analysts, all stress the particular, the idiosyncratic nature of what they have to offer.'* (A.W. Clare & S. Thompson, *Let's Talk About Me*, 1981)

asset stripping *n.* [1972]
the process whereby a financier buys up a company or companies with the intention not of expanding or improving them, but simply of selling off such profitable assets as they still possess, dismissing their employees, and keeping the money thus gained either for investment in unconnected enterprises, or possibly for buying further companies for further asset stripping.

* *'Mr Richardson strenuously denies that this is their intention: "We are not colonial asset strippers".'* (*Independent on Sunday*, 8 April 1990)
* *'The company's interests in property, asset stripping and the loans sector.'* (T. Blacker, *Fixx*, 1989)

assured destruction *n.* [1966]
the philosophy of nuclear deterrence that assures one's enemy that whatever aggression he attempts, you will be able to inflict ➪unacceptable damage upon his forces, and, more importantly, his human population. In essence a form of nuclear blackmail that, for all the fine-tuning of superpower foreign poli-

cies, ensured that the Cold War remained 'cold' from 1945–89.

* *'The deterrent policy has been dubbed MAD, an appropriate acronym which stands for "mutual assured destruction".'* (R.C. Aldridge, *First Strike!*, 1983)

astroturf *n.* [1966]
an artificial surface used primarily for sports fields, especially in US football stadia; from the Houston Astrodome, where the surface was first used.

* *'"What's the difference between grass and Astroturf?"* Joe Namath *"I don't know. I never smoked Astroturf."'* (J.Green & D. Atyeo, *The Book of Sports Quotes*, 1978)

A team *n.* [1980]
a picked team of highly trained and resourceful people, created to tackle a specific problem; 'A teams' were originally devised in Vietnam, where they represented a select group of soldiers, deputed for particular missions.

* *'Why this little history lesson? Because the "A team" was the brainchild of John Wakeham, then the government Chief Whip.'* (*The Independent*, 23 May 1990)

-athon/-ethon *suffix*
all uses of the suffixes -athon or -ethon, come from the Marathon, a race first run in the Olympic games of 1896; its length – 26 miles, 385 yards (which was standardized in 1924) – commemorates the battle of Marathon of 490BC, when the Athenian Pheidippedes ran from Athens to Sparta, a distance of around 23 miles, to alert Spartan aid for the struggle against the invading Persians. Thus the story as recorded by Herodotus, although the race was based on a corruption of this legend: that the run was from Marathon to Athens, bringing news of Persia's defeat. Since then the suffix has denoted any prolonged or extended activity, usually involving a good deal of endurance; examples include *bikeathon* (cycling, 1973), *jigathon* (country dancing, 1978) and *workathon* (intense work, 1977).
See also **telethon**.

ATM *abbrev.* [1988]
automated teller machine: an unmanned terminal, usually activated by a magnetically coded card, which can be used to dispense cash, take instructions on fund transfers, summarize information on the state of an account, etc.

attrit *abbrev.* [1960]
attrition: as used in a military sense to mean death or simply the wearing down of a hostile force; deaths on the nuclear battlefield are measured in 'attrits per second'.
See also **degrade**.

* *'The goal is the "attrit" of his military powers down to half of what it was before the bombardment.'* (*Independent on Sunday*, 10 February 1991)

auntie *n.* [1963]
a nickname for the BBC that dates back to the Reithian era, but has gained far wider use today as used affectionately, if slightly derogatorily, by the commercial network (IBA) towards the state medium.

* *'BBC1: Ben Elton: The Man from Auntie.'* (*Independent on Sunday*, 28 October 1990)

au pair girl *n.* [1964]
from the French 'on equality': a young girl

who is employed as a child-minder/nanny in a foreign country and uses her spare time to learn that country's language. As opposed to the traditional nanny, who was, in theory, a servant, the au pair is meant to be treated as one of the family with whom she lives.

✱ *'The moral forces of the Nanny, as so much else about her, are in disarray. The au pair girl bears little or no resemblance to her.'* (J. Gathorne-Hardy, *The Rise and Fall of the British Nanny*, 1972)

auteur (theory) *n.* [1960]
from the French 'author': a film term beloved of writers in the journal *Cahiers du Cinéma* who preached that the great directors were in fact 'authors' who transformed any scripts they were given into vehicles for their own preoccupations and creative genius. An acceptable theory in moderation, it led too often to the canonization of the third-rate and the arrogant dismissal of any other contemporary talents who might have contributed to the films under discussion.

✱ *'. . . seeing the case as emblematic of the way French auteur cinema was being stifled by mass commercialization.'* (*The Independent*, 30 October 1990)

automatic *adj.*
referring specifically to any make of washing powder deemed by its manufacturers to be ideally suitable for use in automatic washing machines.
See also **biological**.

AWACS *abbrev.* [1979]
an acronym for Airborne Warning And Control System: an aircraft-carried early warning system; by working high over the earth AWACS, operating from converted Boeing 707s, has a far greater range than a static ground-based radar. AWACS replaced the earlier EC-121 radar surveillance planes as from January 1979.

✱ *'AWACS are not armed in the sense that they do not have rockets hanging from their wings or guns fore and aft.'* (C. Lee, *The Final Decade*, 1981)

-aware *suffix.* [1983]
a popular suffix that has moved from describing the 'soft' human world, into that of 'hard' technology. Usually referring to computer systems, programs, etc.
See also **compatible**.

axe *n.* [1969]
a guitar; like much contemporary slang, 'axe' comes from black origins – the jazz players of the 1950s, for whom it meant any instrument; for the rock musicians of the 1960s and beyond, it generally refers to a guitar.

It can also be used, by those who appreciate the musical use, to describe any 'instrument' – e.g. a journalist's typewriter – as an air pilot might call the cockpit his 'office'.

✱ *'I lugged my axe – Smith-Corona, Mr Advertiser! – into the dressing room and set it in a corner.'* (L. Bangs, *Psychotic Reactions and Carburetor Dung*, 1988)

ayatollah *n.* [1979]
from the Arabic 'sign of God': a religious leader of the Shi'ite sect of Islam in Iran; there are around 1200 ayatollahs, who in turn command around 180,000 mullahs. The term was coined in 1963, but came to Western ears after the return to Iran of the Ayatollah Ruhollah Khomeini, religious inspiration

of the revolution against the Shah.

* *'The most effective challenge came from the exiled religious leader, Ayatollah Khomeini, who carried on his campaign from France.'* (J.D. & I. Darbyshire, *Political Systems of the World,* 1989)

Azania *n.* [1976]

the name given to South Africa by African nationalists; it is assumed that were they to gain power, this name would replace the old, 'colonial' one. Azania was an Iron Age civilization, that flourished in what is now South Africa.

* *'The Azanian People's Organization (AZAPO), a militant, socialist party which advocates the exclusion of all whites from any political role in the future "Azania", the name they propose to give to South Africa.'* (P. Brogan, *World Conflicts,* 1989)

B1-B bomber *n.* [1976]
see **stealth.**

✱ *'They say the B1-B has 90 percent the penetration capability of stealth and therefore stealth is not needed so soon.'* (R.C. Aldridge, *First Strike!*, 1983)

Ba'ath *n.* [1963]
the Ba'ath party was founded in 1955, promoting a mixture of socialism and Arab nationalism. The word means 'Arab renaissance'. Its leading exponents today are the regimes that govern Syria and Iraq (although they profess somewhat different versions), and it was the coup in Iraq of February 1963, when the Ba'athist Colonels Arif and al-Bakr overthrew President Kassem, that introduced the term to a non-specialist Western audience. The rise of Saddam Hussein and the Gulf War extended its use even further.

✱ *'In 1963 a government was formed mainly from members of the Arab Socialist Renaissance (Ba'ath) Party, but three years later it was removed in another coup by the army.'* (J.D. & I. Darbyshire, *Political Systems of the World*, 1989)

baby-batterer/battering *n.* [1972]
one who physically abuses a baby or small child, or the act of physical child abuse. The phenomenon is obviously all too old, but the popular term to describe it was not coined until 1972. This in turn was a colloquial version of 'battered child syndrome' or 'battered baby syndrome', which has been used by social workers and similar professions since 1970.

baby boom *n.* [1967]
see **baby boomer.**

baby boomer *n.* [1974]
an adult member of that generation of babies who were born in the aftermath of the Second World War. The original 'baby boom' occurred after the Second World War when the returning soldiers and their wives plunged eagerly into procreation. No-one, however, used the term in the Forties, but it did appear once these babies had come of age in the 1960s. In the 1970s, when that now grown-up generation started making its impact on society, its members found themselves categorized as 'baby-boomers', at least in the US. By extension there is **baby bust** (1972), logically a period of lower-than-average birth rate.

✱ *'This could isolate the company from a generation of baby boomers.'* (*Independent on Sunday*, 8 April 1990)

Babylon *n.* [1969]
white society, especially in its racist aspects, as seen by blacks in general, and (originally) Rastafarians in particular. The word, with its biblical overtones, reflects the religious basis of Rastafarianism.

✱ *'He prowled the streets with Bogart and the boys, went to blues dances where highly amplified black-American music dominated, faced down other gangs, fled the clutches of Babylon, and rode with John Wayne . . . out of places with names like Fort Apache.*' (M. Thelwell, *The Harder They Come*, 1980)

back burner, on the *phrase.* [1973]
awaiting attention, in reserve; the image is of taking a saucepan of food off a fast-burning gas ring and moving it onto a slower one, where it can simmer until required. It can, in context, also mean simply to relegate to the second-rate.

* '*The hostages have been put on the back burner by the American government. . .*' (*Sunday Correspondent*, 10 June 1990)

backchannel *n.* [1975]
secret lines of communication within a government, or between two ostensibly rival governments; such communications – particularly useful as a balance to the formality of summits, arms talks, etc. – can often facilitate political decision-making, especially where the public image of a government means that such otherwise sensible moves cannot be considered; from the CIA's network of clandestine cable channels that run in parallel to the normal traffic between US embassies and Washington.

* '*Moss had handled the so-called backchannel discussions with the Panamanians. Many credited him with having saved the treaty.*' (D. Rieff, *Going to Miami*, 1987)

backhander *n.* [1960]
a tip or payoff; the implication is of a secretive, underhand arrangement.

back up *v., adj.* [1982]
used in computing to describe the process of copying one's data in order to ensure some form of insurance against the corruption of the primary storage system. – **backup**, *adj.*

* '*Datasave ABA/2 5.12, a backup/restore utility for IBM PCs . . . backs up your hard disk onto floppy disks.*' (*Byte*, July 1990)

bad *adj.* [1967]
in a classic slang formation, reversing the meaning of a mainstream word, 'bad' means good, even the very best. It originates in the black jazz world of the 1950s, and moved into white vocabulary *c.* 1970. Pop singer Michael Jackson's hit album 'Bad' gave it a new boost, and introduced it to a younger, prepubescent generation.

* '*Huey P Newton, Minister of the Black Panther Party, the baddest motherfucker ever to set foot in history.*' (B. Seale, *Seize the Time*, 1968)

bag *n.* [1968]
the situation, way of life; an all-purpose ⇨hippie term, with much in common with the equally indefinable ⇨number.

* '*You and I have to get clear, you know? Right up front. I mean you are into this incredibly destructive bag.*' (C. McFadden, *The Serial*, 1976)

baggies *n.* [1965]
baggy shorts, as worn by California's surfers.

bag lady *n.* (1972)
originally a 'shopping bag lady', the term refers to the female tramps who wander the streets burdened down by their vast collections of brimming shopping bags, the contents of which are often taken out, picked over and sorted, but which have little relevance to anyone but the owner.

* *'The shopping bag lady known to locals as Owl (and to the rookie cop patrolling the station as, simply, "one of your cleaner types").'* (A.K. Shulman, *On The Stroll*, 1981)

bagman *n.* [1976]
1. the intermediary in any form of political payoff or corruption – the person who actually carries the bag of money from A to B. Directly taken from criminal use, but always carrying the implication that one user of the 'bag' is an allegedly 'honest' politician, policeman, etc.
2. the officer who continually accompanies the US President and who is charged with carrying the ➪football which holds the nuclear ➪go codes.

Baker day *n.* [1988]
a colloquialism for the regular training days instituted in British schools, which took over teachers' time and paradoxically gave their pupils a day off; named for the then Minister of Education, Kenneth Baker, whose educational reforms had caused this extensive, time-consuming on-the-job retraining.

* *'Days allotted to training – Baker days – we thought would simply formalise the time we already spent in school in the holidays doing preparation and planning.'* (*The Independent*)

balance of terror *phrase.* [1965]
the international stalemate which is based on the ability of both superpowers to wreak nuclear havoc on the other; it was hoped that this has become somewhat less terrifying with the rundown of the Cold War. Probably coined by Canadian PM Lester Pearson in 1955, on the tenth anniversary of the UN Charter, in saying: 'The balance of terror has replaced the balance of power.' The phrase entered more general use during the 1960s when smaller nations began to join the nuclear family.

Balearic *adj.* [1988]
a type of dance music, similar to ➪acid house, but slightly slower, rating at 115–130 beats per minute rather than acid house's 122–135. The music comes from Ibiza and Formentera, which in the 1960s were much haunted by holidaying ➪hippies, keen to escape the package tours of the Costa del Sol, but now the playground of a different clientele.

ball park (figure) *n.* [1962]
an approximate number, an estimated amount; the term comes from baseball, which is played in the 'ball park', thus an estimate of the crowd at the day's game. Often found as 'in that ball park'.

bandit country *n.* [1971]
that area of Northern Ireland that runs next to the border with Eire and as such provides an excellent bolthole for the 'bandits' of the IRA.

* *'Bandit country, the media have called it, and it's not a bad label. The law, as such, does not apply here.'* (A.F.N. Clarke, *Contact*, 1983)

Bangladesh *n.* [1971]
founded as an independent nation in 1971, Bangladesh was formerly East Pakistan.
– **Bangladeshi**, *adj.*

* *'The establishment of a Bangladesh ("Bengal nation") government in exile, in Calcutta.'* (J.D. & I. Darbyshire, *Political Systems of the World*, 1989)

bankable *adj.* [1964]
referring to the financial aspect of 'star quality', the ability of a performer, or possibly a director or cameraman, to guarantee that any film with which he/she is involved will make large profits for its backers; by extension, an individual whose name will help the producer of a film gain the necessary investment for making it.

✱ *'Knowing that her bankability will ensure production, Jackson has exhibited an attractive habit of taking parts in projects in which she believes.'* (*The Independent*, 31 March 1990)

Barbour (jacket) *n.* [1975]
the proprietary name for a type of waterproof oilskin jacket, worn originally by ➪Sloane Rangers for country use only, but gradually adopted by urban ➪yuppies as a badge of their upward mobility.

✱ *'The Barbour. The country jacket for shooting, etc. though of course it does appear in London. The Barbour appeal is its green oily pre-synthetic look.'* (A. Barr & P. York, *The Official Sloane Ranger Handbook*, 1982)

bar code *n.* [1973]
a code of parallel lines of discrete thickness printed on paper and readable by a computer using a scanner. Bar codes have become increasingly popular in stores where they have replaced the traditional price tag; the information they contain is used for stock control and can be tagged and automatically registered on the cash register.
See also **EPOS**.

✱ *'Bar code readers designed for fast, reliable, cost effective data entry. Looks just like keyboard data! Chose from stainless steel wand or laser interface.'* (advertisement for Seagull Scientific Systems, *Byte*, July 1990)

bargaining chip *n.* [1972]
any form of leverage, of concession or compromise, that one might use during negotiations. The term is derived from gambling chips, of which the more one has, the stronger is one's ostensible position, and it is the 1970s successor in international relations to 'trade-offs'. Bargaining chips gained real international currency during the ➪SALT I arms limitations talks of 1969–72 and are generally seen to imply the niceties of nuclear weapons talks. Such 'chips' have taken on increasingly complex forms and while they often refer to actual pieces of hardware – I'll withdraw my rockets if you withdraw your tanks – they can often, as in the case of the ➪Star Wars defensive system (still essentially in its research stage), be based on theoretical advantages alone. Such advantages, realised only on paper, can still be used to extort sacrifices from an opponent, without actually making any material sacrifice – only that of a potential threat – oneself.

✱ *'He reiterated his position that nuclear weapons could not be used as international bargaining chips.'* (R.W. Howe, *Weapons*, 1980)

bargaining counter *n.* [1972]
see **bargaining chip**.

bash *n.* [1989]
an improvised shelter in which one can live; typically the 'homes' created in Britain's ➪Cardboard Cities.

BASIC *abbrev.* [1966]
an acronym for Beginners' All-Purpose Symbolic Instruction Code: simple, albeit somewhat lengthy and inelegant (to programmers) computer language for learners. The usual

starting language for those using microprocessors; thus **tiny BASIC**: a special form of BASIC geared specifically to microcomputers.

✱ *'This book teaches us Elementary and Intermediate BASIC, up to but not including Random and Sequential file handling.'* (D. Lien, *Learning IBM Basic*, 1982)

basket *n.* [1973]
from the French *corbeille*: a group of interrelated issues, especially when such issues are to be discussed in an international conference, such as at Helsinki in 1977; the term is often used in combination with currency as in 'a basket of currencies'.

basket case *n.* [1967]
a nervous wreck, and by extension, an insane person or, most recently, anything or anyone that is failing to function properly. The term was coined in 1919 and originally referred only to physical disabilities – especially as suffered by First World War quadriplegics – but its modern slangy use almost invariably refers to mental, and not physical inadequacy, whether of an individual or of a malfunctioning organization.

✱ *'It was never a near basket case. Its morale and labour relations were never falling through the floor like Jaguar or British Steel.'* (*The Independent*, 21 April 1990)

baton round *n.* [1971]
the official nomenclature for plastic bullets used in riot control.

✱ *'Another white card on the use of PVC baton rounds, and yet another on how M79 grenade launchers can be used.'* (A.F.N. Clarke, *Contact*, 1983)

BCBG *abbrev.* [1975]
an acronym for bon chic, bon genre: the French version of the UK/US ➪yuppie.

beanbag (chair) *n.* [1972]
a chair made of a large bag (often of leather or plastic) filled with small pellets – usually of polystyrene rather than actual beans; such chairs became very popular in ➪hippie homes, where the only other furnishings were probably a few posters, a stereo, and the records to play on it.

✱ *'His rooms were neat but sparsely furnished, with an old couch, a beanbag-type chair, and a bookcase.'* (T. Kidder, *The Soul of a New Machine*, 1981)

bear *n.* [1960]
the general NATO definition of the Soviets and anything pertaining to them, specifically the NATO description of all Russian bomber planes. The term comes from the traditional identification of the Russian state, since at least the 18th century, with a bear.

✱ *'Exit the tanks, but not the Bear. Eastern Europe is in desperate need of a new security order. It is up to the West to provide it with one.'* (*The Independent*, 5 February 1991)

beat box *n.* [1985]
1. an electronic drum machine, central to the creation of ➪hip-hop music.

✱ *'The human beat box is ready and willing.'* (Fat Boys, 'Fat Boys', 1986)

2. another term for ➪ghetto blaster.

Beatle boot *n.* [1962]
see **Chelsea boot**.

Beatlemania *n.* [1963]
the hysterical response (much of it initially engineered by the band's management and record company) that greeted the rise to fame of the Beatles. The term was coined by the *Daily Mirror* who greeted one eruption of fan madness with the headline: 'Beatlemania!'

* *'It was a slightly scaled-down version of the Beatlemania of past days.'* (R. DiLello, *The Longest Cocktail Party*, 1971)

Beaujolais nouveau *n.*
the latest vintage of Beaujolais, which is given only 4–5 days of fermenting and released for sale on the third Wednesday in November. The race to bring the first case of Beaujolais nouveau back to England became for a while an obsession with rugby clubs, subalterns, youthful City gentlemen and the like.

* *'Beaujolais de l'année: The Beaujolais of the latest vintage, until the next. Beaujolais Primeur (or Nouveau): The same made in a hurry.'* (H. Johnson, *Pocket Wine Book*, 1987)

beautiful people, the *n.* [1966]
the chic, the fashionable, the elite of the 1960s youth scene; used especially of the ⇨new aristocracy – the models, photographers and slumming young nobility of 'Swinging London'. Given the prevailing use of drugs, there was an implication of inner, as well as purely surface beauty.

* *'How does it feel to be/One of the beautiful people?'* (The Beatles, 'Baby You're a Rich Man', 1967)

beauty *n.* [1977]
in physics a property of a subatomic particle known as a bottom quark.
See also **charm**, **quark**.

bedhop *v.* [1965]
to sleep around, to lead a sexually promiscuous life.

* *'Never in my less than sheltered career . . . have I ever encountered bedhopping on the scale it took place at Melton Hall.'* (T. Blacker, *Fixx*, 1989)

beehive hairstyle *n.* [1960]
a woman's hairstyle in which the hair is piled up on the head in the shape of a conical beehive. Especially beloved of rocker girls, New York Italian close-harmony groups, and Country and Western chanteuses.

bell bottoms *n.* [1967]
exaggeratedly flared trousers, similar to those worn by sailors, with wide hems. Also used as an adjective, when it drops the final 's'. Bell bottoms were a fashion must in the late 1960s, and reached absurd widths (similar to the Oxford bags of the 1920s) by the early 1970s. They were revived, alongside ⇨tie-dyed T-shirts and other ⇨hippie styles, by the hip young people who touted the Manchester style of 1988–90.

* *'Pam Stacy, 16 years old, a cute girl here in La Jolla, California, with a pair of orange bell-bottom hip-huggers on.'* (T. Wolfe, *The Mid-Atlantic Man*, 1968)

bells and whistles *phrase.* [1985]
in marketing the special features that a given product possesses: it is these features that are most heavily advertised and their existence, or otherwise, is what is expected to influence a customer in making a particular purchase. The phrase is particularly popular in the world of computing, whether referring to a sophisticated piece of hardware, or a program

that hopes to satisfy every potential user.

See also **all singing, all dancing**.

* *'Analysis paralysis – "what happens when you study excessively"; bells and whistles – "hyperbole to sell a system"; horseholder – unhyphenated, "executive assistant".'* (*International Herald Tribune*, 21 May 1990)

belonger *n.* [1986]
one of the system of Values and Lifestyles evolved by advertising agency Young and Rubicam, to define the groups into which society falls; VALs replaced the old system of ABC1C2DE. The belonger is a large, stable, middle-class group, the bedrock of 'normal' society, with conservative, conventional views and attitudes, low on political activism and high on backing the status quo and obtaining material comforts. Other VALs include the survivors – the lowest group; the sustainers – those who are neither well-off nor actually impoverished; the emulators – those who are making their way up the social ladder by aping those whom they would like to be; and the achievers – those who have succeeded.

bends *n.*
see **rapture of the deep**.

benign neglect *n.* [1970]
the deliberate disregard of a problematical issue in the hope that it will go away, or at least right itself unaided. Coined in 1970 by US senator Daniel Patrick Moynihan when he remarked of the civil rights movement that, 'The time may have come when the issue of race could benefit from a period of "benign neglect".' This dismissive response to a major issue attracted a great deal of hostility (and Moynihan always claimed that he had no intention of minimizing the importance of the movement), but it coined a phrase that has stuck.

* *'Benign neglect: a suggestion to allow tension to ease, interpreted as a plot to abandon the civil rights movement.'* (W. Safire, *Safire's Political Dictionary*, 1978)

Bennism *n.* [1975]
any policy that follows the (perceived) hard-left Socialist principles espoused by Tony Benn, MP. At the time of its coinage, Mr Benn had recently emerged from his role as Labour's Minister of Technology – and thus a darling of the pro-progress media – to become a popular bugbear, whose position was seen as well to the left of Stalin. This vilification only ceased when he was defeated in the Labour deputy leadership contest of 1981, since when he has been portrayed as the epitome of the ⇨loony left. – **Bennery** *n.*, – **Bennite** *adj.*

* *'Hence the decision to diminish, it is hoped, the ogre of Bennery without sacking Mr Benn.'* (*Daily Telegraph*, 7 May 1975)
* *'From now on its advance was impaired by the deepening split between the "hard" or Bennite, and the "soft" or Footite, Left.'* (P. Jenkins, *Mrs Thatcher's Revolution*, 1987)

benny *n.* [1981]
in British Army use: an inhabitant of the Falkland Islands; a derogatory reference derived from an intellectually deficient rural character in the TV serial 'Crossroads'.

* *'The islanders presumably latched on to it as a riposte to the derogatory "benny", used of them by the soldiers.'* (J. Ayto (ed.), *The Longman Register of New Words*, 1990)

Bermuda Triangle *n.* [1964]
an area of the North Atlantic, near Bermuda, in which an allegedly disproportionate number of boats and aircraft have disappeared in mysterious circumstances. A number of variously far-fetched theories exist to explain the phenomenon – the bulk of which involve some form of extra-terrestrial interference. Most can be found in Charles Berlitz' best-seller *The Bermuda Triangle* (1974).

best and the brightest, the *phrase.* [1972]
the term comes from David Halberstam's book *The Best and the Brightest* (1972) and originally referred to the American statesmen and soldiers who were recruited first by President Kennedy and then by President Johnson to underpin US involvement in the Vietnam War. Given the fate of many of those individuals, and that of the War itself, the phrase is tinged with not inconsiderable irony.

- *'The Kennedy intellectuals had been praised as the best and the brightest men of a generation and yet they were the architects of a war which I . . . thought the worst tragedy to befall this country since the Civil War.'* (D. Halberstam, *The Best and the Brightest,* 1972)
- *'A sprinkling of the best and the brightest were there – MPs, businessmen, the odd jumped-up journalist.'* (T. Blacker, *Fixx,* 1989)

beta-blocker *n.* [1966]
a drug that prevents the absorption of adrenalin into the heart and blood by blocking the relevant cells' beta receptors. Used medically to stop sudden heart-attacks, beta-blockers have become very popular (albeit outlawed) among sportsmen whose occupation demands intense concentration, notably snooker players.

betamax *n., adj.* [1982]
one of the two rival formats used for ⇨video-recorders; designed by Sony and generally believed to be better than its opposite number ⇨VHS, it is particularly popular in the US.

beta test *n.* [1980]
the completely developed test version of a piece of computer hard- or software, which is given out for their assessment to magazine reviewers, professional testers, etc.
See also **alpha test.**

- *'While the Mac version was being developed I received a great deal of help and advice from a small group of beta testers who were never slow with constructive criticism.'* (*Ace,* December 1990)

beta version *n.* [1980]
see **beta test.**

Bhangra *n.* [1987]
originally the traditional music of the Punjab, but in its modern evocation, as recreated during the 1980s by the young immigrant community in England, the music has been mixed with contemporary rock and dancehall styles and played with a variety of electronic instruments to create a new fusion.

- *'Bhangra is the staple diet of Asian youth, and this exhilarating music provides the central axis of Choranji's show.'* (*Sunday Correspondent,* 4 November 1990)

Biafra *n.* [1967]
a region of Nigeria that seceded from the parent nation in 1967, thus occasioning a three-year war before the stronger federal forces overcame its resistance and reunited the country. – **Biafran** *adj.*

✱ *'The civil war (in which the British sent supplies to the federal forces while the French supported Biafra) dragged on for another twenty months.'* (A. Palmer, *Dictionary of 20th Century History*, 1989)

Big Bang *n.* [1987]
the deregulation of the Stock Exchange on 27 October 1986, whereby stockbrokers could now make markets in shares as well as deal for their clients. Formerly such functions were restricted to separate organizations.

✱ *'In the aftermath of Big Bang, the group was slow to see the need to integrate some of its domestic and international operations.'* (*Independent on Sunday*, 3 June 1990)

big bang theory *n.* [1966]
a theory of the creation of the Universe which posits the massive explosion of a single compact mass of extremely hot matter (in the trillions of degrees), from which spring all the subsequent elements. This explosion occurred around 20 billion years ago and the Universe has been expanding ever since. The big bang, with its concept of infinite expansion from the same origin, is opposed to the earlier steady-state theory, which claims that rather than coming from a single source, the Universe is filled with material that is constantly being replaced.

✱ *'As with so many other concepts, it would be more accurate to speak of the big bang theories, since there are variations on the basic model.'* (D. Kirby, *Dictionary of Contemporary Thought*, 1984)

big C *n.* [1977]
a nickname for cancer, popularized by John Wayne, a victim.

big enchilada *n.* [1973]
the most important person, the boss; presumably a development of the older 'big cheese'. The usage dates from the Watergate era, when H.R. 'Bob' Haldeman used the phrase to describe Attorney-General John Mitchell.

✱ 'Haldeman: *"He is as high up as they've got."* Ehrlichman: *"He's the Big Enchilada".*' (*The Presidential Transcripts*, 1974)

Bigfoot *n.* [1972]
the Sasquatch, a legendary creature, shaggy, humanoid, and with the requisite big feet, that supposedly inhabits the forests of North America's Pacific North-West. Like the yeti of the Himalayas, the Sasquatch exists largely in travellers' tales.

big science *n.* [1961]
scientific research that requires massive capital investment but which should yield concomitantly 'big' results.

biker *n.* [1970]
a motorcycle rider, specifically a member of an outlaw gang such as the Hell's Angels.

✱ *'I played it gleefully and often for a year or so until it was ripped off by some bikers.'* (L. Bangs, *Psychotic Reactions and Carburetor Dung*, 1988)

bikini line *n.*
the limit of pubic hair, thus ensuring that nothing can be seen protruding around the edges of one's bikini. Thus **bikini wax**: the removal of excess pubic hair to ensure a good bikini line.

✱ *'Sex, bikini waxes, pasta recipes and men – it's only Girl Talk'* (C. Blake, *Girl Talk*, 1990)

bimbo *n.* [1988]
a young girl, usually something of a gold-digger and indulged as such by rich and/or powerful older men and the media to whom they tell or sell their tales. The earliest use of bimbo is found *c.* 1900 in America, where it was synonymous with 'bozo' to mean a tough guy. A parallel use was that to mean 'baby', abbreviated from the Italian *bambino.* By the 1920s the word meant young woman, often a prostitute. The current use stems from the revelations of a 'model', Fiona Wright, of her relationship with Sir Ralph Halpern, a millionaire businessman. Bimbos may also be masculine, and as such are synonymous with the slightly older ➪toyboy.

✱ *'Instead of a topless bimbo, Class War's page three usually has a photo of a "hospitalised copper".'* (*The Independent,* 26 June 1990)

bin *v.* [1987]
to discard, to throw away – to throw in the waste-paper bin; the term extends to the military, where it means to discard a weapons system from the inventories after it has been tried in battle and found inadequate.

bio- *prefix.* [1970]
this prefix entered wide use through the current fashion for all things ➪green and environmentally conscious; combinations include *biohazardous* (anything that presents a hazard either to the environment at large or to human beings); *biomotor* (a computer-driven device that mimics the working of the human musculature); *biotech* (abbreviation for biotechnology); and *biopreneur* (anyone who merchandises the environmental movement for profit).
See also **eco-**.

biodegradable *adj.* [1963]
used of matter that will break down naturally through the action of biological agents, especially bacteria.

biofeedback (training) *n.* [1971]
the use of electronic monitoring and measuring equipment, such as a portable electroencephalograph, to teach people to exert conscious control over otherwise unnoticed bodily functions, including heartbeat, blood pressure, stomach acidity, mental and physical tension, etc.

biological *adj.*
referring specifically to any make of washing powder deemed by its manufacturers to be ideally suitable in using its biological properties to eradicate stains. Such powders have their drawbacks – they produce allergies in certain individuals.
See also **automatic**.

biological clock *n.* [1965]
an interior mechanism that regulates the various cyclic and rhythmic activities of an organism; usually used with reference to humans.

bionic *adj.* [1976]
consisting of a blend of electronic and mechanical elements and natural human body structure; the technological upgrade thus created supposedly augments the usual human abilities. Originally coined in 1960 to describe a mechanical or electronic system that could be made to resemble or reproduce the functions of living systems, the popular use of the word came with the television series 'The Six Million Dollar Man' featuring one 'Steve Austin', much of whose body had been

replaced by high-tech robotics. Bionic entered general use as meaning 'extremely strong'.

* '"*No flesh, no bones, everything's turned to ashes except for your boobs. They're bionic. Eternal*"'(C. Hiassen, *Skin Tight*, 1989)

biorhythm *n.* [1964]

a method of analysing and predicting personal performance on the basis of three body/brain cycles: the 23-day physical cycle, the 28-day emotional cycle and the 33-day intellectual cycle. By charting these cycles one can predict highs, lows, peaks, and valleys and plan one's life accordingly for maximum efficiency and benefit.

* '*When the biorhythms were at their lowest ebb, just before dawn, they showed "Dangerous Liaisons".*' (*Independent on Sunday*, 27 May 1990)

Bircher *n.* [1960]

a member of the John Birch Society, America's leading anti-Communist, far right political group. John Birch was a USAF officer killed by Chinese Communists in 1945 and instantly canonized by America's far right as 'the first casualty of the Cold War'. According to the John Birch Society, which was founded in 1958 by a retired sweet manufacturer Robert Welch Jr, Birch's death was deliberately hushed up by left-wing elements in the US government.

* '*Bircher: a member or supporter of the John Birch Society, best known . . . of the ultra-conservative, militantly anti-Communist splinter groups.*' (W. Safire, *Safire's Political Dictionary*, 1978)

black *adj.* [1967]

a popular label of racial identity, it was taken up in the 1960s as a badge of verbal self-awareness by a community that had for the previous sixty-odd years both been called and called itself Negro. It was used in a number of slogans – notably **Black Is Beautiful** – and as the description of certain political and social standpoints – **Black consciousness, Black power**. Its adoption (at first by activists and gradually by the larger community) demoted 'Negro', once an acceptable euphemism for the nakedly racist 'nigger', to the status of a term that would only be accepted by the derided 'Uncle Tom' figure, who was unwilling to recognize the strength of his or her identity, and still happy to kow-tow to white society.

* '*When we say blackness, we mean relating to black culture. These cats, they hang themselves up.*' (B. Seale, *Seize the Time*, 1968)

black box *n.* [1961]

1. *in technological use*: an instrument or component that can be dealt with as a discrete entity, and extended in governmental or business use to define a separate area of knowledge within a larger system which can be dealt with as it is without needing any specialist knowledge of its mechanism or internal structure.

2. *in military use*: modular components (in aircraft, weapons, etc.) that can be moved or changed with speed and simplicity in case of a breakdown.

3. as **black box recorder**: a supposedly indestructible flight data recorder which holds on wire a record of everything that happens on a given journey; most civil airliners have two boxes, one to record the operation of instruments, the other monitoring the cabin crew's conversations both in the plane and with ground controllers. Such boxes are invaluable in reconstructing events immediately prior to a crash. Derived from the RAF slang for any navigational aid.

* *'We break systems down into sub-systems, and sub-systems into electronic entities or black boxes. Then we assign to each of these black boxes an obscure name that has at least five words in its title. Finally . . . we refer to them by an unpronounceable acronym.'* (*New York Times*, 1979)
* *'Black box blues are not just confined to once-competent DIYers.'* (*Sunday Correspondent*, 10 June 1990)

black consciousness *n.* [1967]
a political movement in South Africa that stressed the common heritage of all blacks, irrespective of their tribal affiliations, in the face of the dominant, oppressive, white culture. It was heavily influenced by similar movements in the US.

* *'Another opposition group is the National Forum, organised by survivors of Steve Biko's Black Consciousness movement.'* (P. Brogan, *World Conflicts*, 1989)

black economy *n.* [1979]
the parallel economy of those who perform their normal jobs but outside normal working hours and without admitting to such earnings (usually in cash) for the payment of tax.

black hole *n.* [1970]
a hypothetical 'hole' in space which acts as an all-powerful, ever 'hungry' vortex into which all matter is sucked. Nothing, not even light, has sufficient velocity to escape. A black hole is created when the gravitational force on the surface of a star becomes too great for the interior pressures that otherwise stop it from contracting under that gravitational force, and the star collapses in on itself. This occurs when the star has used up all its energy producing internal nuclear fuels, the absence of which reduce that necessary pressure.

* *'Because light and other forms of energy and matter are permanently trapped inside a black hole by the enormous pull of gravitation, a black hole can be observed only indirectly.'* (*Longman Encyclopaedia*, 1989)

Black Monday *n.* [1987]
the worldwide stock exchange crash of Monday, 19 October 1987 when the Dow Jones Index plunged a record 22.6% and other financial indicators followed suit. All in all it was the worst day since the end of the Second World War.

* *'"We bought the company then a month later, Black Monday, you name it, we lost it. About three million quid went down."'* (*Independent on Sunday*, 21 October 1990)

Black Muslim *n.* [1960]
a member of a black separatist sect, the Nation of Islam, which was founded in 1931 by one Wallace Farad and which from 1934 had been developed and popularized by Elijah Muhammad. The Nation's best-known member was the boxer Cassius Clay who on his conversion in 1964 changed his name to Muhammad Ali.

* *'He remained for four years in Paradise Valley, nurturing a flock of some 8000 souls – the Lost-Found Nation of Islam, later to be disparaged by the press as "Black Muslims".'* (D. Atyeo & F. Dennis, *Muhammad Ali*, 1975)

Black Panthers *n.* [1965]
the militant black organization which emerged in the US in 1965. It took its name from the black panther symbol adopted by the

black civil rights Student Non-Violent Coordinating Committee (SNCC), but took an uncompromisingly militant stand, unlike that of SNCC.

* *'Weatherman stands second only to the Black Panthers in its ability to conjure up the spectre of Revolution within America.'* (H. Jacobs, ed., *Weatherman*, 1970)

Black Power *n.* [1966]
Black Power was developed as a slogan and as a political philosophy by the civil rights campaigner Stokely Carmichael, a leading member of SNCC, and laid out in his eponymous book. The concept embraced all forms of black self-awareness, and the means – whether violent or otherwise – whereby these might be achieved.

* *'The black consciousness which we see as vital to Black Power and to the ending of racism.'* (S. Carmichael & C. Hamilton, *Black Power*, 1967)

black sections *n.* [1987]
the proposed, but as yet unachieved, establishment of a discrete Black caucus in the House of Commons.

* *'A lot of people who say quite happily that they'll vote for black sections, say, are not so good at actually living next door to a black person.'* (J. Green, *Them*, 1990)

Black September *n.* [1972]
a group of Palestinian terrorists formed in summer 1971 and named for the Palestine Liberation Organization's defeat in Jordan in September 1970. As well as Israel, they attacked a variety of Jordanian targets. Their greatest triumph was the murder of 11 Israeli athletes at the Munich Olympics in 1972.

* *'. . . actions usually attributed to George Habash and the PLO's Black September branch.'* (*Independent on Sunday*, 10 June 1990)

blackwash *n.* [1984]
in cricketing use: denotes the outright winning of a test series by the West Indies against England, Australia or New Zealand in which the rival team are unable to score a single victory.

blank generation *n.* [1977]
young people who claimed to have rejected the values, aspirations and other supposed inducements of contemporary society. Modelled, consciously or otherwise, on the 'lost generation' of the 1920s, the term was essentially a synonym for ⇨punk, its theme tune the Sex Pistols' song 'No Future'.

blaxploitation *n., adj.* [1972]
the making of a series of films featuring black stereotypes, albeit as heroes and very macho men, that dominated the production schedules for a period in the early 1970s. The term is derived from ⇨sexploitation – referring to films that emphasize their sexual content. Blaxploitation films included the 'Shaft' series, 'Superfly' and many lesser offerings. In the event, for all the money, sex, and allied vestiges of white liberal guilt/fear/envy, these films made little advance over the era of an earlier black stereotype, the ever-smiling, ever subservient Stepin Fetchit.

* *'This sketch (was) devised and produced by "Black Pack" graduate Keenan Ivory Wynans, director of blaxploitation hit "I'm Gonna Git You Sucka".'* (*The Independent*, 5 September 1990)

bleeper *n.* [1966]
an electronic device that generates telephonic signals; bleepers are carried in all walks of life, notably by doctors, travelling salesmen and other constantly mobile people. They have, to an extent, been replaced by the portable telephone.

bliss out *v.* [1967]
to experience intense bliss or ecstasy; to cause another to have these experiences. The concept originated with the followers of the 1960s' most visible guru, the Maharishi Mahesh Yogi.

blitter *n.* [1986]
a purpose-built chip used in computing to accelerate, and thus improve, the processing of programs that produce animated graphics. The term originated at Xerox PARC (Palo Alto Research Center) as an abbreviation for a technique – then created in ⇨software – known as 'bit block transfer'. In house jargon this became BitBLT, a word that was pronounced 'bitblit' and thence, 'blit'. To use this software was 'to blit'. When the software was incorporated into a chip, that chip became the 'blitter'.

Blitz kids *n.*
see **new romantics**.

blockbusting *n.* [1962]
originally a population shift in the inner city whereby the black population began moving into formerly white areas, causing the whites to flee and turning such areas into increasingly depressed ghettos; in the last decade the process has begun to be reversed, after thirty years of one-way traffic, as young reasonably affluent white bourgeoisie are moving back to ghetto and working-class areas. The first middle-class purchaser in a given street or block is the **blockbuster**.

blocked *adv.* [1962]
intoxicated on drugs, especially amphetamines.

* *'Terry's blocked on pills, tiny blue ones that make you throb like you had a dynamo inside you.'* (N. Fury, *Agro*, 1971)

blotter *n.* [1966]
in drug use: a small square of blotting paper onto which had been dripped a tiny amount of liquid LSD; blotters and sugar lumps (onto which LSD had similarly been dripped) were among the earliest means of taking the drug.

* *'He was rummaging around in the kit-bag. "I think it's about time to chew up a blotter" he said.'* (H.S. Thompson, *Fear and Loathing in Las Vegas*, 1971)

blow *n.* [1970]
a slang term for cocaine.

* *'Lyda called it "crap blow" and John had it more often than not.'* (B. Woodward, *Wired*, 1984)

blow away *v.* [1970]
to devastate, to shock deeply.

* *'Martha's last wedding had just blown Kate away, so she was looking forward to this one too.'* (C. McFadden, *The Serial*, 1976)

blow-dry *v., n.* [1969]
to dry someone's hair while holding the dryer and simultaneously brushing their hair into shape. Blow-drying replaced the old method

of putting curlers into the wet hair and then having the person sit under a dryer.

blow it *v.* [1968]
to fail.

✱ *'There is not much satisfaction in knowing that he blew it for himself, because he took too many others down with him.'* (H.S. Thompson, *Fear and Loathing in Las Vegas,* 1971)

blow job *n.* [1968]
oral stimulation of the penis.

✱ *'If you're going to give forty blow jobs in a night it's no doubt just as well to be blocked.'* (J. Meades, *Peter Knows What Dick Likes,* 1989)

blow out *v.* [1970]
to cancel, to cut off.

blow (your) mind *phrase.* [1966]
originally, to experience the effects of a hallucinogenic drug, and thence more generally to amaze, to alarm, to astound.

✱ *'He blew his mind out in a car/He didn't notice that the lights had changed.'* (The Beatles, 'A Day in the Life', 1967)

bluebeat *n., adj.* [1963]
a type of West Indian dance music, very popular among the ⇨mods of the early 1960s.

✱ *'He would have preferred some reggae, ska or bluebeat, but then they never put anything decent in Juke-boxes.'* (N. Fury, *Agro,* 1971)

blue-rinse set/brigade *n.* [1964]
elderly ladies who have their hair tinted slightly blue, to offset the natural grey; thus ladies who are presumed to share the conservative attitudes inevitably attributed to such a group.

bluey *n.* [1991]
an airmail letter, from the colour of its paper; used by the troops in the Gulf.

blush (wine) *n.* [1987]
a synonym for rosé wine, coined in California as a marketing ploy to shift a surplus of red wine grapes in a market where palates were better attuned to the less demanding flavours of light white wines.

BMX *abbrev.*
bicycle motocross: bicycles built for a variety of stunts; highly popular among the young, BMX bikes preceded ⇨skateboards as a fashionable preteen accessory.

✱ *'Eurosport. 9:00 am BMX. 9:30 Surfer Magazine.'* (*Sunday Correspondent,* Satellite TV listings, 8 April 1990)

boat people *n.* [1977]
Vietnamese refugees, originally political, subsequently often economic, who escaped from Communist Vietnam by sea; these journeys were beset with danger: it was necessary to escape Vietnamese security, then to navigate the inevitably unseaworthy boat, then to avoid the depredations of marauding pirates and, if the natural hazards had been surmounted, to find a country willing to resettle a refugee.

✱ *'The interviews with the Vietnamese, many of them boat people, who often at great peril have made their way to the United States.'* (*New York Review of Books,* 16 August 1990)

bodice-ripper *n.* [1980]
a traditional 'woman's romance', set invariably in a fantasized 18th or 19th century, but enjoying the added sales potential of a salting of sex and violence, possibly even a

rape, whereby once chaste bodices are duly ripped, until, as ever, Mr Right triumphs once again.

* *'Prototype bodice-ripper with 17th-century wild child Lorna (Victoria Hopper, above) falling for her clan's avowed enemy (John Loder).'* (*The Independent*, 30 October 1990)

body *n.* [1986]
a tight form-fitting garment, very similar to a leotard, which is worn by women.

* *'Above: red velour long-sleeved body, also in gunmetal grey or black.'* (*Independent on Sunday*, 21 October 1990)

body armour *n.*
bullet-proof clothing, worn by police and riot squads.

* *'Almost everyone is putting on body armor. It is about half an inch thick and comes with a comforting printed claim by its manufacturer.'* (J. McClure, *Cop World*, 1984)

body bag *n.* [1967]
a specially made zippered rubber container in which battlefield corpses can be stored and transported prior to burial. During the Gulf War the body bag was given a new euphemism: human remains pouch, or HRP. That war also created a psychological phenomenon: the **body bag factor**, which refers to the presumed erosion of public support for a once-popular war when the casualties increase and a regular flow of full body bags begins to come home from the front.

* *'I don't want to know you, because to me you will be just another number when I shovel what's left into a body bag.'* (A.F.N. Clarke, *Contact*, 1983)

body clock *n.* [1970]
an internal bodily mechanism which supposedly regulates one's mental and physical functions and to which are attributed the 'ups' and 'downs' that most people experience during a given time period. The body clock is most noticeable after a lengthy jet flight, when the geographical change outpaces the physical one, and produces ➪jet lag when the 'clock' gets out of synchronization with its physical surroundings.

body-conscious *adj.* [1985]
referring to a fashion style that requires the wearer to have an attractive and above all fit body, honed to perfection by careful exercise and diet.

* *'Space Age. Martine Sitbon's cadets in moulded satin and body-conscious shapes.'* (*Sunday Correspondent*, 25 March 1990)

body count *n.* [1966]
the totalling up, after any level of conventional military engagement, of the numbers of enemy dead. Commanders tend to exaggerate their successes, since a good body count, as in Vietnam, proves to those concerned that one's own side is doing well.
See also **kill ratio**.

* *'The accomplishments of the Phoenix program were subordinated to the military's obsession with high body counts.'* (*New York Review of Books*, 16 August 1990)

body gold *n.* [1975]
see **medallion man**.

body language *n.* [1970]
the way a person demonstrates their feelings through unconscious movements and postures.

✱ *'Something in her body language as she sat in the Eames chair poking her needle in and out, reminded him of Madame Defarge knitting while the tumbrils rolled.'* (C. McFadden, *The Serial*, 1976)

body popping *n.* [1985]
see **break-dance.**

body scanner *n.* [1975]
a machine that produces three-dimensional X-ray pictures – either of the whole body, the brain, or a given area or part – by using Computerized Axial Tomatography (CAT).

body shirt *n.* [1970]
a tight shirt that emphasizes the contours of the (male) body; very popular in the discotheques of the mid-1970s.

bog standard *n., adj.* [1980]
a slang term for average, run of the mill.
See also **vanilla.**

bogusware *n.* [1985]
see **-ware.**

boilerplate *n.* [1965]
in general, a synonym for 'standard', whether of standard legal documents which are used by large institutions for drawing up regularly needed legal papers (especially contracts), or in journalism, when referring to nationally syndicated wire service material that runs unchanged in hundreds of newspapers.
See also **vanilla.**

bomber *n.* [1962]
in drug use. 1. an abbreviation for 'black bomber', a large black capsule containing strong amphetamine.

✱ *'The amphetamine drugs (purple hearts, benzedrine, black bombers, etc)...'* (J. Aitken, *The Young Meteors*, 1967)

✱ *'Keep your voices down and dose him up with those nice brightly coloured bombers.'* (T. Blacker, *Fixx*, 1989)

2. a large cannabis cigarette.

Bond girl *n.* [1962]
any of the pretty young starlets who were recruited by the makers of the 'James Bond' films. These girls, initially no more than extras, became a regular ingredient of all the films, and a role – albeit tiny – as such an adornment added an extra cachet to one's curriculum vitae.

✱ *'Capital City ... is horribly addictive ... because of its lurid comic book characterisations. The bond girls are really just Bond girls, the whiz boys caped crusaders.'* (*The Independent*, 13 October 1990)

bong *n.* [1976]
a pipe used for smoking hashish; the funnel-shaped bong is similar to the West Indian ➪chillum – both give a more intense effect than smoking a regular joint.

bonk *n., v.* [1986]
sexual intercourse, to have sexual intercourse; the most recent graduate of the school of sex as a DIY euphemism – screw, bang, shaft, etc., though before succumbing to the tabloids, bonk meant the feelings of tiredness experienced by competition cyclists.

✱ *'All this bonk on four wheels has spawned an audience of voyeurs who have their own clubs and contact each other through small ads.'*

(J. Meades, *Peter Knows What Dick Likes*, 1989)

* *'The key questions for* Sun *readers are "Is He Bonkers?", "Is She Bonking?"'* (*Sunday Correspondent*, 8 April 1990)

boob tube *n.* [1974]

1. *a disparaging nickname for* television, referring to the 'boobs' who watch it; once abbreviated to 'the tube', however, it seems to have lost its pejorative aspect.

* *'Rad, dudes! Now we can relax an' watch some tube and forget about all the weirdness we just went through.'* (*Teenage Mutant Hero Turtles*, June 1990)
* *'Boob Tube Liberation Front Storms CBS, ABC, PBS & Quaking Independents From Coast To Coast.'* (L. Bangs, *Psychotic Reactions and Carburetor Dung*, 1988)

2. a cylindrical sleeveless garment, often elasticated, worn by women over their breasts or 'boobs'.

boofer box *n.*

see **ghetto blaster**.

book *n.* [1968]

a magazine or newspaper; very popular among media people and those who gain kudos from imitating them; usually found as 'back of the book'/'front of the book' and as such referring to the various sections of the magazine in question: the front tends to hard news, the back to general features and reviews.

boot *v.* [1962]

in computing: to turn on a computer; from bootstrap program, which in turn evolves from 'pulling oneself up by one's own bootstraps': a resident program within the machine's operating system which is activated by turning on the machine; thus **warm boot**: the resetting of the machine without actually turning off the power, but still requiring that application programs, utilities, etc., should be reloaded.

* *'No Warm Boot. My 20-megabyte Seagate hard disk drive won't successfully do a warm reboot anymore.'* (*Byte*, June 1990)
* *'Each virtual machine inherits and can customize the boot DOS session.'* (*Byte*, June 1990)

bootleg *n., v.* [1966]

an illegally recorded record album – sometimes from pirated studio tapes, often from a live concert – which is then sold at a premium price to the fans. Thus 'to bootleg': to make and sell an illegal copy of an album, tapes, or a live concert.

* *'A review for* Rolling Stone *(which never got printed) of a Bob Dylan bootleg.'* (L. Bangs, *Psychotic Reactions and Carburetor Dung*, 1988)

boot money *n.* [1980]

a form of ⊃appearance money that is paid to rugby players for wearing specific pieces of kit, notably their boots. Rugby fans know which boot is made by which maker since the soles – easily visible during play – are often dyed an unmistakable, brand-identifying colour.

born again, to be *v.* [1976]

said of Christians who have been saved, with Christ controlling their lives and Christ's Spirit literally living within them; from John 3:3. – **born-again** *adj.*

* *'"She's also just been born again." Carol dropped her chopsticks. "Martha's gotten religion?"'* (C. McFadden, *The Serial*, 1976)

bossa nova *n.* [1962]
a dance step that enjoyed a brief popularity in the early 1960s; imported from Brazil, where it meant 'new style', it was related to the Samba.

bottle bank *n.* [1971]
a container – often some form of closed, converted skip – into which empty glassware can be placed (often sorted as to colour) ready for recycling.

* *'Sally Kolker is talking about life over the road from a bottle bank, one of the latest hazards for unwitting house buyers.'* (*Independent on Sunday*, 27 May 1990)

bottomless *adj.* [1972]
totally naked, as in *bottomless bar*.
See also **topless**.

bottom line *n.* [1972]
from the Yiddish *di untershte sture*: the end result, the final score. Originally a direct reference to the final tally of figures in a profit and loss account, and popularized by the Jewish employees of New York's garment district, the phrase encompasses both financial and more general usage today. Its increased popularity can doubtless be equated with the money-conscious society of the 1980s.

* *'It would put money on the bottom line, of course. Lots of money. They were going to do it in record time, because the company needed this machine desperately.'* (T. Kidder, *The Soul of a New Machine*, 1981)

boutique *n.*, *adj.* [1987]
small-scale, specialized; the original boutiques (from the Italian *bottega*, meaning small shop) were popularized during the early 1960s by Mary Quant in the King's Road, and such owners as John Stephen and Irving Sellars in Carnaby Street. Used as an adjective the term is by no means restricted to the clothing trade. Implying a specialized business, performing one task very well rather than a number of tasks less efficiently, the modern boutique, as in an advertising agency or bond dealers, may in fact be a discrete organization within a much larger firm.

bovver boys/boots *n.* [1969]
a synonym for ⇨skinheads, who specialized in bovver (the London pronunciation of 'bother'). *Cf.* **aggro**.

* *'He's worried about a gang of boot boys he saw hanging around . . . Bovver is one thing Barney doesn't deal in.'* (N. Fury, *Agro*, 1971)

box *n.* [1983]
in retailing use: refers to a variety of commodities such as televisions, computers, etc. which are regarded by salesmen as no more than boxes bought from the wholesalers and passed on to the consumer.

* *'We won't be selling the software and the add-in board – you have to buy the complete box.'* (*PC World*, April 1990)

bra-burner *n.* [1972]
a feminist, a member of the ⇨Women's Liberation Movement. Among the various canards aimed at the Women's Liberation Movement of the early 1970s was the idea that their main gesture of defiance was to burn their brassieres. The label remains one of the more convenient put-downs, although the actual instances of bra-burning were very rare.

brain death *n.* [1968]
the cessation of all electrical activity in the brain; the trace on an encephalograph will cease to flicker, producing only a flat line. The establishment of brain death is necessary before any organs can be removed from the body for transplantation. – **brain dead** *adj.*

brain drain *n.* [1963]
the loss of highly skilled or qualified people, often academics and usually in the fields of science, technology or medicine, to better-paid jobs; the phrase was coined to categorize such losses from Britain to America and the drain still flows in that direction.

* *'Faced with a cash crisis in universities here, many were lured into the so-called "brain drain" by the promise of plentiful research money across the Atlantic.'* (*Sunday Correspondent*, 22 April 1990)

brand extension (*or* stretching) *n.* [1990]
the use of a famous, best-selling brandname, as a merchandising fillip for non-related products; the customer may not know the new product, but will be attracted by a proven name.

* *'Brand extension, or brand stretching, a practise that allows consumer products companies to capitalise on the popularity of their brandnames by using them to launch new products.'* (*Independent on Sunday*, 8 April 1990)

brat pack *n.* [1984]
the original brat pack were the youthful Hollywood up-and-comers of the mid-1980s; the term is now applicable to any selection of successful young hopefuls – novelists, chefs, black success stories ('black pack'), whatever. Taken presumably from Hollywood's Holmby Hills Rat Pack, a coterie of movie stars and singers led by Humphrey Bogart in the 1950s.

* *'Prix Femina-winning whimsy from a best-selling member of France's brat pack.'* (*Independent on Sunday*, 21 October 1990)

breadhead *n.* [1969]
a ➩hippie term to denote those who cared about money ('bread') rather than revolution or, at least, drugs.

* *'No, Barney's no breadhead. He's strictly street people.'* (N. Fury, *Agro*, 1971)

break-dance (*or* dancing) *n.* [1984]
a form of dancing originated in the black ghettos of America. Highly athletic, it was invariably performed to the complex beat of ➩hip-hop or ➩rap music.

* *'In one corner Indian children proudly showed off their break-dancing and body-popping, unaware that it's six years out of date.'* (*Sunday Correspondent*, 13 May 1990)

breaker *n.* [1963]
1. Citizens Band (➩**CB**) radio code indicating that the speaker wishes to join in or initiate a conversation on the air; from 'break in' meaning interrupt.

* *'They will probably say something like, "Breaker, come on". Then identify yourself.'* (*Complete CB Dictionary*, 1980)

2. used to describe records that are moving up the Top Forty charts, in which context the idea of 'breaking in' is one of breaching defences.

breathalyser *n.* [1960]
from breath + (an)alyser: the breathalyser, 'an American instrument for measuring the

percentage of alcohol in the blood from a breath sample' (*The Times*) was introduced to Britain in 1960, where it was first demonstrated on 18 January. The machine involves the allegedly drunken motorist blowing into a bag which in turn is attached to sensitive crystals, the colour of which alters according to the amount of drink consumed. Measuring by a breathalyser became known as the **breath-test**, a term which is also used as a transitive verb.

bringdown *n., v.* [1967]
a disappointment; also as a transitive verb: to bring (someone) down.

* '*"Some dealers are cooling it." "What a bringdown," sighs Sweetpea.*' (N. Fury, *Agro*, 1971)

British Telecom *n.* [1981]
the public corporation, formerly part of the Post Office, which was set up on 1 October 1981, to provide telecommunications and data-processing services.

* '*The "Code of Practice for Consumers" sets out the standard of service British Telecom aims to give its customers and explains what you should do when things go wrong.*' (*British Telecom Telephone Account*, 1990)

broadbrush *adj.*
rough, within wide limits; often as *broadbrush estimate*; the image is of a housepainter's wide distemper brush which covers a wide area but cannot be used for detailed work.
See also **ball park**.

* '*No. A sketchy broadbrush account should do the trick.*' (T. Blacker, *Fixx*, 1989)

Brompton cocktail *n.* [1978]
a pain-relieving mixture of narcotics, usually based on heroin or morphine, and often supplied in an alcoholic drink (hence 'cocktail') administered to alleviate the pain of those suffering from terminal cancer; derived from the Brompton Chest Hospital, London, where the dose was first created and used.

brother *n.* [1965]
an abbreviation of soul brother and used widely in the black community, especially in a political context.

* '*Early the next morning, 6 April, the brothers and sisters were cooking the food . . . for the rally and barbeque at De Fremery park.*' (B. Seale, *Seize the Time*, 1968)

brownie point *n.* [1972]
merit marks awarded on any assessment of ranking or job evaluation tables; the idea is of a (fictitious) system of awarding points to enthusiastic and well-behaved Brownies, the junior Girl Guides.

* '*Perhaps he was trying to pick up some Brownie points with the local UVF or Tartan gang.*' (A.F.N. Clarke, *Contact*, 1983)

brown sugar *n.* [1974]
a variety of Chinese heroin, known as No. 3; the slang term refers to its colour and consistency.

brushfire wars *n.* [1983]
small wars which, like brushfires, flare up and then die down again quickly. They do not involve the superpowers directly – although the armaments employed will almost certainly have come from one or other of them – but like certain brushfires, they can spread and grow.

brutalism *n.* [1962]
a movement that emphasized the basic ele-

ments of architecture – space, materials and structure – in their most basic, unadorned, unaltered form. The main practitioners were Le Corbusier and Mies van der Rohe, both of whom offered buildings with rough brickwork, open service ducts, exposed floor beams, etc.

BSE *abbrev.* [1989]
see **mad cow disease.**

bubblegum *n., adj.* [1968]
pure pop music aimed straight at the young adolescent and preteen audience; the bubblegum in question is supposedly consumed by such youngsters. Often used as an adjective, either in a musical context, e.g. 'bubblegum band', or simply, as below, denoting the underdeveloped tastes of the audience in question.

* *'Then redo his dome Hitler Youth blond so he resembled a bubblegum Kenneth Anger.'* (L. Bangs, *Psychotic Reactions and Carburetor Dung,* 1988)

bucket shop *n., adj.* [1970]
a cut-rate travel agency. The original use dates back to the 19th century, when a bucket shop was quite simply an illicit betting shop, specializing in stocks and shares, where a sham share broker gambled with his customers on the fluctuations of shares that neither party ever actually possessed. – **bucket-shop** *adj.*

* *'Even travellers on a two-week bucket-shop holiday to the Costa del Sol are beginning to demand a better quality of service.'* (*Independent on Sunday,* 10 June 1990)

buddy *n.* [1983]
a volunteer who acts as a companion and helper to a Person With AIDS.
See **PWA.**

buggy (*or* baby buggy) *n.* [1975]
the pervasive replacement for the traditional pram; pioneered by Mclaren in the mid-1970s, the ubiquitous buggy – a small seat on wheels – has almost ousted the pram. The term originated in the US, where, as well the old stroller it described the old-fashioned perambulator.

* *'A real man – a new man – should be able to . . . say, "I want a Mammas and Pappas buggy combo".'* (*Independent on Sunday,* 24 June 1990)

bulimia *n.* [1963]
an obsessive condition, antithetical to ⇨anorexia, in which the sufferer gorges on large quantities of food, then immediately forces themselves to regurgitate it.

* *'Stranahan had seen some bizarros in his day, but this one took the cake. He looked like Fred Munster with bulimia.'* (C. Hiaasen, *Skin Tight,* 1989)

bulletin board *n.* [1980]
a personal computer, linked to the telephone system by a ⇨modem, that is left open for anyone who knows the number and dials in. The boards, like electronic notice boards, offer a variety of information, from the anodyne to the arcane, from the popular to the illegal.

* *'Computers and bulletin boards have engendered whole new categories of crime, and thus new problems for police agencies.'* (*Sunday Correspondent,* 22 April 1990)

bum bag *n.* [1986]
a small bag that is worn around the waist (and occasionally across the shoulder); originally worn by skiers and windsurfers, and then by a

wide range of tourists, seeking to keep an eye on their cash and passports, the bum bag enjoyed its fashion heyday in more general use *c.* 1989–90.

bummer *n.* [1965]
an unpleasant experience, whether directly drug-related or otherwise; thus the verb **bum out**: to give or have such an experience.

* *'Bummer was the Angels' term for a bad trip on a motorcycle and very quickly it became the hip world's term for a bad trip on LSD.'* (T. Wolfe, *The Electric Kool-Aid Acid Test*, 1969)
* *'All the negative vibes outweigh the good ones and everybody gets constipated and bummed out.'* (L. Bangs, *Psychotic Reactions and Carburetor Dung*, 1988)

bump *v.* [1988]
in airline use: to move a passenger's reservation from one (full) flight to the next one; the simple means of dealing with over-booking.

* *'[Club class] facilities vary, but many include . . . a generous view of excess baggage and a priority position if some passengers have to be "bumped" through over-booking.'* (*The Flier's Handbook*, 1978)

burn *n.* [1968]
the physical pain involved in extending oneself to the full while performing aerobics exercises. Aerobics trainers urge their classes to 'go for the burn', basing their exhortation on the belief that 'there's no gain without pain'.

burn *v.* [1969]
to steal from, especially during a drug deal when one party either runs off with the money without delivering the drugs, or alternatively delivers the drugs, which turn out to be adulterated or completely phoney.
See also **rip off**.

* *'The only bedrock rule is Don't Burn the Locals. Beyond that, nobody cares.'* (H.S. Thompson, *Fear and Loathing in Las Vegas*, 1971)

burn out *v.* [1985]
an occupational ailment of frustrated or exhausted employees; essentially a state of depleted emotions and mental faculties, possibly accompanied by heart attacks, ulcers, high blood pressure, etc. – **burn-out**, *n.*

* *'When you burn out, you lose enthusiasm. I always loved computers. All of a sudden I just didn't care.'* (T. Kidder, *The Soul of a New Machine*, 1981)

bus *n.* [1970]
that stage of a nuclear ➪MIRV missile which contains guidance systems and directional jets and delivers the various 'passengers' (the actual nuclear missiles themselves) onto their targets.

* *'The post-boost vehicle with its dispensing and releasing mechanism (sometimes called the 'bus', because warheads get off along the way).'* (S. Talbott, *Deadly Gambits*, 1984)

busing *n.* [1964]
to take schoolchildren away from their own neighbourhood to attend schools outside that area for the purposes of ensuring a correct racial balance in all the schools. The intention was to combat the drift of white students from the inner cities, and the creation of 'ghetto schools' for those (generally black or Hispanic) pupils who remained. The policy caused a great deal of tension, with resentment voiced on both sides. – **bus**, *v.*

- *'The most controversy-laden code word of the late sixties and early seventies was "busing".'* (W. Safire, *Safire's Political Dictionary*, 1978)

bustier *n.* [1986]
a bodice-like garment worn by women as a top, either without any outer covering or beneath a jacket.

- *'Close encounters of the nicest kind* – Top: *Cacharel's neat grey and white bustier in cool cotton stripes.'* (*Harrods Catalogue*, March 1990)

bute *n.* [1966]
a tradename for phenylbutazone, a painkiller used for racehorses; it does not actually enhance performance, nor does it slow the horse, but by alleviating pain, it is judged to let even injured horses still perform at their best.

butterfly effect *n.* [1987]
a colloquial description for what scientists term 'sensitive dependence on initial conditions': the concept that a tiny cause can have a massive effect, e.g. a butterfly flapping its wings in Japan can, eventually, cause a hurricane over Britain. The idea of the butterfly effect is directly related to the ⇨chaos theory, but is more generally used figuratively.

- *'The butterfly effect – the notion that a butterfly stirring the air today in Peking can transform storm system next month in New York.'* (J. Gleick, *Chaos*, 1987)

buyout *n.* [1980]
from management buyout: a situation where the management of a company (often in financial trouble, or even on the verge of actual liquidation) pool their own economic resources to buy up the firm and start it working again.
See also **LBO**.

- *'What is known in Europe as a management buyout or MBO and in America as a leveraged buyout or LBO.'* (M. Lewis, *Liar's Poker*, 1989)

buzzword *n.* [1970]
a popular jargon word or phrase; buzzwords like 'on-going', 'power', 'parameter', tend to have a short life, but a busy one, and like most of this rather general jargon, give a spurious sophistication to otherwise mundane statements and are thus particularly beloved within the world of business, advertising and similar professions.

- *'Scratch the subject of defence and acronyms, abbreviations, and buzzwords fly out.'* (C. Campbell, *War Facts Now*, 1982)

bypass (surgery) *n.* [1970]
any form of surgery that depends on the creation of a natural or artificial passage or pathway that directs circulation, digestion, etc. away from its normal, malfunctioning or diseased routes.

byte *n.* [1964]
a group of eight consecutive bits which are considered by the computer as a single unit. Multiple bytes are grouped as **kilobytes** (one thousand), **megabytes** (one million), **gigabytes** (one thousand million), and **terabytes** (one million million).

- *'The system will most likely come with 32MB of main memory (expandable up to 256MB); address up to four gigabytes of virtual memory.'* (*Byte*, July 1990)

cabbage patch kid *n.* [1983]
a form of soft-bodied doll which became a massive craze in the US *c.* 1983. Millions were sold, complete with 'adoption papers', but the craze never really extended outside the US.

* *'The dough-faced, chinless, engaging dolls that have become Holy Grail of the the 1983 Christmas shopping season: the Cabbage Patch Kids.'* (*Newsweek*, 12 December 1983)

cable television *n.* [1966]
any system whereby television signals are transmitted to the consumer through coaxial cables rather than to an aerial; cable was originally developed to improve reception where natural features, such as hills and deep valleys, interfered with broadcasting. Today it is seen as an alternative to satellite TV.

* *'With the three networks struggling against cable TV, satellites and home video.'* (*Independent on Sunday*, 10 June 1990)

cache *n.* [1983]
in computing use. a means of speeding up access to the machine's (relatively) slow disk memory: the cache is a buffering system which attempts to work out whatever material the program will need next and to have it extracted from memory (and stored in the cache) ready for instant use.

* *'Like the IP's, the Sys Cache storage consists of expensive memory chips that operate with great speed.'* (T. Kidder, *The Soul of a New Machine*, 1981)

CAD/CAM *abbrev.* [1968]
acronyms for computer aided design/computer aided manufacture: the marriage of computing technology to design and manufacturing processes, especially in the engineering sector.

* *'The new features of RoboCAD, the two-dimensional CAD software package.'* (*Byte*, July, 1990)

Callanetics *n.* [1975]
a proprietar me for an exercise technique, developed b health guru Callan Pinckney, which is designed to improve muscle tone and general fitness. The system gained much favourable publicity when it was revealed that the Duchess of York used it in an attempt to lose weight following the birth of her daughter Beatrice.

camcorder *n.*
from camera + video-recorder: a portable videotape camera with built-in synchronized sound recording; supposedly for the nascent director, but still used mainly for home movies.

* *'If you've ever fancied yourself as Cecil B DeMille, here's the camcorder Cecil B DeMille would have chosen.'* (ad for Panasonic, *Sunday Correspondent*, 10 June 1990)

camp *v., n., adj.* [1965]
1. ostentatious, exaggerated, affected, theatrical; specifically used to describe stereotypical effeminate homosexual behaviour (and as

such dating back to 1909); thus **camp it up**, **camp about**, etc. Its origins remain a mystery.

* *'There's boastful wickedness here, hints of dandyish camp – the double agent adept at using his pristine cuff and well-oiled accent to get away with murder.'* (*Sunday Correspondent*, 22 April 1990)

2. camp came, as it were, out of the closet, in 1964 after Susan Sontag's essay 'Notes on Camp' in the *Partisan Review*. This downplayed the ➪gay element of the word and stressed the aesthetic side: something that is considered clever or amusing not because of its originality or excellence, but because of its banality or (deliberate) lack of sophistication.

* *'The verb "to camp", as soon as it stopped merely meaning to sleep with a lot of soldiers in a field, came to signify the performance of an action not for its intrinsic value to you or anyone else but, rather, to display and to relish your talent in doing it, or, if talent is lacking, your style, or, failing style, your sheer nerve.'* (Quentin Crisp, *How To Go To The Movies*, 1990)

can-do *adj.* [1987]
positive, purposive, ambitious.

* *'The engineers at Westborough, who felt of course that they were good, productive, "can-do" engineers, picked up the* Boston Globe.' (T. Kidder, *The Soul of a New Machine*, 1981)

canned laughter *n.* [1962]
a tape of pre-recorded laughter which is dubbed onto television shows, typically situation comedies, to create the impression of a live audience and to prompt the viewers as to what they ought to find amusing.
See also **laugh track**.

canteen culture *n.*
the philosophies and opinions – usually cynical, right-wing and conservative – that permeate the lower ranks of the British police; such philosophies are given their most regular airing and receive their most enthusiastic reception in the station canteen.

* *'The canteen culture . . . is the below-the-stairs attitude to the job and the world which is a far more powerful influence on a police officer's behaviour and beliefs than the official policies devised at the top.'* (R. Chesshyre, *The Force*, 1989)

CAP *abbrev.* [1967]
an acronym for the Common Agricultural Policy: the programme of price supports for a variety of agricultural products administered by the EC; the CAP is widely blamed for the existence of the numerous butter mountains, wine lakes, etc.

capability *n.* [1965]
the possession of a range of armaments and/or strategic potential by a nation or military force.

* *'For the United States to seek a first strike capability seems implausible when initially considered.'* (R.C. Aldridge, *First Strike!*, 1983)

capital transfer tax *n.* [1975]
a tax imposed on the transfer of money or property from one person to another; inheritance is especially vulnerable.

capitalist roader *n.* [1966]
from the Chinese (pinyin) *Ziben zhuyi daolu*, coined during the ➪Cultural Revolution to vilify those who persisted in maintaining Soviet-style policy and practice: a governmental elite,

'private' elements in industry, bonuses for production, etc.

✱ *'When the young Red Guard fighters rose in rebellion against the handful of capitalist roaders within the Party during the current Great Proletarian Cultural Revolution, the reactionary bourgeois forces . . . got hard blows.'* (*Peking Review*, 30 August 1968)

car bomb *n.* [1972]
a bomb placed in a car and detonated remotely or by suicide bombers; such bombs have become essential terrorist weapons. A new twist on car bombing, known as the **human bomb**, developed in 1990 when the IRA began forcing innocent drivers to drive cars already loaded with explosives, towards their targets. The driver, whose family would be held at gunpoint to ensure he carried out the task, had only seconds to escape.

✱ *'Thinking back to the ten o'clock news and the piece of film about a car bomb in the city.'* (A.F.N. Clarke, *Contact*, 1983)

car-boot sale *n.* [1980]
a jumble sale organized not from the traditional stall, but from the boots of cars; such sales developed alongside the vogue for five-door hatchback cars, which were ideally adapted for the purpose.

✱ *'Damn. It's the Lufthansa Apex shuttle from Cologne. We'll have to delay the Tooting car-boot sale fly past.'* (*Private Eye*, 28 September 1990)

car coat *n.* [1963]
a short coat, usually of sheepskin, designed for use in cars. The point of these coats was both to keep the driver warm and, since they were shorter than the traditional overcoat, to keep their folds from becoming entangled with one's feet, the brakes, gear levers, etc.

card, play the – *phrase.* [1973]
from the older 'playing one's trump card', to augment one's position by emphasizing or playing on one single especially emotive issue; given the varying contexts, among the most popular contemporary 'cards' are the **race card**, the **nuclear card**, and the **green card**.

✱ *'The themes of her speech were Tory innovation and socialist . . . profligacy. She also played the race card.'* (*Independent on Sunday*, 13 May 1990)

cardboard city *n.* [1986]
the cardboard box 'homes' that are used as shelter by the homeless; the original cardboard city was situated on London's South Bank, but rising homelessness has meant that the term now applies to any such gathering.

✱ *'But are the inhabitants of Cardboard City now becoming more used to the sight of camera crews than carers?'* (*Independent on Sunday*, 3 June 1990)

carer *n.* [1987]
anyone who takes care of someone else, whether an orphaned or battered child, an invalid or whoever.
See also **caring professions**.

✱ *'Suzanne has been living with her foster carer since she was born.'* (*The Independent*, 31 March 1990)

caring *adj.* [1975]
a synonym for sensitive, often found combined as in the ➪caring professions.
See also **loving**.

✱ *'Seifert . . . is now perpetrating a new "caring",*

"sensitive", "fitting-in" sort of excrescence.' (J. Meades, *Peter Knows What Dick Likes*, 1989)

* *'The controversy over the redevelopment of Wimbledon town centre (Greycoat versus Speyhawk, or Caring Architects versus Greedy Planners).'* (N. Williams, *The Wimbledon Poisoner*, 1990)

caring professions *n.* [1975]
those professions that have arisen as ancillaries of the welfare state, and particularly of the National Health Service, intended to 'care' for those whom, it is felt, cannot help themselves. Critics of such professions believe either (from the right) that they are merely mollycoddling those who should be able to look after themselves, or (from the left) that for all the earnest ideology and undeniably sincere efforts that the whole concept is little advanced on the traditionally patronizing middle-class 'do-gooders' who help 'the poor' only in an attempt to regiment their individuality.

car phone *n.* [1980]
a mobile telephone operated from one's car; once a luxury of the wealthy, the car phone has become a necessary status symbol for the upwardly mobile.

car sticker *n.* [1967]
stickers, often professing some form of jocular message, which can be attached to the bumpers or windows of cars.

* *'I had to go and browse earnestly through the . . . car stickers ("Baby on Board", "Mother-in-law in Boot").'* (*Independent on Sunday*, 24 June 1990)

cash cow *n.* [1960]
any business that generates a continuous flow of cash; shares that create a similarly dependable income are also cash cows.

cashless society *n.* [1972]
a society in which all cash transactions, whether in shops, banks, booking agencies, or wherever, are administered by computers or other electronic technology.

cassette *n.* [1960]
a small cartridge containing magnetic tape; cassettes are usually used to tape record and play back speech or music, to hold pre-recorded music or, on the lower end of the games computer market, to hold computer programs.

* *'Cream's "Wheels of Fire" was on the cassette, but rotating wearily, as the batteries in Marrakesh are from Shanghai, called White Elephant.'* (R. Neville, *Play Power*, 1990)
* *'Cassettes as used with computers are much the same as ordinary audio cassettes.'* (D. Jarrett, *The Good Computing Book for Beginners*, 1980)

casual *n., adj.* [1986]
a youth cult that emerged in Britain in the mid-1980s, its members were distinguished by their taste for expensive designer clothing which was combined with an equally enthusiastic taste for hooligan violence, often exhibited on the terraces of football stadia.

CAT *abbrev.* [1964]
an acronym for clear air turbulence: one of the main hazards of modern passenger air travel, a violent disturbance in air currents, caused by rapid changes of temperature associated with

the jet stream; CAT is experienced as severe updrafts and downdrafts at high altitudes cause aircraft to plunge hundreds of feet at a time.

- *'Suddenly she was scared to death of clear air turbulence. What would happen if they dropped thousands of feet?'* (C. Blake, *Girl Talk*, 1990)

CAT scanner *n.* [1975]
see **body scanner**.

catalytic converter *n.* [1970]
a device fitted to an automobile exhaust which uses a chemical catalyst – typically composed of platinum and indium – to eliminate the pollution otherwise produced by exhaust vapours; several countries plan to make the devices mandatory, but some experts claim that while they reduce hydrocarbons, they may simultaneously increase the gases that attack the ozone layer.

- *'"So you're not having a catalytic converter fitted to your new car?" "No. I've heard they produce malodorous fumes."'* (*The Independent*, 23 October 1990)

catastrophe theory *n.* [1972]
a mathematical system proposed by the French mathematician Rene Thom for describing a discontinuity or phenomenon of sudden change in a continuous process by fitting the attributes of change into a geometric model consisting of dimensional planes that describe the change; a descendant of the 19th century catastrophism, which suggested that certain geological and biological phenomena were caused by catastrophes, or sudden and violent disturbances in nature, rather than by continuous uniform processes.

Catch-22 *n., adj.* [1961]
a phrase and concept that comes from Joseph Heller's eponymous book, published in 1961, a satire based on his own experiences as a bombardier in the USAF during the Second World War. The basis of Catch-22 is the viciously anomalous law that governs the rights of bomber crews to escape the seemingly endless extension of their tour of duty, flying missions over hostile anti-aircraft emplacements on their way to targets in Italy and beyond. The only way out of a mission was to prove oneself insane; as the definition below points out, merely claiming that continued flying was dangerous and utterly terrifying was quite a rational response. But, since such a response proved one's sanity, it was not one that would keep you grounded.

- *'There was only one catch and that was Catch-22, which specified that a concern for one's own safety in the face of dangers that were real and immediate was the process of a rational mind.'* (J. Heller, *Catch-22*, 1961)
- *'They complain of being in a "Catch-22" situation in which they cannot find work because they are homeless and do not have enough money for accommodation.'* (*The Independent*, 12 September 1990)

catsuit *n.* [1960]
a one-piece garment, usually worn by women, which resembles a tight boiler suit.

CB *abbrev.* [1976]
Citizen's Band radio: a network of personal radio communications used by motorists, especially truck drivers; full of slang and elaborate nicknames CB communications are used to while away the monotony of long journeys as well as to warn fellow travellers of various

hazards, notably the police. CB originated in the US, where it was suited to the vast distances, and spread to the UK in the mid-1970s, where the distances were hardly comparable, but the success of a pop song, C.W. McCall's 'Convoy' pushed hundreds of ➪'breakers' into the CB fold, if only for a while.

✱ *'The United States, a country which has taken CB to its heart since its introduction in 1958.'* (C. Moore, *CB Language in Great Britain*, 1981)

CD *abbrev.* [1980]
➪compact disc: a disk in which sound signals are converted to a stream of binary digits and recorded on an optical disk. The disk is scanned by a laser beam, which exempts it from the wear and tear that a normal acetate LP record suffers from the contact of the stylus. CDs are supposed to produce a finer quality of sound, although there has been a recent backlash against them, with some music buffs claiming that CD sound is actually too perfect and the old albums are still the best.

✱ *'Through a process of osmosis involving many things Japanese (TVs, CDs, cars, hi-fis and so on) . . .'* (*Independent on Sunday*, 10 June 1990)

CD-I(nteractive) *n.* [1988]
➪compact disk – interactive: the next wave of computer gaming, in which players will be able to 'take part' in complex fast-moving stories and adventures that have been programmed onto compact disks.

✱ *'CD-I is "compact disk interactive", and it is based on a Philips design in which the CD drive incorporates a 68000 chip.'* (*Byte*, June 1990)

CD-ROM *abbrev.* [1988]
➪compact disk – ➪read-only memory: a form of compact disk, used in conjunction with a computer rather than an aural stereo system, on which large amounts of information can be stored and accessed, although, like ➪WORM drives, it cannot be altered by the user.

✱ *'The new CD-ROM presentation of Mozart's Magic Flute . . . couples more than 7000 screens of information with 143 minutes of digital music.'* (*Byte*, May 1990)

CD-V *abbrev.* [1988]
➪compact disk – video: the next wave of CD technology, which will offer a compact disk which holds both video and aural data, thus creating a 'home rock video', or reference work which mixes pictures and spoken text, etc.

celebrity *adj., n.* [1985]
as used in *celebrity interviewer, celebrity cook*, etc: any otherwise run-of-the-mill occupation which gains a new degree of importance simply because the person doing it is a 'celebrity'.

✱ *'Nowadays there is not a newspaper that does not feature, flagged on the front page and bannered on its own page, a celebrity interview. The celebrity is not the person who is answering the questions, but the person who is asking them.'* (*The Independent*, 6 October 1990)

cellphone/cell radio *n.* [1986]
a computer-controlled network of portable radio telephones, notably those used in cars.

✱ *'There are a lot of cheap cellphones around. But are you sure that the cellphone you buy will actually do what you want?'* (ad for Nokia-Mobira, *Sunday Correspondent*, 13 May 1990)

centred *adv., adj.* [1975]
a therapeutic term that implies one's awareness of one's own personality and the ability to balance its contrasting demands. Thus the verb **to centre** used both transitively and intransitively.

* *'I mean, all this time I'd thought Bill was centred, and suddenly, wow, it absolutely zapped me, I'd married another MCP.'* (C. McFadden, *The Serial*, 1976)

CEO *abbrev.*
chief executive officer, the senior executive in a firm or organization.

* *'"CEOs [chief executive officers] loved him," says Stephen McGrath, an executive vice president of Warner Lambert Co.'* (*Sunday Correspondent*, 18 March 1990)

CFCs *abbrev.* [1977]
chlorofluorocarbons: any one of a variety of compounds made up of chlorine, carbon, fluorine, and hydrogen, used particularly in refrigerators and aerosols and judged to be harmful to the ozone layer. CFCs have been restricted in a number of countries as part of a greater awareness of such dangers to the Earth's ecology.

* *'CFCs are: (a) Chelsea Football Clubs; (b) Commies for Christ; (c) Ozone damaging chlorofluorocarbons which are used as propellants in . . . aerosols, fridges, . . . and hamburger packaging.'* (*Daily Telegraph*, Student Extra, 1989)

chair *n., v.* [1971]
an abbreviation for chairman, chairwoman or chairperson; a carefully neutral term which simultaneously rules out any complaints of linguistic ⇨sexism, and sidesteps other, more cumbersome formations.

* *'Advice comes under various headings, including "How to be an effective Chair" and "How to enjoy being a Chair".'* (*The Independent*, 25 July 1990)

chairperson *n.* [1971]
the non-⇨sexist alternative to the traditional 'chairman'; coined along with a number of similar neologisms in the early years of feminism.

chalice *n.* [1969]
a pipe used for smoking marijuana or hashish; used originally by Rastafarians (hence the biblical overtones) but quickly spread among the ⇨soft drug consuming public.
See also **bong, chillum.**

challenged *adj.* [1986]
a popular euphemism, originated by social workers but now used widely in the media, for the more pejorative 'crippled'.
See also **disadvantaged.**

champagne socialist *n.* [1970]
a wealthy liberal whose verbal allegiance to ideological purity is belied by his or her lifestyle, in which the privations that beset those with whom they ostentatiously sympathize are notable only by their absence.
– **champagne socialism** *n.*
See also **limousine liberal.**

changes, go through some *phrase.* [1969]
to experience a range of new emotions, usually unpleasant ones; *also* 'put people through changes'.

* *'Oh man, those cats are gonna go through some changes.'* (N. Fury, *Agro*, 1971)

chaos *n.* [1981]
from the Greek *chaos* meaning a gulf or chasm: the irregular and unpredictable behaviour displayed by dynamic systems, and the belief that the basic assumptions of Newtonian physics – that the universe is ordered on a system of mathematically based and thus provable rules – are no longer tenable. To the ancient Greeks chaos was the primeval 'abyss' from which the universe evolved. A state of chaos was a state of confusion, a mixture of parts or elements bereft of any governing system. Modern chaos theory, which sprang from experiments with the computer modelling of weather patterns in the 1950s, deals with the unpredictability of dynamic systems. Based in physics, it touches on many aspects of everyday life: art and economics, biological rhythms, traffic jams, waterfalls, and weather.

* *'A decade later chaos has become a shorthand name for a fast-growing movement that is reshaping the fabric of the scientific establishment.'* (J. Gleick, *Chaos*, 1988)

chapess *n.* [1987]
a facetious term for a woman, used by those who refer to men as 'chaps'.

charge-cap *v.* [1990]
to place a limit, or 'cap' on the amount of poll tax that can be charged by an individual council – such limits are ordered by central government. Charge-capping is the logical replacement for rate-capping, which had the same effect on what were seen by central government as excessive demands for local rates.

* *'Education "will suffer" in charge-capped boroughs.'* (headline in *The Independent*, 5 April 1990)

charisma *n.* [1967]
strong personal appeal, personal 'magnetism' which may have its sexual element, but derives equally from the individual's power and/or abilities; it comes from the Greek word meaning 'the gift of grace' and was a theological term referring specifically to the divine gift of healing. Non-religious usage has developed in the last thirty years, and today's wider use is often synonymous with 'star-quality'.

* *'It must have been a power thing, his charisma, because no-one could have been less attractive.'* (T. Blacker, *Fixx*, 1989)

charlie *n.* [1970]
1. *a slang term for* cocaine; on the same pattern 'henry' means heroin. Similar usages include 'charles' and 'Uncle Charlie'.

* *'Shitnik – that's our word for a beatnik who pushes horse and charlie.'* (J. Aitken, *The Young Meteors*, 1967)

2. *see* **VC**.

charm *n.* [1975]
see **quark**.

chart *v.* [1970]
for a record to enter the Top 40 or similar charts; to do so denotes a certain degree of success.
See also **breaker**.

Charter 77 *n.* [1977]
a petition circulated in 1977 by a number of leading Czechoslovak dissidents, including today's President Vaclav Havel, calling for political and civil rights and full freedom of expression; it cited the Helsinki Final Act of 1975 as the basis for these demands.

* *'In 1977 a number of Czechoslovak intellec-*

tuals issued Charter 77 (Charta 77), a gloss on the progress of the Helsinki Conference (1975).' (J. Green, *Encyclopaedia of Censorship*, 1990)

Charter 88 *n.* [1988]
a petition circulated in the UK by a number of leading liberals – writers, academics, politicians – calling for the establishment of a written constitution, proportional representation, a Freedom of Information Act, and a number of ancillary measures. Consciously echoing Czechoslovakia's ➪Charter 77 the campaign, which has been quietly continuing ever since, has had nothing like the same impact and on the whole has been dismissed as an example of ill thought-out wishful thinking on behalf of the ➪chattering classes.

chase the dragon *phrase.* [1966]
to smoke heroin; the heroin is placed on a piece of kitchen foil, beneath which heat is applied. The heroin liquefies and gives off smoke, this is drawn through a hollow tube (also of kitchen foil) into the mouth. The term is a literal translation of that used in Hong Kong.

chatline *n.* [1983]
the modern version of a party line, a system set up by ➪British Telecom to enable a number of users to carry on a conversation between themselves, each talking on their own telephone. Chatlines are targeted at teenagers, and BT have run into a good deal of complaints, as these youngsters use their parents' phones to run up substantial bills.

chat show *n.* [1970]
any television or radio programme featuring a regular host and revolving cast of guest celebrities, who appear, in most cases, to tout their latest book, film, or other professional attainment; the chat show is by definition entertainment, no hard questions are asked, the conversation is resolutely banal, and everyone – the show and the guests – are allowed to appear to their best advantage.

✱ *'I have heard 'Stop the Week' "admired" as a chat show, and I have heard it derided as a chat show, but both judgements are beside the point as it is not a chat show at all, it is a soap opera.'* (*Independent on Sunday*, 25 March 1990)

chattering classes *n.* [1985]
the opinionated, usually liberal, usually metropolitan middle classes; the main chatterers are employed by the media and are actually paid to express their opinions in print or on screen, but qualifiers are often quite amateur. The implication, much derided by the usually right-wing ➪enterprise culture, that like contemporary lilies of the field, they talk a good deal, but create very little.

✱ *'The absurd idea of a playwright in Number 10. Britain's intellectuals are confined to the "chattering" classes, says Nicholas Faith.'* (headline in *The Independent*, 5 April 1990)

Chelsea boot *n.* [1962]
an elastic-sided boot, on the lines of a cut-down riding boot, which was first worn by members of the 1950s Chelsea set and adopted (and widely popularized) by the Beatles, hence its alternative name of 'Beatle boot'.

✱ *'The Chelsea boot . . . comes in so many permutations this winter (including Jimmy Choo's tangerine and patent versions) that some of them are bound to be comfortable.'* (*Independent on Sunday*, 21 October 1990)

chequebook journalism *n.* [1963]
the payment of large sums of money either to celebrities or, more usually, to individuals – mass murderers, royal girlfriends, etc. – who are currently notorious and newsworthy; such payments are intended to sell newspapers and isolate the recipients from any advances by rival papers.

* *'As the tabloids have hit on hard times, the cheques of chequebook journalism have shrunk.'* (*The Independent*, 5 February 1991)

cherry picker *n.* [1961]
a mobile crane that may be lowered or raised as required.

Chiantishire *n.* [1985]
that part of Tuscany beloved by those of the English middle classes sufficiently well-off to holiday or even purchase homes there; like France's Dordogne, the area has become an English home from home, with more of the Home Counties about it than Italy.

* *'John Mortimer's novel* Summer's Lease *about English carryings-on in "Chiantishire".'* (*The Independent*, 7 July 1990)

child abuse *n.* [1972]
the deliberate harming of children by (primarily) parents, a relation, or another adult; child abuse is usually physical, and can be sexual, but can include the psychological or verbal. *See also* **baby-battering**.

* *'I only relive the strange events . . . in order to cast light on my later life. Child abuse scars for ever.'* (T. Blacker, *Fixx*, 1989)

chill (out) *v.* [1985]
to relax, to take things easy, a suitable pose for one who is 'cool'; originally in US black use, but brought across the Atlantic and extended to white teenagers.

* *'Now Bruce was chillin' one Saturday/Was by himself with nothing to say/When this big hairy creature came from sky/Bruce ran away – thought he was gonna die.'* (Fat Boys, 'Fat Boys', 1986)

chillum *n.* [1969]
from the Hindi *chillum* meaning that part of the hookah used to hold the tobacco and charcoal balls: a pipe used for smoking marijuana or hashish.

China syndrome *n.* [1970]
a catastrophe in a nuclear reactor whereby the cooling system fails causing a resultant meltdown that would create a nuclear lava flow of unassailable intensity; from the concept of the flow burning 'all the way through to China'.

* *'This "fast-breeder reactor" required a large flow of coolant to keep control and prevent the "China syndrome" – a constant worry to technicians, for once she starts melting, she'll melt her way all the way down to China.'* (*Esquire* magazine, June 1970)

Chinese gooseberry *n.*
see **kiwi fruit**.

Chinese walls *n.* [1986]
a variety of rules and safeguards – a 'Great Wall of China' – designed to prevent price-sensitive information, on which the unscrupulous can make profits, from passing between the dealing, fund management and corporate finance areas of the same financial conglomerate or other business enterprise; from the Stock Exchange, which also uses 'green baize doors'.

chip *n.* [1966]
an abbreviation of silicon chip, the basis of modern computer technology: a tiny square or rectangle of thin semi-conducting material – usually silicon, although some companies are trying to push the more efficient, but infinitely more expensive gallium arsenide – which contains a large number of circuit components; a number of chips can be combined to make up a miniaturized integrated circuit.

✱ *'Techniques were developed to hook many transistors together into complicated circuits . . . called integrated circuits or chips (imagine the wiring diagram of an office building, inscribed on your little toe).'* (T. Kidder, *The Soul of a New Machine*, 1981)

chocoholic *n.* [1979]
on the pattern of 'alcoholic', one who is obsessed and addicted to the consumption of chocolate.

✱ *'Happily I am married to a self-confessed chocoholic, and have produced a family who seem more than content to have a chocolate dessert every day.'* (H. Rubinstein, *The Chocolate Book*, 1981)

chopper *n.* [1969]
a motorcycle that has been customized or 'chopped'; the original choppers were customized Harley Davidson 74s, as used by the Hell's Angels, but a chopper can be any bike that has been remodelled, typically with 'ape-hanger' handlebars, specially extended front suspension forks, and similar modifications.

✱ *'Choppers. Beautiful sleek Harley 74s, black against the sky, stripped down to their dynamic steel souls.'* (N. Fury, *Agro*, 1971)

cimetidine *n.* [1977]
an abbreviation of cyano-imidazol-methyl-guanidine ($C_{10}H_{16}N_6S$): the pharmaceutical name for the world's leading blood-clotting agent, which blocks the histamine that stimulates the production of gastric acid; it is used widely for the control of peptic ulcers.

cineplex *n.* [1987]
a cinema that offers a choice of several screens and auditoria.

city *suffix.* [1972]
a variety of hypothetical metropolises which stand as metaphors for certain states; the state in question is delineated by the adjective that precedes 'city'. Particular uses include ➪edge city and ➪fat city.
See also -ville.

city technology college *n.* [1987]
a form of secondary school designed to provide a science-based education and sited in a number of ➪inner city areas.

class action *n.* [1970]
a legal proceeding enacted to take into account not merely the specific defendant and plaintiff involved, but everyone to whom the case might actively refer.

classic *n.* [1965]
a car manufactured between 1925 and 1942; the category that succeeds 'vintage'.

classist *adj.* [1986]
on the pattern of elitist, ➪sexist, ➪ageist, etc., the notion that one class is naturally superior to another.

classless *adj.* [1966]
beyond or outside Britain's stultifying, claustrophobic class system: one of the underlying myths of the 1960s was that the old class system had finally been knocked on the head; this was not so. The ⇨new aristocracy (or those that proved themselves enduring successes) were absorbed by the old, and the mass of consumers, once their months of flash and filigree had passed by, retreated to the same old jobs as clerks and shopgirls. The concept, relatively dormant since its excited beginnings, has been relaunched with the election of John Major – an unassailable son of the lower middle classes – as Prime Minister.

* *'The swinging elite (i.e. the self-styled classless society) talks so much about being cool.'* (J. Aitken, *The Young Meteors*, 1967)
* *'You think you're so clever and classless and free/But you're all fucking peasants as far as I can see.'* (J. Lennon, 'Working Class Hero', 1970)

clean *n.* [1960]
a nuclear device that produces maximum blast and thermal effects but keeps radiation fallout to a minimum and thus, in theory, produces most of the deaths immediately, rather than slowly over the succeeding months or years.

clean up one's act *phrase.* [1970]
to alter one's lifestyle, especially if one has purged it of what are seen as its antisocial aspects.
See also **get one's act together**, under **act**.

* *'Whatever he once was like he has cleaned up his act. Like everyone else in the Eighties he wears a suit, wears it with zealous negligence.'* (J. Meades, *Peter Knows What Dick Likes*, 1989)

clear air turbulence *n.* [1964]
see **CAT**.

clone *n.* [1986]
in computing: a machine that resembles the industry standard, and which will perform all the same functions, but which is cheaper, and may be assembled from parts supplied by less reputable manufacturers; clones are invariably of IBM machines, usually the 'AT' model.

* *'Other computer companies soon started to produce lower cost copies, machines which generically became known as "clones".'* (*PC World*, April 1990)

clout *n.* [1960]
power or influence. The term was originally used in politics and government, and clout accrued to an individual, whether or not they stood for election; indeed, sufficient clout makes the process of offering oneself for election wasteful of time and (in the US) money, as well as an unnecessary risk. When applied to an elected politician it implies the power to see his programmes carried through; when applied to his fellow citizens, it implies the influence to determine what those programmes shall be. Clout is no longer restricted to politics, but can be found in any institution or organization where power struggles go on.

* *'Clout, in its power sense, applies to the ability of an individual or a group to put across a program, decide a nomination, sway votes.'* (W. Safire, *Safire's Political Dictionary*, 1978)
* *'Dell, NeXT and, in the UK, Acorn, all lacked the clout necessary to kick the market into life.'* (*PC World*, April 1990)

club *adj.* [1975]
an intermediate class between first and economy provided by many airlines. The target customer for such tickets is the businessman or woman, whose flight, with its attendant perks – wider seats, better meals – is paid for by the company.

* *'Competition for the rich lode of commercial traffic runs high, so many airlines offer special "club" facilities for regular customers.'* (*The Flier's Handbook*, 1978)

COBOL *abbrev.* [1970]
an acronym for Common Business-Orientated Language: the most popular and widely recognized of the high-level languages developed for commercial (rather than technical) computing.

cock-up (*or* conspiracy) theory *n.*
the two rival theories of why things happen, usually used as a pair: the cock-up assumes that things are the result of blundering humans, the conspiracy that they are down to scheming ones.

* *'Most accidents can be explained by cock-up rather than conspiracy theory.'* (*The Independent*, 31 March 1990)

co-counselling *n.* [1970]
an abbreviation of re-evaluation co-counselling: a form of resolutely non-authoritative therapy that is based on mutual supportiveness and appreciation, and aims to help people by infusing them with optimism, love and cooperation. Based on non-qualified, 'ordinary people' – the co-counsellors – who simply listen to one's problems, it appears remarkably similar to talking things over with a sympathetic friend. – **co-counsellor**, *n.*

* *'In co-counselling, as in any effective therapy, the individual is encouraged to assume responsibility for his distress and not perceive it as caused by a conspiracy.'* (R.D. Rosen, *Psychobabble*, 1977)

code word *n.* [1965]
a euphemism for any one of a number of offensive or sensitive words; thus 'law and order' disguises (if one believes Gore Vidal) the more honest, if pernicious 'get the niggers' and to the diplomat 'defensible borders' mean 'no turning back'.

* *'The most controversy-laden code word of the late sixties and early seventies was "busing".'* (W. Safire, *Safire's Political Dictionary*, 1978)

coffee-table book *n.* [1962]
a large book, almost invariably illustrated, rendered in a wealth of glossy colour, and usually highly priced, which is intended primarily to be displayed, and only secondarily to be opened or read.

coin-op *n.* [1986]
a computer game that was originally designed for use in an arcade, where players must feed coins into the machines for each go, and has now been reprogrammed for home use.

* *'Most coin-ops score well here because they are designed for instant satisfaction.'* (*Ace*, August 1990)

collateral damage *n.* [1966]
in military jargon, a euphemism for: civilian casualties that will inevitably accompany warfare (especially large-scale bombing or missile attacks), no matter how far the targeting is supposed to hit military forces and establishments only.

* *'Collateral damage: physical harm done to persons or property near targets such as missile silos.'* (C. Campbell, *War Facts Now*, 1982)

collectible *n.* [1976]
any object deemed worthy of being collected; often a modern artefact of some type, rather than an antique.

* *'If your child simply grows up to be someone who does not use the word "collectible" as a noun, you can consider yourself an unqualified success.'* (F. Lebowitz, *Social Studies*, 1981)

colour field painting
see **hard-edge painting**.

colourize *v.* [1986]
the colouring of classic black and white movies of the 1930s and 1940s in what many film buffs feel is the mistaken belief that the mass audience is unable to appreciate the monochrome originals. – **colourization** *n.*

* *'Media mogul Ted Turner has announced his intention to "colorize" (that's "computerized tinting" to jargophobes) old MGM black and white movies.'* (Charles Shaar Murray, *Crosstown Traffic*, 1989)

colour man/announcer *n.* [1971]
a broadcaster employed to add colour to commentary, or backup/editorial material to news programmes. Sometimes, derogatorily, as 'colour babbler'.

colour supplement *n.* [1962]
any supplement to a newspaper which features large coloured illustrations and advertisements; colour supplements had existed for some time in the US and UK, but the concept of such supplements as being able to define ways of life, and create a discernible 'colour supplement lifestyle', came with the *Sunday Times* colour supplement, first published on 4 February 1962.

* *'Anxious to start a colour supplement for his paper, he approached Mark Boxer through his editor.'* (J. Aitken, *The Young Meteors*, 1967)

come out *v.* [1969]
an abbreviation of the slang come out of the closet: for a homosexual to declare him or herself in their true sexual orientation. The term was well known in ➪gay circles, but did not fully enter mainstream use until the growth of ➪Gay Liberation in the late 1960s and beyond. *See also* **out**.

coming from, where you're *phrase.* [1970]
the way you feel, what your emotional state is. *See also* **where you're at**.

* *'Well, I can dig where you're coming from.'* (B. Woodward, *Wired*, 1984)

comint *n.* [1969]
an acronym for communications intelligence: all forms of intelligence derived from satellites, the monitoring of foreign radio, and other broadcast media (both public and military), listening in to foreign codes and telephone calls, etc.

comms *abbrev.* [1982]
in computing: communications.

community charge *n.* [1986]
the official name for the poll tax, introduced to Scotland in 1989 and England and Wales in 1990, and officially abandoned in 1991.

✱ 'From April 1 1990 the existing rating system will be replaced by the community charge and a national business rate.' (Westminster City Council leaflet, April, 1990)

community politics *n.* [1967]
a synonym for grass-roots politics; the local issues and personalities that make up politics at the community level. **Community** can also be used as an all-purpose adjective:

✱ *'A so-called 'community garden' in Seven Sisters was brought up to help the local populace.'* (T. Blacker, *Fixx*, 1989)

compassion fatigue *n.* [1987]
the feeling that world events are so distressing and thanks to the media we are so heavily exposed to them that as earthquake follows earthquake, and famine succeeds famine, each will blend into the other and the battered viewer will lose his or her ability to extend compassion to the myriad victims.

✱ *'One danger of showing young children the beauty of the world and the mess their parents . . . have made of it so far, is that they will get compassion fatigue before reaching puberty.'* (*The Independent*, 31 March 1990)

-compatible *suffix.* [1982]
in computing use: denoting systems that will work with each other. Thus **downward compatible**: a piece of ➪software that will work with previous (less complex) versions; **upward compatible**: a piece of software that will work with a later version; **plug-compatible**: pieces of ➪hardware that will work simply by plugging them into each other. – **compatibility** *n.*
See also **-aware, -friendly**.

✱ *'These outfits went by the names of "plug-compatibles" and "third-party peripheral manufacturers".'* (T. Kidder, *The Soul of a New Machine*, 1981)

✱ *'A package that includes desk accessory software for Windows-compatible desktop publishing with Presentation Manager.'* (*Byte*, May 1990)

✱ *'Naturally we thought that maximum IBM compatibility would be gained by buying an IBM computer. Fools!'* (*PC World*, March 1991)

compliance *n.* [1986]
in economic use: acting in accordance with the Financial Services Act of 1986, which provided an new and extensive set of rules, designed to eliminate corrupt practices within Britain's financial institutions.

computeracy *n.* [1982]
see **computer literacy**.

computer crime *n.* [1972]
any form of crime that requires a computer for its success; it includes the placing of destructive ➪viruses in programs and systems, but refers more specifically to a variety of larcenous financial transactions which are achieved simply through the manipulations of bank accounts, credit cards and other instruments that are nowadays held electronically.

✱ *'Whereas burglary is a familiar crime with well-established procedures, computer crime is not.'* (*PC World*, March 1991)

computer dating *n., adj.* (1968)
the finding of a new partner through consulting a computer database of suitable individuals; these databases are held by a number of companies, who take customers through a questionnaire and attempt to find a number of suitable dates for them.

* *'A questionnaire by Dateline – the biggest computer dating agency with 35–40,000 clients on its books – showed 93 per cent of its members are looking to wed.'* (*The Independent*, 7 February 1991)

computerize *v.* [1965]
to introduce computers into a workplace.

computer literacy *n.* [1982]
the ability to understand and use computers.

* *'Of course it has its imitators. Some limited by their capabilities. Others restricted by their memory. Many requiring computer literacy.'* (ad for Sharp in *The Independent*, 26 May 1990)

comrade *n.* [1986]
a member of a group of young black radicals who play a leading role in the politics of South African townships.

* *'In the townships the comrades had petrol-bombed 7700 buses, torched 1447 schools and 985 black-owned businesses.'* (R. Malan, *My Traitor's Heart*, 1990)

concept *n.*
a philosophy of marketing that creates a whole range of interlocking interests, all of which can be grouped together; essentially a synonym for 'idea', concept has the added 'sexiness' required of the profession that uses it.

concert party *n.* [1967]
1. *in banking use*: a method of evading the UK law (the Companies Acts 1967, 1976) that states that any single shareholder with 5% or more of a company must inform the company in writing at once: a number of purchasers 'acting in concert' all buy less than 5% shares, then consolidate their holdings, thus gradually taking over a company.

* *'The Companies Act (1981) has attempted to remedy this by declaring such gradual takeovers as illegal and stating that any 'concert party' must by law inform the target company of their joint interest.'* (F.E. Perry, *Dictionary of Banking*, 1983)

2. *in management use*: a term employed by the (UK) City Code on Take-overs and Mergers to refer to 'persons acting in concert' to cooperate in the purchase of shares with a view to gaining control of a company; a pun on the traditional show business term.
3. *in stock market use*: a group of people who agree secretly (and, in some countries, illegally) to make separate purchases of shares in a given company, with the intention of amalgamating all their shares in a single holding later.

* *'The officials believed that Tiny Rowland . . . was engaged in a "concert party" with the Fayeds to purchase Harrods.'* (*Private Eye*, 16 March 1990)

condo/condominium *n.* [1962]
a type of shared-ownership apartment block, popular in the US, where the tenants buy a building jointly, then divide up the apartments between them.

* *'He found a terrific crash pad right away, a one-bedroom condo on Eliseo Drive overlooking the Greenbrae Canal.'* (C. McFadden, *The Serial*, 1976)

conglomerate *n.* [1967]
a large business group, often international, which has been formed from a wider variety of diverse commercial enterprises.
See also **multinational**.

* *'And here I've observed the successful conglom-*

erates (whose structure is inevitably networked to some extent) like Owen Green's BTR and Chris Hogg's Courtaulds.' (*Independent on Sunday*, 8 April 1990)

connectivity *adj., n.* [1985]
1. *in military use*: the improvement of the command and control of nuclear forces to ensure that in the event of an actual nuclear conflict, despite its magnitude and potential chaos, the war-fighting plans would succeed as required.

* *'In the new Pentagon buzzword, those reviews are referred to as "connectivity" studies.'* (D. Ford, *The Button*, 1985)

2. *in computing use*: the ability for computers of different types to communicate with each other and to run each other's programs.

Consciousness I/II/III *n.* [1970]
the three types of cultural consciousness, as set down in Charles Reich's best-selling *The Greening of America* (1970): **I** 'is the traditional outlook of the American farmer, small businessman or worker trying to get ahead'; **II** 'represents the values of an organizational society ... the machinelike rationality of the corporate state'; **III** 'which is spreading rapidly among wider and wider segments of our youth . . . is the process of revolutionizing the structure of our society.' Reich espoused Consciousness III with all the enthusiasm of an ageing convert. Time has shattered the myth, although one can see certain parallels in the work of another futurologist, Alvin Toffler, whose *The Third Wave* (1980) bears certain similarities, although from a very different standpoint.

* *'The contrast to her own oppressively regimented childhood made her feel truly optimistic about the future of humanity in the hands of Consciousness III.'* (C. McFadden, *The Serial*, 1976)

consciousness-raising *n.* [1969]
essentially the greater awareness of one's own position in the world, and with it one's needs and one's potential as a human being, the phrase was swiftly coopted into the women's movement to the exclusion of all else. Thus a risen consciousness now means the fulfilment of one's true femininity, and is not open for use by other groups. Often found as an adjective, especially in *consciousness-raising group*.

* *'Carol had been the first woman in their conscious-raising group . . . to wear black fingernail polish.'* (C. McFadden, *The Serial*, 1976)
* *'Costa-Gavras makes films that are more or less uneasy mixes of entertainment and political consciousness-raising.'* (*The Independent*, 14 June 1990)

consumerism *n.*
1. (1969) the protection of the consumer, as advocated by the great consumer advocate of the 1960s, Ralph Nader and his 'Raiders'.
2. (1960) the belief in the paramountcy of consumption as the basis of a sound economy, and (especially in the 1980s) of the ideal life.

* *'The dissatisfied 1960s generation who dropped out of the blatant consumerism of the "me decades".'* (*Sunday Correspondent*, 3 June 1990)

consumer terrorism *n.* [1989]
the deliberate and dangerous tampering with foodstuffs, e.g. putting ground glass into certain jars – often as displayed in bulk on

supermarket shelves – by those who wish to extract large payments from the shops and manufacturers concerned.

container ship *n.* [1966]
a ship that has been specifically designed to transport container units, up to 40 feet long, which can then be offloaded onto purpose-built trucks and thus distributed around a country. Thus **containerization**: the shipping of cargo in such containers.

contextualize *v.* [1972]
to place in context.

Contra *n.* [1981]
a member of the opposition forces recruited from supporters of the deposed Somoza regime, who until 1989 fought a bitter, bloody guerrilla war (with substantial US backing) against the left-wing government of Nicaragua.

* *'The Contras never had more than 4000–5000 men in Nicaragua and were thus outnumbered by approximately 16:1.'* (P. Brogan, *World Conflicts*, 1989)

convenience food *n.* [1961]
any form of frozen, dried, vacuum-packed or similar foodstuff, prepared in the factory and sold ready-to-eat, with little consumer input other than opening the packet and heating the contents.

* *'Master Foods is a successful and expanding producer of quality convenience foods, including many exciting new lines.'* (*Independent on Sunday*, 8 April 1990)

convenience store *n.* [1965]
a general store which combines extended opening hours with a wide range of foods and household items; the classic example is the 7–11 chain.

Convoy, the *n.* [1983]
a group of modern gypsies – ex-hippies, punks, a variety of ➪dropouts from mainstream society – who move around England in a convoy of rundown trucks, vans, and buses, appalling the locals and, by their own account, desiring nothing more than a peaceful, if ➪alternative, life.

* *'Over such shells our ancestors stretched turves, hanks of bark, peat. The Convoy stretches tarpaulins and thick agricultural polythene instead.'* (J. Meades, *Peter Knows What Dick Likes*, 1989)

cook-chill *v., adj.* [1987]
a method of mass-catering in which meals are cooked, flash frozen and then defrosted as and when required.

cookware *n.* [1988]
the contemporary description of cooking utensils and equipment; possibly drawn on the high-tech world of computing hardware and software.

cop out *v., n.* [1967]
to give up, especially by betraying one's anti-establishment ideals, when it becomes a synonym for ➪ sell out.

* *'The time had come to pull back . . . to retire, hunker down, back off and "cop out", as it were.'* (H.S. Thompson, *Fear and Loathing in Las Vegas*, 1971)

Used as a noun and hyphenated it is essentially 'an excuse', although the grounds for that excuse are presumed to be somewhat shameful and certainly indicative of moral cowardice.

-core, *suffix.* [1987]
an all-purpose rock music suffix: it includes **thrashcore, grindcore** and **grunge core**.

* *'The sound is dancecore, the heaviest dance/hardcore crossover in the world.' (The Independent,* 4 October 1990*)*
* *'Hardcore: Pornography with oodles of fucking and sucking, usually supplied by those sexy Scandies . . . Sometimes foolishly applied as a tag for yankee punk music.' (Britcore: The Street Suss Encyclopedia,* 1990*)*

corporate hospitality *n.* [1985]
a form of business entertaining that is linked to major sporting or cultural events; a firm purchases a box at Lords or Ascot, the best seats at Glyndebourne, etc., and offers them, gratis, to favoured clients.

* *'Company guests arrive via the hospitality village, with separate access from the 16,000 spectators.'* (*Independent on Sunday,* 10 June 1990)
* *'There'd be headhunters roaming the floors of the conference in search of young engineers, whom they'd take back to "hospitality suites", ply with liquor and caviar, and talk into defecting.'* (T. Kidder, *The Soul of a New Machine,* 1981)

corporate state *n.* [1970]
a state that is less a political entity than a business one, written enormously large. The corporate state, according to the term's coiner Charles A. Reich, is beyond human control and cares nothing for human values; it prescribes and proscribes as dictated by current market forces.

corporate welfare *n.*[1987]
used in the US to describe the compulsory funding of welfare programmes by large corporations.

corporatize *v.* [1987]
the reverse of nationalize: to return a large public institution to private ownership. – **corporatization,** *n.*

Cosa Nostra *n.* [1963]
from the Italian meaning 'our thing' or 'this thing of ours': *a synonym for* the Mafia. The term was revealed in 1963 by former Mafia 'soldier' Joe Valachi.

* *'Joe Bananas . . . had ordered the deaths of the Cosa Nostra's entire top board members and elder statesmen: the dons, the consigliere who ruled America's crime empire.'* (J.R. Nash, *Bloodletters and Badmen,* 1973)

cost effective *adj.* [1967]
referring to any piece of work, proposal or piece of equipment that pulls its economic weight and repays in profit the investment that has been made in it.

Costa del Crime *n.* [1980]
on the pattern of the Costa del Sol, the tourist centre of south-eastern Spain, that area of the country which attacts a disproportionate number of British criminals, often dependent on the proceeds of their crimes, who are able to live there safe from the fear of extradition back to the UK.

* *'The sunny "Costa del Crime" also attracted retired CID officers and it was rumoured that both sides used to spend time together reminiscing.'* (*The Independent,* 15 May 1990)

cot death *n.* [1970]
the unexplained death of a baby in its sleep; no consistent cause of cot deaths has yet been established, although theories abound as to breathing patterns, sleeping postures, the type

of sheet or blanket on which the baby rests, and many more. Thus **cot death syndrome**: the phenomenon of cot deaths, which has yet to be explained.
See also **SIDS**.

couch potato *n.* [1986]
an inveterate television watcher.

* *'[The programme is] a novel experience for any couch potato – and heaven in the sitting room for the sports fan.'* (TV listing in *The Independent*, 23 May 1990)

council tax *n.* [1991]
The Conservative replacement for the ill-fated ➪community charge or ➪poll tax. Introduced in April 1991, the council tax, designed like its predecessors to raise revenue for local government spending, is to be levied from 1994. Based on house prices, it will be assessed in seven different bands with house owners paying +/– a predetermined average.

counter-culture *n.* [1968]
also known as the ➪'alternative society' (to its devotees) or the ➪'underground' (to the media), the counter-culture was a coverall brandname for the world the 1960s hippies aimed to create. In many ways similar to 'straight' society, with newspapers, shops, restaurants, and small businesses of many types, its enterprises were infused with a set of cultural values that ran contrary to the mainstream.

* *'Apart from the lightning evolution of a counter-culture, the One Great Youth Unifier has been Vietnam.'* (R. Neville, *Play Power*, 1970)
* *'Our first job is to convince the younger generation, and ourselves, that the counter-culture was an enriching and educational experience.'* (*Independent on Sunday*, 27 May 1990)

counterforce *adj., n.* [1960]
a nuclear strike against the enemy's weapons rather than at his centres of population; thus *counterforce weapons, counterforce option, counterforce strike*, etc.

* *'As a nuclear strategy, counterforce means aiming attack missiles at military targets.'* (R.C. Aldridge, *First Strike!*, 1983)

counter-insurgency *n., adj.* [1962]
any form of military action aimed at guerrillas or other insurgents. Also found as an adjective, as in *counter-insurgency actions*.

* *'He has [the] user's manual right there in his desk, written by an American counter-insurgency expert whose research has clearly established the water cannon's effectiveness. To intimidate and discourage white riots, you put green dye in the water.'* (R. Malan, *My Traitor's Heart*, 1990)

countervalue *adj., n.* [1960]
a nuclear strike against the enemy's cities and population; thus *countervalue option, countervalue strike*, etc.

* *'A stream of terms befuddling even to those familiar with military jargon . . . counterforce, countervalue, and damage limitation.'* (P. Pringle & W. Arkin, *SIOP*, 1983)

coupling *n.* [1983]
usually known as **strategic coupling**: the linking of low-level conflict – Soviet/Warsaw Pact aggression in Europe – to the threatened use of US nuclear weapons.

* *'Extended deterrence has been a way . . . of "coupling" American and West European defenses.'* (S. Talbott, *Deadly Gambits*, 1984)

cowboy *adj., n.* [1979]
second rate, probably illicit, almost certainly part of the ⇨black economy; the term is usually applied to plumbers, builders, and similar occupations – who may be the 'cowboys' themselves, or known generically as 'cowboy builders' or 'cowboy plumbers' – who promise gullible customers cut-price work, but often end up leaving them with a whole new set of bills for the work that has to be performed by genuine professionals in clearing up the cowboy's mess.

✱ *'These cowboy outfits are bottom of the jousting pile, just as jousting itself is fairly near the bottom of the equestrian hierarchy.'* (J. Meades, *Peter Knows What Dick Likes*, 1989)

CPA *abbrev.* [1960]
see **critical path analysis.**

CPS *abbrev.*
Crown Prosecution Service: the civilian service that has taken over the prosecution of criminal cases from the police.

✱ *'The handing over of court prosecution to the Crown Prosecution Service (CPS) had been matched by the creation of crime support groups (CSG) within divisions.'* (R. Chesshyre, *The Force*, 1989)

CPU *abbrev.* [1967]
Central Processing Unit: that part of the computer's system which controls all its operations and performs the arithmetical and logical functions.

✱ *'Among these new CPUs will be several new Macintosh Portables, including models that are actually portable.'* (*Byte*, June 1990)

crack *n.* [1988]
a purified and potent form of cocaine which, unlike the normal powdered form, is smoked rather than snorted; crack, a mixture of cocaine, baking powder, and water, is heated and then resultant pellets are smoked through a small glass pipe. Its strength, alleged addictiveness, and destructive popularity have made it the current bête noire among narcotics agents and government officials.

✱ *'When I was dealing in crack I was told I could keep one rock for every four I sold. But I got greedy.'* (*Sunday Correspondent*, 8 April 1990)

crash *n., v.* [1968]
in general slang used as a verb meaning to sleep.

✱ *'I'd crashed Friday afternoon – I hadn't completely recovered from the infection.'* (*Byte*, June 1990)

also in computing use: as a noun, meaning a situation in which the machine has stopped working. This is an abbreviation of 'head crash': the accumulation of even a tiny amount (a few microns) of dust between the read/write head of the computer and the disk which can destroy the information on that disk.

✱ *'File access from all computers on the network; user customization; and crash protection.'* (*Byte*, July 1990)

Here too the term is found as a verb, both intransitive – 'The PC just crashed' and transitive – 'X crashed the system'.

crash barrier *n.* [1970]
a barrier erected along the centre of a motorway to prevent cars skidding across into the opposite lanes.

crash pad *n.* [1968]
a temporary home where hippies could 'crash', or sleep, usually for no more than a few nights.

✱ *'Hippies took a lot of crap. Illegal busts of crash pads and communes in the Lower East Side.'* (A. Hoffman, *Woodstock Nation*, 1969)

creation science *n.* [1981]
the belief that scientific evidence affirms rather than (as scientists tend to feel) denies the biblical version of the creation.

✱ *'Adherents of this view . . . seek to have creation science taught as a scientific theory no less valid than the theory of evolution.'* (*American Speech*, 1983)

creative accountancy (*or* **accounting)** *n.* [1969]
inventive or imaginative accounting procedures, in which figures are manipulated so as to bend, but never actually break the tax rules in favour of the firm or client. This slightly ironic use of 'creative', meaning manipulative or deceitful, is occasionally found in other combinations, but the primary meaning always implies the somewhat underhand.

✱ *'Hobbies: Hunting, shooting, fishing, propagation of lysteria, drinking, cruelty to animals, creative accountancy, mad cows.'* (*Sunday Correspondent*, 10 June 1990)

cred *n., adj., adv.* [1977]
an abbreviation of credibility, e.g. 'Cliff is seriously low on cred.' It is also used as an adjective either referring to objects, e.g. 'a cred pair of boots', or people, 'she's well cred', and as an adverb, synonymous with 'appealing to' or 'accepted by'.
See also **street cred**.

✱ *'He has cardigan-cred, granny appeal – whether this will endure as he ages is questionable.'* (J. Meades, *Peter Knows What Dick Likes*, 1989)

credibility *n.* [1965]
the concept of making an ally or an enemy believe that you mean what you say, will do what you promise or threaten, and have the weapons to carry it out.

✱ *'According to Haig's evidence to a US Senate Hearing in 1981, "Strategic nuclear forces affect the quality and credibility of deterrence".'* (M. Dando & P. Rogers, *The Death of Deterrence*, 1984)

credibility gap *n.* [1968]
coined during the Vietnam War to underline the American public's growing inability to take the statements (as opposed to the actions) of the Johnson Administration at face value, and since used to point up the discrepancies between the actions and words of any government. Coined properly in 1968, when the television-viewing public witnessed the perceived (if not actual) defeat of US forces in the Tet Offensive, the term possibly originated as early as 1966. A series of pieces in the *New York Times*, filed from Hanoi, made it clear that the Administration's positive assessment of the war was some way from the negative reality. A Pentagon spokesman termed the reports 'a credibility disaster'.

✱ *'But it was a crucial moment for [Walter Cronkite] because for the first time the credibility gap had surfaced in front of everyone's eyes.'* (D. Halberstam, *The Powers That Be*, 1979)

CREEP *abbrev.* [1972]
an acronym for the Committee to Re-Elect the

President: a body organized by the White House to ensure the re-election of Richard Nixon in the 1972 presidential elections; so assiduous was CREEP, and so careless of the legal norms, that while Nixon was elected in 1972, he was forced to resign, the first US president so to do, two years later, the most important victim of the Watergate Affair.

* *'It was going to be another year before CREEP was finally revealed as the crucial mechanism used to distort democracy in the United States.'* (C. MacCrystal, L. Chester, *et al.*, *Watergate*, 1973)

crew *n.* [1969, 1987]
a gang of young men, used both by ⇨skinheads in the late 1960s and by black ⇨hip-hop fans in the 1980s.

* *'He's the only member of the crew wearing one, so everyone can see he's the leader.'* (N. Fury, *Agro*, 1971)
* *'They got a wacky-wack record with a wacky-wack crew. Yo! What about the lyric? That shit's wacky-wack too.'* (N.W.A., *Compton's In The House*, 1988)

cricket test *n.* [1990]
devised by right-wing populist Norman Tebbit who proposed in a debate on the admission of Hong Kong refugees to the country that the loyalty of immigrants to the UK could and should be judged by the side they chose to support in a Test match between England and their native country.

crimper *n.* [1967]
a hairdresser, who 'crimps' one's hair.

* *'Mane Man. Leonard the Crimper.'* (J. Meades, *Peter Knows What Dick Likes*, 1989)

crisis management *n.* [1961]
1. originally a military usage, coined after the Cuban Missile Crisis (1961) by US Secretary of State Robert MacNamara who declared that 'there is no longer any such thing as strategy, only crisis management'. Thus, the concept that foreign relations is in essence a process of keeping such international crisis that must occur beneath such a level at which actual conflict would be inevitable.

* *'According to Haig's evidence to a US Senate Hearing in 1981, "Strategic nuclear forces affect . . . our ability and success in crisis management and the conduct and results of American diplomacy".'* (M. Dando & P. Rogers, *The Death of Deterrence*, 1984)

2. now in general use, extending the basic meaning to civilian affairs.

* *'The ultimate test of Carter Van Pollen's crisis management skills.'* (*Independent on Sunday*, 25 March 1990)

critical path analysis (CPA) *n.* [1960]
the analysis of the most important sequence of the individual stages of an operation, thus determining the time required to perform the whole of the operation.

Crombie *n.*, *adj.* [1969]
a type of overcoat, named for its manufacturer, which had once been the province of the well-heeled, but by the late 1960s had been usurped by its many ⇨skinhead wearers.

* *'He's got on a black Crombie coat, the type you only used to see in the Burlington arcade.'* (N. Fury, *Agro*, 1971)

crossfader *n.* [1988]
a device used by DJs who operate twin turntables: it permits them to lower the volume on one record while simultaneously raising it on the other, thus achieving a seamless transfer of sounds.

crossover *adj., n.* [1972]
1. *in film*: a film that can attract a number of different specialist audiences; thus *crossover star*: a performer who can attain the same multiple success.
2. *in music*: music that crosses over from one specialized area into another; often used of black stars who appeal to the white audience, but also of country-and-western material that is enjoyed by pop fans, etc.

* *'I've just signed this heavy band with a pedal steel guitarist – real HM/Country crossover stuff.'* (T. Hibbert, (ed.), *Rockspeak*, 1984)

cru *n.* [1966]
an international monetary unit designed to ease the strain on gold and hard-currency reserves in settling accounts between nations.

crucial *adj.* [1985]
the mass market's equivalent to yuppiedom's 'serious'; originally promoted by American ⇨rappers, it joined the mainstream youth vocabulary, alongside 'rad'(ical), 'wicked' (as in excellent), 'distress' (cause unpleasantness), etc.

cruise missile *n.* [1977]
essentially a small, pilotless aeroplane that hugs the ground and uses its on-board radar and guidance system to deliver a nuclear (or, as in the Gulf War, ⇨conventional) warhead over great distances and with sufficient accuracy to threaten ⇨hard targets. Relatively slow by missile standards it can, as was seen in the Gulf War, be shot down by conventional anti-aircraft fire. Nonetheless its accuracy and comparative cheapness of production makes it in military eyes almost the ideal modern weapon. Cruise missiles include the ⇨ALCM ('alkum': Air-Launched Cruise Missile), ⇨SLCM ('slickem': Sea-Launched Cruise Missile) and ⇨GLCM ('glockem': Ground-Launched Cruise Missile).

* *'Because the cruise missile is so small it can be adapted to a great number of mobile carrier vehicles.'* (R.C. Aldridge, *First Strike!*, 1983)

crumbly *n.* [1972]
see **wrinkly**.

cryonics *n.* [1962]
the process of freezing a dead body as soon as possible after decease, and preserving the corpse in the assumption that at some future date science will have made it possible to revive the preserved organs and tissues.

* *'Cryonics is the American pastime of freezing the departed in readiness for the happy day when science unlocks the secret of everlasting life.'* (*The Independent*, 6 October 1990)

CSE *abbrev.* [1963]
Certificate of Secondary Education: an examination equivalent to the lower grades of O Level pass and which, with O Level, was replaced by the GCSE.

cuisine minceur *n.* [1975]
cuisine minceur (cooking for slimmers) and its close cousin **cuisine nouvelle** appeared in the 1970s as cookery's answer to the small is beautiful philosophy that lies behind the

exercise and diet fads of the period. Such French chefs as Paul Bocuse and the Troisgros Brothers jettisoned the creams, liqueurs, and animal fats of traditional haute cuisine for a new regime of lighter-than-light, fatless, aesthetic cookery, using the finest ingredients and heavily influenced by the minimalism and artistry of Japanese cooking. Unfortunately this innovatory style has all too frequently paled into the insubstantial, cliched imitations served up by second-rate artisans in the rash of restaurants capitalizing on this new culinary fashion.

See also **nouvelle cuisine**.

* *'In the Cuisine Minceur version, whatever the butcher may say, veal and beef should be cooked "naked" and not wrapped up in layers of fat.'* (M. Guérard, *Cuisine Minceur*, 1976)

cuisine nouvelle *n.* [1975]
see **nouvelle cuisine.**

cult *adj.* [1966]
any thing or person that is the subject of adulation from a specific group of mutually fascinated fans. The term is usually used in such combinations as *cult figure, cult hero, cult movie,* or *cult object.*

* 'Superstar – The Karen Carpenter Story *(1987) – a quasi-documentary shot over two weekends and acted entirely by Ken and Barbie dolls – was a cult hit.'* (*The Independent*, 1 March 1991)

cultural *adj.* [1970]
traditional, pertaining to West Indian culture, especially as practised by Rastafarians.

* *'This mellow and very successful reggae club. The emphasis is on cultural rather than Dance Hall reggae.'* (*The Independent*, 29 May 1990)

cultural icon *n.* [1980]
like the religious icon, which represented the religious ideal, a cultural icon represents the peak symbolic achievement of a given cultural form; typical contemporary icons are the late film stars James Dean and Marilyn Monroe.

Cultural Revolution *n.* [1966]
the cultural, political, social and concomitantly economic upheaval in China between 1965 and 1969, launched by Chairman Mao to regain some of his depleted power, lost through the failure of the Great Leap Forward. Intended to crush the bureaucracy and install true egalitarianism, the Cultural Revolution, with its massive purges, its violence and its growing personality cult devoted to Mao, proved a major disaster for China and its people – and one from which the nation has yet fully to recover.

* *'The scale and momentum of the Great Proletarian Cultural Revolution . . . have no parallel in history and the tremendous drive and momentum and boundless wisdom of the working people . . . exceed the imagination of the lords of the bourgeoisie.'* (*People's Daily*, 1 June 1966)

* *'The fear of chaos . . . remains deeply entrenched in the minds of people who remember only too well the torments of the Cultural Revolution.'* (*The Independent*, 16 May 1990)

culturati *n.* [1966]
on the pattern of 'literati', the cultured class.

* *'Thousands of straight intellectuals and culturati and square hippies, North Beach style, gawking and learning.'* (T. Wolfe, *The Electric Kool-Aid Acid Test*, 1969)

culture shock *n.* [1967]
the sense of confusion and alienation often experienced by those suddenly exposed to a culture and society which is totally outside their previous experience. Often it appears that the 'hosts' have no sense or logic in their ways of living and communication.

* *'I had travelled so there wasn't as great a culture shock as there might have been, but there was some confusion.'* (J. Green, *Them*, 1990)

cursor *n.* [1972]
a small square or line of flashing light that can be moved around a computer screen and indicates where a letter may be inserted, a command indicated, etc.

* *'The cursor changes shape according to the part of the screen and the mode you're in.'* (J. Cavuoto & J. Berst, *Inside Xerox Ventura Publisher*, 1989)

curtain track *n.* [1971]
a track on which curtains are fixed and on which they can be pulled and drawn smoothly.

cut it *v.* [1970]
to manage, to achieve; an abbreviation of the older 'cut the mustard'.

* *'If I can't cut it at work, I may as well give up now.'* (*Independent on Sunday*, 25 March 1990)

cutting edge *n.*
the forefront, the most advanced position, used of businesses, technological development and similar areas of activity.

* *'Our success comes from using top quality professionals to work directly at the cutting edge with clients.'* (ad for Kinsley Lord management consultants in *Independent on Sunday*, 3 June 1990)

cyberpunk *n.* [1984]
a form of science fiction in which the imagined future world is post-apocalyptically grim, and concomitantly violent, all subject to some faceless computer which controls humans and machines alike.

* *'The big movement in science fiction in the middle of the 1980s was called cyberpunk. It promoted a stylish techno-noir atmosphere that owed more to Raymond Chandler than to Isaac Asimov.'* (*The Independent*, 31 October 1990)

cyborg *abbrev.* [1964]
cybernetic organism: a predecessor of bionic, a human body that has been taken over either in whole or in part by electronic or electromechanical devices.

daisywheel *n.* [1972]
in computing, a printer that was introduced by Diablo System in 1972; it uses a removable font element in the shape of a disk, the characters are placed at the end of small metal stalks that are arranged around the central hub – creating, for the fanciful, a metal 'flower'.

* *'The early honours have been taken by the daisywheel or petal printers.'* (D. Jarrett, *The Good Computing Book for Beginners,* 1980)

Dalek *n.* [1964]
the principal 'baddies' in the Dr Who television series; the name for these robots, whose oft-repeated motto 'Ex-ter-min-ate' was echoed across Britain's playgrounds during the show's heyday, allegedly came from the spine of a dictionary: DA-LEK.

damage limitation *n.* [1985]
1. *in general use:* any attempt in business, bureaucracy, government, etc. to deal with an unavoidable crisis by minimizing its effects to the best extent possible. The damage has been done, all that the 'survivors' can hope to do is establish what controls are feasible.
2. *in military use:* the concept that judicious planning can limit the damage, and thus the virulence of the conflict and the deaths it must cause, incurred in a nuclear war. The damage that is to be limited is that sustained by one's own side, and such thinking lies behind the current belief in 'winnable' nuclear wars.

* *'Including super-accurate missiles, damage limitation policies, and anti-submarine warfare.'* (R.C. Aldridge, *First Strike!,* 1983)

DAT *abbrev.* [1986]
an acronym for digital audio tape: the latest form of sophisticated audio tape which records sound in a digital format.

* *'1 trillion bytes of data in a single package just slightly bigger than a digital audio tape cartridge.'* (*Byte,* July 1990)

database *n., adj.* [1970]
any collection of information kept on an electronic file, though if taken literally, even a file of yellowing press cuttings could comprise a database. Thus **database management system,** a feature of the 'electronic office': a software package geared to arranging, sorting, and retrieving information and generally managing the operation and accumulation of a database.

* *'Informix is the only company in the Unix world able to provide true integration between its own corporate database products and its PC software.'* (ad for Informix software in the *Sunday Correspondent,* 8 April 1990)

dawn raid *n.* [1980]
a method of forcing a takeover by the surreptitious purchasing of as many shares as possible of the company in which one is interested at 'dawn' – starting as soon as the stock exchange opens for business and com-

pleting one's purchases by 10am. One can purchase up to 29% of a company using such methods before legally being forced to announce one's intentions. All purchases over 30% must be declared.

dayglo *adj.* [1968]
the proprietary name of a range of highly fluorescent colours – notably red, yellow, and green.

* *'There is a panel truck parked just outside, painted in blue, yellow, orange, red dayglo, with the word BAM in huge letters on the hood.'* (T. Wolfe, *The Electric Kool-Aid Acid Test*, 1969)

DBS *abbrev.* [1986]
direct broadcasting by satellite: a system that broadcasts television programmes directly into one's home via a satellite rotating in the earth's orbit.

de-accession *n.* [1987]
also known as ***de-acquisition***: the selling off of all or part of its treasures by a museum or similar institution. Such sales are presumably arranged in order to make up for financial shortfalls in the institution's budget.

death squad *n.* [1969]
any of a number of vigilante groups who operate (especially in the countries of South America); right-wing, and often sanctioned, if not acknowledged by the relevant government, these squads specialize in the abduction and murder of prominent liberals and left-wingers.

* *'Blanca de Rosal was celebrating her own escape from the death squads.'* (Amnesty International, *Voices for Freedom*, 1986)

decapitate *v.* [1974]
in military use: to launch an attack, often as a pre-emptive strike, which might be able to 'decapitate' the war effort, i.e. by knocking out the massively computerized command and control systems that dominate each side's war-planning; if this concept proved true, then the military 'torso' would be rendered powerless once its 'head', containing the ➪high-tech and human facilities essential to warfighting, was lopped off. – **decapitation** *n.*

* *'A nuclear strike to decapitate Soviet leadership and its political infrastructure dates back at least to the Ford administration.'* (R.C. Aldridge, *First Strike!*, 1983)

decay *n.*
the date of re-entry of a satellite into the earth's atmosphere, either through natural causes or on human/computer-activated command.

decimalize *v.* [1970]
to change a national currency to a decimal system. – **decimalization** *n.*

decision tree *n.* [1968]
a flow chart or similar visual aid designed to aid in the analysis of complex situations in which various alternative strategies are advanced and which should make available data on the possible outcome, profitability, potential problems, and any other information pertinent to such a situation.

deck *n.* [1977]
a record turntable.

deconstruction *n.* [1972]
a philosophy of criticism (usually of literature

or film) that seeks to expose the deep-seated contradictions in the work being considered by delving beneath the surface meaning – the rhetoric – and setting out the deeper implications of what has been written or filmed. According to its guru, Jacques Derrida, deconstruction is a practice of reading that 'must always aim at a certain relationship, unperceived by the author, between what he commands and does not command of the patterns of language he uses' (*Dissemination*, 1972).
See also **structuralism.**

* *'It engages in fact and speculation in the most eccentrically provocative manner. This is free-range deconstruction, dense and funny.'* (*Sunday Correspondent*, 10 June 1990)

decoupling *n.* [1981]
the decision by the US to sacrifice Europe, and the forces it holds there, rather than permit an international conflict to affect the US itself. Such a decision would fly in the face of the ➩'coupling' theory, which presumes that the permitting of the US to base missiles in Europe will act as an extra guarantee against Russian incursions. Thus European leaders continue to encourage the deployment of missiles on their national soil. The logical extension of this European fear is that both superpowers might choose to fight a nuclear war outside their own boundaries, pitting NATO against the Warsaw Pact and each preserving their own territory.

* *'Cancellation of the NATO deployments . . . would risk decoupling the American nuclear deterrent from the defense of Europe.'* (S. Talbott, *Deadly Gambits*, 1984)

decriminalize *v.* [1972]
to remove from the category of a crime; most commonly used by those who argue for and against the legalization of cannabis. – **decriminalization** *n.*

* *'Somebody could sign the ad without necessarily being in favour of legislation, and the basic idea was decriminalization.'* (J. Green, *Days in the Life*, 1988)

dedicated *adj.* [1981]
in computing: a machine or program or a single part of a machine or system that is completely given over to a specific task; thus 'dedicated word processor', etc.

* *'I remain unconvinced as to whether or not there is a market for the dedicated word processor, post Amstrad PCW.'* (*PC World*, April 1990)

deep throat *n.* [1973]
the original Deep Throat was the super-confidential high-level source used by reporters Carl Bernstein and Bob Woodward in their investigation of the Watergate Affair for the *Washington Post*; the name was taken from 1972's popular 'art porn' film of the same name, starring Linda Lovelace as a girl whose clitoris is sited in her throat. Since Watergate the term has been used for any secret source.

* *'When Deep Throat heard Woodward's voice, there was a long pause. This would have to be their last telephone conversation . . . Both the FBI and the White House were determined to learn how the Post was getting its information.'* (B. Woodward & C. Bernstein, *All the President's Men*, 1974)

de-escalation *n.* [1965]
the reversal of escalation, thus the defusing of a situation that is moving towards military conflict.
See also **escalation**; **re-escalation.**

def *adj.* [1987]
definitive: excellent, first-rate.

* *'Hey what about the scratching, is it def? Fuck, no.'* (N.W.A., *Compton's In The House*, 1988)

defensible space *n.*
the area in which one lives and which, in an increasingly hostile world, requires defending with a variety of gates, entry phones, etc. against incursion from outside.

* *'Probably the best the present tenants can hope for is a fair share of "personal defensible space".'* (*Independent on Sunday*, 17 June 1990)

defensive medicine *n.* [1987]
a style of medicine characterized by its ultra-cautious methods and resistance to innovation; such methods have been adopted in the face of a surge of costly malpractice suits by patients in the US, who sue at the slightest opportunity, and the huge price hikes in medical insurance that have accompanied the trend.

degrade *v.* [1965]
in military jargon: to wear down an enemy's offensive capability.

degradable *adj.* [1965]
capable of being broken down by natural processes.

demi-veg *n.* [1989]
a vegetarian who eats fish, eggs, and poultry, none of which would be permitted to a strict observer, let alone a vegan.

demo *abbrev.* [1963]
demonstration: a demo disc (latterly a demo tape) contains the rough recording of a song by a new band, which can be hawked around the record business in the hope of finding professional interest and, thus, a contract.

* *'I would spend hour after hour listening to tapes and demo discs in the hope of finding a hit.'* (T. Blacker, *Fixx*, 1989)

deniability *n.* [1973]
the ability of any high official to disassociate themselves from any illegal or improper activity performed by a subordinate.

denial *n.* [1965]
in military use: any aggressive operations directed at securing a military position; thus denial of space would mean the immediate destruction of any hostile attempts to place satellites and/or weapons in what was claimed as 'one's own' space-based areas.

Denver boot *n., adj.* [1986]
the clamp used to immobilize illegally parked cars, both by the police and by an increasing number of private clamping firms. The 'boot' takes its name from the city where it was first used, Denver, Colorado.

* *'Finding the Denver Boot brigade still at work, the motorists vented their frustration, setting about the clamper and his 22 year-old female assistant.'* (*Sunday Correspondent*, 21 October 1990)

dependency culture *n.* [1987]
a derogatory synonym for the very poor and most socially disadvantaged: a coinage of right-wing Conservatives, who deplore what they see as a culture in which people find it easier to fall

back on the various financial provisions of the welfare state rather than 'get on their bike' and look for work, and in general take responsibility for the inadequacies of their lives.

✱ '"*Dependency culture", with its connotations of something nastily non-human growing in a petri dish, along with "enterprise culture", has been one of the great successes of the Tory New Right in the jargon war.*' (*Sunday Correspondent*, 23 September 1990)

deprogram *v.* [1973]
to release a member of a religious cult – whether an adherent of the Revd Moon, Bhagwan, or whoever – from the psychological control that is being exerted over their free will; such cults ensnare their members with an intense programme of ideological brainwashing. Deprogramming reverses the process with an equally intense period of indoctrination back into the 'real world'. – **deprogramming** *n.*

✱ '*We really flipped out when Joannie pulled that whole Moonie number, but it came out okay after we got her deprogrammed.*' (C. McFadden, *The Serial*, 1976)

deregulate *v.* [1974]
to remove from controls; especially when those controls have been governmental or legislative. The term became particularly widespread when the US and later the British stock exchanges were freed from earlier restrictions and opened up to a far wider membership. – **deregulation** *n.*

deschool *v.* [1970]
to abolish traditional schooling, and thus to eradicate the philosophies of such schooling from the teaching process; the term was coined by Ivan Illich in 1970 and popularized in his book *Deschooling Society.*

✱ '*The radical deschooling of society begins, therefore, with the unmasking by cultural revolutionaries of the myth of schooling.*' (I. Illich, *Saturday Review*, 17 October 1970)

deselect *v.* [1985]
under the rules of the British Labour Party, for the local constituency party to decide to withdraw their support from a sitting member and to opt for a replacement who will fight the next by- or general election. – **deselection** *n.*

✱ '*Ron Brown MP was deselected by his local Edinburgh Leith Labour party as a candidate for the next election.*' (*The Independent*, 6 April 1990)

designer *adj.* [1980]
an all-purpose adjective, developed in the image-conscious 1980s and denoting unashamed display, whether quite literally of the designer's label or not. Hitherto labels had been a secret for the wearer alone, a source of quiet self-satisfaction if suitably grand, but certainly not to be attached to the outside of the garment. 'Designer' epitomized an era determined to advertise its devotion to conspicuous consumption. Labelling was all and the adjective embraced not merely clothes (Armani, Gaultier), but water (Perrier), drugs (⇨ecstasy) and even stubble. The word stems from US millionairess Gloria Vanderbilt, whose name was featured on the well-turned (and expensive) jeans promoted as her special creation.

✱ '*Loosely termed the designer-wally, these figures became unpleasantly prominent in the 1980s.*' (*Sky*, December 1989)

✱ '*The Hans Crescent shop . . . is reckoned by*

many to be the most influential designer boutique in the land.' (*The Independent*, 9 June 1990)

* *'The real perils of 20th century designer living – for the beautiful people of California at any rate.'* (*The Independent*, 22 June 1990)

designer drug *n.* [1986]
any of a variety of illegal recreational drugs that have been created by chemists specifically for a variety of effects. The best known is ⇨ecstasy, but there are many others.

desktop (computer) *n.* [1985]
a computer system that sits on one's desk, the most popular and widely-used type of ⇨personal computer.

* *'The systems are packaged in three basic models: desktop, deskside (or tower) and rack-mount.'* (*Byte*, April 1990)

desktop metaphor *n.* [1985]
a concept popular in computer design whereby the screen is supposed to simulate one's office desktop – with calculator, notepad, files, address book, etc.; the idea is also known as a 'pen and pencil idiom' (*The Independent*, 9 April 1990).

* *'Desktop metaphors are great, if they are fast enough.'* (*PC World*, May 1990)

desktop publishing *n.* [1988]
essentially high-level word-processing, using ⇨dedicated ⇨programs and printing out copy on a sophisticated ⇨laser printer. DTP (as it is generally known) supposedly gives the user the opportunity of rivalling professional typesetting and magazine production from the comfort of their own desk. The technology is certainly sophisticated, but, unless it takes advantage of the skills of a professional designer, the product rarely is.

* *'CAD and desktop publishing continue to be improved with ever new and faster PCs.'* (*PC World*, April, 1990)

des res *abbrev.* [1987]
desirable residence: once no more than (widely understood) estate agent's jargon, the term has come to mean no more than a desirable property, which one might wish to own.

destabilize *v.* [1974]
the using of clandestine methods by the intelligence services of a major power to undermine and ultimately to destroy an incumbent foreign government which is unfriendly to one's policies and to have it replaced by one which is more amenable. This process can include the use of propaganda (both press and radio), the financing and advising of opposition parties, the arming and advising of their military wings, and a variety of black operations up to and including the assassination of heads of state. – **destabilization** *n.*

* *'He begins to give you a bad name. So you destabilize him. You get rid of him.'* (*Independent on Sunday*, 27 May 1990)

detente *n.* [1972]
a policy which encouraged a degree of mutual understanding between the superpowers and even created some short-lived ⇨de-escalation of the nuclear arms race; encouraged in particular by Dr Henry Kissinger, the policy flourished between 1972 and 1973, with its highest achievement being the ⇨ABM Treaty of 1972. The term originated *c.*1908 when it had the general meaning of easing political relations. It was not, however, until the 1970s that it

gained its specific modern use. During the Reagan period detente was vilified as 'a sell-out' and was replaced by an increasingly icy Cold War, 1980s style. The winding down of that Cold War in 1989 led to a renewed use of detente, although the general view is that detente implied only a pause, whereas the status quo might indicate the absolute end of hostilities.

* *'It was . . . under the aegis of detente and arms control that the United States seemed to acknowledge temporarily its loss of nuclear advantage.'* (R.C. Aldridge, *First Strike!*, 1983)

deterrence *n.* [1960]
literally 'dissuasion by terror', deterrence – 'the highest priority task of the strategic forces' (Herman Kahn) – sets out to prevent an enemy from doing something through fear of the consequences that will inevitably follow such an act. Deterrence is in effect psychological – and the metaphors surrounding it refer to chess, bridge and poker – but the threat may require a material backup. **Nuclear deterrence**, planning not for World War III but to ensure that such hostilities never occur, is based on the possession and deployment of ⇨ICBMs and ⇨SLBMs, the heavyweights of the nuclear armoury.

* *'There is a semantic abyss created by the word "deterrence".'* (R.C. Aldridge, *First Strike!*, 1983)

developing (countries) *n.* [1962]
a euphemism for poor nations which has replaced 'under-developed', which in turn replaced 'backward' and which, in its turn, is being rivalled by ⇨Third World and the ⇨South. It is always assumed that 'developing' countries are gradually creating some form of wealth/stability along Western capitalist lines.
See also **South**; **Third World**.

devolution *n.* [1976]
the granting of an increased degree of self-government, particularly as regards the splitting off of Scotland and Wales from England and their developing discrete legislative bodies.

dice *v.* [1963]
to jostle for position in a race.

diet *adj.*
a less sweet than usual version of a given commodity, often a soft drink, e.g. *Diet Coke, Diet Pepsi.*
See also **lite**.

dietary fibre *n.* [1976]
the roughage contained in vegetables and fruit; dietary fibre became quite literally the dieter's ⇨flavour of the month around 1978 when it was touted as the latest cure-all, cutting down weight and promoting good health.

diethylene glycol *n.* [1984]
a chemical that was found to be used for adulterating a large amount of Austrian wine.

digital audio tape *n.* [1987]
see **DAT**.

dinky *abbrev.* [1985]
an acronym for dual income no kids yet: the most desirable of 1980s states, although somewhat tarnished by the fashion for offspring which (as much biologically as sociologically) has overtaken the dinkies as they move into

the 1990s. The opposite to a dinky was a nilky: no income lots of kids.
See also **yuppie**.

dinosaur *n.* [1977]
a slang term for an ageing rock musician, usually of the 1960s generation and resolutely impervious to suggestions that they should hang up their guitars.
✱ *'Dinosaurs walk the earth again next Sunday at Knebworth Park . . . Genesis, Cliff Richard and the Shadows, Elton John.'* (*Independent on Sunday*, 24 June 1990)

dirty *adj.* [1960]
referring to a nuclear explosion that carries the maximum fallout.
See also **clean**.

dirty tricks *n.* [1973]
illegal activities by a political party or its hirelings (notably the great trickster of 1960s campaigns – Dick Tuck) which are designed to sabotage the smooth progress of their rival's political campaign. It derived from the CIA's 'Department of Dirty Tricks' (actually the Directorate of Plans), which specialized in covert operations, allegedly restricted to overseas targets.
✱ *'This was the side of the CIA that lived and operated under the wraps of maximum security and which figured in Communist demonology as the "dirty tricks" extension of "US imperialism".'* (C. McCrystal, L. Chester *et al.*, *Watergate*, 1973)

disadvantaged *adj.* [1962]
a blanket term, some say euphemism, for those suffering from poverty, inadequate parenting, mental inadequacies, environmental deprivation and all the other problems that are considered as detrimental to living the idealized social role. *cf.* **challenged**.
✱ *'Not poor, not rich, we were nonetheless more disadvantaged than all of those around us.'* (T. Blacker, *Fixx*, 1989)

disappear *v.* [1976]
a literal translation of the Spanish *desaparecer*, and as such used to refer to the arrest and subsequent disappearance of many alleged members of opposition groups in Argentina (prior to the Alfonsin government), El Salvador, Chile, and other South American states. Once disappeared it is assumed that those concerned, known as **the disappeared**, are dead, imprisoned, suffering torture, etc.
✱ *'The children are Anatole and Victoria Julien, who "disappeared" with their parents when security forces invaded their home in Buenos Aires.'* (Amnesty International *Newsletter*, November 1981)

disaster film/movie *n.* [1975]
any film that concentrates on one of a variety of natural or technological disasters, notably *Earthquake* and *The Towering Inferno*. Filled with major stars in cameo roles, they capitalize on special effects and, despite a good deal of obligatory death, comfort the audience with an equally obligatory happy ending.

disco *n.* [1975]
1. in general, the music played in ⇨discotheques; specifically a style of music popular for dancing, accentuating a regular rhythmic beat, coupled to banal or non-existent lyrics.
See also **House**.
✱ *'One reason for the popularity of rap music, like disco and punk before it, is that it's so utterly*

annoying.' (L. Bangs, *Psychotic Reactions and Carburetor Dung*, 1988)

2. *an abbreviation of* ⇨discotheque.

discotheque *n.* [1965]

a club which features recorded, rather than live music for dancing.

* *'Down in the throbbing ultra-violet bowel of a discotheque, Terry and a few of the lads are backed to a wall.'* (N. Fury, *Agro*, 1971)

discourse *n.* [1977]

a mode of systematic representation of the world, what Marx called 'consciousness' and what Michel Foucault has termed the systems of linguistic representations through which power sustains itself. The discourse is used to order and arrange an otherwise random world, and in so doing to exert one's mastery over it. On a more general level this bedrock term of structuralist criticism is a synonym for the way we see a given topic, discipline, or just a way of talking about things.

* *'We codified his likes and dislikes. We deconstructed his discourse. We analysed his doodles.'* (*Independent on Sunday*, 17 June 1990)

disinformation *n.* [1966]

1. *in business use*: the deliberate spreading of inaccurate information about designs, sales, marketing, etc., which is intended to confuse and worry trading rivals.

2. *in espionage or military use*: distorted or false information deliberately disseminated either at home to confuse foreign agents operating in one's own country, or in a foreign country to confuse its inhabitants.

* *'The policy of "disinformation", supplying the other side with deliberately misleading information, reached its apotheosis during the early 1970s.'* (T. Blacker, *Fixx*, 1989)

disinvest *v.* [1986]

to end or withdraw one's investment; thus the ending or withdrawal of investment; specifically the withdrawal of investment in South Africa by countries who have hitherto braved the wrath of the anti-apartheid lobby but now see a move towards ideological purity as a good commercial move. – **disinvestment** *n.*

diss *abbrev.* [1986]

disrespect: to undermine another person's self-esteem; current liberal philosophy in the US attributes lack of self-esteem as the cause of many crimes.

* *'The man alleged to have started the murderous fire . . . claimed he did it because his girlfriend had "dissed" him. "Getting dissed ain't good for your self-esteem", explained one young man.'* (*The Times*, 7 April 1990)

DMT *abbrev.* [1967]

dimethyltryptamine: a synthetic hallucinogenic drug allied to LSD-25.

* *'Hooking down mathematical lab drugs, LSD-25, IT-290, DMT, instead of soma water . . .'* (T. Wolfe, *The Electric Kool-Aid Acid Test*, 1969)

do a number *v.* [1967]

to make emotional demands upon, or deliberately to try to mystify or bamboozle. Also to subject to deceit or confidence trickery.

docking *n.* [1965]

in spaceflight terminology the linking together of two vehicles in space; thus **undocking**: the disengagement of two vehicles.

Doctor Martens *n.* [1969]
the proprietary name for large high-laced workman's boots, featuring their unique air-cushioned sole (with or without steel toe-caps), which were adopted by the first generation of ➪skinheads *c.*1969. Since then Doc Martens (as they are generally known) have put their name to a number of fashion designs, and their original boots have been adopted as popular street fashion in the 1980s, but they remain the footwear of choice for the youthful hooligan.

* *'Dr Martens, Cherry reds, Tuf! Heavy-heeled, tank-soled, lace-up soul boots.'* (N. Fury, *Agro*, 1971)

docudrama *n.* [1960]
from docu(mentary) + drama: a television dramatization, using actors, sets, and a script, which is based on facts. It is often presented in the style of a documentary to intensify the sense of authenticity. *cf.* **faction**.

Other uses of the prefix docu- include *documusical* (1974), *docuhistory* (1981), and *docurecreation* (1983).

docutainment *n.* [1960]
see **infotainment**.

doggy-bag *n.* [1968]
a bag into which a diner can have the remains of a restaurant meal placed in order that they may be taken home 'for the dog'.

dog(s) of war *n.* [1960]
a mercenary; popularized by the eponymous novel by Frederick Forsyth, who in turn took his title from Shakespeare: 'Cry "Havoc!" and let slip the dogs of war.' (*Julius Caesar*, III. i.), although Mark Antony was referring to the general phenomenon of war, rather than to its paid fighters.

* *'A dog of war who had his day'* (headline in the *Sunday Correspondent*, 22 April 1990)

Dolby *n.* [1969]
a patented electronic device that reduces peripheral noise on a recording; the name is taken from Ray Dolby (*b.* 1933) who patented his Dolby System in 1969.

dolly (-bird) *n.* [1965]
the quintessential description of young, pretty, usually working-class girls in the 1960s; the customers of Biba and Bus Stop, the temporary secretaries, etc. Often found in contemporary media with the obligatory adjective 'mini-skirted'.

* *'Our biggest source of customers are the dolly birds . . . working class girls.'* (J. Aitken, *The Young Meteors*, 1967)

dontopedalogy *n.* [1964]
a coinage of the royal consort Prince Philip and meaning the ability to put one's foot in one's mouth.

doomwatch(er) *n.* [1972]
on the pattern of China-watchers and Russia-watchers, one who surveys and analyses current events for signs of impending doom, usually of an environmental nature.

do one's own thing *v.* [1967]
the core curriculum of the hippie 1960s: stay untrammelled by the demands of 'straight' society, live out one's life as one wishes and create one's own world.

* *'One could do this thing, live together with*

other kids – Our own thing!' (T. Wolfe, *The Electric Kool-Aid Acid Test*, 1969)

* *'Just thought I'd let you know what I mean when I say, "I'm just doin my thing".'* (A. Hoffman, *Woodstock Nation*, 1969)

doorstep *v.*
for a reporter to wait on a person's doorstep in order to attempt to gain an interview when that person either arrives home or goes out.

doper *n.* [1967]
a drug user.

* *'It had long been clear to everybody except a handful of rock industry dopers and the national press.'* (H.S. Thompson, *Fear and Loathing in Las Vegas*, 1971)

Dormobile *n.* [1963]
a small van which has been equipped for mobile living; it often has a roof that can be raised to offer space for a bunk bed, as well as a kitchenette; the word is an elision of dormitory and automobile; known in the US as a camper.

dot-matrix printer *n.* [1980]
a printer that creates each character from an array of dots that are usually formed by transferring ink by mechanical impact; the print head is formed of a number of wires, which produce the actual dots as programmed by the word-processing software; clarity and print quality differs as to the number of dots – current models offer 9, 18, 24 or 48 dot printers.

* *'It supports dot-matrix printers, ink jet printers, laser printers and phototypesetters.'* (J. Cavuoto & J. Berst, *Inside Xerox*, 1989)

double-digit *adj.* [1974]
any figure from 10 to 99; usually used of inflation statistics.

doublespeak *n.*
any form of language which pretends to communicate but doesn't, ameliorative language which makes the bad seem good (slums are the 'inner city'), the cheap seem expensive (second-hand is 'preowned'), and the negative positive (the poor are 'fiscal underachievers').

* *'In the world of doublespeak dying is "terminal living".'* (C. Ricks & L. Michaels (eds.), *The State of the Language*, 1990)

do up (*or* do) *v.* [1969]
to consume, usually drugs and implying (though not invariably) the use of a needle, with which one 'shoots up'.

* *'To this end you spend tomorrow morning doing up brandies in a bad-oil gaff in the Plaza Real.'* (J. Meades, *Peter Knows What Dick Likes*, 1989)
* *'You have stuff to do, but so do we – the best stuff any Army helicopter can carry in.'* (B. Woodward, *Wired*, 1984)

dove *n.* [1962]
anyone who prefers negotiations to armed conflict in the conduct of international relations; coined by US political writers Stewart Alsop and Charles Bartlett in 1962.

down *adj.* [1980]
1. *in the technical use:* not working, out of commission; the general use springs from computer-speak and like similar adoptions confers upon the speaker a certain technological sophistication.
2. *in the emotional sense:* depressed, unhappy.

downer *n.* [1970]

1. an unfortunate, depressing, saddening experience.

See also **bummer**.

✱ *'I recollect another mighty sad downer stretch about the beginning of the seventies.'* (L. Bangs, *Psychotic Reactions and Carburetor Dung*, 1988)

2. depressant drugs, especially barbiturates (the opposite of ⇨upper).

✱ *'Coupled with alcohol, downers can wipe out reality completely.'* (M. Farren, *Watch Out Kids*, 1972)

downmarket [1973]

1. *adj.* aimed at the lower income consumer.

✱ *'A growing desire to discourage what is bluntly referred to as the "downmarket holidaymaker".'* (*The Times*, 6 October 1990)

2. *v.* to adopt a merchandising/packaging/marketing strategy firmly aimed at the poorer end of the market, including the altering of an otherwise 'up-market' product so that it will appeal to the lower income groups.

downscale *v.*

see **upscale**.

downside *adj.* [1985]

referring to the negative aspect of a given situation; thus *downside risk*: an estimate that a given share will decline in value, as well as an estimate of the extent of that decline, taking into account all the relevant factors.

downsize *v.* [1987]

to shrink, especially of a workforce.

Down's syndrome *n.* [1971]

the current description of what was known as mongolism, a relatively common form of mental deficiency caused by chromosome abnormality and characterized by physical signs which might be seen to resemble the characteristics of Mongolians; the term was considered both racist and pejorative, and has generally been replaced by this one, which is taken from the medical researcher J.L.H. Down (1828–96) who first specialized in the condition.

downward compatibility *n.* [1964]

see **upward compatibility**.

Dr Feelgood *n.* [1972]

any easy-going, complaisant doctor who prescribes drugs without asking any difficult questions.

✱ *'A couple of Dr Feelgood's gaily coloured pills which had become so much a part of Mila's life.'* (T. Blacker, *Fixx*, 1989)

dread [1968]

1. *n.* a generic term for any Rasta man.

2. *adj.* implies seriousness, importance – whether positive or negative. There is an overtone, as in ⇨Babylon, of a Biblical element.

dreadlocks *n., adj.* [1969]

the distinctive hairstyle worn by Rastafarians – long, matted 'locks' that are often concealed beneath large woolly hats.

✱ *'Natty dread lock in a fifth street/And then I skip one fence to sixth street/I've got to reach seventh street'* (B. Marley, 'Natty Dread', 1975)

drive-by *n., adj.* [1987]

a killing (usually as reported from the US) which takes place when the killer drives by in their car, pausing only to shoot dead the target. Drive-by deaths (the models for which can be seen in a variety of classic gangster movies of the 1930s) are especially widespread among the warring gangs of Los Angeles.

-driven (*or* -led) *suffix.* [1980]
despite their opposite meanings in general use, for jargonauts both state the same thing: a technospeak way of saying impelled by a given force. Usually as *market-led, design-driven,* etc.

* *'There was little doubt . . . which manufacturer was design and engineering driven rather than led by men in snappy suits.'* (*Independent on Sunday,* 3 June 1990)
* *'We have a vision and it's market-driven in the sense that're always keeping the user in sight.'* (*PC World,* November 1990)
* *'A good demand-led idea is rapidly turning into a speculative farce.'* (*The Independent,* 15 May 1990)

drop *v.* [1968]
to take a drug, from dropping a pill down one's throat; especially common as **drop acid**: to take LSD.

drop-out *n.* [1960]
one who chooses to quit mainstream society; particularly those who, in the 1960s, began leaving universities and colleges before they had finished their courses, preferring to drop formal education for the alternative lifestyle.
– **drop out** *v.*

druggie *n.* [1970]
rarely used by actual drug-takers, the term is popular among the uniformed, notably the pundits who write or talk about drugs in the media.

* *'Not only has he been labelled a "druggie" . . . but he also faces a third consecutive year of record-breaking losses.'* (*Independent on Sunday,* 8 April 1990)

dry *n.* [1979]
in political as in metereological use, the opposite of ⇨wet and essentially a back-formation from that term of schoolboy (and thence political) slang: a Conservative politician who followed the political ideology of former prime minister Margaret Thatcher, especially as regards her monetarist policies which the wets saw as causing great misery, and the dries praised as being necessary, if nasty medicine.

DTP *n.* [1987]
see **desktop publishing.**

dual track *adj., n.* [1979]
originated at a meeting of NATO leaders on Guadeloupe in January 1979, the policy that NATO deployment of new weapons would proceed in parallel to the continuous seeking of arms limitation talks with the Russians to reduce, limit, or even eliminate the very weapons that were to be deployed.

* *'Not to the point of thinking that the dual track decision be scrapped altogether; such a recommendation, he said, would be "unhelpful".'* (S. Talbott, *Deadly Gambits,* 1984)

dub *v., n.* [1970]
for disc jockeys to improvise their own lyrics over a soundtrack. Taken from the much earlier film use.

* *'Trying to join my fanclub/Lip-synchin' over one of my dubs.'* (N.W.A., *Compton's In The House,* 1988)

dude *n.* [1970]
slang for boy, man, fellow. Dude began life as rural US slang for a city slicker or dandy; it gained its first resurgence in the late 1960s, when, as a more general term, it had its moment of popularity in the hip community; its most recent use was concentrated among preteen fans of the 'heroes in a half shell', the Teenage Mutant Ninja (Hero in the UK) Turtles, who use the term continually.

* *'Carol had been having some problems with the dude when she joined their consciousness-raising group.'* (C. McFadden, *The Serial,* 1976)
* *'Robots! Ya-hoo. Let's rock, dudes!' Teenage Mutant Hero Turtles* comic, 1990)

dumb terminal *n.* [1972]
attached via a network to a mainframe computer, it has no computing capacity itself, and can be used purely to access material. Typical are the screens found at airport check-ins. The opposite, the **smart terminal**, is similarly attached to a mainframe, but can perform some computing functions by itself.

dump bin *n.* [1972]
a display unit, usually made of strong cardboard, that is placed in a bookshop to show off a given title.

* *'Would you be pleased at the prospect of its going on sale in dump bins?'* (*Independent on Sunday,* 24 June 1990)

dune buggy *n.* [1965]
a cross between a jeep and an automobile with large tyres and high suspension, designed for travelling over sand-dunes and deserts.

* *'It's the richest off-the-road race for motorcycles and dune buggies in the history of organised sport.'* (H.S. Thompson, *Fear and Loathing in Las Vegas,* 1971)

Dungeons and Dragons *n.* [1980]
a fantasy ⇨role-playing game, drawing its primary inspiration like most of its kind from J.R.R. Tolkien's 'sword and sorcery' epic *Lord of the Rings* (1954). 'D&D' games have been modified for computer use, but the essential game is played with dice, maps, model characters, their weapons and other implements, and a good deal of additional paraphernalia.

* *'The Dungeons and Dragons game system provides a framework within which the imagination can turn lifeless numbers into characters and gives them a world to live in.'* (J. Butterfield, P. Parker, D. Honigman, *What Is Dungeons & Dragons?,* 1982)

dusty *n.* [1972]
see **wrinkly**.

E *n.* [1987]
see **ecstasy.**

earner (nice little) *phrase.* [1979]
a slang term for a profitable (and probably illegal) job or deal; the use, which certainly goes back to the Second World War in police and criminal circles, was given vast popularity with Thames Television's hit series *Minder*, which began life in 1978, and owed much of its appeal to the lowlife slang paraded by its chief character Arthur Daley.

earth shoes *n.* [1970]
square-toed shoes with thicker soles in the front than the back, designed to adapt to the contours of the Earth and by lowering the heel, give the wearer greater comfort. The shoes were launched in Denmark on 22 April ('Earth Day') 1970.
See also **flip-flop, thong.**

EC *abbrev.* [1987]
European Community: an abbreviation of the original European Economic Community that has become increasingly popular in the last five years, especially since it was chosen as the regular term by the new *Independent* newspaper.

- ✱ *'Yet she jibs at the best antidote – a more tightly knit EC – and seeks refuge in visions of wider . . . European cooperation.'* (*The Independent*, 31 March 1990)

eco- *prefix.* [1972]
denoting various combinations that refer to events, occupations, and concerns keyed to ecology.
See also **green.**

- ✱ *'Actions like these have made Foreman a wanted but respected man, says eco-activist and postman Bob Kaspar.'* (*Sunday Correspondent*, 3 June 1990)
- ✱ *'Edward Abby's 1975 novel about eco-saboteurs,* The Monkey-Wrench Gang.*'* (*Sunday Correspondent*, 3 June 1990)

ecodoomsters *n.* [1975]
those who watch for and forecast the imminent collapse of the world's ecology.

- ✱ *'Somebody was bound . . . to bring out a book named for the new decade, gesture at millenial anxieties (button pushers in Washington, eco-doom, disease) . . . '* (*Independent on Sunday*, 25 March 1990)

economic refugee *n.* [1986]
a refugee who leaves his or her native country in the hope of finding a better life; such refugees, who have every right to seek such material improvements, are often looked down upon by their peers, the political refugees.

ecopolicy *n.* [1970]
any policy that concentrates on ways of modifying or preserving the ecology.

eco-terrorism *n.* [1991]
the deliberate destruction of the environment during a war. The term, which had previously applied to sabotage carried out by ecology activists (⇨**eco-**), was reworked in the context of the 1991 Gulf War, when it described the release of large quantities of oil into the Persian Gulf and burning of Kuwaiti oilwells by Iraqi troops under the orders of Saddam Hussein.

- ✱ *'In the US radical greens are turning to eco-terrorism.'* (*Sunday Correspondent*, 3 June 1990)
- ✱ *'The fact that . . . it was still uncertain whether Saddam was trying to make a political point or hamper the allies' military operations indicates the strategic futility of this "eco-terrorism".'* (*The Independent*, 1 March 1991)

ecstasy *n.* [1986]
a slang term for the drug known officially as MDMA or methylene dioxymethamphetamine. Ecstasy existed in the 1960s as one of many synthetic hallucinogens, but only reached its apotheosis as the ⇨acid of the late 1980s.

- ✱ *'Soft drugs were common, but there was talk of how ecstasy . . . was now hard to find and had been replaced by cannabis and amyl nitrate.'* (*Independent on Sunday*, 3 June 1990)

ECU *abbrev.* [1972]
an acronym for European Currency Unit, usually printed in lower-case as 'ecu' (which already meant 'coin' in French). This 'euro-currency' was created in 1972 to help EC members settle their debts and to act as a standard against which the various national currencies could be measured.

- ✱ *'To sign up for monetary union, for a single currency, an ecu note without a portrait of the Queen, would split her [Margaret Thatcher's] party.'* (*The Independent*, 30 October 1990)

edge city *n.* [1969]
the extremes of experience, whether physical or spiritual, drug induced or whatever; often carrying overtones of fear and challenge.
See also **city, Fat City, -ville.**

- ✱ *'327,000 horsepower, a whole superhighway long and soaring, screaming on toward . . . Edge City, and ultimate fantasies.'* (T. Wolfe, *The Electric Kool-Aid Acid Test*, 1969)

EFL *abbrev.* [1963]
English as a Foreign Language.

EFT/POS *abbrev.* [1985]
an acronym for electronic funds transfer at point of sale: any form of electronic payment for goods. As opposed to a credit card which delays payment, these charges, as in the Switch system, are instantly debited to the account holder.

EFTS *abbrev.* [1973]
an acronym for electronic funds transfer system: any computerized system which enables its user to transfer funds by electronic rather than paper means.

ego trip *n.* [1969]
self-aggrandisement, boasting, egocentricity; a mix of the analytic Freudian 'ego', with the hallucinogenic, Learyesque ⇨trip.

- ✱ *'It's not like I'm on any kind of a personal ego trip, I mean I'm not asking for anything for myself.'* (R. DiLello, *The Longest Cocktail Party*, 1971)

A similar combination is **power trip**, using trip

to mean 'the way in which one acts'.

* *'Rule number one is no power tripping. Nobody needs power tripping, Harvey.'* (C. McFadden, *The Serial*, 1976)

ekistics *n.* [1970]
the science of human settlements: ekistics collates the relevant information from many disciplines, including economics, anthropology, social sciences, urban planning, a variety of technologies, etc. Coined by the Greek architect C.A. Doxiadis, ekistics posits megalopolises of fifty to one hundred million inhabitants, as well as ecumenopolises that stretch from London to Beijing.

electronic cottage *n.* [1987]
the ➪high-tech country home, replete with personal computer (plus ➪modem), ➪fax, Xerox machine and whatever else is required, that makes it possible for one to conduct one's working life far away from the city while in no way sacrificing the technological and informational facilities hitherto unavailable outside the metropolis.

electronic office *n.* [1980]
the office of the future, laden with ➪high-tech electronic equipment – computer, ➪modem, ➪fax, ➪laser printer, etc.

* *'The electronic office will mean a revision of existing office procedures and job roles.'* (D. Jarrett, *The Good Computing Book for Beginners*, 1980)

electronic tagging *n.* [1989]
a system of tagging convicted prisoners, originated in the US by a judge who first saw the idea in a children's comic; a band which emits an electronic signal is fixed around the subject's ankle, he or she can be traced by this signal and thus, since the band cannot be removed, held as secure in their own home as if they were in a prison.

elint *n.*
Electronic Intelligence: the monitoring, measuring, identifying and analysing of all varieties of hostile communications and radar activity.

E-mail *n.* [1986]
electronic mail: transmitted between individuals via their computer screens.

* *'Our new building will have all the new information technology – desktop computers, E-mail (electronic messaging) – and the offices will be open-plan to facilitate the team process.'* (*Independent on Sunday*, 8 April 1990)

Eminent Persons Group *n.* [1986]
the original EPG consisted of seven Commonwealth statesmen who in May 1986 visited South Africa in the hope of pushing forward a negotiated settlement of the country's political crisis; since then the term has been extended to describe a number of such high-ranking deputations.

* *'Last month, I went back to the Soviet Union as part of an Eminent Persons Group, sponsored by the Student and Academic Campaign for Soviet Jews.'* (*The Independent*, 31 March 1990)

EMP *abbrev.* [1970]
an acronym of electromagnetic pulse: the result of a nuclear explosion – the release of intense bursts of energy across the electromagnetic spectrum. These bursts can temporarily or permanently damage or destroy all kinds of

electronic equipment, both on the ground and in space and could be fatal to satellite, as well as earth communications systems. It is quite feasible that the EMP alone that results from a first strike impact would be sufficient, irrespective of the concomitant and devastating heat and blast damage, to wreck the greater proportion of all communications and render further organization – defensive or offensive, civil or military – virtually impossible.

* *'The tremendous speed of an incoming warhead . . . would generate a higher electromagnetic pulse (EMP) in its circuitry.'* (R.C. Aldridge, *First Strike!*, 1983)

EMU *abbrev.* [1988]
an acronym for European Monetary Union: a system, which it is hoped will come on stream by 2000, in which the various separate currencies of the EC will be united in a single currency which will be legal tender throughout the member states. This may be the ecu (which is certainly the most likely name for the currency), or it may be that each country keeps their 'pounds', 'marks', or 'francs' and prints its own design of note, even though each individual name will only mask a local version of the same basic system.

* *'As with her [Margaret Thatcher] objection to EMU, this is because government and parliament lose direct control of interest rates.'* (*The Independent*, 30 October 1990)

encounter group (*or* **session**) *n.* [1970]
a group of people who meet under the guidance of a trained therapist in order to use the situation to bring out their own feelings through interacting, often in a highly emotional manner, with others in the group.
See also **group therapy**.

end-user *n., adj.* [1963]
1. the customer or purchaser of a given item; or if not the actual purchaser, then the individual who will actually use the computer, the weapon, etc.

* *'It can't hurt to let the people who are designing OS/2 and Windows . . . to come to the oldest computer show of the lot and talk to end users.'* (*Byte*, June 1990)

2. *in government use:* those on the receiving end of all bureaucratically and politically created programmes and ideas: the public; from the industrial use, referring to the customer of a given line of goods or consumer durable.
See also **end-user certificate**.

end-user certificate *n.* [1963]
1. *in military use:* a declaration that must be made by private arms dealers citing those who will actually be using their wares; this is intended to prevent such arms falling into terrorist hands but in reality is of little use against the many methods of avoiding such restrictions.
2. *in commercial use:* a declaration that must be signed by the user of a licensed product – especially computer hardware or software – that is intended to prevent piracy and breach of copyright.

enemies list *n.* [1973]
a list of 'enemies' compiled by the Nixon White House in 1972; this list included political and cultural enemies (notably the liberal establishment), who were seen as a threat to the administration.

* *'At its peak the enemies list contained the names*

of over two hundred individuals and eighteen organizations, loosely divided into different categories.' (C. McCrystal, L. Chester, *et al.*, *Watergate*, 1973)

energy crisis *n.* [1970]
1. the acute shortage of energy-producing fuels, especially of oil; this crisis emerged in 1973, after the Yom Kippur War in the Middle East led to massive price rises from OPEC, and continued under the Carter presidency from 1976–80.
2. the idea that our main source of energy – oil – is damaging the environment so badly as to cause a crisis, and thus the belief that alternative sources of energy must be created.

engine *n.* [1985]
in computing: the basic technology that lies at the heart of hard- or software; thus the 'Canon engine' is used as the basis for a wide variety of ➪laser printers, although they are each badged under an individual manufacturer's name.

* *'Nelson Taylor looks at a hypertext engine for the computer age.'* (*PC World*, April 1990)

English (*or* British disease) *n.* [1969]
the original use of English disease was by the French who, returning the xenophobia embodied in the term 'French pox', used it to mean venereal disease; today it usually refers to the alleged propensity of the British worker to indulge in injurious strikes, and that of their managers to resist gaining proper knowledge of the business of which they are in charge; taken together, it can be seen as the continuing class struggle that dominates English life.

* *'The second, broadcast directly afterwards, is the "British Disease", which is diagnosed here as class.'* (*The Independent*, 4 September 1990)

enterprise *adj.* [1981]
a keyword for the supposed age of the (Tory) entrepreneur, role model for a much-touted 'enterprise culture'; thus the *enterprise zone*, backdrop for such skills, the decaying inner city, thrown open for tax-free deregulated profit-making.

* *'An avenging angel cypher who solves enterprise culture crime while looking good in a fast-changing world.'* (*The Independent*, 29 May 1990)

entry-level *adj.* [1986]
basic, primary level; used in computing to describe the first machine (or specific piece of ➪software) a user either purchases or learns to use.

* *'Tell them Dell have systems and everything that goes with them, from entry-level 286s to mighty networking 486 models.'* (ad for Dell Computer Corporation in *The Independent*, 16 October 1990)

entryism *n.* [1981]
the infiltration of democratic institutions by those who use such democracy to gain admission, but once in control of them ensure that such democracy is no longer available to their opponents. The charge of entryism has typically been raised against the Trotskyist left, e.g. ➪Militant, but the political right is equally culpable.

E-number *n.* [1986]
an abbreviation of European number: a variety of coded numbers, all preceded by the letter

'E', which denote a range of ⇨additives that are to be found in a given food; E-numbers are mandatory on all packaging. Thus **E-free**: a food that contains no additives.

envelope, back of an *phrase.* [1973]
quick and easy; usually of calculations; the idea is of jotting them down on the back of an envelope or similar small piece of paper.

environment *n.* [1972]
as well as its widespread ecological/conservationist use, environment is commonly used as a chic synonym for 'area', a redundant usage that is reminiscent of the older 'situation'.

* *'You ought to send John-John to Camp Middle Earth . . . It's five hundred a week, but it's a nurturing environment.'* (C. McFadden, *The Serial*, 1976)
* *'An impressive graduate-calibre individual with proven experience of the retail sales environment.'* (recruitment ad for Master Foods in *Independent on Sunday*, 8 April 1990)

EPG
see **Eminent Persons Group.**

EPOS *abbrev.* [1973]
an acronym for electronic point of sale.
See also **bar code.**

equal opportunity *adj.* [1963]
nondiscriminatory hiring which promises equality of employment regardless of race, creed, or colour; the phrase is often found as 'EOE' in recruitment ads.
See also **affirmative action, positive discrimination.**

* *'Trinity College is an Equal Opportunities Employer.'* (ad for Trinity College, Dublin, in *Independent on Sunday*, 3 June 1990)

ERA *abbrev.* [1970]
an acronym for Equal Rights Amendment, a proposed amendment to the US Constitution which was to guarantee equal rights to all citizens, irrespective of sex. The first ERA was proposed in 1923, following on women being given the suffrage in 1920, but it was rejected. Feminist groups continued to campaign for ERA without success until 12 October 1971 when the House of Representatives approved it; the Senate followed suit on 22 March 1972. One final hurdle was not surmounted: for the amendment to be passed two-thirds of the states had to ratify it within seven years; despite intense lobbying by the Women's Movement (and due in part to equally intense opposition from the conservative right) the ERA was not ratified in time.

ERM *abbrev.* [1979]
exchange rate mechanism: established as part of the European monetary system to promote cooperation and currency stability in the ⇨EC, the ERM is designed to keep the fluctuations in value between member currencies to a minimum.
See also **snake.**

* *'The discipline imposed by the ERM is going to be at least as distressing for British chancellors as for British industrialists.'* (*The Independent*, 17 October 1990)

escalation *n.* [1965]
a military coinage as early as 1938, but popularized by nuclear futurologist Herman Kahn (*b.*1922) in the 1950s and 1960s: the concept of a build-up of military forces and inter-

power conflict that leads from a minor crisis through a series of major crises and thence to nuclear war, itself developing in intensity from merely 'exemplary' explosions, probably on theatre troops, to full-scale no-holds-barred, no-targets-excluded 'spasm war'.

escalation control *n.* [1965]
also known as ⇨**de-escalation**: a concept central to contemporary ideas of 'winnable' and 'limited' nuclear wars: the belief that the ⇨escalation of such wars – even after the missiles have been fired – can still be held in check. De-escalation from the lower rungs of Kahn's ⇨escalation ladder seems feasible – the stepping back from any crisis that threatens the use of nuclear weapons is likely to be greeted with relief, albeit with the proviso that something must be done to make sure that such an event does not recur – and that 'something' need by no means be simply appeasement. De-escalation from the higher rungs, once missiles are actually exploding, seems less likely.

escalation dominance *n.* [1965]
the theory that, all things being equal, one side must possess the capability to mount the ⇨escalation ladder one step ahead of the opponent and thus reach the top, or at least the highest rung prior to ⇨**de-escalation** (*see* **escalation control**) in the dominant position. Escalation dominance is 'a function of where one is on the . . . ladder. It depends on the net effect of the competing capabilities on the rung being occupied, the estimate by each side of what would happen if the confrontation moved to other rungs and the means each side has to shift the confrontation to these other rungs.' (Herman Kahn, *On Escalation*)
See also **escalation ladder**.

✱ *'The United States seeks to use its nuclear advantage to achieve what the strategists call "escalation dominance", that is, to make the Soviet Union back down.'* (R.C. Aldridge, *First Strike!*, 1983)

escalation ladder *n.* [1965]
proposed in Herman Kahn's *On Escalation* (1965) as 'a generalised or abstract scenario [for nuclear war]': an 'escalation ladder', described as 'a linear arrangement of roughly increasing levels of intensity of crisis' divided into 44 'rungs' grouped in seven categories, moving through six thresholds. From rung 1 (ostensible crisis) to rung 44 (spasm or insensate war) the progress of a putative Third World War runs from Sub-Crisis Manoeuvring (Don't Rock the Boat Threshold) through Traditional Crises (Nuclear War is Unthinkable Threshold), Intense Crises (No Nuclear Use Threshold), Bizarre Crises (Central Sanctuary Threshold), Exemplary Central Attacks (Central War Threshold), Military Central Wars (City Targeting Threshold), Civilian Central Wars and thence to Aftermath.

ESDI *abbrev.* [1980]
an acronym for Enhanced Small Drive Interface: a low-level serial interface that was initially designed to work with minicomputers. It is one of the fastest hard disk interfaces available, although no disk as yet produced can utilize the speeds it offers.

✱ *'The Ultra-Max 386–33 is an inexpensive system . . . that comes with a 64K byte cache, 4 MB of RAM, a 160-MB 28-ms ESDI hard disk drive, VGA graphics (including the monitor).'* (*Byte*, May, 1990)

esky *n.* [1974]
Eskimo: a portable container for food and drink, which originated in Australia, where the name is a trademark.

Essex man *n.* [1990]
a derogatory description of the lower middle class and working class Conservatives whose votes had been drawn away from their traditional allegiance to the Labour Party by the social and economic policies of Thatcherism. The term refers to the culture and opinions of that population, originally east Londoners, who since the war have moved out of the inner city and into the dormitory towns of south Essex. Epitomized in their favourite son Norman Tebbit, they err to the right wing, promoting old-fashioned Little England nationalism, disapproving of excessive immigration and deploring anything – notably any form of intellectual culture – that smacks of the middle class.

* *'I suggested that perhaps what people meant was that Mr Hurd lacked Essex appeal. He enjoyed this thought and poured us a drink.'* (*The Independent*, 27 November 1990)

est *abbrev.* [1971]
an acronym for Erhard Seminars Training: the creation of Werner Erhard (formerly John Rosenberg), an eclectic package of 'self-realization' which is on offer to those who desire it during a course comprising three weekends of abuse, sensory deprivation and psychological processing, all geared to creating in the devotee an improved state of mind. This basic course can be followed by more intense immersion, which mixes more conditioning with varieties of game-playing and physical challenges.

See also **co-counselling; Rolfing.**

* *'The presence of Erhard Seminars Training is undeniable. Est has by now claimed over 90,000 graduates, among them corporate executives, politicians, actors, educators, and members of the mental health profession.'* (R.D. Rosen, *Psychobabble*, 1977)

Euro- *prefix.* [1962]
denoting European within the context of the ➪EC, this prefix has created a number of combinations including *Eurobanking*, *Eurodebt*, *Eurodeposit*, and *Euromarket*.

eurobond *n.* [1965]
a bond, especially that of a US corporation, sold outside the US on the European markets, but which is denominated and paid for in US$ and which yields interest in dollars.

Eurocrat *n.* [1962]
one of those bureaucrats, culled from the member states of the Common Market (EC) who staff the myriad agencies of the ➪EC headquarters in Brussels; the term carries with it much of the same disdain that attaches to its root 'bureaucrat'.

euro-currency *n.* [1965]
see **ecu.**

Euro-dollar *n.* [1965]
deposits of US$ held with banks outside the US; these overseas banks need not necessarily be sited in Europe. Such currency is barred from being re-imported into the US.

EW *abbrev.* [1965]
electronic warfare:

* *'The use of a wide range of electronic systems*

and subsystems to conduct active or passive measurement of an enemy's offensive or defensive electronic capabilities, attack or defend against those systems, and reach tactical or strategic mission objectives using personnel and/or weapons that include ground forces, ships, submarines, air-craft and missiles.' (C. Campbell, *War Facts Now*, 1982)

executive *adj.* [1987]
once referring specifically to the senior management of large corporations, and the lifestyle that was perceived as theirs, the word is now used as a general adjective, synonymous with luxury.

executive flu *n.* [1986]
see **ME.**

executive toys *n.* [1970]
a variety of gadgets created for the amusement of office-bound executives and the West's equivalent to the Eastern 'worry beads'. Typical are the chromed balls suspended in a line from a metal framework.

Exocet *n.* [1982]
an anti-ship missile (which can be carried either by other ships or by aeroplanes) which gained worldwide prominence during the Falklands War of 1982, when the Argentine forces used them with great effect against the Royal Navy. The missile is the brainchild of Emile Stauff, a French engineer. Stauff began designing such missiles in the early 1960s – the first trials came in 1967. The type used in 1982 was the improved AM39, a 'fire and forget' missile with its own guidance system, travelling ten feet above the waves at 680mph, to deliver a warhead of 363lbs of high explosive. *See also* **Scud.**

* *'He failed to recognise what it was, but then neither he nor anybody else had ever seen an Exocet approaching head on at near supersonic speed.'* (*The Sunday Times* Insight Team, *The Falklands War*, 1982)

expert system *n.* [1985]
a computer system which reflects the decision-making processes of a human specialist. The system embodies organized knowledge of a defined area of expertise and is intended to work as a skilful, cost-effective consultant. Such a system comprises a knowledge base, the distilled and codified knowledge of the human experts, often the result of years of sophisticated experience; an inference machine, the ⇨program which drives the system; an explanation program, which 'queries' the rules laid down by the expert and makes them acceptable to the user; a knowledge refining program which enables the expert to update the knowledge base; and a natural language processor, which enables the user to communicate with the machine in a natural manner. While expert systems are currently limited, the fifth generation (*see* **first generation, fourth generation**) of ⇨artificial intelligence (⇨AI) computers should make their deployment and development far greater.

* *'An expert system, that is, a program which organises and presents pre-existing knowledge.'* (*PC World*, April, 1990)

expletive deleted *phrase.* [1974]
an expression that indicates an obscene word or phrase has been cut from printed material; the term originated during the Watergate Affair, when the official transcript of the White House Tapes was littered with such delicate parentheses.

* *'Mr Nixon: (expletive deleted) Of course I am not dumb and I will never forget when I heard about this.'* (*The Presidential Transcripts,* 1974)

exploitation *n.* [1960]
in films: 1. all phases of publicity, advertising and promotion to market the finished product. 2. the making of films that depend on one specific topic – aimed directly at a specific audience – which is worked hard for a number of decreasingly successful attempts, and then abandoned, e.g.: ➪sexploitation, ➪blaxploitation. Such films lack any intrinsic value other than the possibility of spectacularly vulgar promotional techniques.

extra-terrestrial *n.* [1982]
any form of non-human life that may or may not exist in the Universe. The term became widely popular with the release of the film *ET* in 1982.

fab *abbrev.* [1961]
fabulous: a vogue word along with ➪gear, ➪grotty, and other linguistic artefacts of ➪Beatlemania.

face time *n.* [1989]
that period of the working day in which one is visibly present in the office; those who put in most face time are seen as the hardest workers.

✱ *'Another, more insidious factor, is that of spending "face time" in the office.'* (*Independent on Sunday*, 25 March 1990)

faction *n.* [1966]
a work of fiction that derives with only minimal alterations from events that actually happened; the printed version of a TV docudrama.

factoid *n.* [1973]
a published statement that takes on the reality of the 'fact' purely by virtue of its having been published and thus assimilated into the public consciousness. Often referring to unsubstantiated events that have developed into modern myth, it was coined in 1973 by Norman Mailer as a defence of such factoids in his heavily criticized 'biography' of Marilyn Monroe.

fag hag *n.* [1972]
a pejorative term for any woman, often middle-aged or older, who prefers the company of homosexual men to that of heterosexuals.

✱ *'I'd had a deadly relationship the previous summer with another media maiden who was a self-declared faghag so gee whiz.'* (L. Bangs, *Psychotic Reactions and Carburetor Dung*, 1988)

fail-safe *n., adj.* [1962]
1. *in aerospace, industry, etc.* an in-built mechanism that should in theory take over in the case of mechanical breakdown and restore the system to safety.
2. *in military use.* the US strategic bomber force has a fail-safe point whereby when alerted they fly only so far towards their targets and then loiter there until issued a code ordering them either to proceed or to return to base. This makes bombers, already the slowest means of weapons delivery, also the safest: unlike them, ground or submarine launched ➪ICBMs cannot be recalled if the emergency turns out not to have led to war.

✱ *'Inside the airplane the six men of the crew were looking forward now to turning at their fail-safe point.'* (P. George, *Dr Strangelove*, 1963)

3. *in international relations.* the concept of establishing a series of precautions, agreed by both sides, that will ensure that a nuclear war cannot be triggered 'by mistake' or by some lone psychotic.
4. used generally as an extension of **2**.

✱ *'What follows is not only the sole fail-safe account of segments and offsets I've seen, it's also the most useful exposition of what CPU registers do.'* (*Byte*, July 1990)

Falklands factor *n.* [1982]
initially proposed by Mrs Thatcher as the modern equivalent of the Dunkirk spirit – the belief that the nation could and should pull together in times of crisis – it developed into the idea that public perceptions of Mrs Thatcher's role during the Falklands war substantially boosted her popularity and (in 1983) won her her second term as prime minister.

* *'The Falklands factor was the spirit of a new age, she told the Cheltenham Tories. What the country had done in war . . . it could surely do in peace.'* (H. Young, *One Of Us*, 1989)
* *'Not only was the Falklands factor making the trains run on time, it was – it seems – rallying the nation behind the Medium Term Financial Strategy.'* (P. Jenkins, *Mrs Thatcher's Revolution*, 1987)

fallback (position) *n.* [1960]
a tacitly accepted position which a politician or negotiator accepts from the outset of a new policy or of talks, that he will be willing if needs be to retreat to. The term originates in military use.

fallout *n.* [1970]
any unpleasant side-effects that accompany a political decision, statement, or allied activity; fallout is not invariably negative, and can simply apply to a variety of knock-on effects, by-products, contingent ideas, responses, etc. The term was originally used to refer to the radioactive refuse of a nuclear bomb explosion and the process of the deposition of such refuse on the surrounding land and human and animal population. The extent of this fallout differs as to the type of explosion: an ➪air-burst will be limited as to local effects, but with the greater dispersion into the atmosphere will have far greater potential as a global pollutant.

family credit *n.* [1988]
introduced under the Social Security Act of 1988, family credit has replaced family income supplement, and provides a social security payment for Britain's low-income families. Calculated on net rather than gross income (as was the case with family income supplement) only those who work less than 24 hours per week and have at least one child are eligible.

* *'Single mothers on family credit, though, will be allowed to keep £15.00 of their maintenance.'* (*The Independent*, 30 October 1990)

family jewels *n.* [1978]
from the slang 'family jewels' (male genitals): used by the CIA to denote such internal and potentially embarrassing secrets that the agency would prefer were never disclosed in public; skeletons in the espionage closet, e.g.: CIA assassinations and allied illegal forms of ➪destabilization.

farout *adj.* [1969]
extreme.
See also **way out.**

* *'He was really on a farout trip . . . he was like so wise . . . y'know he knows so much.'* (J. Meades, *Peter Knows What Dick Likes*, 1989)

fare *n.* [1980]
this 'olde worlde' term for food can be found in many British pubs, underlining the country's move into ➪theme park ➪heritage culture; it has some ➪foodie credibility however: André Simon, doyen of the Wine and Food

Society, headed one handwritten menu in 1953, 'The Fare'.

fashion victim *n.* [1985]
anyone who is obsessed by fashion and permits its vicissitudes to dominate those of their own life.

* *'New Age hippies don't care for labels. They love fashion but don't want to be fashion victims.'* (*The Independent*, 19 July 1990)

fastback *n.* [1962]
a type of car style that slopes backwards in a continuous line from the top of the car to the rear bumper.

fast food *n., adj.* [1970]
any form of quickly cooked commercially provided food, notably hamburgers and pizzas; fast food is the industry's polite description of what critics would term ⇨junk food.

* *'He started a fast food chain and operated taxis, long-distance lorries, and petrol stations.'* (*Independent on Sunday*, 3 June 1990)

fast lane (*or* track) *n.* [1976]
the way to the top, with plenty of scope for overtaking, the image is of motorways, where the term 'fast lane' originated *c.* 1966 and is synonymous with 'overtaking' lane.
See also **high flier**.

* *'The perils of life in the fast lane.'* (headline in the *Independent on Sunday*, 25 March 1990)
* *'Bill had a feeling he was on a fast track. "Listen, Martha, I don't feel guilty. I didn't turn Kate on to bargello".'* (C. McFadden, *The Serial*, 1976)

fat city *n.* [1965]
prosperity, material comfort, and satisfaction, although as below, the term can be used ironically.
See also **city**; **edge city**; **-ville**.

* *'Harvey had . . . watched the needle on the scale swing slowly to the right, shaken his head and hit her with, "Wow . . . Fat City".'* (C. McFadden, *The Serial*, 1976)

fatwa *n.* [1989]
an edict as proclaimed under the sharia, or Muslim religious law. This otherwise obscure term came to worldwide notice on 14 February 1989 when the late Ayatollah Khomeini pronounced a fatwa on the author Salman Rushdie, condemning him to death for the alleged blasphemy of his novel *The Satanic Verses*.

* *'14 Feb. 1989 Ayatollah Khomeini of Iran proclaims a fatwa on Salman Rushdie.'* (L. Appignanesi & S. Maitland, *The Rushdie File*, 1989)

fave rave *n.* [1963]
slang for favourite person, experience or occupation.

fax *abbrev.* [1985]
facsimile: originally the transmission by wire or radio of graphic material from one newspaper to another, or from a remote source to a newspaper, the fax machine has become a staple of business and professional life, whether in an office, a home, or as a vital adjunct of the ⇨electronic cottage. The noun is often used as a verb, as in 'Fax me the contract . . . ' etc.

* *'It just spewed out of my fax machine, this torrent of filth, saying what this person would like to do to me.'* (*The Independent*, 6 April 1990)

feedback *n.* [1970]

1. *in new therapy*: one person's reaction to another person's action or speech, conveyed by analysing, criticizing, rejecting or agreeing, but always in some way modifying the original statement or action by their response.

2. *in politics*: the response from one's peers, supporters, potential voters, and opponents that emerges as the response to a politician's action or statement. Such a response is available both during a campaign and after an election to office, although the candidate's own feedback may well differ as to his/her altering status.

3. *in commercial use*: any reviews, comments, or opinions from the media, retailers, or consumers concerning a new product.

* *'Mr Ross says that despite a tumultuous week for VPI, he is touched by the overwhelming positive feedback from the Carter Organization's 173 active clients.'* (*Independent on Sunday*, March 1990)

fighter *n.* [1982]

any of the guerrilla forces engaged in the civil war in Lebanon, or in fighting either the Israelis or Syrians.

* *'He shouted defiantly at a Phalangist fighter and was instantly shot in the belly.'* (*Independent on Sunday*, 30 September 1990)

Filofax *n.*

a 7" x 5" ring binder stuffable with supposedly vital information that was a long-running merchandising hit during the 1980s. The binders had existed since their launch in 1941, but very few would hear of them for the next four decades. Given Filofax's possession of its name, the various imitations were forced to coin a synonym: ➪personal organizer.

* *'Filofax Group, manufacturers of the eponymous personal organizer, is desperate to throw off "the wretched tag of being a yuppie product" according to chairman David Collischon.'* (*The Independent*, 6 April 1990)

Fimbra *abbrev.*

an acronym for Financial Intermediaries, Managers, and Brokers Association.

* *'Fimbra wanted it to be cheap and simple, and asked several large companies to tender for the contract.'* (*Independent on Sunday*, 8 April 1990)

Finlandization *n.* [1969]

neutrality; especially when, as in the case of Finland which is ostensibly Western but abuts onto the USSR, a country is caught between the demands of two major powers.

* *'In the Expert Level game, you attempt to encourage or discourage Finlandization among the nations of the world. You have two weapons to help you: pressure and treaties.'* (C. Crawford, *Balance of Power*, 1988)

firmware *n.* [1980]

a handwired logic circuit that can perform the functions of a ➪program.

See also **-ware**

* *'Firmware is essentially software fixed in the computer in Read-Only Memory (ROM).'* (D. Jarrett, *The Good Computing Book for Beginners*, 1980)

first generation *n., adj.* [1960]

that series of computers and calculating machines designed between 1940–55 and which are characterized by electronic tube (valve) circuitry and delay line, rotating or electrostatic memory. Most had primitive input/output, using punched paper tape, punched card, magnetic wire, magnetic tape, and primitive printers. Despite this, such prototype machines performed admirably for their mainly scientific and military users. *See also* **fourth generation**.

first strike *n., adj.* [1962]
the first attack in a nuclear war; thus **first strike capability**: the ability to launch a first strike with the intention of destroying at the outset of the war any capacity the enemy may have to retaliate.

* *'The first strike capability is intended mainly to intimidate adversaries.'* (R.C. Aldridge, *First Strike!*, 1983)

first use *n.* [1962]
the first use in war of a specific intensity or type of military measure: thus if a first strike were conventional, a nuclear retaliatory strike would still represent the first use of such weapons. – **first-use** *adj.*

* *'Such use of nuclear weapons would be on a first-use basis, before any nuclear attack from Warsaw Pact forces.'* (M. Dando & P. Rogers, *The Death of Deterrence*, 1984)

First World *n.* [1974]
the major industrialized nations: most of Western Europe, the US, USSR, and Japan. *See also* **Second World; Third World.**

fish finger *n.* [1962]
a popular convenience food consisting of a small rectangular shaped chunk of fish, approximating the size of a (large) finger, which has been dipped in egg and breadcrumbs and must be fried or grilled before eating.

* *'Only the fish finger has ever seriously challenged the baked bean.'* (*Independent on Sunday*, 19 August 1990)

flaky *adj.* [1967]
a slang term (mainly in the US) meaning unconventional, eccentric or actually crazy. Thus the noun **flake**: one who has these qualities.

* *'Seven African men she couldn't talk to and a notoriously flaky daughter.'* (*Independent on Sunday*, 25 March 1990)

flares *n.* [1971]
an abbreviation for flared trousers (*cf.* loon pants).

* *'Heavy, flapping denim spreading from the hip not the knees, nearer Oxford bags than flares.'* (*Independent on Sunday*, 3 June 1990)

flashback *n.* [1966]
the recurrence of part or all of an LSD trip; such flashbacks could be terrifying, certainly, since one could never prepare for them, they were extremely disorientating.

* *'It came stuttering out through a fog of tears and obscene acid flashbacks.'* (H.S. Thompson, *Fear and Loathing in Las Vegas*, 1971)

flash on *v.* [1970]
to have an inspiration, to realize (used transitively).

* *'She just flashed on it: for once in her life she ought to put her own needs right up front and then get behind them.'* (C. McFadden, *The Serial*, 1976)

flavour of the month *phrase.* [1986]
a derisory reference to a contemporary and, it is presumed, short-lived fashion or fad.

* *'The Greenhouse Effect. Television's flavour of the month enjoys another airing.'* (*Independent on Sunday*, 25 March 1990)

flexible response *n., adj.* [1967]
the concept of meeting aggression with a suitable level of counter-aggression and in the relevant environment; always, unless the initial aggression is a nuclear ⇨first strike, leaving the options of ⇨escalation and ⇨de-escalation available if required or feasible. It was first accepted by NATO forces in Europe in 1967.

* *'It surfaced . . . in Jimmy Carter's endorsement of a "flexible response" doctrine in Presidential Directive 59.'* (R.C. Aldridge, *First Strike!*, 1983)

flex(i)time *n.* [1973]
the staggering of working hours in an attempt to improve an employee's working standards by offering a more relaxed 'day' than the traditional 'nine to five'. Research has shown that this choice (within certain limits) of one's working hours has improved both the quality and quantity of productivity, since the workers are using those hours at which they themselves are most alert and efficient.

* *'Flexible time, or flexitime allows an employee to choose, within guidelines, his own starting and finishing times.'* (*New York Times*, 4 February 1973)

flight recorder *n.* [1962]
otherwise known as the ⇨'black box', a wire recorder that is placed in every commercial aeroplane and keeps track of the relevant technical details of each flight, including the actual conversations between the crew and air-traffic control, and the progress of on-board computers and other technology.

flip-flops *n.* [1970]
a plastic or rubber sandal, usually worn at the beach. The sandal is secured simply by the strap that crosses the toes, thus when walking it makes a 'flip-flop' sound, creating its onomatopoeic name.

flirty-fishing *n.* [1985]
see **love-bombing.**

floating point *n.*
see **scientific notation.**

floppy disk *n.* [1975]
a flexible storage medium, either 5.25 (the most popular), 8 or 3.5 inches in diameter, on which data can be stored, memorized and retrieved by a computer. The average double-sided, double-density 5.25" floppy can store approx. 360,000 ⇨bytes or at best 1.2MB of data; the 3.5 inch version offers either 720KB or 1.44MB, with plans to expand this to 2.8MB in the very near future. Despite this, any floppy disk remains greatly inferior in capacity, and in operational speed to the larger ⇨hard disks or ⇨Winchesters with storage in the millions of bytes.

* *'The code would exist on the so-called floppy disk, like a 45 rpm record, not in unalterable ROM inside the machine.'* (T. Kidder, *The Soul of a New Machine*, 1981)

FLOPS *abbrev.* [1968]
an acronym for floating-point operations per second: the measure of power used for extra-powerful computers; this is always qualified by a statement of the precision to which the operations are carried out.
See also **MIPS.**

floptical *n., adj.* [1987]
usually combined with disk, and referring to a form of electronic storage that is read by an optical reading device and which is capable of storing many times more data than is the normal ⇨floppy disk.

flower children *n.* [1967]
the ⇨hippies, whose most widespread (and commercialized) symbol of the love and peace they espoused was a flower. Thus the hippies themselves became known (mainly to the media) as the flower children. At the height of hippie optimism, in 1967's 'Summer of Love', it was fondly believed that with love and peace paramount, flower power rather than military or political power, would take over in a new better world.

* *'A phosphorescent fascist fandango, King Herod spavanning the Flower Children, O Fuck & Corruption, G-narl, G-nash.'* (T. Wolfe, *The Electric Kool-Aid Acid Test*, 1969)
* *'The three-day Festival of the Flower Children faded out at Woburn Abbey . . . to the tinkling of necklace bells and cash registers ringing up more than £20,000 profits.'* (*Daily Telegraph*, 29 August 1967)

flower power *n.* [1967]
see **flower children**.

fly-by/flyby *n.* [1960]
a space mission, usually undertaken by a long-distance space probe, that flies past a planet or similar heavenly body, taking pictures and relaying them back for analysis on earth.

fly-by-wire *adj.* [1986]
a computerized control system in which commands – typically to a missile – are transmitted electronically.

fly-drive (holiday) *n.* [1976]
a package holiday in which one flies to and from a main foreign destination, then uses a car to tour the local areas. Thus the **cruise drive**: one flies to join a ship in, say, the Caribbean, and then cruises around before returning home by air.

flyover *n.* [1962]
a road bridge that crosses another road.

folk-rock *n., adj.* [1966]
a mixture of folk music and rock 'n' roll; a creation of the 1960s, its first and best-known exponents were the band Fairport Convention. – **folk-rockers** *n.*

* *'Like most of the early acid bands they started as folk rockers, Marty Balin . . . had taken the same inspiration from "A Hard Day's Night" as the Byrds and Lovin' Spoonful.'* (*The Rolling Stone Illustrated History of Rock & Roll*, 1976)

foodie *n.* [1985]
spawned by the ⇨nouvelle cuisine boom of the late 1970s, the professional eater, culinarily and sociologically several courses ahead of the merely hungry; you are, *pace* the 1960s, what you eat.

* *'Such gems are not designed for foodies; they are destined for the millions of us who love Good Bad Food.'* (*Independent on Sunday*, 19 August 1990)

food processor *n.* [1977]
an electrical appliance that, with the help of various attachments cuts, slices, chops, shreds,

minces and generally replaces a variety of human kitchen tasks with a single high-speed machine.

* *'After just three months, a first prize of £500! And now, a food processor, a £100 gourmet hamper, and would you believe it, a Renault GTX!'* (ad for *Competitor's Companion* magazine in the *Sunday Correspondent*, 10 June 1990)

food stamp *n.* [1962]
stamps that are issued to the badly off, allowing them to gain a substantial discount on food purchases in designated stores.

football *n.* [1960]
the attaché case holding the day's nuclear launch codes that is carried by an officer whose duty it is never to leave the president's side.

footprint *n., adj.* [1966]
1. *in nuclear warfare:* the pattern into which it is calculated that the descending warheads of a ➪MARV bus will fall when completing their intercontinental trajectory on target.
2. *in computing:* the space a given machine or ➪peripheral takes up on the desk.

* *'AMT packs its 486 Personal Mainframe into a small footprint case.'* (*PC World*, April 1990)

Footsie *abbrev.* [1984]
an acronym for Financial Times – Stock Exchange 100 Share Index. Established on 3 January 1984 the Index monitors the fluctuations in share prices of the 100 largest companies in the UK.

* *'Footsie follows close behind the galloping Dow'* (headline in *The Independent*, 15 May 1990)

for openers *phrase.* [1960]
a colloquialism for to begin with; probably taken from the idea of making an opening bet or ante in card games.

FORTH *n.* [1969]
a programming language especially popular in the control of a scientific instrument by means of its flexibility and compactness. As opposed to such languages as ➪BASIC the user is not forced to work with pre-set symbols, but can define words as required, which words then can be used in expressions on equal terms with the system operators. FORTH is written in reverse Polish notation. FORTH was created by Charles Moore in the late 1960s as the language for ➪fourth generation computing. The machine on which he worked would accept only five-letter words, thus the mis-spelt FORTH appeared.

Fosbury flop *n.* [1968]
a style of high-jumping in which the jumper approaches the bar backwards and stretches out faceup, landing on his or her back; originated by the US jumper Dick Fosbury, winner of the Olympic gold medal in 1968.

found object *n.* [1963]
from the French *objet trouvé*: in Surrealist theory, the taking of any random object and presenting it as art, worthy of comparison with more respectable traditional art.

fourth generation *n., adj.* [1980]
the current generation of computer designs, covering those that appeared after 1970 and which feature integrated circuit technology and very large (1 MB+) main memory. Fourth generation machines also offer networking

facilities and support a wide variety of languages.
See also **first generation.**

Fourth World *n., adj.* [1974]
the world's poorest and most underdeveloped countries.

fractal *n.* [1977]
any of a class of highly irregular and fragmented shapes or surfaces that are not represented in classical geometry.
See also **chaos.**

- ✱ *'At $25 this is the fastest and cheapest way to find out if you like playing with fractals.'* (*Byte*, June 1990)

franglais *n.* [1964]
a mix of French and English, most notably parlayed in a series of successful books by humorist Miles Kington.

fratricide *n.* [1971]
the theoretical result of the detonation of a number of ⇨MIRV/MARV warheads out of absolute and simultaneous synchronicity – which, given the distance travelled to their targets would most likely be the case: the various massive explosions would tend to destroy other incoming warheads or at least interfere seriously with the accuracy of their guidance systems.

- ✱ *'No one knows enough about fratricide to reliably predict what will happen, let alone to incorporate this effect into a system design.'* (R.C. Aldridge, *First Strike!*, 1983)

freak *n.* [1965]
an extreme ⇨hippie, less of a ⇨flower child than a ⇨hardcore ⇨counter-culturist, who tended to reject 'peace and love' in favour of a ⇨high-profile assault on 'straight society'.

- ✱ *'Freak referred to styles and obsessions, as in "Stewart Brand is an Indian freak", or, "the zodiac – that's her freak" or just to heads in costume.'* (T. Wolfe, *The Electric Kool-Aid Acid Test*, 1969)
- ✱ *'The crowd was yelling for the Freaks. By the end of the film everyone was jumpin up and down, hissing the cops, laughing their asses off.'* (A. Hoffman, *Woodstock Nation*, 1969)

freak out [1965]
1. *v.t.* to alarm or amaze a third party (often used simply as 'freak').

- ✱ *'Paul and Harvey were still alive and well and freaking the locals. No way to get any peace here.'* (A.F.N. Clarke, *Contact*, 1983)

2. *v.i.* to become alarmed or worried, especially as a result of drug use.

- ✱ *'Some of the girls told me there was this really weird guy in here who's kind of freaked out and I should come in.'* (R. DiLello, *The Longest Cocktail Party*, 1971)

3. **freaked out**, *adj.* disturbed, terrified, disorientated.
4. **freakout**, *n.* a breakdown or a notably bizarre experience (probably caused by drugs).

- ✱ *'Owsley's freakout! Owsley became obsessed with it himself.'* (T. Wolfe, *The Electric Kool-Aid Acid Test*, 1969)

freaky *adj.* [1965]
weird, bizarre, probably with connotations of drug use – although given the drug-hazed tenor of the era, the term was by no means an automatic pejorative.

freebase *v.* [1972]
a fashionable method of taking cocaine:

instead of the usual 'snorting' of powdered lines, the user consumes cocaine base, which must be heated first and is then smoked. The 'high' is much more intense, but the equipment, given that it requires a stoned drug-user to operate a naked flame, may prove dangerous.

* *'All the apparatus, including a blowtorch, for freebasing cocaine.'* (B. Woodward, *Wired*, 1984)

Freedom ride *n.* [1961]
an organized ride through areas of the US south – in buses or cars – by anti-segregationist civil rights campaigners (the **Freedom Riders**).

* *'Over 300 Freedom Riders arrested in Jackson, Mississippi, in May and June 1961 were sentenced.'* (Amnesty International, *Voices for Freedom*, 1986)

free-range *adj.* [1960]
the opposite of battery-farming: poultry that is allowed to forage freely for food, rather than being penned in a shed and fed as and when the farmer decides.

freeze-dry *v.* [1962]
a method of drying foodstuffs, blood plasma, pharmaceuticals, etc., and then freezing them; this retains the physical structure. To restore the material it is warmed in a high vacuum.

freeze-frame *n.* [1969]
a device whereby the action on film appears to freeze into a still; accomplished by printing one frame a number of times.

FRELIMO *abbrev.* [1964]
an acronym for Frente de Libertação de Moçambique: the leftwing guerillas who from 1964–74 fought for Mozambique's independence from the Portuguese colonial government.

* *'Instead of trying to develop into a mass party, Frelimo remained a small tightly organized cabal.'* (P. Brogan, *World Conflicts*, 1989)

fridge-freezer *n.*
a combination of refrigerator and freezer, usually in the form of a large cabinet divided into two 'boxes', each with its own door.

* *'A dishwasher, a microwave, a fridge-freezer, a food processor, a cordless kettle and a £200 Breadsmade.'* (ad in the *Sunday Correspondent*, for *Competitor's Companion*, 10 June 1990)

-friendly *suffix.* [1986]
in favour of, kind to, in sympathy with; the original -friendly suffix was *user-friendly*, referring to computer hard- or software that was (relatively) easy to use; the term has been extended to several other uses, e.g. *environmentally-friendly*; *computer-friendly*; etc.

* *'What about tampons that say on the packet they're "environmentally-friendly"?' I ventured.'* (*The Independent*, 5 April 1990)
* *'Because San Jose cops are, in McNamara's phrase, "computer-friendly", the suggestion . . . was generated from within the rank and file.'* (*Sunday Correspondent*, 22 April 1990)

Friends of the Earth *n.* [1972]
an organization of conservationists and environmentalists, founded in 1972.

✱ *'Friends of the Earth kept its head in all the Green hype.'* (*Daily Telegraph*, Student Extra, 1989)

fringe theatre *n.* [1970]
experimental, low-cost theatre; the equivalent of America's 'off-off Broadway', the fringe takes its name from the annual Edinburgh Festival where its productions are seen to take place on the fringe of the mainstream activities.

✱ *'I especially dislike fringe theatres as places in which to pass an evening – uncomfortable seats, sycophantic audiences, etc.'* (J. Meades, *Peter Knows What Dick Likes*, 1989)

Frisbee *n.* [1968]
a small plastic disk that can sail through the air; playing with frisbees was popular with the hippies of the 1960s, and has become a sport, albeit on a relatively small scale.
See also **aerobie**.

✱ *'Which does not mean that we should reject our traditional games and throw ourselves wholeheartedly into frisbee.'* (D. Atyeo, *Blood and Guts*, 1979)

frisée *n.* [1987]
from the French, meaning 'endive': along with radiccio and lamb's lettuce frisée became one of the chic staples of 1980s cookery, and moved on from the ⇨nouvelle cuisine restaurants to the supermarket shelves.

frit *adv., adj.* [1983]
a veteran of many English dialects and meaning no more than 'frightened', frit rose to national prominence when on 19 April 1983 Margaret Thatcher used it in the House of Commons to taunt her opponents on the Labour benches whom she said were 'afraid of an election – frightened – frit!'. The term then became a part of British political vocabulary, most often used by the Opposition to taunt the then prime minister herself.

fromage frais *n.* [1978]
a variety of curd cheese, the consistency of double cream, which became popular in England during the ⇨nouvelle cuisine boom of the late 1970s and 1980s.

✱ *'Fromages Frais, Tome de Vache, Jean Jemet sells on farms at Preau on Mondays and at Wednesday and Saturday markets at Lafayette, Angers.'* (P. Rance, *The French Cheese Book*, 1989)

front-end *adj.* [1987]
originally an abbreviation of 'front end processor' – a secondary unit designed to back up the functioning of the main processor by taking on a variety of basic tasks and performing them ready so that the main unit can take advantage of this spade-work and concentrate on performing major tasks. Latterly a euphemism for ⇨user-friendly ⇨interface, some form of graphical system (⇨GUI) designed to help the less computerate deal with running ⇨programs and dealing with the often problematical operating system.

✱ *'Nelson Taylor looks at the alternative graphical interface to Lotus 1-2-3 which offers a graphical front-end and extending graphing capabilities.'* (*PC World*, May 1990)

frontlash *n.* [1964]
the reverse of a backlash, coined by President Lyndon B. Johnson in 1964 to explain how the threatened racist backlash against his civil rights legislation would be submerged in the frontlash of its many supporters.

front line *n.* [1981]
from the military definition of a line of confrontation: certain streets in the UK's West Indian areas (e.g. Railton Road, SW9 and All Saints Road, W11 in London) where the black community feel that their rights and freedoms are most heavily under assault, and where, in white/police eyes, such rights and freedoms are paraded most provocatively.

* *'So while the rest of us were living dangerously on the front line, taking chances. . .'* (T. Blacker, *Fixx*, 1989)

frontline (states) *n.* [1976]
those black African nations that border South Africa and, formerly, Rhodesia before it became Zimbabwe.

* *'President Kenneth Kaunda of Zambia, chairman of the southern African frontline states.'* (*The Independent*, 22 March 1990)

front money *n.* [1972]
a deposit, an advance; especially used in drug dealing where 'front' has become a verb: 'You have to front some bread.'

frug *n.* [1964]
a modern dance, of the same era as such peers of the ⇨Twist as the Swim, the Monkey, and the Watusi; like them its signature was that the partners never touched.

* *'Kids dancing not rock dances, but the frug and the – what? – swim, mother, but dancing ecstasy, leaping, dervishing.'* (T. Wolfe, *The Electric Kool-Aid Acid Test*, 1969)

fudge and mudge *n.* [1986]
the failure of policymakers to come to a decision; a phrase coined by Lord Jenkins and popularized by the words and deeds of successive permutations of the 'fruit salad' party – Social Democrats.

funky *adj.* [1970]
originally a black slang term meaning smelly (with overtones of post-coital odours); from there it moved into meaning messy or dirty, but its current popular meaning errs towards pleasantly eccentric or unconventional.

* *'The fabric . . . will be made into children's clothes and looks quite funky despite the serious message.'* (*Sunday Correspondent*, 10 June 1990)

funny money *n.* [1960]
counterfeit money; also money obtained through crime, fraud, or similar dishonest means, which is put through the Isle of Man and similar ⇨offshore banks for ⇨laundering.

* *'We have suggested that the Isle of Man forget all the "funny money" – and simply concentrate on the honest people who are not afraid to show their bank statements.'* (*Independent on Sunday*, 13 May 1990)

fun run *n.* [1976]
a run undertaken purely for pleasure, albeit in a crowd; fun runs were initiated by the *Sunday Times* as the paper's contribution to the newly health-conscious 1970s.

* *'One could easily imagine him beginning the 24th mile in second place and . . . stopping to*

assure the reporter that he is on a lone fun run, nothing to do with the race.' (*Sunday Correspondent*, 13 May 1990)

fusion *n.* [1976]
any blend of two disparate streams of music, notably jazz and rock.

future shock *n.* [1970]
coined in Alvin Toffler's eponymously titled book, published in 1970: a state of stress and disorientation occasioned by an excess of dramatic and continuing changes in society – especially the technological changes that alter the entire social basis and assumptions of that society.

✱ *Future shock arises from the superimposition of a new culture on an old one. It is culture shock in one's own society.'* (A. Toffler, *Future Shock*, 1970)

fuzzbox *n.* [1968]
a small electronic device used to distort amplified guitar sounds.

fuzzy logic (*or* theory) *n.* [1965]
a form of logic in which the variables may assume a continuum of values between 1 and 0. This branch of logic is especially amenable for the representation of knowledge and human reasoning in terms useful for computer processing. Fuzzy logic is applicable to ➪expert systems, knowledge engineering and ➪artificial intelligence (➪AI).

Gaia theory *n.* [1990]
the idea that the Earth's life forms are part of a great living being that regulates its own stability. Modern industrial society is a suicidal process. Progress is measured simply in the flow of money – Gaia, the earth mother, is ignored.

* *'Amazonia is at the heart of Dr Lutzenberger's near-mystical doctrine of a sentient global being, Gaia, developed by the British scientist James Lovelock.'* (*Independent on Sunday*, 22 April 1990)
* *'And try playing Sim Earth with the Gaia principle turned off – that's when it really starts getting difficult.'* (*Ace*, August 1990)

game plan *n.* [1969]
derived from the US football term for a strategy prepared for a given game: taken by politicians (especially the Nixon White House, where the president actually sent in a play to the Washington Redskins – which play resulted in their opponents scoring) and by businessmen to mean a planned strategy aimed at achieving given goals within defined rules.

* *'A game plan goes into unscheduled turnaround, we're talking major short-term depression.'* (T. Blacker, *Fixx*, 1989)

games console *n.* [1988]
in computing: a purpose-built computer, such as the Nintendo Gameboy or the Sega Megadrive, which contains its own screen and controls and which is used specifically for playing a variety of computer games, available on ⇨dedicated disk or ⇨cassette.

* *'What, no games console? It's one of the more winning evocations of the power of youthful thought, a nostalgia that doesn't have to apologize for its indulgence.'* (*The Independent*, 26 October 1990)

Gang of Four *n.*
1. in China (1976): the former leaders of the ⇨Cultural Revolution who were immediately pilloried after the death in October 1976 of Mao Tse Tung. They were: Wang Hun-Wen (vice-chairman of the cultural committee of the Party and sentenced to life imprisonment); Chang Ch'un Chiao (politburo member sentenced to death); Chiang Ch'ing – Jiang Qing (pinyin) – (Mao's widow and cultural supremo sentenced to death, commuted to life imprisonment) and Yao Wen-Yuan (sentenced to 20 years in gaol). All four were tried between 1980–81 for 'counter-revolutionary revisionism' and duly found guilty.

* *'In October 1976, one month after Mao's death, Jiang and her three colleagues were arrested, expelled from the Party and accused (as the Gang of Four) of committing numerous crimes.'* (*International Dictionary of 20th Century Biography*, 1987)

2. in the UK (1981): four leading members of the Labour Party who broke away in 1981 to found the Social Democratic Party (SDP): Roy Jenkins, David Owen, William Rodgers and Shirley Williams; their nickname was mod-

elled facetiously by the British media on their Chinese 'counterparts'.

* *'Had the Gang of Four stayed, the chances are that Dennis Healey would have been elected leader.'* (*The Independent*, 8 June 1990)

garage sale *n.* [1967]
a sale of old or worthless belongings, traditionally held in the garage.

gas guzzler *n.* [1968]
the traditionally over-sized American automobile of the 1950s and 1960s, which ran at relatively few miles to the gallon at a time when petrol was cheap and environmental concerns as to exhaust pollution were the preserve of a few 'cranks'.

* *'"Making the world safe for gas-guzzlers" was Thomas Friedman's summary of American aims in the Gulf crisis.'* (*Independent on Sunday*, 19 August 1990)

-gate *suffix.* [1974]
the Watergate affair of 1972–74 created, *inter alia*, a new linguistic suffix which has been attached to a wide range of proper nouns to denote a form of political or allied scandal. Among the best known are **Muldergate** (1979, the scandal in South Africa centred on government official Cornelius Mulder), and **Irangate** (1986, the sale of arms to Iran by the US and the investment of the profits in the Nicaraguan Contras); other, lesser '-gates', have included **Billygate** (problems for Billy Carter, President Carter's brother), **Abdulgate** (referring to the fictional Abdul Enterprises of the 1980 Abscam scandal), and many others.

* *'Then we hear about Irangate . . . I think we should talk openly and honestly to Syria and Iran.'* (*Sunday Correspondent*, 10 February 1990)

gay *adj.* [1969]
homosexual; as a slang term the word dates back to the late eighteenth century, when it meant a promiscuous woman, even a prostitute. The use of gay by homosexuals originates during the Second World War, when it was probably an abbreviation of the old US tramps' slang 'geycat'; the wider use in the heterosexual world began around 1970, with the emergence of the ➪Gay Liberation Front, first in the US and subsequently in the UK.

* *'This book would never have reached the publishers without the perseverance and encouragement of Jim Anderson . . . I look forward to his first book* Gay Power.' (R. Neville, *Play Power*, 1970)
* *'Up at Balboa Park the Gay Pride Day rally and pop concert is reaching its climax.'* (J. McClure, *Cop World*, 1984)
* *'A homosexual, (he loathed the word "gay") in a straight world.'* (*Independent on Sunday*, 10 June 1990)

gay liberation *n.* [1969]
on the pattern of ➪women's liberation, the movement to improve the status of homosexuals through a programme of self-definition, assertion, and the refusal to be bound by the traditional negative stereotypes.

* *'From the Stonewall riot, on the last weekend of June 1969, the gay liberation movement was born, peopled by angry women and men.'* (R. Shilts, *And the Band Played On*, 1987)

gazump *v.* [1971]
originally used by Jewish tradesmen to mean 'cheat or swindle' (which is what the word

means in Yiddish) it spread during the 1920s into the motor trade, where it described the fraudulent technique whereby the salesman closed a sale with one buyer but then, realizing that another buyer would pay more, offering the same vehicle to that buyer before the first one was able to pay for and collect the vehicle. The modern use stems from the early 1970s, when the UK property market was booming: estate agents and their clients adopted the term (and the practice); as prices calmed down, so did the practice, but it will doubtless continue to parallel their fluctuations.

GCSE *abbrev.* [1986]
General Certificate of Secondary Education: the replacement (as of 1986) for O-level (it-self a substitute for the older School Certificate). With its greater emphasis on course-work and practical experience GCSE is seen by its supporters as a better way of testing real learning than the more academic O-level; its opponents suggest that it merely panders to the inadequacy of the less intelligent and gives them a false sense of their own (limited) abilities.

* *'Around 8.7 per cent more girls than boys got GCSE grades A to C in craft, design, and technology.'* (*Sunday Correspondent*, 8 April 1990)

gear *adj.* [1963]
wonderful, excellent, good; a traditional piece of Liverpudlian vocabulary, brought into the mainstream by the Beatles' popularity.

* *'The* Sunday Times *commented on how they had enlarged the English language, bringing Liverpool words like "gear" (meaning good or great) into general usage.'* (H. Davies, *The Beatles*, 1968)

gear *n.* [1965]
a slang term for clothing, as in the HughLloyd/Terry Scott sitcom 'Hugh and I' in which the pair shopped at 'Fab Gear' of Tooting.

gender-bender *n.* [1986]
a synonym for transvestism or transexuality: bending or eroding the line between the two sexes; the term was popularized during the rise to fame of the pop star Boy George, whose outrageous clothes and ostentatious makeup managed to disturb many observers.

* *'Gender-bending version of Pygmalion myth.'* (*Sunday Correspondent*, 13 May 1990)

generation *n.* [1962]
successive developments of a piece of equipment – a computer, hifi, weapons systems, etc. – in which each new generation can be assumed to be more sophisticated, efficient, capable, etc.
See also **first generation**.

* *'The Qi 300 delivers 386SX power for around the price of IBM and Compaq 286 machines, which are a generation behind.'* (ad for Apricot computers in *PC World*, May 1990)

* *'Japan's Ministry of International Trade and Industry will spend $46 million on its Fifth Generation Computer Project this year.'* (*Byte*, July 1990)

generation gap *n.* [1967]
cultural and attitudinal differences between successive generations, especially as experienced between teenagers and their parents. Generational differences have always existed, but it took the 1960s, with its premium on youth and its plethora of sociological jargon, to create a suitable phrase.

* *'How to build confidence across the generation*

gap.' (headline in the *Independent on Sunday*, 25 March 1990)

gene-splicing *n.*
see **recombinant DNA.**

genetic code *n.*
see **RNA.**

genetic engineering *n.* [1969]
the scientific alteration of genes or genetic material either to produce desirable new traits in the given organism, or to eliminate undesirable ones.

* *'Making these or other agrichemicals from genetically engineered bacteria is no different from making other chemicals this way.'* (*Christian Science Monitor*, 7 July 1981)

genetic fingerprinting *n.* [1986]
a means of identifying an individual by checking the pattern of repeated DNA sequences that are unique to each individual.

gene transplantation *n.*
see **recombinant DNA.**

gentrification *n.* [1973]
in property development, the taking over – usually by young, upwardly mobile, professional middle-class people – of former slums or similarly run down 'inner city' housing (which may in its earlier days have in fact been smart, bourgeois homes) and renovating them back towards their former status. – **gentrify** *v.*

* *'What is perhaps best about Coney island, and most nostalgic, is that it has escaped the gentrification so prevalent in Manhattan.'* (*The Independent*, 26 May 1990)

get behind *v.* [1970]
to back up, to approve of, to support.
See also **relate.**

* *'Weddings were much less conformist now that people were getting behind marriage again.'* (C. McFadden, *The Serial*, 1976)

get in touch with (oneself) *phrase.* [1972]
to understand one's inner feelings.

* *'I asked how things were going and received this reply: "I've really been getting in touch with myself lately. I've struck some really deep chords".'* (R.D. Rosen, *Psychobabble*, 1977)

get it on (with) *phrase.* [1969]
to make love (to).

* *'Maybe the answer to her dissatisfactions with Harvey was to get it on with somebody else.'* (C. McFadden, *The Serial*, 1976)

get off on *phrase.* [1973]
to enjoy, appreciate; to find sexually stimulating.

ghetto blaster *n.* [1980]
also known as ➪**beat box, boofer box, wog box:** a large, portable tape-recorder-cum-radio; as the various names imply, particularly beloved in their early-1980s heyday by youths in ghetto or inner city areas.

* *'Market economy: streets, open spaces, even whole sports stadiums have been turned into vast bazaars, selling everything from shoelaces to ghetto blasters.'* (*The Independent*, 2 November 1990)

GIGO *abbrev.* [1966]
an acronym for garbage in garbage out: a dictum that states that if one puts worthless data

into a computer the machine can only give worthless data back; it possesses no alchemical ability to transmute the 'garbage' into 'gold'.

* *'GIGO: acronym for garbage in garbage out, signifying that a program working on incorrect data produces incorrect results.'* (*Sphere Dictionary of Computing*, 1983)

give *v.*
to operate, to put across, as in 'give good meeting', 'give good phone'; the term stems from the slang term for fellatio: to 'give head'.

* *'This woman gives such good phone she should be a Hollywood agent.'* (*The Independent*, 19 July 1990)

glam-rock *n., adj.* [1973]
a form of rock music in which the externals – dress, make-up – are as important if not even more important than the actual music and lyrics themselves. The main message was of a contrived sexual decadence, and was epitomized by David Bowie in his 'Ziggy Stardust' persona (*c.* 1973), the New York Dolls, Jobriath, and others.

glasnost *n.* [1987]
from the Russian, meaning 'openness', and as such the central tenet of Mikhail Gorbachev's attempt to introduce into Russia the greatest revolution in Soviet life since the last war and possibly since the Revolution itself.
See also **perestroika.**

* *'The era of "perestroika" or economic restructuring, and "glasnost" or openness, represents a new and positive phase in the US-Soviet relationship.'* (*Chronicle of America*, 1990)

glass cockpit *n.* [1989]
computer-based aircraft navigation, in which the old systems of dials and switches have been replaced by ➪VDU screens on which the relevant information is displayed and monitored.

* *'The computer systems that run "glass cockpits" are also subject to question after two crashes of the world's most advanced computerised airliner.'* (*The Independent*, 23 May 1990)

GLCM *abbrev.* [1977]
an acronym for Ground-Launched Cruise Missile (pronounced 'glockem'): 464 of these ➪cruise missiles were deployed in the UK and Europe, after this deployment was agreed by NATO in 1979. The missile has a range of 2500 km, a speed of 550 mph and delivers a 200 kiloton warhead to an accuracy of 30m. It was against the GLCM that Europe's anti-cruise campaigners focused their attentions.

* *'With their 1600 nautical mile range, GLCMs could reach all Warsaw Pact countries from England.'* (R.C. Aldridge, *First Strike!*, 1983)

glitch *n.* [1962]
a hitch or snag, a malfunction: first popularized by US astronauts, 'glitch' originates in electronics jargon, where it refers to a sudden change in voltage that results in the addition of a new load to the circuit. Such ➪spikes, as they are known, can cause a malfunction, especially in the sensitive circuits of a computer. There are thus a number of usages:
1. *in computing*: from Yiddish *glitchen* (slide): any form of unexpected electronic interference that involves the computer, either in the power supply or in the ➪program function. Possibly first used by German scientists working at NASA for the US space programme.
2. *in politics*: a situation when an unexplained but crucial electronic breakdown or burst of

interference can result in major problems for a candidate or an office-holder; e.g. faulty transmissions of speeches, especially those in translation, can ruin otherwise satisfactory communications or conferences; similarly badly printed campaign literature, malfunctioning microphones, etc., all take their toll.
3. *in astronomy*: a sudden change in the rotation of any heavenly body, planet, or star.
4. as well as in the computing use this term for a slight and unexpected error is used throughout technology, including TV, radio, radar, motor racing (where the Yiddish 'to slide' is most literally interpreted), space flight and more.

glitter *n., adj.* [1973]
a style of rock music popular in the early 1970s; it mixed its banal lyrics and cliched tunes with brightly-coloured, glitter-bedecked costumes, awash with cosmetics and facepaint; its two stars were Marc Bolan, a former star ⇨mod, and the suitably named Gary Glitter, the former Paul Raven.

* *'He, like most of this audience, leaned much farther to denims than to glitter.'* (L. Bangs, *Psychotic Reactions and Carburetor Dung*, 1988)

glitterati *n.*
a combination of ⇨glitz and ⇨literati, the smarter sections of the literary world; typically, the Booker Prize-giving audience.

* *'But he brought in a new elite of glitterati . . . as betrayers of right-wing populism.'* (*New York Review of Books*, 19 July 1990)

glitz *n.* [1968]
dazzling superficiality, meretricious gloss.
– **glitzy** *adj.*

* *'Trump is a master of glitz – a talent he displayed to the full at Thursday night's official opening.'* (*Sunday Correspondent*, 8 April 1990)
* *'A glitzy maze of shops which . . . will sell you nothing you really want at prices your bank manager will not thank you for paying.'* (*Independent on Sunday*, 25 March 1990)

global music *n.*
see **world music.**

global village *n.* [1967]
the concept, popularized by Marshall McLuhan, that rather than living separately in our various houses, towns, countries and continents, the entire world is unified in a single 'global village', thanks to the proliferation of the mass media – available to all and with access to everything.

* *'"Time has ceased; "space" has vanished. We now live in a global village . . . a simultaneous happening.'* (M. McLuhan, *The Medium is the Message*, 1967)

global warming *n.* [1988]
the phenomenon whereby due to two centuries of industrial production, and the concomitant erosion of the protective ozone layer, the earth is gradually heating up, a process that may, if left unchecked, lead to a full-blown ⇨greenhouse effect.

* *'Last month in Washington, President Bush outlined to another ministerial meeting on global warming a strategy consisting largely of masterly inaction.'* (*Independent on Sunday*, 13 May 1990)

glue-sniffing *n.* [1963]
the sniffing of various forms of plastic cement for their narcotic effects. – **glue-sniffer** *n.*

* *'Michael Hurley, a former glue sniffer, who is now a professional former glue sniffer.'* (J. Meades, *Peter Knows What Dick Likes*, 1989)

goalposts, shift (*or* **move) the** *phrase.* [1986]
to change the target, to alter the rules, especially when that alteration is perceived as somewhat underhand and the agents of change, who might otherwise have found themselves in some degree of embarrassment, are able to emerge undeservingly unscathed.

gobsmacked *adv.* [1986]
an increasingly popular synonym for shocked or appalled; deriving from the age-old 'gob' (mouth), it implies an earthy, possibly northern origin. – **gobsmack** *v.t.*

* *'I was slightly flummoxed. Well, totally gobsmacked.'* (*Independent on Sunday*, 27 May 1990)

go codes *n.* [1963]
the US codes that would be transmitted in the event of launching a nuclear war or in response to a hostile attack: these codes, which change daily, are carried in a briefcase called the ⇨football by an officer who must never leave the president's side. Only on receiving these codes, which must match with counter codes and similar security devices, can the military begin a nuclear strike.

gofer *n.* [1970]
a corruption of 'go for' and originally identifying anyone around a TV or film studio, theatre, or record company (now the term extends to any place of employment) who is employed basically to run errands, make coffee, and serve as a general dogsbody. Some gofers, like newspaper copy boys, can rise high, but the description is essentially derogatory, especially when used of executives who would not like to admit that they occupy so lowly a position.

* *'If you are a 22 year-old man you get promoted to editor, if you're a woman you're a gofer all your life.'* (*Sunday Correspondent*, 25 March 1990)

go for it *phrase.* [1980]
an all-purpose exhortation to energy and effort; certainly Californian, and probably taken from the devotees of ⇨aerobics (Hitler's 'strength through joy' for the 1980s) and their motto 'Go for the burn!'.

* *'Go for it, Henry! he said, once again to himself. Go for it! the evening has a new agenda, detoxification followed by strangulation. Go for it, Henry! he said.'* (N. Williams, *The Wimbledon Poisoner*, 1990)

go-go *adj.* [1965]
1. exciting, plentiful, *see* **a go-go**.
2. as in **go-go dancer**: a girl who is hired to dance – often on a bar or in a cage – in a discotheque.

* *'Go-go dancer, topless waitress, massage parlor, call girl . . . it all boiled down to the same thing.'* (L. Bangs, *Psychotic Reactions and Carburetor Dung*, 1988)

go-go (fund) *n.* [1968]
risky, short-term, volatile and above all speculative investment dealing; the implication is of the frenetic atmosphere of a discotheque, the home of ⇨go-go dancing.

* *'In the late 1960s, the period memorialized in John Brooks's* The Go-Go Years, *venture capital (among other things) abounded.'* (T. Kidder, *The Soul of a New Machine*, 1981)

gold *adj.* [1969]
referring to a record – single or album – that has sold one million units; thus to 'go gold' is to sell one million records.
See also **platinum, silver**.

gold card *n.* [1982]
the superior form of credit card, issued first by American Express in 1982 and soon afterwards by such rivals as Diners Club, Visa and Mastercard. The gold card is available to those on higher incomes (£30,000+), and offers a substantial line of credit and various concomitant perks. So popular were the gold cards that they soon forfeited their initial exclusivity and Amex followed them up with the even more rarefied platinum card.

golden *adj.* [1960]
referring to any large sum of money directly related to one's employment; the first such term was **golden handshake** (coined in 1960), but the others, all mimicking the original, developed during the boom years of the 1980s. Thus **golden hello** a joining-up bonus; **golden handcuffs** high bonuses and commissions which, if one leaves the firm, must be (in part) returned; **golden parachute** major pay rises paid out to themselves by executives who fear for their jobs with a takeover looming; **platinum handshake** an even more remunerative farewell than the golden version.

* *'And of course, everybody understands what they call the "golden handcuffs" clause.'* (*Sunday Correspondent*, 1 April 1990)

* *'Inventing golden parachutes, wilder buyouts, trickier S&L investments.'* (*New York Review of Books*, 19 July 1990)

golden oldie *n.* [1966]
anything old, long-established and well-beloved; often used of old hit pop records.

golden parachute *n.*
see **tin parachute**.

Golden Rose/Silver Rose *n.* [1961]
the television awards presented at the annual International Television Festival at Montreux and presented to the year's best light entertainment programme.

* *'The Pythons gained respectability in the eyes of the BBC by winning a Silver Rose at the Montreux festival, with a special compilation edition.'* (R. Wilmut, *From Fringe to Flying Circus*, 1980)

Golden Triangle *n.* [1972]
the opium-growing area of South-East Asia, responsible for the production of the bulk of the world's heroin, approximately contained by China's Yunnan province, northeastern Burma, northern Thailand, and northern Laos.

gonk *n.* [1964]
an egg-shaped doll, often 'clothed' in brightly coloured material, which was briefly popular amongst teenage girls during the early 1960s. The predecessor, perhaps, of the ➲cabbage-patch doll.

gonzo *adj.* [1971]
bizarre, eccentric, unrestrained; the word is most frequently found in 'gonzo journalism',

a phrase coined by the writer Hunter S. Thompson in 1971 to describe his own brand of reporting, a sub-division of the ⇨New Journalism, where the usual intrusion of the reporter's ego into the reporting of the story was additionally fuelled by what appeared to be superhuman degrees of multiple drug and drink consumption.

* *'Horatio Alger gone mad on drugs in Las Vegas. Do it now: pure gonzo journalism.'* (H.S. Thompson, *Fear and Loathing in Las Vegas*, 1971)

go public *v.* [1965]
to reveal a plan to the public gaze; also, for a hitherto private company to offer its shares for public purchase on the Stock Market.

Gorbymania *n.* [1988]
on the pattern of Beatlemania, the near hysterical adulation that greets Soviet premier Mikhail Gorbachev when he visits foreign countries, especially Germany and the US; such enthusiasm is not, however, repeated in his home country.
See also **Beatlemania.**

gorillagram *n.*
see **kissagram.**

goth(ic) (punk) *n.* [1986]
a subgroup of ⇨punk rock fans who dress in austere black and enjoy a suitably grim joyless music.

* *'Goth, like punk, is a predominantly gestural genre, in this case indicative of a fondness for the darker side of life.'* (*The Independent*, 26 October 1990)

gourd, out of one's *phrase.*
see **skull, out of one's.**

go with *v.* [1970]
to accept, to tolerate, to permit life to sweep one along; the term is often combined as 'go with the flow', the image here is of the Beatles' 'Tomorrow Never Knows': 'Turn off your mind, relax and float downstream . . . '

* *'This is the Aquarian Age and the time to be yourself, to love one's beauty, to go with one's process.'* (R.D. Rosen, *Psychobabble*, 1977)
* *'By now I'm ready to go with the flow, with anything, as it has begun to seem to me, delusory or not.'* (L. Bangs, *Psychotic Reactions and Carburetor Dung*, 1988)

graceful degradation *n.* [1981]
1. *in military use:* the concept inherent in positing a possibly 'winnable', 'limited' nuclear war: that one's own command, and control and communications facilities, and the weapons that they administer will survive longer, or at least collapse less speedily than those of the enemy. They will thus continue (albeit damaged) to work to a greater effect than those of the enemy. It is accepted that massive loss and destruction on both sides will accompany this process; thus it would seem that such a victory would merely go to the side that was last to die of its wounds.

* *'Systems which will be resistant to enemy attack and which will degrade gracefully . . . after the initial clash.'* (P. Pringle & W. Arkin, *SIOP*, 1983)

2. *in computing:* a synonym for 'failsoft' – programs or machines that can tolerate a degree of failure or breakdown without impairing the running of the complete program or stopping the machine from running.

grannex
see **granny annexe.**

granny *adj.* [1966]
descriptive of a type of 'antique' style adopted for a while in the 1960s by the fashionable young; typical combinations were **granny glasses** wire-rimmed spectacles, worn by both sexes and **granny dresses** long lace dresses which, with such accessories as crushed velvet shawls, were all supposed to give a flavour of Victoriana and thus one's grandmother.

- ✱ *'"Hoo wot," repeats the girl in the granny dress, pulling on the negro's arm.'* (N. Fury, *Agro*, 1971)

granny annexe (*or* **flat)** *n.* [1978]
also known as **grannex**: the extension to a house in which one's elderly parent(s) can be housed in adjacent privacy.

granny battering *n.* [1988]
on the pattern of ➲baby-battering or wife-battering, the systematic beating of the old carried on within the family situation.

gray (*or* **grey)** *adj.* [1974]
used since the 1960s to denote pensioners or senior citizens, usually those formed into pressure groups or advocating some form of activism, on the analogy of the US ➲Black Panthers who fought and demonstrated for the black cause. Thus the **Gray Panthers** (founded in the US *c.* 1972) who demand attention for the elderly in the areas of health, housing, protection from crime, finance and utilities; and a study on elderly homosexuals published in 1982: 'Gay and Gray'.

- ✱ *'The file is updated each month and all WWAV's mailings targeted at the "grey" market will be run against it.'* (*Independent on Sunday*, 3 June 1990)

grebo *n.* [1963]
a British youth cult featuring a cultivatedly sordid appearance, a boorish manner, and a devotion to ➲heavy metal music.

green *adj.* [1972]
current shorthand for ecologically/environmentally concerned. Germany's Green Party emerged after the 1960s (and gained substantial successes in the national elctions of 1982), but British concerns, and the success of the homegrown Greens, are a more recent phenomenon.

- ✱ *'I own only two of those new green cleaning products.'* (*Independent on Sunday*, 25 March 1990)
- ✱ *'The typical Green voter is youthful, lives in the south, and he or she (neither gender predominates significantly) prefers green wellies to green terrorism.'* (*Daily Telegraph*, Student Extra, 1989)

green channel *n.* [1968]
see **red channel.**

green cross code *n.* [1969]
the highway code as applied to crossing roads, a development of the traditional 'Look right, look left and look right again'.

- ✱ *'The green cross code grows up.'* (heading in *The Independent*, 24 May 1990)

green currency *n.* [1977]
see **green pound.**

greenfield (site) *n.* [1962]
those rural and undeveloped sites, often near

towns or cities but not designated as part of the protected green belts – the strips of land that surround the urban centres and prevent one large town simply sliding into the outskirts of another through builders' continuing greed for new land.

* *'An explosion of business parks on greenfield sites – 800 are in the pipeline – has swept away distinctions between office and factory.'* (*The Independent*, 15 May 1990)

greenhouse effect *n.* [1962]
the major current environmental worry – the 'heating up' of the planet due to pollution – increased carbon dioxide in the atmosphere allows the sun's heat in, but no longer lets it out. The greenhouse effect was originally a theory of post-nuclear civilization whereby the effect of multiple explosions would have caused the ozone layer in the atmosphere to be destroyed and would thus permit the harmful rays of the sun to penetrate; the result of this would be akin to living in a superheated greenhouse, water supplies would dry up, plants would 'burn' away and humanity would duly collapse without vital liquids and crops. Its current usuage embraces the effects of non-nuclear waste products.

* *'Also let me stress that the CO2 greenhouse effect is a long-term trend.'* (P. Ehrlich, C. Sagan *et al*, *The Nuclear Winter*, 1984)

green monkey disease *n.* [1967]
also known as **Marburg disease**: a contagious, even fatal disease characterized by high fever and haemorrhaging, transmitted by West African monkeys of the species *Cercopithecus aethioops*. It gained the name 'Marburg disease' after a number of W. German laboratory technicians who were researching the virus died of the disease after handling green monkeys in 1967.

Greenpeace *n.* [1977]
a militant environmentalist movement whose high profile activities in opposing whaling and the dumping of toxic waste at sea have brought them into worldwide renown.

* *'The image Greenpeace carries is of heroics on board inflatable boats.'* (*Daily Telegraph*, Student Extra, 1989)

green pound *n.* [1974]
the British version of the green currency by which agricultural transactions are made through the EC. Sterling is thus the 'green pound' and there are similarly 'green lire', francs, deutschmarks, etc.

green revolution *n.* [1970]
originally the increase in production of cereal crops in developing countries after the introduction of high-yield varieties and the application of scientific and planned methods to their cultivation. Now referring to the worldwide interest in 'green' (environmentalist) issues that emerged during the 1980s.

green sweater worker *n.* [1990]
anyone involved in conservation or environmentalism. (*Sunday Times*, 25 March 1990)

grey imports *n.* [1982]
see **grey market**.

grey market *n.* [1982]
on the pattern of black market and grey area: the importation of computer goods (usually manufactured in the US) before they are fully

available in the UK. Such imports are not actually illegal, but while they benefit the enthusiastic consumer, they go against the policy of companies who have deliberately chosen to postpone their official launch of the product outside the US. The first big grey market emerged with the launch in the US in 1981, but not for a further year in the UK, of the IBM PC.

✱ *'One of the problems of ordering Apple equipment through the grey market . . . is that there are no guarantees.'* (*PC World*, July 1990)

gridlock *n., v., v.* [1983]
a complete and extensive traffic jam in which traffic has become interlocked at a road junction and cannot move in any direction; also used figuratively to imply any deadlocked situation. Occasionally used as a verb, e.g. 'Traffic has gridlocked'.

✱ *'If US management and labor could break the economic gridlock . . . what would the resulting new American economy look like?'* (*Atlantic*, April 1982)

grief therapy *n.* [1963]
supportive therapy for the recently bereaved, often carried out between an 'encounter group' of four or five similarly bereaved individuals, under the direction of a highly motivated counsellor.

GRIT *abbrev.* [1962]
an acronym for Graduated Reciprocated Reduction in Tension: the strategic version of 'turning the other cheek', a version of conflict management that implies not weakness but the desire to avoid all out conflict and initiate some process of de- escalation. GRIT was developed in 1962 by US professor of psychology Charles E. Osgood in his book *Alternative to War or Surrender*. Under a GRIT scenario, the major problems of international relations – notably the weapons themselves – should be put aside, and nations should concentrate on removing lesser, but more easily accessible, sources of tension. The intent of GRIT is to draw from the opponent a similar degree of restraint, pulling further and faster away from the potential war.

grockle *n.* [1960]
a tourist; the term originated in Torbay, where a local remarked that the stream of visitors to the town resembled little Grocks, or clowns, but spread throughout Britain's holiday resorts.

grok *v.* [1961]
to understand, to communicate meaningfully; coined by science fiction author Robert Heinlein in his novel *Stranger in a Strange Land* (1961).

✱ *'In his movie – right right right – and they all grok over that. Grok – and then it's clear, without anybody having to say it.'* (T. Wolfe, *The Electric Kool-Aid Acid Test*, 1969)

groovy *adj.* [1966]
a general term of hippie approbation.

✱ *'If he can bring himself to approve of what's happening, he becomes groovy.'* (H.S. Thompson, *Fear and Loathing in Las Vegas*, (1971)

gross *adj.* [1968]
a slang term for utterly disgusting, especially referring to the physically unpleasant – vomit, blood, grotesque injuries, etc.

gross-out *adj.* [1973]
disgusting, highly distasteful. – **gross out**, *v.*

- ✱ *'His early gross-out comedies earned enough to set him up as Hollywood's golden boy.'* (*The Independent*, 27 July 1990)

groupie *n.* [1968]
a girl who follows and sleeps with rock groups. The phenomenon of groupiedom is hardly new, but it gained a universal currency when *Rolling Stone* magazine ran an entire 'Groupie Issue' (no. 27) early in 1969. The term is also used figuratively, to mean a particularly devoted fan.

- ✱ *'Known as groupies, these people are a sexological phenomenon of the Sixties, as fashionable anthropological specimens as were the Trobriand islanders in their day.'* (R. Neville, *Play Power*, 1970)
- ✱ *'I used to be a bit of a groupie. I thought they had glamour, but all they wanted was money and a mock Tudor mansion.'* (J. Meades, *Peter Knows What Dick Likes*, 1989)

group sex *n.* (1964)
a synonym for the traditional orgy, albeit touted in the 1960s as some form of personal liberation.

- ✱ *'When she and one of her husbands tried to experience group sex by answering an advertisement in a swingers' magazine, the only result was a rendezvous . . . with a portly burgher wearing a Goldwater button.'* (G. Talese, *Thy Neighbor's Wife*, 1980)

group therapy *n.* [1970]
the treatment of a number of psychotherapeutic patients in a group, rather than as individuals; the individual therapies are seen as being augmented by the dynamics of the group.
See also **encounter group**.

- ✱ *'Only this was group therapy not for the middle-aged and fucked-up but for the Young! and Immune!'* (T. Wolfe, *The Electric Kool-Aid Acid Test*, 1969)

groupuscule *n* [1964]
a very small group, usually a splinter group of an already minuscule political party (usually of the left).

grungy *adj.* [1965]
bad, ugly, inferior, boring.

- ✱ *'It sounds just as grungy and jumbled now as it did way back in 1967.'* (L. Bangs, *Psychotic Reactions and Carburetor Dung*, 1988)

grunt *n.* [1965]
a US infantryman, a nickname supposedly derived from his inarticulacy, and the grunts of effort as he strains to carry a heavy pack.

- ✱ *'Sometimes an especially smart grunt or another correspondent would even ask me what I was really doing there.'* (M. Herr, *Dispatches*, 1977)

G spot *n.*
that area of the female anatomy which, if suitably stimulated, will create the maximum of sexual pleasure. Thus used figuratively.

- ✱ *'Most of Prince's work heads straight for the aural G-spot, consistently breaking pop's cast-iron taboo against naming the dirty bits it's so obsessed with.'* (*The Independent*, 14 June 1990)

guerrilla (theatre) *n.* [1965]
spontaneous street theatre that aims to make a political point and thus take the same role in the theatre as does a real guerrilla in conventional warfare.

* *'The aim of the Yippies, as described by Rubin was "guerrilla theatre media politics".'* (F. Wheen, *The 1960s*, 1982)

guesstimate *n., v.*
a rough estimate, with a large element (as has the combination word) of guesswork.
See also **ball park**.

GUI *abbrev.* [1981]
Graphic User Interface: a method of operating the computer via the manipulation of screen ⇨icons rather than by typing lengthy and often convoluted script commands; *also known as* ⇨WIMPs (windows, icons, mice and pointers). GUIs were pioneered in the early 1980s by Xerox (Palo Alto Research Corporation) but came to real prominence with the launch of the Apple Corporation's Macintosh machines in 1985 and with that of 'Windows 3.0' (a GUI designed for the IBM-PC and its ⇨clones) in 1990.

* *'As easy to use as the non-graphical-user-interface (GUI) DESQview (although Apple is moving forward to its own updates).'* (*Byte*, June 1990

gulag *n.* [1974]
from the Russian *Gulag* – *G*lavnoye *U*pravleniye *Lag*erei (Chief Administration of Corrective Labour camps): the network of camps initiated by Lenin, vastly expanded by Stalin, and still maintained (albeit in fast shrinking numbers) by the Soviet authorities. The word was brought to Western ears by author Alexander Solzhenitsyn in his trilogy *The Gulag Archipelago* (1974).

* *'That amazing country of Gulag which, though scattered in an archipelago geographically, was, in the psychological sense, fused into a continent – an almost invisible, almost imperceptible country inhabited by the zek preople.'* (A. Solzhenitsyn, *The Gulag Archipelago*, Vol.1, 1974)
* *'I might be languishing today, pale and unshaven, in some distant gulag.'* (T. Blacker, *Fixx*, 1989)

gut *adj.* [1964]
visceral, deeply felt, instinctive; 'gut' is usually found in such combinations as *gut feeling*, *gut reaction* and *gut issue*, where the word is extended to mean 'core' or 'basic'.

* *'Gut sensibility leads us all to work with what is familiar to us, or with what we think we can make our own.'* (J. Meades, *Peter Knows What Dick Likes*, 1989)

gypsy (cab) *n.* [1966]
the US version of a minicab: an unlicensed cab that can be called to take a passenger from one place to another but may not cruise the streets for fares.

* *'Finally the boat docked. They whisked Don Johnson into a limousine and we looked around and found a couple of gypsy cabs.'* (A. Warhol, *Diaries*, 4 July 1986)

hack *n., v.* [1960]
1. the exploitation of a computer's potential for the pure delight of its technical abilities; to perform such operations.
See also **hacker, 1.**

* *'A project undertaken or a product built not solely to fulfil some constructive goal, but with some wild pleasure taken in mere involvement, was called a "hack" . . . to qualify as a hack, the feat must be imbued with innovation, style, and technical virtuosity.'* (S. Levy, *Hackers*, 1984)

2. *see* **hacker, 2.**

* *'Ten year-olds can hack into NATO; a cat can fax to a king.'* (*Sunday Correspondent*, 10 June 1990)

hacker *n.* [1960]
1. anyone who enjoys computing for its own sake rather than for its applications; those who learn about both hard- and software with the intention of stretching and modifying both to their greatest extent.
2. computer enthusiasts who devote their energies and abilities to penetrating major computer networks, notably those of banks, defence systems, and the like. In their own eyes simply adepts of a 'recreational and educational sport', they are widely condemned as at best a nuisance and at worst as criminals.
See also **virus.**

* *'5 out of 5 hackers prefer other software protection methods to Hardlock E-Y-E.'* (ad for Fast Electronic GmbH in *Byte*, February 1991)

hack it *v.* [1969]
to manage, to get along.
See also **cut it.**

* *'"I just can't hack it back in the World," he said.'* (M. Herr, *Dispatches* 1977)

hair gel *n.* [1977]
a jellylike substance that is applied to the hair so that it retains the style.

hair implant *n.* [1974]
the grafting of strands of artificial hair (usually made of an acrylic fibre) stitched into a bald area of the scalp or attached to small metal barbs forced into the scalp under pressure.

hair lacquer *n.*
a mix of shellac and alcohol that is sprayed onto the hair to hold it in place.

hair transplant *n.* [1973]
a graft or grafting of one's own hair by removing follicles and inserting them in a bald area of the scalp.

hairy *adj.* [1962]
exciting, but dangerous; hair-raising.

hammer *n.* [1975]
as used by ⇨CB radio broadcasters: the accelerator; thus **put the hammer down**: to accelerate.

* *'Smoking into Texas with the hammer down.'* (S. Earle, 'Guitar Town', 1988)

hand-bag *v.* [1985]
to hit with a handbag; the original 'handbagger' was 'Miss Piggy' of the Muppets, but the term became far more widely applied to the former prime minister Margaret Thatcher, whose dressings down of various figures, international or Parliamentary, are likened to the flailings of the latex prima donna.

* *'Dorn's face collapsed into a variety of rubbery emotions, like Kermit the Frog being handbagged by Miss Piggy.'* (*Independent on Sunday*, 10 June 1990)

handle *n.*
a particular aspect of an advertising or marketing campaign, geared to make the maximum impact and attract as many as possible of the target audience; the marketing equivalent of the media's 'angle' and the recording industry's 'hook'.

hands-on *adj.* [1971]
personal practical involvement in a job; the implication is of sleeves rolled high and hands covered in oil; although the original use is in computing, where the user, not the machine, controls the program.

* *'Hands-on management, extensive consultation, plenty of commitment and networking at all levels throughout the group.'* (*Independent on Sunday*, 3 June 1990)

hang-glider *n.* [1972]
a suspension glider, controlled and stabilized by the movements of the pilot, who is suspended beneath the framework of the glider's wing. The first hang-glider appeared around 1930, but the contemporary sport only emerged in the early 1970s. – **hang-gliding** *n.*

hang in there *v.* [1968]
to hold on, to hang on; to maintain one's position despite the odds. Often used as a cry of encouragement, 'Hang in there, man . . . ' See also **hang tough**.

hang (*or* stay) loose *v.* [1968]
the opposite of being ➪uptight: to coast through life taking good or bad as one finds them and letting neither disturb one's equilibrium.
See also **go with the flow**.

* *'"And remember," he told him, waving, "stay loose".'* (C. McFadden, *The Serial*, 1976)

hang tough *v.* [1968]
a variation on 'toughing it out', first coined to encourage heroin addicts who were attempting to withdraw from drugs at the Synanon Foundation in California: used by politicians to stress that once they have adopted a position or stance, they intend to stick by it. Politicians also refer to ➪hanging in there, in much the same way.

hang-up *n.* [1965]
a problem or difficulty, usually emotional and often in the form of an inhibition or an obsession. – **hung up** *adj.*

* *'I feel hung up and I don't know why.'* (The Beatles, 'I Want To Tell You', 1966)
* *'Cassady brought in a Scandinavian-style blonde who was always talking about hang-ups. Everybody had hang-ups.'* (T. Wolfe, *The Electric Kool-Aid Acid Test*, 1969)

happening *n.* [1962]
a spontaneous or improvised public perfor-

mance, often involving the audience; happenings originated in the US around 1959, they arrived in England in 1962, when at that year's Edinburgh Festival a nude girl was wheeled across a theatre stage, much to the consternation of the assembled audience.

* *'Smoke billows through a resulting aperture. A previously unnoticed object above her head repeatedly explodes. The happening is over.'* (R. Neville, Play Power, 1970)
* *'Yoko's 1960s happening isn't everyone's bag.'* (*Independent on Sunday*, 25 March 1990)

hard *adj.* [1960]
in military use: referring to bases, silos, and similar missile installations or military command posts which have extra protection, usually in the form of reinforced concrete defences and the construction of subterranean bunkers, against incoming nuclear weapons; such hardening must be reinforced to keep pace with advances in the strength and accuracy of new weapons and it is generally accepted that if the hardened silo is to be anything but a static concrete shroud rather than a useful asset to a weapons system, it cannot realistically be expected to survive a direct hit.

* *'Neither side, however, can presently destroy the opponent's hard military targets, such as missile silos.'* (R.C. Aldridge, *First Strike!* 1983)

hardball, play *v.* [1973]
from professional baseball's use of the correct hard ball, rather than that used in the amateur, if popular game of softball: used in politics to imply a tough, no-nonsense attitude to governmental problems in general and confrontations in particular; equally popular in business use, often referring to the refusal to give way easily on a contract or similar deal.

hard copy *n.* [1964]
copy that has been printed out from the electronic records held in any of the retrieval systems held in the machine's memory; the opposite of the 'magnetic' records held either on tape or disc.

* *'Hard copy is computer output on paper, printing or graphics.'* (D. Jarrett, *The Good Computing Book for Beginners*, 1980)

hard-core *adj.* [1960]
1. hardline, extreme, uncompromising, aggressive. This (essentially US) use, often found as a self-description by tough young men, is probably a back-formation from **2**.
2. specifically (and found more frequently) the most extreme pornography, invariably involving some form of violence, portraying (usually on film or video, but also in books and magazines) such activities as child abuse, bestiality, sado-masochism, etc.

* *'Women's groups and Labour women MPs claim there is a direct link between hard-core porn and sexual violence.'* (*Independent on Sunday*, 3 June 1990)

hardcore
see -**core**.

hard disk *n.* [1983]
a rigid storage disk made from aluminium substrate plated or coated usually on both sides, with a magnetic material; it is used for the mass storage of computerized data and offers retrieval times far faster than those of ⇨floppy disks.
See also **Winchester**.

* *'Server-based LAN operating systems typically can handle very large hard disks.'* (*Byte*, June 1990)

hard drugs *n.* [1968]
drugs that are judged to be physiologically or psychologically addictive, e.g. heroin and cocaine (and its derivatives such as ⇨crack).
See also **soft drugs**.

hard-edge painting *n.* [1966]
also known as **colour field painting**: colour field painters replace tonal contrasts and brushwork by solid areas of colour which usually extend across the canvas from edge to edge and imply that the fields of colour stretch on to infinity, far beyond the confines of the canvas; a type of painting that views the entire picture surface as one unit and thus has no division between the 'ground' and 'figures' on it; paintings that are crisp, geometrical, and have no apparent interest in personal emotional statements.

✱ *'The indirect lights spotting an assortment of hard-edge paintings in silver frames.'* (R. DiLello, *The Longest Cocktail Party*, 1971)

hard landscaping *n.*
permanent features in landscape architecture. An extension of the figurative use of ⇨**hard-wired**.

✱ *'Hard landscaping – paving, ornaments and brickwork – is regarded with deep suspicion.'* (*Independent on Sunday*, 3 June 1990)

hard landing *n.* [1967]
a sudden downturn in the economy after a period of relative prosperity; the reverse, **soft landing** is an improvement in the economy after a period of austerity and falling prices.

hard-line *adj.* [1962]
rigid, inflexible, especially in industrial or political relations. Those who adopt such positions are **hard-liners**.

✱ *'Thus some professional Jewish hard-liners offer us an Israel, not as a home for Israelis, but as one big museum of martyrdom.'* (A. Oz, 'The Slopes of Lebanon', 1987)

hardware *n.* [1965]
1. *in computing*: the actual machinery – electrical, mechanical, structural – that comprises the working parts of a computer, as opposed to the ⇨software with which it is programmed and otherwise made to work.

✱ *'As the head of Oracle's engineering department you will be responsible for co-ordinating the work of our team of highly skilled hardware and software engineers.'* (*Independent on Sunday*, 8 April 1990)

2. *in military use*: a general term for military materiel, weapons, and equipment; in these terms software tends to imply the human beings involved in wars.

✱ *'It really showed what you could do if you had the know-how and the hardware.'* (M. Herr, *Dispatches*, 1977)

✱ *'The Soviets have chosen to concentrate on simpler, more redundant, and more durable hardware.'* (D. Ford, *The Button*, 1985)

hard-wired *adj.* [1971]
in computing: any circuit that is directly wired into the computer; it can be used figuratively to mean 'permanent'.

✱ *'A computer in which the stairway ends there, at the level of assembly language, is said to be "hard-wired".'* (T. Kidder, *The Soul of a New Machine*, 1981)

Hare Krishna *n., adj.* [1969]
the International Society for Krishna Con-

sciousness, a sect devoted to the Hindu God Krishna, whose devotees, often white, can be seen in their saffron robes, parading through the world's great cities, banging drums, chanting and asking for money; the Hare Krishnas appeared in England around 1969, directly imported by Beatle George Harrison.

* *'Student sitters-in have had their ranks swelled by visitors from the local Arts Lab, Hare Krishna chanters,* et al.' (R. Neville, *Play Power,* 1970)
* *'A Hare Krishna combo is in full wail, competing with a chain-smoking woman evangelist, who shouts about what Jesus has done for her.'* (J. McClure, *Cop World,* 1984)

hash *abbrev.* [1964]
hashish.
See also **Acapulco gold**.

* *'Only two quid deals and a ten bob deal of hash still . . . chafe against his balls in their tight crinkly silver paper wrapping.'* (N. Fury, *Agro,* 1971)

hatchback *n., adj.* [1970]
a design of car that has dispensed with the traditional boot and replaced it with a sloping rear which is a single door that can be lifted to open.

* *'Fickle buyers turned to dynamically superior hatchbacks – wolves in sheep's clothing, rather than the other way about.'* (*Independent on Sunday,* 10 June 1990

have-a-go *adj.* [1971]
a term used of any member of the public who voluntarily attempts to hinder the performance of a crime – grabbing a bankrobber, knocking down a mugger, etc. The term, and the practice, was encouraged by a Commissioner of the Metropolitan Police who suggested that the public should 'have a go' and thus help the official police; in an increasingly violent society, current police chiefs stress that the public should resist such heroics and let the professionals work as best they can.

* *'A wages snatch in which a "have-a-go" hero was battered.'* (*Sunday Correspondent,* 8 April 1990)

hawk *n.* [1962]
an advocate of an aggressive posture and policy on foreign relations. Coined in 1798 as 'war hawks' by Thomas Jefferson, to describe those who wanted a war with France, and later for those who actually promoted the War of 1812 with England, and revived in 1962 by US writers Stewart Alsop and Charles Bartlett, in a piece on the Cuban Missile Crisis. With its opposite ➪'dove' hawk has gained a permanent place in the political/military lexicon ever since.

* *'Influential right-wing "hawks" in the United States voiced much concern over the possibility of Soviet nuclear superiority.'* (M. Dando & P. Rogers, *The Death of Deterrence,* 1984)
* *'Bush holds back hawks on Lithuanian crisis.'* (*Independent on Sunday,* 25 March 1990)

Hazchem *abbrev.* [1976]
Hazardous Chemical: used to label any container of potentially dangerous chemicals or the vehicle or building in which they are kept.

head *n.* [1968]
a drug user, thus a general term for a ➪hippie, all of whom were presumed to use some form of (usually ➪soft) drug. Head can be suffixed to the drug names or types themselves, thus *acid head; pill head; hash head;* etc. There were

also **head shops**, the first of which was the ➩Psychedelic Shop, opened in San Francisco in 1967, which specialized in drug paraphernalia.

✱ *'A . . . pair of shiny low cut black shoes doesn't set them all to doing the Varsity Rag in the head world in San Francisco.'* (T. Wolfe, *The Electric Kool-Aid Acid Test*, 1969)

✱ *'Embroiled in a freaking mass of amphetamine-heads.'* (N. Fury, *Agro*, 1971)

✱ *'Drugs served . . . to give the pill head confidence in himself to the point of feeling rightness and omnipotence.'* (M. Farren, *Watch Out Kids*, 1972)

✱ *'Leonard's office in the back of a remodelled ark he shared with a head shop.'* (C. McFadden, *The Serial*, 1976)

✱ *'A yuppie cokehead who dodges the heat by hiding out in a de-tox clinic.'* (*Sunday Correspondent*, 3 June 1990)

✱ *'For "crack heads" in need of a "fix" even the poorest churches represent an oasis of prosperity.'* (*Independent on Sunday*, 24 June 1990)

headbanger *n.* [1970]
a fan of ➩heavy metal music, whose enthusiasms lead him to bang his head against hard surfaces, in or out of time with the music. – **headbang** *v.*

✱ *'They were singing about them in ghastly raucous voices to deeply proletarian, headbanging, drunken crowds.'* (*The Independent*, 26 May 1990)

headhunt *v.* [1970]
to search out and recruit top executives, often with the implication of stealing them from their current employer in order to capitalize on their special abilities, rather than waiting for them to tire of that job and make an approach themselves; thus **headhunters** the individuals or firms who perform such recruitment. They may be either regular employees of the headhunting firm, or may operate as consultants, with specific knowledge of the executives in question and hire themselves out to any interested party.

✱ *'There'd be headhunters roaming the floors of the conference, in search of young engineers, whom they'd . . . ply with liquor and caviar, and talk into defecting to other computer companies.'* (T. Kidder, *The Soul of a New Machine*, 1981)

head, out of (one's) *phrase.* [1966]
intoxicated with drugs or drink.

✱ *'I'd been out of my head for so long now, that a gig like this seemed perfectly logical.'* (H.S. Thompson, *Fear and Loathing in Las Vegas*, 1971)

head up *v.* [1960]
to lead, organize; often as, 'X heads up the project'.

head-up (display) *n.* [1960]
a projection of instrument readings – in a car, aircraft cockpit, or any equipped vehicle – that is taken off the actual dials and appears on the windscreen so that drivers, pilots, etc., can read the information without taking their eyes off the road or sky ahead.
See also **glass cockpit**.

✱ *'Flight deck instruments. Flight control systems. Electronic displays. Military controls. Head-up displays. Multi-purpose colour displays.'* (ad for Smiths Industries, Aerospace and Defence Systems, *Independent on Sunday*, 25 March 1990)

heavy *adj.* [1970]
giving an emotional charge, whether positive or negative; intense, important, or notably unpleasant. Like ➪'wicked' in the late 1980s, 'heavy' was an all-purpose word for the ➪hippies, and meant whatever it had to mean according to context.

* *'I've been able to meet some very heavy dealers, like the guy who produced most of the STP in the world and has a network of ten laboratories.'* (A. Hoffman, *Woodstock Nation*, 1969)

heavy metal *n., adj.* [1975]
a type of rock music (in full 'heavy metal music') which is invariably played very loud, depends on a succession of repeated sound-alike riffs; its main audience is composed of adolescent boys, slightly too old for computer games, who revel in its images of macho men and yielding beauties, set against the bloodier end of the sword and sorcery market.

* *'Drag racers do it to heavy metal music.'* (*Independent on Sunday*, 22 April 1990)

hegemony *n.* [1970]
from the Greek *hegemon* (leader or ruler).

1. *in politics*: term that describes the sort of superpower policies used in dealing with smaller nations, which is seen by its critics as similar to traditional imperialism.

2. *in China*: used by Mao Tse Tung specifically to attack the Soviet Union's neo-colonialism especially as regarded parts of China.

3. as **bourgeois hegemony**: in Marxist terms, the aspirations of any one class (especially the bourgeoisie) to rule the others, particularly by conditioning the masses to accept such rule as 'natural' and 'common sense'.

Heimlich manoeuvre *n.* [1975].
a first-aid technique that dislodges a given object (usually food) from a person's throat. The rescuer embraces the victim from behind, clasping his or her hands just below the rib cage and presses the closed fist under the breastbone with a quick upwards thrust.

* *'Here are the instructions for the Heimlich manoeuvre, which has just been officially endorsed by the AMA as a lifesaving rescue device.'* (*House & Garden*, January 1976)

helpline *n.* [1980]
any of a variety of public access information services, whether dealing with legal problems, ➪child abuse, housing queries, ➪AIDS advice, or any similar service – available either on a specially manned telephone line, or as phone-in services run by radio stations.

* *'Dial-a-solicitor, night or day. Sue Fieldman looks for advice from some of the Samaritan-style legal helplines.'* (*The Independent*, 6 April 1990)

her indoors *n.* [1979]
a synonym for wife, a term popularized by the television series *Minder*.

* *'Today the kids are round the computer and Dad is watching the telly with a pint, while Her Indoors has nothing to say to anybody.'* (*Independent on Sunday*, 10 June 1990)

heritage *n., adj.* [1985]
traditional history as interpreted by Disneyworld, the commercial exploitation of a nation's past, justified by its supporters as offering greater access for the mass market.

* *'What is our "heritage"? Surely more than whatever is pretty, pompous or ancient . . .'* (*Private Eye*, 16 March 1990)

* *'This decade has seen the tectonic accumulation that we have learned to call "the heritage" less threatened than at any time since the War.'* (J. Meades, *Peter Knows What Dick Likes*, 1989)

hermeneutics *n.* [1965]
the theory and method of interpreting meaningful human action; the word was coined to describe the problem of discovering the authentic version of a text at a time when books were still hand-copied and thus filled with many errors; its use subsequently developed to deal with the way in which lived human experience is studied by looking both at individuals and the world view of which they are a part.

herstory *n.* [1978]
the feminist response to the traditional 'history'; both a linguistic and an ideological alteration, which uses a pun to change the word (on the lines of ⇨wimmin for women, etc.) and stresses the masculine bias that informs the bulk of traditional historical study.

* *'The rewriting or respeaking of history as herstory – coined by some feminists in the 1970s – is guaranteed to annoy most men, many women, and almost all linguists.'* (J. Mills, *Womanwords*, 1989)

heterosexism *n.* [1986]
on the pattern of ⇨sexism, ⇨ageism, etc.: the belief that heterosexuality is inherently superior to any other sexual predilection.

heuristic *adj.* [1960]
1. *in computing*: in essence, trial and error: a situation in which a computer, faced with a set problem, will analyse all the possible solutions before coming up with the ideal one and then, if necessary, move onto the next stage of its activity.
2. *in education*: especially of science teaching; the emphasis that such teaching must centre on practical methods of experimentation and investigation.

hex *n.* [1968]
any mathematical system that uses the decimal number 16 as a base for calculations, the norm for computer arithmetic systems which use binary – base 2 – arithmetic which is further organized into 8-bit chunks, also using a base of 2. – **hexadecimal** *adj.*

* *'Hex is a number system to base of 16, just as decimal is to the base of 10, binary to the base of 2, and octal to the base 8.'* (D. Jarrett, *The Good Computing Book for Beginners*, 1980)

hidden agenda *n.* [1975]
originally used as a management term to denote those matters that are vitally important to an individual at a given meeting but which are neither on the official agenda nor can they be placed there since they arise from that individual's emotions rather than the company's business, e.g. the personal antagonisms between two members of the board/committee etc. Now more frequent in political use, where the implication is of devious long-term plotting.

* *'The obvious question which might be overlooked by interviewers more preoccupied with their own hidden agenda.'* (*Sunday Correspondent*, 1 April 1990)

high five *n.* [1966]
ritual palm slapping, originated by US blacks, and now popular among a wide range of individuals, especially sportsmen who raise their

hands and slap palms together to celebrate a victory or on-field success.

* *'West Germany: Voller and Klinsman make with the high fives in Milan.'* (*Independent on Sunday*, 17 June 1990)

high flier *n.* [1970]
originally the top ranks of the civil service, often selected early in their career, both on the instinct of their superiors as well as on the indication of their potential, and groomed from their early twenties onwards as future mandarins; now in general use to describe any potential star.

* *'He was a high-flyer in the straight establishment; I had the "alternative" world at my fingertips.'* (T. Blacker, *Fixx*, 1989)

hi(gh)-tech *adj.* [1975]
a design fashion popularized in the mid-late 1970s in which styles more usually found on or around the factory floor – exposed pipes, steel staircases, heavy duty materials for floor and wall-coverings, etc. – were transmuted into the home or office where one would now find various technical artefacts – dentists' trolleys, hospital-style taps, etc., all unearthed from wholesalers' catalogues – in place of the traditional domestic supplies. This factory/workshop style originally used the actual materials employed in the 'tech' environments, but soon degenerated into **slick tech** when the look was mass produced for easy purchase.

* *'The entire legal bulletin . . . was intened to bring together individuals with unusual sexual preferences, a kind of high-tech dating service for the kinky.'* (*Sunday Correspondent*, 22 April 1990)

Thus its opposite **low tech** [1972].

* *'Low tech against high tech; the barrow boy approach against the public school way.'* (*Independent on Sunday*, 25 March 1990)

hip capitalism *n.* [1969]
capitalism as practised by the ➪hip entrepreneurs of the ➪alternative society, typical hip capitalists were the illustrator Peter Max and the Thelin brothers, who in 1967 opened the world's first ➪Psychedelic Shop in San Francisco.

* *'A cultural revolutionary – not a cultural nationalist, for that would embrace a concept of hip capitalism which I reject.'* (A. Hoffman, *Woodstock Nation*, 1969)

hip-hop *n.* [1985]
a musical form, originated in New York, that mixes a heavy ➪disco beat, often played on drum machines and synthesizers, with spoken, rhymed lyrics, sometimes of a political/sociological nature, but equally often celebrating the ➪rapper's strength, verbal agility or sexual prowess; thus the youth subculture that grew up around and is typified by the musical style. *See also* **rap**.

* *'"About a year ago things started to happen in hip-hop and rap," says Billboard's Latin music writer Carlos Agudelo.'* (*The Independent*, 27 July 1990)

hippie (*or* hippy) *n.* [1966]
the 1960s ➪counter-culture made flesh, that decade's youth cult, resplendent in beads and bells, proffering flowers and murmuring of peace, love, and 'getting it together in the country'. The word descended directly from hip, a black coinage of the 1930s (if not earlier) and the style descended from that of the beatniks, middle-class white youth's previous attempt to break away from established society.

* *'In almost all cases the hippie is a schizophrenic who leads a double or even triple life in his head.'* (S. Grunwald, *The Great Hippie Hoax*, 1967)

hippie trail *n.* [1969]
the ➲alternative tourist route, taking in India, Afghanistan, and Nepal, with excursions to the Balearic Islands, North Africa, and South East Asia, which was popular among the hippies of the mid-1960s to mid-1970s, at which point many national governments (notably that of Nepal) took measures to bar the ever-increasing influx. The hippies often claimed to be looking for the mental stimulation of the east, but on the whole went for the cheap (semi-) legal drugs.

* *'Most people had taken the boat, but I got very much sucked into the hippie trail, which was just beginning.'* (J. Green, *Them*, 1990)

hog *n.* [1967]
a customized motorcycle, usually a Harley Davidson, also known as a ➲**chopper**, and ridden primarily by the Hell's Angels and other outlaw motorcyclists.

* *'The hard core, the outlaw elite, were the Hell's Angels . . . wearing the winged death's head on the back of their sleeveless jackets and packing their "mammas" behind them on big "chopped hogs".'* (H.S. Thompson, *Hell's Angels*, 1966)

hold *n.* [1961]
a delay or postponement, originally in space launch use, thus **on hold**.

* *'It was time to put love on hold, lust on the back burner.'* (T. Blacker, *Fixx*, 1989)

holism *n.* [1970]
coined in 1926 by Gen J.C. Smuts (1870–1950) to define 'the one synthesis which makes the elements or parts act as one or holistically' and revived in the 1970s by a variety of ➲new therapies, all of which like to emphasize the relationship between biological and psychological well-being which together make up the 'whole' person. – **holistic**, *adj.*

* *'As gem, talisman or touchstone, or for use in holistic and alternative medicine.'* (*The Independent*, 31 March 1990)

Holocaust *n.* [1965]
The mass murder of Jews by the Nazis during the Second World War, especially as part of the 'Final Solution' which was set in motion at the Wannsee conference of 1941. It comes from the Greek word meaning 'whole burning', and was used, in general, to mean mass human destruction as early as 1833.

* *'The systematic attempt to destroy all European Jewry – an attempt now known as the Holocaust – began in the last week of June 1941, within hours of the German invasion of the Soviet Union.'* (M. Gilbert, *The Holocaust*, 1986)

home beat officer *n.*
a policeman who, in the traditional manner, walks a beat round a regular pattern of streets, this should enable him to be better known, and have better relations with his local community.

* *'The house had been targetted as a result of information from the local home beat officer.'* (R. Chesshyre, *The Force*, 1989)

homeboy *n.* [1985]
a synonym for friend or ally, literally someone from one's home town or, given its urban origins, from one's street or block. Primarily used

by US black youth, it has spread, as has their culture, to the UK.

* *'The homeboys in the place are holding up the wall/While the girls are on the floor/Giving their all.'* (Fat Boys, 'Crushin'', 1987)

home computer *n.* [1979]
often used (especially in the US) as a synonym for ➪personal computer, and referring to any microcomputer that is used in the home. In the US, where prices are lower and incomes higher, this often meant the relatively expensive IBM PC, while in the UK home users, at least in the early 1980s, tended to have machines such as the Spectrum, which used tape cassettes rather than the more sophisticated ➪floppy disk. In the last five years, with the growing popularity of the Amstrad computers, which offer cheaper versions of the IBM machines, the British too, have brought these more powerful computers into their homes.

* *'You're not going to believe this, but a home computer is a computer which can be used in the home.'* (D. Jarrett, *The Good Computing Book for Beginners*, 1980)

homeland *n.* [1963]
any of the autonomous areas of South Africa that have been set aside by the white government as separate (but totally dependent) black states; such areas were originally known as Bantustans but were relabelled in the 1970s, ostensibly to offset charges of racism in the name.

* *'South Africa's dependencies consist of four so-called "independent" Bantu homelands and the state of Namibia. The homelands were created as part of the racial separatism policy (apartheid).'* (J.D. & I. Derbyshire, *Political Systems of the World*, 1989)

home watch *n.*
see **neighbourhood watch.**

homophobia *n.* [1969]
the hatred of homosexuals, engendered like arachnophobia, as much by irrational, blind fear as by any logical reason.

* *'I was dismayed by your leading article "Homophobia and the Underclass" [14 May].'* (*The Independent*,16 May 1990)

honcho *n. v.* [1964]
from Japanese *han cho* (squad leader):
1. *n.* the boss, the senior figure.

* *'She wasn't into making coffee for the head honcho.'* (C. McFadden, *The Serial*, 1976)

2. *v.t.* to take care of something personally and ensure that it is carried out.

honkie (*or* honkey) *n.* [1965]
originally in US black use meaning a white man or woman; it gained widespread use in the 1960s and inferred an element of racism or general prejudice in the person so described. Honkie is a direct descendent of the earlier 'hunkie', which was coined in Chicago to describe Baltic or Slavic immigrants working in the stockyards.

* *'And with our entrance into the straight media we have demonstrated to the honkies that anything they do to fuck with us will be exposed to their children.'* (MC5 album note, 'Kick Out the Jams', 1969)

hook *n.* [1970]
1. *in music:* a catchy 'jingle' or musical phrase that sticks in the brain and keeps one humming the tune.
2. *in marketing and advertising:* any aspect of a campaign that has been deliberately inserted

to beguile the consumer and lodge in his or her mind.

3. *in television drama*: a cliffhanger, any aspect of a script that deliberately sustains an audience's fascination; among the great hooks was the 'Who shot J.R?' furore deliberately implanted in an episode of Dallas.

horizontal *adj.*
see **vertical**.

hormone replacement therapy *n.*
a therapy which is given to replace those hormones which are no longer produced in sufficient quantities during or after the menopause. It helps prevent such conditions as osteoporosis (a disease which renders the bones porous or spongy).

* *'The Royal College of Physicians . . . sent a special report . . . describing hormone replacement therapy as "the only effective means of prevention" to counter the "osteoporosis epidemic".'* (*The Independent*, 23 October 1990)

horse opera *n.*
see **oater**.

host *n., adj.* [1970]
1. a host computer which is attached to a ➪network and provides other services than simply acting as a store-and-forward processor or communication switch. Such computers are divided into 'servers', which provide resources within the network, and 'users' which access them.

2. in a network, the computer that controls a multiple computer installation.

* *'It seems that using modems and a mouse and connecting to a host all require more and more communications ports.'* (*Byte*, June, 1990)

hostile merger (*or* **takeover**) *n.* [1970]
a merger of two companies which is created not through mutual consent, but because one (the stronger) targets the other and sets about manipulating the market, the financial and trade media, and any other necessary levers to attain its end.

* *'The quintessential hostile takeover . . . in which companies were consumed without their consent.'* (D. Halberstam, *The Reckoning*, 1986)

hot line *n.* [1963]
1. (*often caps.*) a telex link between the White House and the Kremlin designed for use during any international crisis and specifically during a potential ➪escalation towards nuclear war. Established by President Kennedy and Premier Khruschev in the Hot Line Agreement (1963) the Hot Line Moderation Agreement of 1971 added two additional circuits which use satellite communications systems. Current moves are aimed to update the hot line with modern computer technology, but this decision has not been finalized.

2. in general use; a telephone line to be used for a specific purpose, implying that the caller will receive help or information promptly.

* *'Real customer service . . . and real customer support (toll-free telephone hotlines as a starter).'* (*Byte*, June 1990)

hot pants *n., adj.* [1970]
ultra-short shorts worn by women in the early 1970s.

* *'Thierry Mugler's multi-coloured Star Trek jerseys and hotpant suits and silver astronaut jackets.'* (*Sunday Correspondent*, 25 March 1990)

hot tub *n.* [1973]
a large tub, often made of wood, which contains heated water and in which a number of people may bathe together, more for relaxation than for actual washing.

* *'More recently, a form of folliculitis attributable to contamination of communal hot tubs and whirlpool baths is being seen.'* (N. L. Novick, *Super Skin*, 1988)

House *n.* [1987]
the most popular form of contemporary dance music, originated at Chicago's Warehouse Club and spread across the Western world; a direct descendant of ⇨disco, it features similarly mindless rhythms and banal lyrics, with the sole difference that electronic special effects – synthesizers, ⇨sampling, drum machines – have replaced the original instrumental playing.
See also **acid house**.

* *'A loose, trace-like hand-flail popularised in the House clubs.'* (*Independent on Sunday*, 3 June 1990)

househusband *n.* [1970]
a man, either the husband or live-in partner, who takes over the running of the household – traditionally the female role – from the woman with whom he lives. Househusband is the deliberate reverse of housewife; both have been, in some instances, replaced by houseperson. *See also* **new man**.

house, in the *phrase.* [1986]
here, in the same place (usually an auditorium or club).

hovercraft *n.* [1961]
any form of vehicle or craft that is supported on a cushion of air which is ejected downwards against the surface (solid or liquid) beneath it.

HRT *abbrev.*
see **hormone replacement therapy**.

human potential movement *n.* [1970]
an amalgam of various mental therapies, including the many cults that seem invariably to start in California, and a number of simplified theories that have trimmed classical psychoanalysis of the need for any real dedication by patient, replacing it with a simple 'cure' available to anyone who is able to pay the fees and which is somewhat removed from Freud's original conception.

* *'Meanwhile, from another side of the youth movement, the human potential movement and the New Age Consciousness was emerging.'* (B. Miles, *Ginsberg*, 1990)

humint *abbrev.* [1969]
human intelligence: the traditional intelligence network of spies who collect information themselves, rather than the impersonal surveillance by electronic technology that has become increasingly common.

humongous *adj.* [1976]
enormous, gigantic, tremendous; presumably a mixture of huge and monstrous.

hung up *adj.*
see **hang-up**.

hydrofoil *n.* [1975]
a narrow steel plane which can be attached to the bottom of a vessel and which, by reducing

the natural drag of the water, enables that vessel to move faster.

hype *n.* [1969]
the building up of an act, a record, a film, a performer, or any other saleable commodity by the exaggeration of its potential appeal, and the maximum possible use of promotion and advertising. The image is always one of slightly fraudulent huckstering: the hype that succeeds is a major merchandising success, but the one that fails is simply a hype.

The word stems from a number of sources: essentially an abbreviation of 'hyperbole', it encompasses two US slang usages. Hype, as an abbreviation of hypodermic syringe, and thus the idea of being 'hyped up' or high on drugs; hype as the giving of short change, and thus any form of confidence trick or deception.

* *'"Hype!" shouted the commentators as IBM launched its RS/6000. Well, the news may be that it wasn't hype.'* (*PC World*, April, 1990)

hype *v.* [1969]
to promote – a product, an individual performer, or any saleable commodity – beyond its intrinsic merits. Sometimes found as the transitive verb, to 'hype up'.

hyper *adj.* [1970]
an abbreviation of hyper-active: over-intense, obsessive.

* *'Rapping at her in this very hyper way about how he was into corporal punishment.'* (C. McFadden, *The Serial*, 1976)

hypercard *n.* [1988]
a proprietary brand of computer ⇨database which is based on ⇨hypertext, the linking of disparate pieces of information in a non-linear way.

* *'We plan to include software and an interface that will make it easy to get things started, like radio buttons in a Hypercard stack.'* (Byte, 5, 1990)

hypermarket *n.* [1970]
a very large supermarket, usually sited outside a town, possibly in a ⇨shopping mall; the word is a direct translation of the French *hypermarché*.

* *'Who are we? Just the UK's biggest hypermarket chain – with eight stores already open and more planned.'* (ad for Savacentre in *The Independent*, 14 June 1990)

hypertext *n.* [1988]
a multi-layered system of ⇨database storage, whereby a wide variety of documents and graphics can be linked to each other and accessed in a random way, each single piece of data being linked to every other one that relates to it.

* *'The term hypertext originated more than 23 years ago when Theodore H. Nelson formed his ideas of a fabulous literary utility which he called Xanadu.'* (*PC World*, July 1990)

hypothetical *n.*
a variety of television programme in which a panel of experts debate a given problem under the guidance of a moderator; each expert plays him- or herself, and the moderator poses them a variety of 'what-if' questions in order to elicit their response, and that of others of opposing views on the topic.

* *'At their best hypotheticals provide genuine insights into professional bias; the different preconceptions and vested interests.'* (*The Independent*, 2 May 1990)

ICBM *abbrev.* [1960]
Inter-Continental Ballistic Missile: a missile that is capable of penetrating targets in either the USA or the USSR after being fired from a site on the territory of the opposite superpower or from a strategic submarine. As defined by both sides in the ⇨SALT II talks: 'land based launchers of ballistic missiles capable of a range in excess of the shortest distance between the north-east border of the US and the north-west border of the continental part of the USSR, that is, a range in excess of 5500 kilometres'.

* *'There would still be over 250 US ICBMs unscathed and ready to launch.'* (R.C. Aldridge, *First Strike!*, 1983)

icon *n.* [1967]
in computing: a small graphic, representing a given application or function, which is used in a ⇨GUI to facilitate the running of such ⇨programs. *See also* **WIMP**.

* *'When he clicked on a video display icon, the slide show ran with full animation and digital sound.'* (*Byte*, May 1990)

identikit *n., adj.* [1961]
a composite picture of a police suspect which is put together from a number of pre-existing parts – noses, eyes, chins, etc. – on the basis of eye-witness testimony.

idiot testing *n.* [1963]
any form of test that allegedly reproduces the sort of handling a given object – typically a piece of technology – would receive from the lowest common denominator of user, 'the idiot', who has not read the instructions, has no understanding of the item in question and thus subjects it to a variety of problems that a more intelligent user would manage to avoid.

in *adj.* [1965]
popular, fashionable, chic; thus **in-crowd**: fashionable people. Also used by itself, e.g. 'Motorcycle jackets are in this year'.

* *'I'm in with the in-crowd. I go where the in-crowd go.'* (Dobie Gray, 'The In-Crowd', 1965)

-in *suffix.* [1965]
the use of -in as a suffix began with the 'teach-ins' of the mid-1960s: informal debates, originally on university campuses and usually concerning the Vietnam War. The use spread, particularly in the ⇨hippie community, where 'be-ins' and 'love-ins' became synonyms for any form of large-scale get-together, alternatively termed, when sufficiently grandiose, a 'gathering of the tribes'.

* *'Anyway, just a couple of weeks before, the heads had held their first big "be-in" in Golden Gate Park.'* (T. Wolfe, *The Electric Kool-Aid Acid Test*, 1969)
* *'I was present at a yippie meeting in Union park at which a department store loot-in was being planned.'* (R. Neville, *Play Power*, 1970)

income support *n.* [1988]
introduced under the Social Security Act of 1988, income support has replaced supplementary benefit; simpler than the old system, it requires no means test and has replaced the multiplicity of different special needs allowances with far fewer broad categories of eligibility.

incomes policy *n.* [1963]
a policy introduced by the Labour government in 1964 in the hope of curbing inflation by controlling wage and price increases.

index-linked *adj.* [1970]
any payment (especially wages or pensions) that is adjusted in accordance with the fluctuations of the cost-of-living index.

* *'In the case of a low-paid public service worker on an index-linked pension scheme, there will simply not be enough money.'* (*Independent on Sunday*, 3 June 1990)

indie *n., adj.* [1977]
an abbreviation of independent:
1. *in the film industry*: independent: any independent production company, and the films which they make; such companies are the opposite of the ⇨majors. Cinemas, distributors and any other parts of the industry not directly connected to a major corporation are also 'indies'.
2. *in the record business*: independent record companies, usually small and depending on the major companies for distribution, which, although currently in eclipse, have been responsible for the bulk of the rock industry's innovations in the last decade.

* *'A performance by "indie" contenders the Heart Throbs.'* (*Independent on Sunday*, 17 June 1990)

industrial action *n.* [1971]
a euphemism for a strike, an event epitomized, in the eyes of its critics, by its industrial inaction.

in-flight *adj.* [1964]
referring to a variety of services provided during a commercial air flight. Typically *in-flight magazine; in-flight catering;* etc.

* *'On one domestic US service, the in-flight entertainment begins on the ground, where passengers can watch flight-deck activity . . . on short-circuit TV.'* (*The Flier's Handbook*, 1978)

INF Talks *n.* [1980]
an acronym for Intermediate-range Nuclear Forces Talks: a series of eventually abortive talks, initiated by the Carter Administration in 1980, which attempted to deal with the problem of intermediate-range nuclear weapons, notably US cruise and Tomahawk missiles, based in Europe and threatening the USSR. Both sides preferred a series of propaganda coups to real initiatives and the talks foundered in late 1981.

* *'With strains developing between them, it became all the easier for Richard Burt to take command of INF policymaking.'* (S. Talbott, *Deadly Gambits*, 1984)

informatics *n.* [1967]
information science: a branch of science that concentrates on the procedures whereby information, especially that which deals with technical or scientific subjects, is collected, transmitted, stored, processed or displayed.

information technology *n.* [1971]
a popular generality that covers many innova-

tions in the abilities of computers, microelectronics and telecommunications to produce, store, and transmit a wide spectrum of information in ways that are supposedly destined to revolutionize contemporary society.

* *'Six core skills: communication, problem solving, personal skills, numeracy, information technology, modern language competence.'* (*The Independent*, 17 May 1990)

Infotainment *n.* [1960]
also known as **docutainment**: a type of news broadcasting which minimizes factual information and its import, and places everything within a context more akin to a purely entertainment programme. Low on 'importance' but easily assimilable by those who cannot bear too many demands on their intelligence. *See also* **docudrama**.

In-house *adj., adv.* [1966]
anything that is created/designed/built and otherwise originated within a company, rather than being contracted for elsewhere.

* *'He is keen to use outside experts to develop new systems . . . a change from the old policy of developing it all in-house.'* (*Independent on Sunday*, 25 March 1990)

Ink-jet (printer) *n.* [1973]
a type of printer, usually used in conjunction with a computer, in which jets of ink are broken up into magnetized droplets and directed by the program to form letters, numbers, and other symbols on paper.

* *'Ink-jet printers are still expensive, though, and that alone prevents them from competing with the daisywheels.'* (D. Jarrett, *The Good Computing Book for Beginners*, 1980)

In-joke *n.* [1964]
a joke that is only understood and appreciated by a small group.

Inner city *n., adj.* [1968]
a euphemism for the slums; run-down areas of once prosperous city centres which have declined since their Victorian heyday and have now been abandoned by the majority of those who can afford to live elsewhere; thus inner city also refers to those who tend to live in these areas, usually coloured immigrant groups.

* *'The 75 rule tends to punish inner-city councils (mainly Labour-controlled)'.* (*Sunday Correspondent*, 8 April 1990)

Inner space *n.* [1961]
the subconscious, often used by ⇨hippies to refer to that part of the mind which is affected by hallucinogenic drugs, meditation, or similar mind-expanding methods.

* *'The centre of the infinite black expanse spanning the inner space between his ears.'* (N. Fury, *Agro*, 1971)

Insider trading/dealing *n.* [1966]
the use of privileged information by members of the Stock Exchange to line their own pockets; definitely illegal, if increasingly widespread.

* *'Some are worried about the SEC's attempts to crack down on insider trading. But most are trying to lie low.'* (*Independent on Sunday*, 8 April 1990)

Instamatic *n.* [1964]
the proprietary name for Eastman-Kodak's lightweight, fixed focus camera with a non-adjustable lens; the direct descendant of the 'Box Brownie'.

instant book *n.* [1968]
any book that is produced in response to a recent event: the Falklands War, the massacre in Tiananmen Square, satanic abuse in Rochdale; such books are usually produced by the same journalists who originally covered the story; long on fact, short on analysis, they satisfy the immediate demands of those who want an expanded news story, if not a considered assessment; the idea of 'instant' creativity comes directly from that of instant food, which dates back to the turn of the century.

instant replay *n.* [1973]
an immediate replay of televised action (usually sporting) by using videotape.

* *'You can see the graphics but just avoid the instant replay.'* (XOR Corporation, *NFL Challenge User's Guide*, 1985)

integrated battlefield *n.* [1980]
a battlefield in which any combination of conventional, nuclear, chemical, and biological weapons may be employed.

intelligent *adj.* [1974]
equipped with some form of computer guidance, usually an integral ⇨chip or chips.
See also **smart**.

-intensive *suffix.* [1970]
a number of combinations have been created by the addition of -intensive to a variety of words, all modelled on **capital-intensive** (1959), and implying the need for a large quantity or an accentuation of whatever is specified in the first word; examples include **calorie-intensive** (1980, filled with calories, fattening); **export-intensive** (1971, accentuating the need for exports); **research-intensive** (1976, depending heavily upon research); and **technology-intensive** (1972, dependent on technology, incorporating a high level of technology).

intensive care *n.* [1963]
a form of medical care during which a seriously ill patient is kept under continual observation. Most hospitals carry out such observation in an **intensive care unit**.

interact *v.* [1967]
popular among sociologists and psychologists as a jargoneering way of saying relate to, or have a relationship with.

interactive *adj.* [1972]
used originally of video, but also applied to TV, computers, computer games, etc.

1. any video product that requires some degree of physical involvement by the user to complete its function; videogames are the obvious example.
2. any kind of video hardware (the actual recorder or disc player) that allows a viewer to make decisions as to the course of a program, as in pausing the tape, playing back scenes, slow motion, etc.

* *'The cable franchises which prosper will be those that develop telephony and interactive services such as home shopping.'* (*The Independent*, 23 May 1990)

interactive fiction *n.* [1988]
a form of fiction that is available on computer disk: each story is composed of a set of interlinked branching plot lines, which can be assembled according to taste by each individual user.

interface *n.* [1966]

strictly any thing or area that connects two systems in a machine; in general use no more than 'meeting' (both physical and conceptual), but given a little technological fillip.

* *'A word much loved by the jargon writers, an interface is the boundary between two systems.'* (D. Jarrett, *The Good Computing Book for Beginners,* 1980)
* *'My interface with Marjorie was not going at all as planned.'* (T. Blacker, *Fixx,* 1989)

interferon *n.* [1961]

a protein produced in the cells of many vertebrates and which prevents the replication of viruses through its sensitivity to foreign nucleic acid; interferon is among the many 'cures' put forward for both ➩AIDS and some cancers.

* *'Dormont described the comparative benefits of AIDS drugs on trial, such as isoprinosine, interferon, ribavirin, and HPA-23.'* (R. Shilts, *And the Band Played On,* 1987)

intermediate technology *n.* [1973]

a form of technology that combines small-scale simplicity and self-sufficiency with modern technology; such technology is often seen as suitable for introduction into developing nations where traditional methods can thus be preserved, but augmented by modern technological expertise.

intifada *n.* [1987]

the Palestinian uprising on the West Bank and the Gaza strip, started in December 1987 and still going strong; 'people power' where twenty years of PLO efforts are seen to have failed.

* *'The intifada began in a Jabalaya refugee camp in Gaza on 9 December 1987, when four Arab workers returning from their jobs in Israel were killed in a collision with an Israeli truck.'* (*New York Review of Books,* 29 March 1990)

into *adv.* [1969]

strongly involved with, interested in, concerned with, fascinated by, etc.

* *'About ten years ago, when I was into psychology stuff, I bumped into a guy I knew from high school days.'* (A. Hoffman, *Steal This Book,* 1969)

investigative journalism *n.* [1972]

the use of methods more usually associated with the solving of crime to cover a news story; the phrase entered popular use during the Watergate Affair of 1972–74 when Bob Woodward and Carl Bernstein, two young reporters on the *Washington Post,* set about tracking their way through the maze of ➩disinformation to publish the details of a story that eventually brought down a president.

* *'With the kind of investigative journalism that won their newspaper the Pulitzer Prize for its Watergate coverage . . . the authors portray the participants in this backstage drama.'* (blurb for B. Woodward & C. Bernstein, *The Final Days,* 1976)

invisible earnings *n.* [1969]

that part of a country's balance of payments that is composed of receipts and payments for services (as opposed to material goods). This includes cash gifts (e.g. legacies), and other transfers for which no services are performed, the tourist industry, and (for a financial centre like London) the two-way flow of the international money markets.

* *'The bulk of Britain's invisible export earnings*

come from this sector.' (*Independent on Sunday*, 8 April 1990)

Irradiation *n.* [1986]
a means of preserving food by exposing it to low levels of radiation; mooted in 1986, the scheme ran into a storm of opposition and, openly at least, it has yet to be widely employed.

ISBN *abbrev.* [1972]
International Standard Book Number: a number that has been assigned to all new books (usually seen as a ⇨barcode on their back cover) to facilitate stock taking, ordering, etc. The codes were adopted in 1972 at a meeting of the International Standards Organization Technical Committee at Scheveningen in Holland.

IUD *abbrev.* [1966]
intrauterine device: a contraceptive loop or coil which is placed within the uterus as a physical barrier to sperm.

jacket crisp *n.* [1988]
a form of potato crisp which is made from potatoes which have not been peeled and thus includes the allegedly nutritious skin.

jacuzzi *n.* [1966]
a trade name for a device that creates swirling water in a bath; thus the bath that incorporates that device.

Jesus freak/people *n.* [1970]
one of the many cults the followed ➩hippie disillusionment with the ➩counter-culture at the end of the 1960s, and replaced a search for a better world through peace, love and drugs, with one based on religion. Despite their avowedly intense relationship with the Christian saviour, and their espousal of such Pentecostalist phenomena as speaking in tongues and healing by faith, the Jesus people have no actual affiliation to any established church.

jet lag *n.* [1969]
the sense of exhaustion and disorientation that for many people follows a lengthy jet flight that crosses two or more time zones; the ➩body clock fails to keep up with the flight and the body requires several days to adjust to its new regime. – **jet-lagged** *adj.*

✱ *'She wished Georgia would concentrate on the road ahead. "I'm tired and jet-lagged, I'm sorry".* (C. Blake, *Girl Talk*, 1990)

jet set *n., adj.* [1963]
a set of smart rich people, beloved of the gossip columns, who travel the world by jet, seeking a succession of expensive pleasures. Also used as an adjective, e.g. 'jet set travellers'. Jet travel began on 2 May 1952 when the first jet airliner flew from London to Johannesburg, but the term itself did not develop until the early 1960s.

✱ *'Right in the middle of a glug of champagne at some jet-set hot spot the ineluctible truth hits him.'* (L. Bangs, *Psychotic Reactions and Carburetor Dung*, 1988)

job centre *n.* [1971]
a government-sponsored centre where workers (usually the unemployed) can check on the availability of local work; the euphemism for what in Britain was originally called the Labour Exchange.

jobsworth *n.* [1970]
a time server, a petty official, anyone who refuses a request or prohibits an activity with the stock intonation 'It's more than my job's worth . . . '

✱ *'The midget jobsworth sort of smiles in confirmation . . . And you sibilate gratitude.'* (J. Meades, *Peter Knows What Dick Likes*, 1989)

jogging *n.* [1968]
a popular form of exercise, especially among the overweight and middle-aged, which requires one to move at a gentle pace some-

where between running and walking; the proliferation of combinations – jogging shoes, jogging suit, etc. show the extent to which the exercise has been commercialized. Those who enjoy jogging are **joggers**, and the verb form is **to jog**.

✱ *'However, my critic charmingly tells me jogging is part of her new exercise regime.'* (*The Independent*, 16 May 1990)

joint *n.* [1964]
a cannabis cigarette in which tobacco and cannabis – whether as hashish or marijuana – is 'joined' to tobacco. The term originated in the US in the 1930s, but did not properly cross the Atlantic until the mid-1960s.

✱ *'Have a seat or have a cigarette or have a joint and I will be back in three minutes.'* (R. DiLello, *The Longest Cocktail Party*, 1971)

joystick *n.* [1980]
in computing: modelled on the original aircraft steering control, a moveable stick controller that can be attached to the computer and used in the playing of many games.

✱ *'Floppy disk drives; keyboard, mouse, MIDI, joystick and analog device control support.'* (*Byte*, June 1990)

juggernaut *n.* [1969]
a large truck, 35–40 feet long, often used for moving containers; the original Juggernaut, an Indian idol, was a corruption of the Sanskrit word *Jagannatha* meaning Lord of the Universe and referring to Krishna. It was dragged through the streets at an annual celebration, carried on a large wheeled carriage, surrounded by worshippers who, in the hope of attaining a devout death, threw themselves beneath the wheels.

jumbo (jet) *n.* [1964]
a Boeing 747 aircraft; the original 'Jumbo' was an elephant, kept at London Zoo and sold in 1882 to Barnum and Bailey's Circus. He weighed 6.5 tons and was accidentally killed by a railway engine in 1885.

✱ *'Or, most poignant of all, a jumbo jet flying noisily overhead.'* (T. Blacker, *Fixx*, 1989)

jump-jet *n.* [1964]
colloquial name for the vertical or short take-off/landing jet aircraft.
See also **V/STOL**.

jump-suit *n.* [1965]
a one-piece garment modelled on the traditional suits worn by pilots.

✱ *'He also has four hand-crafted rhinestone jumpsuits and a devoted following.'* (*Sunday Correspondent*, 10 June 1990)

junk bond *n.* [1981]
the dubious underpinning of much of the high-profit takeover market of the 1980s; a company raises money for a takeover by issuing bonds whose security is the current value of the company which it intends to purchase. Such bonds form the basis of the ➪LBO (leveraged buy-out).

✱ *'An acceptable form of financing known as "junk bonds", which one stock analyst called paper whose worth lay somewhere below cash and above Monopoly money.'* (D. Halberstam, *The Reckoning*, 1986)

junk food *n.* [1970]
any of a number of ➪fast foods, usually sold as ➪takeaways, which provide minimal nutritional value but satisfy the taste buds and, for a while, the pangs of hunger: MacDonald's

hamburgers, Pizza Hut pizzas, Kentucky Fried Chicken, etc.

* *'Maisie finished her last chocolate and got to work on a packet of crisps, a tube of Rollos, half a pound of jellybabies and a jumbo bar of Turkish delight . . . Sometimes Henry wondered whether the junk food industry was going to be able to take the kind of demands Maisie was going to make on it.'* (N. Williams, *The Wimbledon Poisoner*, 1990)

junk mail *n.* [1967]
unsolicited commercial advertising, posted to millions of homes, couched in highly appealing prose, and rarely taken further than the waste paper bin; the proliferation of the fax machine has now added a new version: **junk faxes**.

* *'Take all the junk mail and then the package and open it. Leave through the window.'* (*Ace*, August, 1990)

K *abbrev.* [1970]
from kilo-, meaning one thousand: one thousand pounds or dollars.

✱ *'Marketing Services. £15k–£22k + benefits'* (recruitment ad for *Yellow Pages* in *Independent on Sunday*, 8 April 1990)

Kabouter *n.* [1970]
a member of a Dutch group of political activists who promoted pacifism and anarchism; the kabouters – literally the 'dwarves' – were best known outside Holland for their 'white bicycles' scheme of the mid-1960s: white bicycles were left all over Amsterdam, free for anyone to use.

✱ *'With this money the Kabouters started their own newspaper, the Kabouterkrant, and set up various free and cut-price services throughout the city.'* (P. Stansill & D. Z. Mairowitz (eds.), *BAMN*, 1971)

kalashnikov *n.* [1970]
the brand name of a type of automatic rifle made in the USSR; the kalashnikov has become synonymous with urban guerrilla movements, whether in Beirut or Belfast.

Kampuchea *n.* [1975]
the official name of Cambodia since the Khmer Rouge took power in 1975; the name has been maintained, although after the Vietnamese invasion of 1979 the country's official name was changed from Democratic Kampuchea to the People's Republic of Kampuchea.

✱ *'Opposing them is a loose grouping known as the Coalition Government of Democratic Kampuchea.'* (P. Brogan, *World Conflicts*, 1989)

karaoke *n.* [1989]
the term means 'empty orchestra' in Japanese, and the 'karaoke machine' was designed originally to provide backing tracks for solo cabaret performers. It has been taken up in the UK, but with more of a music hall feel, or a hi-tech version of the family singing round the piano, a loud and raucous singalong rather than that of Japan, where bars are full of determinedly jolly businessmen fighting their way through 'My Way'.

✱ *'A spirited "Teddy Bear" accompanied by a backing tape on a karaoke machine.'* (*Sunday Correspondent*, 10 June 1990)

Kevin *n.* [1986]
see **Sharon.**

keyboard (*or* **key (in))** *v.* [1961]
to type material – copy, spreadsheet figures, other data – into a computer. The performing of this operation is **keyboarding**.

✱ *'An ATC centre can request the crew . . . to key in data, but most of the exchanges between ground and aircraft will be automatic.'* (*PC World*, November 1990)

key club *n.* [1962]
a members-only club which required a key – a form of membership card – to gain entry.

Such clubs had existed for some time before Hugh Hefner, creator of Playboy magazine, took over the idea for his Playboy Clubs.

* 'Playboy *published a story, in 1959, about the new "Gaslight" key clubs, which featured buxom cocktail waitresses laced into saucy costumes said to be inspired by the gay nineties.'* (R. Miller, *Bunny*, 1985)

keypad *n.* [1967]
a small console with a set of buttons which operate a telephone, an electronic calculator, or any similar machine.

Khmer Rouge *n.* [1970]
the force of Communist guerillas, formed *c.* 1970, in opposition to the then ruler of Cambodia, the pro-American Lon Nol. The Khmer Rouge took power in 1975, and over the next four years subjected their country to an unparalleled degree of brutality, killing several million people in their drive to impose absolute ideological purity on the population.

* *'The Khmer Rouge began their rule by driving the entire population of Phnom Penh – 2.5 million people – into the countryside.'* (P. Brogan, *World Conflicts*, 1989)

kick-start *v., n.* [1988]
to set going with an initial sudden impetus; from the kick-starting of a motorbike.

kiddie porn *n.* [1985]
pornography that features the sexual exploitation of young (sometimes very young) children. The practice has been going on for many years, the term emerged into wider use during the mid-1980s.

* *'I'm looking for a certain picture. Kiddie porn. My client is concerned that a picture was taken of a certain kid.'* (A. Vachss, *Strega*, 1987)

killer bee *n.* [1976]
the African honeybee *Apis mellifera* which is known for its exceptional aggressiveness; the bees, which are hard workers and excellent producers of honey, were imported into Brazil in 1956. There they interbred with the native bees to produce a particularly vicious strain; this hybrid has been spreading north, into the southern US since the early 1960s. Its propensity to attack anything that disturbs it gave it the name killer bee or **Mau Mau bee**.

killing fields *n.* [1984]
the rural killing grounds of the ⇨Khmer Rouge, where hundreds of Cambodians were murdered as part of the ideological purging of the country; the term gained worldwide acceptance with the release of an eponymous film in 1984.

* *'Less important Cambodians were taken to the killing fields, and butchered. The skulls were set out in rows and their bones piled in heaps together.'* (P. Brogan, *World Conflicts*, 1989)

kill ratio *n.* [1968]
the difference between the number of hostile troops and of one's own forces killed in an engagement.
See also **body count**.

kinky *adj.* [1960]
bizarre, eccentric, usually with a sexual overtone and as such a synonym for 'bent'; kinky apppeared around 1960, and gained its popularity with the television series *The Avengers*, in which the female star Honor Blackman was regularly outiftted in a variety of 'kinky'

costumes – high boots, leather, etc. Blackman, with co-star Patrick Macnee pushed the word further with their pop song 'Kinky Boots' – which returned to the charts in 1990.

* *'Depending on your morals and such, I guess we could go find the necessary ingredients but that would be real kinky!'* (*Sunday Correspondent*, 22 April 1990)

kipper (tie) *n.* [1966]
an ultra-wide tie, often decorated with paisley patterns, flowers, or other gaudy motifs; its exaggerated shape was roughly that of a kipper.

* *'Remember Union Jack T-shirts and flares, and kipper ties and Aldermaston?'* (B. Humphries & N. Garland, *The Complete Barry McKenzie*, 1988)

kir (royale) *n.* [1966]
a drink composed of dry white wine and creme de casis; a kir royale substitutes champagne for the white wine. The drink was invented by Canon Felix Kir (1876–1968), a former mayor of Dijon, and has become particularly popular in the last two decades.

kissagram *n.*
a human greetings telegram, delivered as a surprise to the recipient by a (usually) scantily clad girl or boy. Other 'grams' include ➪strippagram (the donor performs a quick striptease), ➪gorillagram (using a 'King Kong' outfit), and many others. The stripping policewoman or traffic warden is particularly popular.

kiss and tell *adj.* [1970]
a form of confessional memoir in which the hero or (more usually) heroine details his or her amours, usually with a variety of celebrities who might well have preferred their bedroom antics to remain secret. A subgroup of kiss-and-tell is **snort-and-tell**, in which the memoirs are similarly revelatory, but the confessions centre on drugs (usually cocaine, hence 'snort') rather than sex.

* *'As a kiss-and-tell account from Sartre's harem, Liliane Siegel's memoir . . . may be a disappointment.'* (*Independent on Sunday*, 10 June 1990)

kiss of life *n.* [1961]
the colloquial version of 'mouth to mouth resuscitation'; also used figuratively as a synonym for rescue.

kiwi fruit *n.* [1972]
an edible fruit, grown in New Zealand (hence 'kiwi') and resembling a large furry gooseberry (and also known as a **Chinese gooseberry**). Kiwi fruit were one of the principal ingredients of the nouvelle cuisine of the early 1980s.

* *'As one speaker said, "There's nothing like the kiwi fruit looming up".'* (*The Independent*, 31 March 1990)

kludge *n.* [1961]
at best an improvised, do-it-yourself 'lash-up', at worst a poorly engineered machine in which inadequate shortcuts fail to hide the essential imperfections in the technology and design.

* *'Kludge is perhaps the most disdainful term in the computer engineer's vocabulary; it conjures up visions of a machine with wires hanging out of it, of things fastened together with adhesive tape.'* (T Kidder, *The Soul of a New Machine*, 1981)

kneecapping *n.* [1975]
a modern version of tarring and feathering

and as such the most popular punishment meted out by ➪urban guerrillas in Northern Ireland; both the IRA and the Protestant extremist groups use the technique; essentially it involves shooting the victim in the legs, the kneecap as such is not usually touched. – **kneecap** *v.*

✱ *'The methods used to control them [are] just the same as the IRA use. Kneecappings, beatings and in some instances, torture and death.'* (A. F. N. Clarke, *Contact*, 1983)

The word may also be used figuratively:

✱ *'It's a threefold assault . . . Heath's very good at kneecapping lazy ideas.'* (J. Meades, *Peter Knows What Dick Likes*, 1989)

knock-off *adj.* [1966]
originally used in fashion to describe cheap copies of best-selling lines and models (e.g. a royal wedding dress) which are aimed at the mass market. Now extended to general use, especially in publishing. where the term denotes quick hack productions that either echo a current fiction best-seller, or, as non-fiction, are tied into a major event, e.g. the Gulf Crisis, and attempt to cash in on the public's appetite for all material related to it.

✱ *'Cheap knock-off products from the Pacific Rim and a cutthroat sales climate make entry into this market tough.'* (*Byte*, July 1990)

knowledge base *n.*
see **expert system**.

knowledge engineer *n.* [1986]
the builder of an ➪expert system.

komiteh *n.* [1979]
a revolutionary committee, with wide-ranging disciplinary powers, formed to put into practice the Islamic Revolution in Iran.

✱ *'These . . . gangs developed into the 'komitehs', the Revolutionary Guards, the Foundation of Martyrs and similar militantly Islamic groups, urging the absolutes of the faith and the dictates of the Ayatollah.'* (J. Green, *Encyclopaedia of Censorship*, 1990)

kook *n.* [1960]
an eccentric or otherwise bizarre person.

✱ *'Yes! And heads, kids, kooks, intellectual tourists of all sorts, started heading for Kesey's in La Honda.'* (T. Wolfe, *The Electric Kool-Aid Acid Test*, 1969)

kook(y) *adj.* [1965]
bizarre, eccentric, weird.

krugerrand *n.* [1967]
a South African gold coin which carries the picture of President Kruger. The coins were minted for external use only; there grew up a flourishing market in the coins which as legal tender, albeit of a foreign country, were not eligible for capital gains tax.

kung fu *n.* [1966]
a form of martial arts, the Chinese form of karate; kung fu outstripped virtually every other martial art in popularity when a rash of kung fu movies (known in the trade as 'chop-socky' movies) which are regularly made in Hong Kong, were distributed in the West; especially popular were those starring 'The Little Dragon' – superstar Bruce Lee.

✱ *'Kung Fu is not a game! Kung Fu is a highly skilled art which, if misused by the untrained, can be deadly.'* (F. Dennis & D. Atyeo, *Bruce Lee King of Kung Fu*, 1974)

ladies who lunch *n.* [1980]
coined by John Fairchild the influential editor of New York's *Woman's Wear Daily*, the term describes those rich fashionable women whose daytime existence, unencumbered by the need to earn a living, centres on their lunching with other ladies of a similar persuasion.

✱ *'John Fairchild would like to see himself as a bit of a Tom Wolfe. Certainly his "ladies who lunch" . . . does have a certain ring to it.'* (*The Observer*, 10 February 1991)

lager louts *n.* [1985]
young men, of conscriptable age and often synonymous with football supporters, whose late adolescent excesses are allegedly fuelled by quantities of heavily advertised lagers.

✱ *'Standard lagers, whose association with lager loutism has given the drink a bad name.'* (*Sunday Correspondent*, 10 June 1990)

laid-back *adv.* [1969]
calm, distanced, unruffled; the original hippie use implied that such nonchalance had been reached with the help of drugs

✱ *'A clientele so laid back their collective energy level couldn't run an electric toothbrush.'* (C. McFadden, *The Serial*, 1976)

Laingian *adj.* [1967]
pertaining to the psychiatric theories of R. D. Laing, whose ⇨'anti-psychiatry' movement of the 1960s provided an important intellectual underpinning to many ⇨counter-cultural theories. For Laing there was no such thing as classical 'madness': schizophrenia, for instance, was caused by a variety of social, usually family pressures, and any successful treatment was dependent on the removal of those pressures.

lambada *n.* [1990]
a type of disco dance, considered in some quarters to be overly sexual, which originated in Brazil and had a brief vogue in the summer of 1990.

LAN *abbrev.* [1986]
an acronym for local area network: a communications ⇨network linking a number of stations.

language laboratory *n.* [1963]
any classroom, equipped with tape recorders, headphones, etc., in which languages are learnt through repeated oral practice.

laptop *n.* [1986]
any (relatively) lightweight computer, that can, in theory, be balanced on the lap, and thus rendered suitable for use on planes, trains, etc.
See also **luggable**.

✱ *'The Dell System 316LT laptop. Other laptops pale by comparison. An opinion shared by PC magazine which recently named the Dell system 316LT Editor's Choice.'* (ad for Dell Computer Corporation in *Byte*, June 1990)

laser *n.* [1960]
assumed to be a simple noun, laser is actually an acronym of Light Amplification by the Stimulated Emission of Radiation: any device that is capable of emitting a very intense narrow parallel beam of highly monochromatic and coherent light. This beam is used to stimulate the emission of more light of the same wavelength and phase by atoms or molecules that have been excited by some means.

laser printer *n.* [1987]
a non-impact printer that employs a ➪laser to fuse toner to paper to create near-typeset quality text and graphics. The technology involved is almost identical to that used in a photocopier.

* *'Finally, for less than $3000, you can have a PostScript laser printer right at your desk.'* (ad for Texas Instruments in *Byte*, May 1990)

lateral thinking *n.* [1966]
any method of thinking that uses unorthodox methods, especially in making connections that would fall outside the lines of logical thought processes, to cut through apparently intractable problems; the concept was popularized by Dr Edward de Bono.

Laugh-In *n.* [1968]
Rowan and Martin's *Laugh-In*, a television programme of gentle satire with overtones of commercialized ➪psychedelia, broadcast from 'beautiful downtown Burbank' starting in 1968.

* *'After all, when Michaels was a writer on Laugh-In in 1969, President Nixon had come on.'* (B. Woodward, *Wired*, 1984)

laugh track *n.* [1962]
a tape of pre-recorded laughter which is dubbed onto a comedy show to create the effect of a live audience.

launch window *n.* [1965]
that period when the Earth and a target planet are in a mutually favourable position for the launching of a rocket and/or capsule.

launder *v.* [1970]
to transfer any funds that have been obtained illegally into a bank, usually in a foreign country, and then to withdraw those funds through legitimate means.

* *'He may be what he says he is – a veteran of the CIA's world of front groups . . . an "asset" of the money-laundering and gun-running milieu.'* (*Sunday Correspondent*)

laundry list *n.* [1968]
a detailed and often lengthy list of plans, priorities and other political intentions, often included in a speech.

law and order *phrase.* [1970]
a popular right-wing slogan, demanding the return of a greater degree of social discipline in order to curb a supposed rise in crime and violence; more often than not such demands are seen (by their critics) as code words for attacks on minority groups.

* *'"Isn't it about time we had some LAW and ORDER?" Which is simply a more polite way of saying "Kill those fuckin hippies".'* (A. Hoffman, *Woodstock Nation*, 1969)

layering (or layered look) *n.* [1972]
1. a fashionable clothing style in which the overall effect was achieved by the wearing of

layers of garments, each of a different length and type.

2. A style of cutting hair popular in the early 1970s, where the differing lengths of hair, or layers, gave a shaggy look, typically as sported by pop star Rod Stewart.

LBO *abbrev.* [1980]

see **leveraged buyout**.

- ✱ *'A well connected, often outrageous investment banker who played key roles in the decade's two largest leveraged buyouts.'* (*Sunday Correspondent*, 18 March 1990)
- ✱ *'Johnson ultimately chose to launch his LBO with a Drexel competitor.'* (*Sunday Correspondent*, 18 March 1990)

LCD *abbrev.* [1973]

Liquid Crystal Display: the device used in digital watches, computer games, etc. to display numbers and letters. A display uses groups of segments which can be combined to form individual characters; application of an electric field across the segments – each a normally transparent anisotropic liquid sandwiched between two electrodes – causes the reflectivity of the liquid to change and the segment to become opaque. Individual segments can thus be manipulated to form characters.

- ✱ *'The main reason for the thickness is the backlit display which . . . is considerably bulkier than a conventional LCD.'* (*PC World*, May 1990)

leader board *n.*

a board mounted at the side of a golf course listing the leading players in a tournament.

leading edge *adj.* [1987]

a synonym for state of the art, ultra modern, the latest.

- ✱ *'A leading edge product today could be obsolete next week.'* (*Byte*, July 1990)

lean-burn *adj.* [1986]

an internal combustion engine specifically designed to minimize the inevitable pollution that accompanies the working of such engines. This is done by using less fuel in the fuel-air mixture that creates combustion.

learning curve *n.* [1967]

the learning process as represented on a hypothetical piece of graph paper; the curve may be steep (requiring a good deal of fast assimilation of complex material) or shallow.

- ✱ *'Your learning curve will be steep, as will the demands on your ability to provide innovative solutions.'* (ad for J. P. Morgan, *The Independent*, 12 July 1990)

learning disability *n.* [1960]

any form of nervous disability which interferes with the normal process of learning, particularly of reading and arithmetic.

learning-disabled *adj.* [1989]

a piece of sociological euphemism denoting mentally backward or educationally subnormal.

See also **challenged**; **disadvantaged**.

Lebanese gold *n.* [1967]

see **Acapulco gold**.

Lebanese red *n.* [1967]

see **Acapulco gold**.

Leboyer birth *n.* [1975]

a form of 'natural childbirth' named after its originator the French obstetrician Frederick

Leboyer, that became especially popular in the late 1970s, following the publication of Leboyer's book *Birth Without Violence* in 1975. The basics of his system required peace and quiet in the delivery room, low lights, the placing of the infant in a warm bath (mimicking the recently abandoned amniotic fluid) on delivery and the complete absence of such traditional events as the slapping of the newborn to start him or her breathing.

LED *abbrev.* [1970]
an acronym for Light Emitting Diode display: a device used in some digital watches, calculators, etc., to display individual characters. LEDs are semi-conductor diodes which can be manipulated to create numbers and/or letters.

* *'Most digital read-outs on laboratory instruments, calculators and watchs use LED display.'* (D. Jarrett, *The Good Computing Book for Beginners*, 1980)

legionnaire's disease *n.* [1976]
a high-risk strain of pneumonia *Legionella pneumophilia*, which often kills, and is typified by high fever, chills, lung congestion, and stomach pain. The disease was so named after its first outbreak, at a US Legion Convention in Philadelphia in June 1976. Since then it appears regularly, often as a result of contaminated air conditioning ducts, in which the virus that causes it tends to develop, before being flushed around a building.

* *'Legionellosis has so far been seen in two basic forms: legionnaire's disease and pontiac fever.'* (*Scientific American* October 1979)

leg warmers *n.* [1976]
knitted coverings for the legs that extend from the ankles to the upper thighs; leg warmers were originally used by dancers to protect themselves from the chill of bare rehearsal rooms; they entered mainstream fashion in the mid-1970s.

* *'A travelo whore dressed in mules, legwarmers, and a sort of psychedelic nappy came out of the bushes.'* (J. Meades, *Peter Knows What Dick Likes*, 1989)

leisure pounds *n.* [1989]
a synonym for disposable income.

* *'Between 100,000 and 150,000 people will have parted with a number of what are referred to in the marketing offices – and nowhere else – as "leisure pounds".'* (*The Independent*, 27 April 1990)

leisure suit *n.* [1986]
a popular style of garment, something along the lines of a tracksuit, worn by those who prefer to eschew more traditional forms of dress.

leisure wear *n.* [1986]
a line of casual clothing that most nearly approximates to sportswear, especially in the ◇leisure suit which, but for its garish colours and modern synthetic fabrics, is to all intents and purposes no more than the traditional tracksuit.

* *'The colossal investment made over the past decade in the design of sports equipment, sports fashion, and leisure wear.'* (*The Independent*, 31 March 1990)

LEM *abbrev.* [1962]
an acronym for lunar excursion module: a vehicle capable of moving across the lunar surface, probably equipped with cameras and similar recording equipment.

* *'The Lem . . . a complex mechanical craft or creature which had the look of a particularly nasty insect. It was the astronaut's first glimpse in space of the Lunar Module, or Lem.'* (N. Mailer, *A Fire on the Moon*, 1970)

let it all hang out *phrase.* [1970]
to be uninhibited or relaxed, to be absolutely honest.

* *'Ah yes, the late sixties. Pot, permissiveness, let it all hang out, take time to smell the flowers.'* (T. Blacker, *Fixx*, 1989)

leverage *adj.* [1968]
1. borrowing money at a fixed rate of interest and then investing it to yield enough money to deal with that interest and still leave a profit. The term was coined within the business community in the 1950s, but only entered the mass consciousness a good deal later.

* *'A homeowner is leveraged when he takes out a mortgage to buy his home. A corporation or government is leveraged when it issues bonds.'* (M. Lewis, *Liar's Poker*, 1989)

2. of a company's capital, the relation of the amount of its loan capital (money borrowed at a fixed rate of interest) to its ordinary-share capital.
3. to use as a lever, to gain impetus from; thus 'I leveraged off their promotion', etc.

leveraged buyout *n.* [1981]
the takeover of a company by using borrowed funds, for which collateral is provided by the assets of the company one intends to take over; the US version of Britain's ➪'management buyout'.

* *'What is known in Europe as a management buyout or MBO and in America as a leveraged buyout or LBO.'* (M. Lewis, *Liar's Poker*, 1989)

libber *n.* [1971]
a slightly derogatory, diminishing description for a member of the ➪Women's Liberation Movement.

liberate *v.* [1969]
a ➪hippie/radical euphemism meaning to steal; the theory was that property was theft and thus the fact of ownership merely rendered one a bigger thief than those who 'liberated' your possessions for the greater good.

* *'I think we ought to liberate these . . .Rock belongs to the people, not the pigs.'* (N. Fury, *Agro*, 1971)

liberated *adj.* [1970]
socially, politically, or sexually uninhibited.

* *'That summer's day of liberated rhythms, unchained energies, the new geology, the restless, wild, electric warnings of a change in lifestyle.'* (R. Neville, *Play Power*, 1970)
* *'Groups where liberated friends were encouraged to share their assets in an uninhibited way.'* (T. Blacker, *Fixx*, 1989)

liberationist *adj.* [1970]
any advocate of ➪women's liberation.
See also **libber**.

liberation theology *n.* [1971]
a primarily South American theological standpoint whereby leftwing Catholic priests ally themselves with the aspirations (and sometimes actions) of the oppressed masses, despite the official denunciation of such support both from the Pope and the various national authorities.

* *'Liberation theology, invented by and most attractive to male, middle-class intellectuals, cannot compete.'* (*The Independent*, 16 May 1990)

libertarian *n.* [1966]
the original meaning of libertarian, suitably coined in 1789, referred to one who set the doctrine of the freedom of will above that of freedom of necessity; this meaning was approximately that which was used in the 1960s, when libertarian was usually applied to those who voted for ⇨gay rights, abortion on demand, and an end to censorship. By the 1980s the meaning had shifted, and as coopted by the Conservative right-wing, had been perverted into a philosophical equivalent of the market economy: everyone should lead their own lives and take the consequence for them, unprotected by any social or governmental agencies; thus heroin addiction was quite acceptable, as long as the addict appreciated that the logical consequence was death, from which the new libertarian would make no effort to save him.

- *'In measured tones, he precisely minimized the contribution of "libertarian elements" in the Paris uprising.'* (R. Neville, *Play Power*, 1970)
- *'Portillo, who is a regular guest of "libertarian" (extreme right-wing) David Hart at his Suffolk mansion.'* (*Private Eye*, 16 March 1990)

Librium *n.* [1960]
a minor tranquillizer, the trade name for chlordiazepoxide; like other ⇨minor tranquillizers such as Valium, Librium was developed specifically to replace the barbiturates which had proved addictive to their users.

lifeboat ethic(s) *n.* [1974]
a set of values which, in a crisis, assigns its priorities according to urgency or expedience, rather than looking at longer-term moral or humanitarian considerations.

lifestyle *n., adj.* [1980]
literally, the way in which individuals or groups choose to live, and the commodities and attitudes that influence the given choice; 'lifestyle' dates back some time, but its widespread use is as a term that ranked high on any list of 1980s' buzzwords, notably in such advertising/marketing usages as *lifestyle concept; lifestyle segmentation*; etc.

- *'During the early fifties a new lifestyle began to evolve.'* (M. Farren, *Watch Out Kids*, 1972)
- *'In an ironic reversal of underlying materialism of the term, Britain's April 1990 poll tax riots revealed the lifestylists who were 'recognizable by matted hair, combat clothes and emaciated dogs' and made up a large proportion of those calling themselves anarchists.'* (*Sunday Correspondent*, 8 April 1990)
- *'I am tired of media-fed middle-class restraint and discrimination, tired of the simplest act of consumption generating a thousand lifestyle connotations.'* (*Independent on Sunday*, 13 May 1990)

life-support system *n.* [1962]
specifically, any equipment used to maintain human life, especially in a hospital or an alien environment such as space; extended to figurative use to mean any combination of circumstances without which life would be unbearable.

LIFFE *abbrev.*
an acronym for the London International Financial Futures Exchange.

- *'First quarter volumes on Liffe, which specialises in futures and options currencies, government bonds and interests, almost doubled from last year.'* (*Independent on Sunday*, 8 April 1990)

ligger *n.* [1969]
a freeloader, especially in the rock business. The etymology is debatable, but may come from the old Yorkshire dialect *ligger* meaning one who lazes about in bed and contributes nothing to the communal effort; the verb *lig* (often as 'lig about' or 'lig around') also meant to gossip or talk too much.

* '*"You mean about last night?" "Yeah. That guy was a bleedin' little ligger".*' (L. Bangs, *Psychotic Reactions and Carburetor Dung*, 1988)

light show *n.* [1965]
a popular form of backdrop for rock performances of the 1960s, created by projecting light through slides covered in coloured oils; as the heat of the projector warmed the oil it would start to move, creating swirling ➩psychedelic patterns on and around the band.

* '*The Beatles produced* . . . Sergeant Pepper *and the light show made its appearance as an art form.*' (M. Farren, *Watch out Kids*, 1971)

Likud *n.* [1973]
Israel's coalition of right-wing parties; formed in 1973 in opposition to the dominant Labour party, Likud came to power under Menachim Begin in 1977 and has remained, now led by Yitzhak Shamir, as Israel's government ever since.

* '*Likud was formed in 1973 as an alliance of several right-of-centre groupings. Under its present leadership it has adopted a much harder line that the Labour party towards its Arab neighbours.*' (J. D. & I. Darbyshire, *Political Systems of the World*, 1989)

limousine liberal *n.* [1969]
a wealthy liberal whose verbal allegiance to ideological purity is belied by his or her ➩lifestyle, in which the privations that beset those with whom he or she ostentatiously sympathizes are notable only by their absence.

line *n.* [1969]
a portion of a powdered drug, usually cocaine, heroin, or amphetamine sulphate, which is chopped up and layed out in thin lines, usually on a mirror.

linkage *n.* [1976]
the linking within superpower relations, especially in the field of arms negotiations, of progress in military and diplomatic accords with that in humanitarian and social issues, especially as regards Soviet interests in the ➩Third World; particularly espoused by the Carter Administration (1976–80) during which Congress refused to ratify ➩SALT II until Russia showed itself willing to take real steps to improve domestic policies on dissidents and human rights, to set up a grain deal with the US, to moderate imperialistic ambitions in Africa, etc. Linkage gained a more general use during the Gulf Crisis and the War that followed, when it was used to describe Saddam Hussein's attempts to link an Iraqi withdrawal from Kuwait with the Israeli–Palestinian problem.

* '*He had come into office espousing the concept of linkage, vowing to hold arms control talks subject to Soviet good behaviour.*' (S. Talbott, *Deadly Gambits*, 1984)

listeria *n.* [1961]
a bacterium of the genus *Listeria*, formerly known as *Listerella*, which can be harmful and

even fatal to human consumers; listeria was actually coined in 1940, but reached an audience larger than that of the medical and food professions in 1989 when it joined salmonella as one of the much-touted food contaminants that were allegedly undermining the British table.

* *'Three-quarters of ready-to-eat salads contained unacceptably high levels of bacteria including listeria and a fifth of frozen dishes contained other food poisoning organisms.'* (*The Independent*, 5 April 1990)

lit. crit. *abbrev., adj.* [1962]
literary criticism: especially when seen as a profitable media-oriented industry for sophisticated self-promoting ⇨talking heads.

* *'Like, say, the academic lit-crit industry, these are ridiculous and risible, but their decadence is of little moment to the outside world.'* (J. Meades, *Peter Knows What Dick Likes*, 1989)

lite *n.*
1. a low-alcohol, ostensibly non-fattening form of beer or soft drink (e.g. 'Miller Lite').
2. cut down in a variety of general uses.

* *'PC Write Lite, an inexpensive, speedy word processor from Quicksoft.'* (*Byte*, February 1990)

literati *n.* [1965]
fashionable members of the literary world, including the authors themselves, plus critics, literary editors, publishers, and allied hangers-on.
See also **glitterati**.

* *'The short stories . . . have been the laughing stock of the New York literary community for years, but only because so few literati have really understood Shawn's purpose.'* (T. Wolfe, *Queen*, 1965)

live-in lover *n.* [1969]
one of a variety of more or less clumsy terms created to describe individuals who live together but have not been married. Others include 'partner' and the statistical acronym POSSLQ (pronounced posselkew: Persons of the Opposite Sex Sharing Living Quarters).

live now, pay later *phrase.* [1963]
from the eponymous Jack Trevor Storey novel published in 1963: the hedonistic philosophy of the early days of hire purchase, when one had the material things one desired at once, and paid for them at some later date.

* *'I rapidly became known among the live-now-pay-later set as a sophisticated sort of odd-job man.'* (T. Blacker, *Fixx*, 1989)

liveware *n.* [1966]
see **-ware**.

living history *n.* [1973]
the recreation for study and research, but primarily for tourism, of the everyday activities of the past, sometimes set within a genuine relic of the past – a castle, a country house – but also created within museums, purpose-built buildings, etc.

* *'Schedule a day at Stone Mountain Park . . . or drive to Plains for some living history.'* (*New York magazine*, 30 April 1979)

loadsa- *prefix.* [1988]
an all-purpose synonym for 'plenty of'.
See **loadsamoney**.

* *'Lots of speed, a bagful of weaponry for*

the taking, loadsabonuses, and plenty of challenge.' (Ace, August, 1990)

loadsamoney *n.* [1988]
the name of a character, a cockney plasterer, created by comedian Harry Enfield on the television programme *Saturday Night Live.* This grotesque figure, waving his money and preaching that 'Wad is God' was designed to mock contemporary excess, especially as perceived as a creation of the ⇨Thatcherite 1980s, but many viewers failed to appreciate the satire, and Loadsamoney turned on his creator to become ⇨Thatcherism's shameless golem. Enfield also created 'Buggerallmoney', an unemployed northerner, but he never had the same success.

* *'Hey! Wozzat then! What is thaaaaattttt!!?? I'll tell you what that is, right. That is Loadsamoney!!!! And it's all mine, right. Loadsamoney!!!! You can't have a penny of it. And it's all mine!'* (Harry Enfield on *Saturday Night Live,* 1988)

lobby-fodder *n.* [1970]
members of the House of Commons who are considered as having little influence on a party's conduct of affairs, but who still count when it comes to the vote by walking obediently into the correct 'Yes' or 'No' lobby.

lo-cal (*or* **low-cal)** *adj.* [1969]
an abbreviation for low calorie and usually combined with a variety of words like yoghurt, dessert, meal, etc. *See also* **diet; lite; slimline.**

locks(man) *n.* [1960]
a Rastafarian, whose membership of the religion is easily identified by his wearing of 'locks', long strands of uncombed hair.

locomotion *n.* [1962]
a dance popularized by the record 'Locomotion' performed by Little Eva in 1962 and revived in the 1980s by Kylie Minogue.

log on *v.* [1982]
to turn on one's computer and access the program with which one wishes to work.

* *'For the first year he couldn't even log on. In those days he had the personal computer on a table across the office.'* (*Independent on Sunday,* 8 April 1990)

logic bomb *n.* [1986]
a fault which can be deliberately programmed into a system, usually by an employee who operates or programmes that system, with the deliberate intention of wrecking its proper functioning; such 'bombs' are often placed by a dissatisfied or soon to be made redundant employee.

* *'A "logic bomb" or "time bomb" is a destructive program activated by a certain combination of circumstances, or on a certain date.'* (*PC World,* July 1990)

longhair *n.* [1969]
a ⇨hippie, one of whose identifying badges was notably long hair.

* *'The two guys right behind me were acid people. Longhairs. They'd been picked up for vagrancy too.'* (H. S. Thompson, *Fear and Loathing in Las Vegas,* 1971)

longlife *adj.*
referring to a type of milk, given special heat treatment, which lasts many times longer than its fresh equivalent.
See also **UHT milk.**

loon pants *n.* [1969]
excessively flared trousers, either cotton or corduroy, which were popular in the late 1960s and early 1970s.
See also **flares**.

loony left *n.* [1981]
coined by the tabloids to describe Tony Benn, Ken Livingstone, Bernie Grant, and a variety of hard-left activists; possibly predated by *Private Eye's* condemnation of the SWP as 'Vanessa [Redgrave]'s loonies'.

* *'Ken Livingstone has been a friend to many people and causes. Newts, subsidized gays, Colin Wallace . . .On Friday, he moved to a dark place, where the loony left and loony right cannot easily be distinguished.'* (*Independent on Sunday*, 13 May 1990)

loop, in the *phrase.* [1979]
to be one of an administration's inner circle of advisers, privy to top-level restricted information; especially under US President Reagan.

love-bombing *n.* [1975]
also known as **flirty-fishing**: the softening-up process which is aimed at a potential convert to the 'cult' religions, e.g. Moonies, Children of God, whereby its members saturate the neophyte with affection, optimism, Utopian theories, etc., and thus, usually manage to effect the seduction into the cult. At this point the affection is replaced by less appealing but equally intense conditioning processes, from which escape is far less simple than was the initial induction.

love generation *n.* [1967]
a synonym for the ⇨hippies, who proclaimed love and peace.

* *'Just another ugly refugee from the love generation, some doom-struck gimp who couldn't handle the pressure.'* (H.S. Thompson, *Fear and Loathing in Las Vegas*, 1971)

loving *adj.* [1975]
in new therapies/social work: usually found as **loving relationship**: the emphasis is on emotional rather than physical love, although the inference is a full integrated relationship (heterosexual or homosexual) in which the needs, feelings and any other desires of both individuals are accepted and nurtured by the other.
See also **caring**.

low intensity conflict *n.* [1969]
originally referring to the use of restrained force to contain terrorism, the contemporary usage still means restrained or unobtrusive but has lost its exclusively military connotations.

* *'At the same time . . . he or his lieutenants are running a low-intensity campaign for the leadership.'* (*Independent on Sunday*, 13 May 1990)
* *'But of course it doesn't actually put it like that. It talks of "low intensity conflict".'* (*Independent on Sunday*, 27 May 1990)

low rise *n.* [1966]
a one or two storied building, the opposite of a high rise or tower block and often used to identify a design of public housing.

LSD *abbrev.* [1966]
Lysergic Acid Diethylamide-25: the basic hallucinogenic drug of the ⇨psychedelic 1960s; LSD had been discovered by Dr Albert Hofmann, working at Sandoz Laboratories in Switzerland in 1943. The drug had spread into psychiatric practice during the 1950s, but not

until its dedicated proselytizer Harvard University's Dr Timothy Leary began touting it as a spiritual cure-all in the early 1960s did it gain worldwide attention, and many hundreds of thousands of young consumers.

* *'Thousands of kids were moving into San Francisco for a life based on LSD and the psychedelic thing.'* (T. Wolfe, *The Electric Kool-Aid Acid Test*, 1969)

ludes

See **methaqualone**.

luggable *n., adj.* [1986]

a computer, advertised as portable, but which has dimensions which fall between a true portable, and a normal (and thus heavier) ⇨desktop machine.

See also **laptop; notebook.**

M0, M1, M2, M3, M4 *abbrev.* [1974]
a series of terms that cover different forms of money supply:

M0: a money aggregate consisting of notes and coins, both in circulation with the public and held in banks' tills and banks' operational balances with the Bank of England.

M1: the basic money supply, consisting of currency in circulation, plus demand deposits held in current (cheque) accounts.

M2: the money supply of a country, including M1, as well as commercial bank time deposits, but not certificates of deposit.

M3: the overall money supply of a country, including M2, plus deposits in savings and loan associations (including building societies) and certificates of deposit.

M4 (not usually used by economists): savings bonds and credit union shares.

✱ *'The growth of the narrow money measure, M0, which the Treasury believes is a good guide to spending in shops.'* (*Independent on Sunday*, 10 June 1990)

mace *n.* [1966]
an abbreviation for chemical mace: a chemical weapon, akin to tear gas, which is packed into aerosol cans and can be used for self-defence when sprayed into an assailant's face.

✱ *'Shit, there's nothing in the world like a Mace high – forty-five minutes on your knees with the dry heaves, gasping for breath.'* (H.S. Thompson, *Fear and Loathing in Las Vegas*, 1971)

macho *adj.* [1969]
from the Spanish meaning masculine or vigorous, thus manly or virile; **machismo** is the quality of being macho. While macho remains an estimable characteristic in Latin cultures, elsewhere macho men have come to be mocked in the post-feminist world for their strutting masculinity and 'tough guy' posturing. The word has been used by English speakers since the 1920s, but its change of meaning is very much a product of feminist criticism.

✱ *'Hiaasen seems to be uneasy about satirising dumb, macho, redneck attitudes.'* (*Sunday Correspondent*, 10 June 1990)

macro *n., adj.* [1983]
1. *in computing*: a means of reducing a number of complex instructions (and thus multiple keystrokes) to the pressing of a single key.

✱ *'A very good macro recorder which deals equally with mouse movements and keystrokes.'* (*PC World*, July 1990)

2. *in general use*: the 'big picture', the broad view.

✱ *'I was busy enough with the broadbrush strategy, what I call the "macro" issues.'* (T. Blacker, *Fixx*, 1989)

macrobiotics *n.* [1965]
a diet that ostensibly draws on Zen Bhuddist culinary traditions; based on pure vegetables, brown (untreated) rice, and similar natural foods, it is designed to prolong life, purge the body of impurities and possibly bring spiritual

enlightenment. – **macrobiotic** *adj.*

✱ *'Macrobiotics has almost nothing to do with Zen. Its central concept, yin and yang, is borrowed from Taoism.'* (R. Christgau, *New York Herald Tribune*, 1965)

mad cow disease *n.* [1989]
a popular nickname for. bovine spongiform encephalopathy (BSE): a disease that in 1989 began to be reported as attacking British cattle; it apparently comes from the practice of feeding cattle with food made up of the brain and offal of other diseased cattle.

✱ *'This unhappy creature was found to have contracted spongiform encephalopathy, known as "mad cow" disease or BSE when it occurs in cattle.'* (*The Independent*, 15 May 1990)

magic bullet *n.* [1967]
a drug or other medicinal agent that can destroy disease-carrying bacteria.

magic mushroom *n.* [1969]
the psilocybe mushroom, a mild organic hallucinogenic, popular in the 1960s, and still regularly consumed by those who bother to collect them from Britain's fruitful fields.

✱ *'No magic mushrooms or carefully distilled electric banana skins.'* (N. Fury, *Agro*, 1971)

magic realism *n.* [1970]
from the German *magischer Realismus*: originally coined in 1925 by Franz Roh in an essay dealing with the artists of the Neue Sachlichkeit or 'new objectivity'. He described the way in which such painters often portrayed the imaginary, the improbable, or the fantastic in a realistic or rational manner. The term was taken up in the US to describe an exhibition in 1943 that featured the work of Charles Sheeler (1883–1965) and Edward Hopper (1882–1967). Its current use refers to literature, notably the works of such Latin Americans as Borges and Garcia Marquez, Europeans like Gunter Grass and Italo Calvino, and Britons Salman Rushdie and Angela Carter, offering a strong narrative, in which the unexpected and the inexplicable are treated in a paradoxically down-to-earth manner, combining the everyday with phenomena better linked to dreams and fairy tales. – **magic realist** *n.*

✱ *'In political terms he sees himself as a realist, not a magic realist, and wants to preserve Peru from . . . utopian solutions.'* (*Sunday Correspondent*, 1 April 1990)

mail(ing) shot *n.* [1968]
the sending out of large-scale mail order campaign material.

✱ *'The mailshot boom is bringing a flood of 2 billion postal items a year.'* (*Independent on Sunday*, 3 June 1990)

mainframe *n., adj.* [1964]
the largest type of computer installation, with great capacity, large and static equipment and which requires installation in air-conditioned, ultra-clean rooms and a variety of other special criteria for their use. Originally used to describe the main framework of the central processing unit within a large computer but now, with the development of ⇨minicomputers and ⇨microcomputers, to mean the whole large central machine.

major *n.* [1963]
any leading company. When used non-specifically, the term usually applies to a multinational conglomerate; when referring to a specific industry, it describes the various field

leaders; specifically the large film companies – MGM, Paramount, Columbia, etc., as opposed to the independents.

major tranquillizer *n.* [1969]
those tranquillizers – the barbiturates – which, while effective, were found to render habitual users addicts. They were largely replaced by such ➲minor tranquillizers as ➲Librium and Valium.

male bonding *n.* [1972]
the traditional male 'buddy' relationship, surpassing, as Rudyard Kipling once put it, the love of women.

male chauvinism (*or* supremacism *n.* [1970]
feminism's derogatory term for a man who regards himself, and all other men, as naturally superior to all women and adopts the traditional ➲sexist attitudes towards them. Chauvinism dates from the Napoleonic era, and is named for Nicolas Chauvin of Rochefort, a veteran soldier whose displays of adulation for the Emperor led to his being cited in Cogniard's play *La Cocarde Tricolore* (1831) as a byword for excessive patriotism.
– **male chauvinist**, *n.*
See also **MCP**.

* *'He's also dumped on the male chauvinism (abuse born of fear) that the working class is prone to.'* (J. Meades, *Peter Knows What Dick Likes*, 1989)
* *'A classical beauty, which could make her, in the eyes of the average male chauvinist, very much out of place in a police uniform.'* (J. McClure, *Cop World*, 1984)

male chauvinist pig *n.* [1970]
see **MCP**.

management buyout *n.* [1980]
a situation whereby the management of a liquidated company use their own cash to buy up the firm and start it working again.

Mandelbrot set *n.* [1988]
a fascinating visual object, which can be demonstrated on a computer screen and is the function of the iteration in the complex plane of the mapping z – < z² + c, which can be set down as 'take a number, multiply by itself and add the original number'. The set is named for Benoit Mandelbrot, a mathematician who discovered the set, only to have it ignored for some time, since the complex and laborious mathematics it involved proved impossible until the advent of ➲number-crunching computers. The visual representation of the set, which is central to the currently fashionable, and barely explored ➲chaos theory, offers a 'coastline' of infinite complexity, which, however much one magnifies even the smallest section, remains exactly the same.

* *'The Mandelbrot set is a collection of points. Every point in the complex plane . . . is either in the set or outside it.'* (J. Glieck, *Chaos*, 1988)

man manager *n.* [1967]
anyone who is seen as good at human relations within the working environment.

* *'A goal orientated man manager with a proactive mind, capable of controlling the production and technical complexities of the accounting requirements.'* (ad for Commercial Resources recruitment advisers in *Independent on Sunday*, 8 April 1990)

man management *n.* [1967]
the practice of conducting human relations within the workplace.

✱ *'These are qualities that those who do not have them call man management. Sir John, who does, subtitles his book* "Making It Happen", *"Leadership".'* (*The Independent*, 21 April 1990)

mano a mano *adv.* [1975]
from the Spanish 'hand to hand': single combat, also known as 'one on one'; used for any direct confrontation between two individuals.

✱ *'Harvey had this mano a mano with a Langendorf bread truck he was sure had his number on it.'* (C. McFadden, *The Serial*, 1976)

Mandrax
see **methaqualone**.

Mao jacket *n.* [1967]
see **Nehru jacket**.

mao tai *n.* [1965]
1. a vodka-like clear spirit based on sorghum and produced in China.
2. a cocktail that originated in Hawaii and is based on rum.

Marburg disease
see **green monkey disease**

margarita *n.* [1965]
a fashionable cocktail of the 1970s: it was made of tequila and citrus fruit juice, and drunk from a glass with its rim dipped in salt. The margarita was a successful attempt to capitalize on the fashionable taste for tequila, which was traditionally drunk in a ritual that involved licking salt, tossing off a shot of alcohol, and finishing off by sucking a lemon quarter.

marginalize *v.* [1986]
to render powerless by removing from the centre of affairs. – **marginalization** *n.*

market forces *n.* [1970]
the bedrock of ⇨monetarist economics and of ⇨neo-Conservative government: the belief that the market must be allowed to dictate the way that not just the ecomnomy, but society at large functions; this extends to arts funding, diminished provision for the welfare state, and many other measures where the lowest common denominator of taste is allowed to take precedence, simply because quantity must prevail, irrespective of any qualitative judgment.

market maker *n.* [1986]
the post- ⇨Big Bang name for the traditional jobber: a stock exchange firm which commits itself to being ready at any time to deal in the range of stocks for which it is registered.

✱ *'The move into market-making is one example of a higher risk area.'* (*Independent on Sunday*, 3 June 1990)

MARV *abbrev.* [1983]
an acronym for Manoeuvrable Re-entry Vehicle: any missile of which the warhead can be steered electronically, usually by internal inertial navigation guidance systems. MARVed weapons can rely on mid-course and terminal guidance options that include television, imaging infra-red laser, and distance-measuring equipment (DME). Such weapons are also able to take evasive action if targeted by another missile. MARVing has added appreciably to the accuracy of ⇨MIRVed missiles which would otherwise be susceptible to atmospheric conditions.

* *'MARVs were ostensibly being designed to evade enemy interceptors during reentry.'* (R.C. Aldridge, *First Strike!*, 1983)

MAS *abbrev.* [1985]
an acronym for Mutually Assured Survival: coined by Max M. Kampelman, a leading negotiator in the 1985 arms control talks in Geneva, the favoured gospel of the originators of the High Frontier study, the foremost supporters of 'star wars' development. While deterrence by ⇨assured destruction is 'a time worn and morally bankrupt doctrine' (Gen Daniel O. Graham, 1985), the ⇨SDI with its space-based super-defences would ensure that under the stern but necessary umbrella of US omnipotence, neither side would need to launch an attack and thus both would be assured of survival – an extreme example of the Orwellian 'war is peace' philosophy.

mascarpone *n.* [1978]
a soft Italian cream cheese, usually eaten as a dessert, possibly with fruit, sugar, etc. *See also* **fromage frais.**

massage *v.* [1966]
a financial or political term that means to improve upon the facts, or figures.

* *'Talbot would stay behind the desk . . . massaging the figures if necessary, Mr Nobody to my Sunshine Superman.'* (T. Blacker, *Fixx*, 1989)

master class *n.* [1963]
a tutorial given by an expert in a given field; the original master classes tended to be conducted by classical musicians, but the term and the activity have gained much wider currency.

* *'The analogy we have been using is the musical master class, the chance to work with someone who is 10 or 15 years further down the line.'* (*The Independent*, 31 March 1990)

mau-mau *v.* [1970]
to threaten, to terrorize, especially as in the way minority pressure groups capitalize on liberal guilt to extract a variety of material benefits for their cause; the original Mau-Mau was an African secret society who in 1950 launched a guerrilla war against the British colonial government in Kenya.

* *'The poverty program encouraged you to go in for mau-mauing. They wouldn't have known what to do without it.'* (T. Wolfe, *Radical Chic & Mau-Mauing the Flak-Catchers*, 1970)

Mau Mau bee *n.*
see **killer bee.**

maxi *n., adj.* [1966]
a full-length skirt which, in the late 1960s, challenged the omnipresent ⇨mini-skirt for fashion supremacy.

* *'Women laid them to rest with all the other relics of the decade: purple nail varnish, maxi coats and tank tops.'* (*Sunday Correspondent*, 13 May 1990)

maxiseries *n.* [1971]
on the pattern of ⇨miniseries, a television series that runs to a large number of episodes.

* *'If the maxiseries left something to be desired, there were new miniseries of high quality.'* (*Newsweek*, 19 February 1979)

MBFR talks *abbrev.* [1973]
Mutual and Balanced Force Reduction talks:

begun in Vienna in 1973, these talks aimed to set up controls for non-nuclear forces based in Europe. Direct participants were Benelux, W Germany, the UK, and the US; Czechoslovakia, E Germany, Poland, the USSR. While both sides of negotiators have put forward a massive variety of possible restructuring of the balance of forces, none have yet appeared realistic to each party. The talks were suspended shortly after the Russian walk-out from the nuclear ➪START and ➪INF talks, in January 1984.

* *'The Pentagon recommended postponing a number of other, non-nuclear arms control negotiations, such as the Mutual Balanced Force Reduction talks in Vienna.'* (S. Talbott, *Deadly Gambits*, 1984)

MC *abbrev.* [1985]
master of ceremonies: in a ➪hip-hop ➪crew, the member who actually sings or ➪raps the lyrics.

* *'MC Hammer couldn't be there to accept his award as Best International Newcomer.'* (*The Independent*, 12 February 1991)

McLuhanism *n.* [1967]
pertaining to the theories of Canadian media guru Marshall McLuhan (1911–80), essentially that the spread of mass media across the 'global village' tends to diminish the critical faculties of individuals and to create a world in which, thanks to instant mass communication, the differences between those individuals are continually decreasing.

* *'What is McLuhanism? . . . Arthur M. Schlesinger Jr answered, "It is a chaotic combination of bland assertion, astute guesswork, fake analogy, dazzling insight [and] hopeless nonsense"'* (M. McLuhan & Q. Fiore, *The Medium is the Message*, 1967)

MCP *abbrev.* [1969]
male chauvinist pig: the most popular term of feminist abuse in the early days of the movement. *See* **male chauvinist**.

* *'She thought taking shorthand "from some MCP with a big desk" one more variation on the master–slave relationship.'* (C. McFadden, *The Serial*, 1976)

ME *abbrev.* [1986]
myalgic encephalomyelitis: known to the unsympathetic as 'yuppie flu' or 'executive flu', a long-term, as yet incurable viral disease. Its defiance of scientific understanding has made critics equate it with malingering; euphemists have coined the synonym 'post-viral syndrome' to sidestep their attacks. Originally noted at London's Royal Free Hospital, it was known for a while as 'Royal Free disease'.

* *'Like that other disease of the 1980s, yuppie flu or ME, it is something of a mystery.'* (*Independent on Sunday*, 25 March 1990)

medallion man *n.* [1975]
a 'real man', who underpins such a self-image by wearing of gold chains and medallions and similar 'body gold', displayed to maximum effect across a hairy chest revealed by a tight shirt that has been left unbuttoned to the navel. *See also* **macho**.

medevac *n.* [1966]
from medical evacuation: a military helicopter used to carry the wounded away from the battlefield to a field hospital.

* *'That's when I left, riding a medevac with a lieutenant who was covered with blood-soaked bandages.'* (M. Herr, *Dispatches*, 1977)

media *n.* [1962]
a collective noun that covers a variety of forms of communication: print, radio and television; the word had been used since the 1920s as advertising jargon, when discussing the outlets through which advertising should be channelled to the consumer, but its contemporary use developed in the 1960s.

* *'I have straddled the line between "the movement" and "the community". .. between the world of "the street" and the world of "media". I have doubts that I can go on balancing these forces.'* (A. Hoffman, *Woodstock Nation*, 1969)

media event *n.* [1976]
any event of supposed importance that is staged less for any real effect than for its potential impact on the TV, radio, and print journalists who have been carefully mustered to record it.
See also **photo opportunity; sound bite.**

* *'When Steve Jobs left Apple . . . it was a media event in California, somewhere around 8.0 on the Richter scale.'* (*PC World*, April 1990)

media mix *n.*
in planning an advertising campaign or product promotion, the combination of media outlets that are chosen for maximum efficiency.

mega *adj.* [1983]
from the Greek prefix, meaning 'great'; now applied to legions of nouns and adjectives, and frequently used as a stand-alone approbation/description: 'It's mega.'

* *'The same Swing-beat wave that washed up the mega-successful Bobby Brown.'* (*Sunday Correspondent*, 10 June 1990)

me generation *n.* [1973]
a concept, describing the young people of the 1970s, ➪yuppie prototypes with ➪Filofaxes yet to come, who had transmuted the inner contemplation advocated by the 1960s' hippies into a simple obsession with self, as seen in the proliferation of health clubs, 'quick-fix' therapies and allied ego-oriented indulgence. The idea was coined by writer Tom Wolfe (1931–) in an essay, 'The Third Great Awakening', subsequently rechristened 'The Me Decade' in *The Critic*, May/June 1973, in which he compared this exaltation of the self with a new theology, 'with the mightiest holy roll of all, the beat that goes . . . Me . . . Me . . . Me . . .'

* *'Those who agree with Tom Wolfe's assessment of the seventies as the self-promoting "Me Decade" have in a sense not looked deep enough; these people seem barely to be talking to themselves at all.'* (R.D. Rosen, *Psychobabble*, 1977)

mellow *adj.* [1967]
a synonym for ➪laid-back; the overtone was that the feeling was drug-induced.

* *'The first major crack occurred in my plastic dome which by now was beginning to feel sort of mescalin-mellow.'* (A. Hoffman, *Woodstock Nation*, 1969)
* *'Rock band managers in narrow-waisted white suits . . . scarfing up brown rice and veggies . . . It was a mellow scene.'* (C. McFadden, *The Serial*, 1976)

meltdown *n.* [1965]
the collapse of the core of the reactor at a nuclear power station, possibly through the malfunction of its cooling system, when it has become heated above its melting point. Such a meltdown may cause a major disaster if it

develops a critical mass of fissile fuel which can sustain a chain reaction and thus cause a nuclear explosion.

* *'Experts have not ruled out the possibility of a complete meltdown, but they claim that the accident is being brought under control.'* (*Chronicle of the 20th Century*, 1988)

Mensa *n.* [1962]
an association of intellectuals, whose membership qualification is an IQ of 148 or above.

* *'Can you solve this puzzle faster than Einstein? If you solve this puzzle you could be eligible for Mensa. The High IQ Society.'* (ad for Mensa in the *Sunday Correspondent*, 4 November 1990)

menu *n.* [1986]
the commands that drive a computer program, which can be accessed on the screen in a series of linked lists, which (fancifully) resemble a restaurant menu and from which choices can be made in the same way. If the computer is equipped with one, the menu can be revealed by a ⇨mouse pointing device and can be 'pop-up' (the mouse merely touches the top line of the menu and the remaining lines appear on screen) or 'pull-down' (the mouse touches the top line, but the extra commands will not appear until the user clicks the mouse). Thus **menu-driven**: a program which functions according to the menu item that the user selects.

* *'The Menu selector allows you to instantly eject up to the Ventura menus when you need to tag text and use other menu functions.'* (*The Soft Kicker Plus manual*, 1989)

MEP *abbrev.* [1976]
Member of the European Parliament.

merchandising *n.* [1973]
merchandising as a commercial word goes back at least 50 years, but the merchandising of a person, who is treated as a commodity rather than as an individual, is a more recent phenomenon.

meth(edrine) *n.* [1967]
methedrine was synthesized in 1939 and was usued initially as a means of raising sluggish blood pressure; in the 1960s it enjoyed a brief vogue as the ultimate in ⇨'speed', drugs that made one 'go faster'. Methedrine derivatives reappeared in the late 1980s, known as 'crystal' and 'ice'.

* *'Speed kills. It really does. Methedrine and amphetamine . . . can and will rot your teeth, freeze your mind and kill your body.'* (R. Neville, *Play Power*, 1970)

methaqualone *n.* [1961]
a hypnotic or sedative drug, sold as **Mandrax** in the UK and **Quaalude** in the US; known as '**Mandies**' or '**Ludes**' the methaqualones were enjoyed both for their relaxing qualities and the lowering of inhibitions, especially as to casual sex, that these promoted.

* *'Not that he deals in anything fiercer than hash, LSD, STP, mandies and . . . some speed.'* (N. Fury, *Agro*, 1971)
* *'I've got plenty of Mandrax and cigars, and I'm ready.'* (L. Bangs, *Psychotic Reactions and Carburetor Dung*, 1988)
* *'Lou Reed looking younger, innocent, fingering his lip wide-eyed in a Quaalude haze.'* (L. Bangs, *Psychotic Reactions and Carburetor Dung*, 1988)

metri(fi)cation *n.* [1965]
the conversion of any systems of weights and measures to a metric base.

Mexican green *n.* [1969]
see **Acapulco gold.**

Mexican wave *n.* [1986]
a sequential wave produced in a large crowd. The original one appeared when soccer's World Cup was staged in Mexico in 1986, when sections of that crowd stood up in turn and waved their arms before sitting down, when they were replaced by the next section in line.

MIA *abbrev.* [1968]
missing in action. On the pattern of KIA (Killed In Action).

micro *prefix.* [1961]
an all-purpose prefix taken from Greek and meaning 'miniature'. The form has been used for many years, and among its latest combinations are **microcode**: microinstructions used in a computer as an alternative to hard-wired circuitry to implement given functions of parts of the system or of the processor; **micromarketing**: a method of analysing a marketing situation by looking only at a single, individual firm or consumer; **microteaching**: a teacher-training technique developed at Stanford University, California, in 1960: a teacher takes a small class (5–10 pupils) for a specially constructed lesson of 10–30 minutes; an observer assesses this lesson, and the observer and teacher, possibly with the aid of videotape, analyse it together afterwards.

microchip *n.* [1969]
see **chip.**

microcomputer *n.* [1972]
a synonym for personal computer or ➪desktop computer, epitomized by the IBM-PC or the Apple Macintosh.

✱ *'Microcomputer companies sold equipment as if it were corn, in large quantities; they spent most of their money making things.'* (T. Kidder, *The Soul of a New Machine*, 1981)

microelectronics *n.* [1961]
that branch of electronics that deals with integrated circuits, built on a very small scale. – **microelectronics** *adj.*

✱ *'They did do some business, using the beautiful and, to me, inscrutable language of the microelectronic era.'* (T. Kidder, *The Soul of a New Machine*, 1981)

microlyte *n.*
a small lightweight aircraft with room for a single pilot; in many ways a more sophisticated, powered ➪hang-glider.

✱ *'Microlyte pilot Brian Milton touched down in Darwin, Australia 51 days after leaving London docklands in his 440cc aircraft Dalgety Flier.'* (*Chambers Book of Dates*, 1989)

microprocessor *n.* [1970]
a small ➪silicon chip which contains all the circuitry required in the central processing unit of a computer.

✱ *'A microprocessor is just a small processor. Actually that doesn't do it justice . . . a microprocessor represents a major technological advance.'* (D. Jarrett, *The Good Computing Book for Beginners*, 1980)

microwave *n., v.* [1965]
an oven in which the food is cooked by passing microwaves through it – this makes for quick

and uniform cooking, reducing normal cooking times to a fraction of their traditional length. Thus the adjectival use, e.g. *microwave cookery; microwave meals.*

* *'A dishwasher, a microwave, a fridge-freezer, a food processor, a cordless kettle and a £200 Breadsmade.'* (ad for *Competitor's Companion* in the *Sunday Correspondent*, 10 June 1990)

midi system *n.* [1984]

a mid-range medium-sized stereo system, positioned between the diminutive micro systems and the fullsize ⇨stack system; in common with its peers, it comprises the usual record deck, amplifier, tape system, and speakers, plus possibly a ⇨CD player.

midi-skirt *n.* [1967]

a skirt that reaches mid calf, neither a ⇨mini (above the knee) nor a ⇨maxi (down to the ankles).

midlife crisis *n.* [1972]

a crisis experienced (especially by men) as they reach their forties and reluctantly abandon youth for middle age.

* *'Just another mid-life crisis haunted by passing time and lost opportunity.'* (T. Blacker, *Fixx*, 1989)

Militant *n.* [1977]

the Militant Tendency, a far-left Trotskyite revolutionary political group who emerged *c.* 1977 and for a period in the 1980s made substantial (and massively divisive) inroads into the Labour Party. Their greatest success was the running of Liverpool Council.

* *'The paper's defence was that, while the Labour candidate may not have been a member or public supporter of Militant, he was so leftwing that he was as good as in the Trotskyist organization.'* (M. Hollingsworth, *The Press and Political Dissent*, 1986)

milk round *n.* [1970]

the annual recruitment drive carried out by major corporations and other businesses, touring universities and colleges and interviewing final-year students in the hope of finding suitable graduate employees.

* *'The "milkround" goes mostly to universities, rather than to the polytechnics, which have a far higher proportion of ethnic minority graduates.'* (*The Independent*, 14 June 1990)

mind-blowing *adj.* [1967]

phenomenal, remarkable, astounding; originally a ⇨hippie term, relating to anything that produced an equivalent effect to consuming ⇨LSD, the basic 'mind-blowing' hallucinogenic.

minder *n.* [1979, 1981]

1. a bodyguard, employed by a criminal: the term gained widespread currency after the success of the late 1970s Euston Films television series *Minder*.

2. in the Falklands and Gulf wars, the foreign office or military officials who were deputed in theory to assist the working journalists but who, as those journalists made clear, actually acted as on-the-spot government or military censors.

* *'The men charged with the main burden of imposing censorship were the Ministry of Defence press officers accompanying the task Force, the "minders" as they became known.'* (R. Harris, *Gotcha!*, 1983)

3. by extension from **2.** anyone acting to

ensure that a politician is kept well away from the press and can therefore make no overly honest statement.

✱ *'One of her minders did most of the talking on the doorstep, and another took me aside.'* (*The Independent*, 31 March 1990)

mind-expanding *adj.* [1963]
referring to the properties of ⇨psychedelic or hallucinogenic drugs which were able, it was claimed, to expand the mind's abilities beyond their usual constraints.

mind set (*or* **head set)** *n.* [1967]
a state of mind, especially as felt by a particular interest group.

✱ *'I can't take the whole Marin head set anymore. Angela. Marlene.-Natural foods. Cocaine.'* (C. McFadden, *The Serial*, 1976)

minicab *n.* [1960]
an unlicensed taxicab, allowed to pick up passengers from their homes or offices, but not to cruise the streets looking for trade.

✱ *'I called a minicab, put her in, and when we got home I phoned the Citizens Advice Bureau.'* (*Sunday Correspondent*, 13 May 1990)

mini (car) *n.* [1961]
the proprietary name for a small car designed by Sir Alex Issigonis and made by British Leyland; there were a variety of minis, including the **Mini-Cooper** a souped up sports version, and the **Mini-Moke**, which resembled a small jeep.

✱ *'Speeding around the metropolis in Aston-Martin, motor-bike or Mini-Moke.'* (J. Aitken, *The Young Meteors*, 1967)

mini (skirt) *n.* [1965]
a very short skirt, or dress, reaching mid-thigh and higher (when it could be called a 'micro').

✱ *'She was all decked out in the most mini of minis, a silver see through thingie, and she had no underwear on at all.'* (A. Hoffman, *Woodstock Nation*, 1969)

✱ *'For the customer who insists on wearing the micro-mini despite one knee tuck operation too many.'* (*Independent on Sunday*, 21 October 1990)

minicomputer *n.* [1972]
the second level of computer, a cut down version of the ⇨mainframe, but much more powerful (at least in the early days) than the micro- or ⇨personal computer.

✱ *'After mainframes, as the big computers were known, came the cheaper and less powerful minicomputers.'* (T. Kidder, *The Soul of a New Machine*, 1981)

minimalism *n.* [1965]
a major art movement of the 1960s, first described by Richard Wolheim and initially restricted to sculpture, which promoted clarity and simplicity over ornamentation and the emotional self-expression of abstract expressionism.

minimum deterrence *n.*
the smallest quantity of nuclear weapons required to assure a potential attacker that they will suffer unacceptable national damage in a retaliatory strike. Such a form of ⇨deterrence (in effect the policy of assured destruction cut back to the barest necessary arsenals), would dispense with all but the vital warheads, thus making obsolete any 'war-fighting' or 'limited' capabilities, especially the short-range 'battlefield' nuclear weapons.

minipill *n.* [1970]
any pill that contains a very low dosage of a drug, used specifically to describe a brand of an oral contraceptive that contained only one tenth of the usual dose of progesterone, and none of the estrogen found in larger pills.

miniseries *n.* [1973]
a television series, usually taken from a best-selling popular novel, that runs to three or four episodes; such series rate high on superficial glamour and second-rank celebrity actors, they are often financed by companies based in several different countries and their overall blandness and low production values reflect the need to make international sales.
See also **maxiseries**.

* *'Of course I have to think about taking an option for a miniseries. Am I a fool?'* (C. Blake, *Girl Talk*, 1990)

miniskirt *n.* [1965]
see **mini (skirt)**.

minisupercomputer *n.* [1988]
a scaled down ➪supercomputer, with many of the high-speed calculating functions of the true supercomputer, but priced somewhat more accessibly.

minor tranquillizer *n.* [1969]
any of a group of mild tranquillizers e.g. Valium and ➪Librium, which were created to replace the ➪major tranquillizers, the barbiturates, which had been found to render their users addicts.

MIPS *abbrev.* [1974]
an acronym for millions of instructions per second; a measure of computing power.

* *'The base machine's already impressive 27.5 MIPS and 7.4 MFLOPS.'* (*PC World*, April 1990)

Miranda (ruling) *n.* [1966]
based on the case of Ernesto A. Miranda vs. the State of Arizona (1966): a set of rules established by the US Supreme Court whereby the US police, on arresting a suspect, must inform him/her of all due rights and privileges before beginning any subsequent interrogation – the equivalent of the 'caution' in the UK. Thus **Miranda card**: a card with the suspect's rights written down on it; **Miranda rights; Miranda warning.**

* *'"He says that a lot", said Luis Cordova. "It's one of his favourite things. All during the Miranda, he kept saying it.'* (C. Hiaasen, *Skin Tight*, 1989)

MIRV *abbrev.* [1967]
an acronym for multiple individually targeted reentry vehicle: a nuclear missile that carries a number of warheads, each of which can be programmed to hit a separate target.
See also **ICBM, MARV**.

* *'MIRVs changed the concept of one missile destroying one target to one missile being able to destroy many targets.'* (R.C. Aldridge, *First Strike!*, 1983)

missionary position *n.* [1969]
the face-to-face position in sexual intercourse; the man is on top; an apocryphal etymology stems from the belief that it was the one position permitted by Christian missionaries.

mission control *n.* [1964]
the ground-based command centre from which space flights are controlled.

* *'Over the radio came the dialogue of Mission Control talking to Collins in orbit overhead.'* (N. Mailer, *A Fire on the Moon*, 1970)

mix *n.* [1986]
the final version of a recorded song, created by the mixing of the various tape tracks, each of which records a different instrument or vocal to create the finished effect. These mixes, using the same basic tape, can vary as to their final use, whether for a short single record, a longer track that accentuates the rhythm for dancing, etc.

* *'The extended club mixes . . . allow vocalist Pauline Henry ample space to prove she is the first Brit-soul singer to emulate . . . Chaka Khan.'* (*Sunday Correspondent*, 10 June 1990)

mixed media *n.* [1965)]
any entertainment or work of art which combines a variety of media, usually including tape recordings, film projection, etc.

* *'"Mixed media" entertainment – this came straight out of the Acid Tests' combination of light and movie projections, strobes, tapes, rock 'n' roll, black light.'* (T. Wolfe, *The Electric Kool-Aid Acid Test*, 1969)

mock (exams) *n.* [1960]
an internal test examination given by a school to prepare its pupils for the real public examination that will follow. Often known as **mocks**.

mod [1966]
1. *adj., in the US:* smart, fashionable, especially as regards clothes.

* *'The flag design is a current mod-fashion among the rich.'* (A. Hoffman, *Woodstock Nation*, 1969)

2. *n., in the UK:* a working class youth cult that originated in the late 1950s and peaked around 1964; the original mods liked cool jazz, existentialism, and sharp Italian-influenced clothes; by the second generation the clothes were all that remained. The mods reached national prominence when on successive bank holidays in 1964 they fought their rivals the ⇨rockers (who wore leathers and rode motorbikes as opposed to the mods' Italian scooters) on a variety of Britain's seaside beaches.

* *'While the rockers clung to the past, the mods sought an identity in what amounted to an almost grotesque parady of consumer capitalism.'* (M. Farren, *Watch Out Kids*, 1972)

modem *n.* [1980]
an abbreviation of Modulator and Demodulator: a device that makes it possible to transmit messages between computers through a suitable communication channel, often the public telephone system. The modem modulates the transmitted digital bit stream into an analog signal that can be transmitted, and then demodulates back to the digital state at the receiving station.

* *'BIX itself has a good deal of C and Unix software available on-line . . . where it can be downloaded by anyone with a modem.'* (*Byte*, June 1990)

mole *n.* [1976]
a deep cover agent, put in place many years before he/she can be of use, but on the assumption that such an agent will gradually gain greater access to the centres of power, and become increasingly useful and damaging as time passes. 'Mole' stands as the perfect example of the blurring of fact and fiction:

while Sir Francis Bacon uses it first in his *History of the Reign of King Henry VII* (1622), it has otherwise been found in the world of John le Carré, notably *Tinker, Tailor, Soldier, Spy* (1974). In a BBC-TV interview Le Carré claimed that mole was a genuine KGB term, but it was the televising of *Tinker, Tailor, Soldier, Spy*, – plus the revelations of the 'Fourth Man' (Anthony Blunt) in October 1979 that took mole out of fiction and put it into the headlines for good.

* *'One day, it's a discreet chat over port and cigars with a senior civil servant and mole.'* (T. Blacker, *Fixx*, 1989)

moment in time, at this *phrase.* [1972]
a synonym for now, beloved by those who like to infuse the commonplace with an element of pseudo-technological jargon.

Monday Club *n.* [1962]
a right wing Conservative party club, founded in 1962 and originally meeting regularly on Mondays. The aim of the club was 'to keep the Conservative Party Conservative'.

monetarism *n.* [1963]
an economic theory, epitomized by the teachings of Milton Friedman and his fellow-members of the 'Chicago school' of economists, that is based on the belief that increases in inflation can be traced directly to those in the money supply; thus cut the money supply and inflation will fall as well. – **monetarist**, *adj.*

* *'Prominent among these were Patrick Minford, an inflexibly ideological monetarist at Liverpool University; Brian Griffiths, a professor at City University whose monetarism was seductively spiced with Christian morality.'* (H. Young, *One of Us*, 1989)

monokini *n.* [1964]
a one piece swimsuit, comprising only the bottom half of a bikini; the etymology is specious since there is no such thing as a 'kini', 'mono' or 'bi', but only Bikini Atoll, the name of which was appropriated for the swimming costume.

Monteneros *n.* [1970]
Argentine guerillas, operating from the countryside, who fought against the right-wing dictatorship of Juan Peron.

* *'The extremists, disillusioned with Peron and exasperated by 30 years of Fascist or quasi-Fascist misgovernment, turned to terrorism, calling themselves Monteneros.'* (D. Brogan, *World Conflicts*, 1989)

moog *n.* [1969]
an abbreviation of Moog synthesizer, an electronic musical instrument, invented by the US engineer R.A. Moog, on which could be produced the full range of instrumental sounds, plus many that were beyond normal instruments played by humans.

* *'Martha somehow rounded up a Moog synthesiser and two guitars.'* (C. McFadden, *The Serial*, 1976)

Moonie *n.* [1973]
a nickname for the Unification Church, an evangelistic religious and political organization, largely seen as a somewhat sinister cult, founded in 1954 by the Revd Sun Myung Moon, a South Korean. It spread through the US (and to a lesser extent the West) during the 1970s, mopping up a variety of 1960s' casualties and kindred naive individuals.

* *'But most people didn't understand that you were a Moonie. If they ask you outright if you*

are raising money for Reverend Moon, you deny it, don't you?' (E. Heftmann, *Dark Side of the Moonies*, 1982)

moonwalk *n.*, *v.* [1969]
1. an exploratory walk on the moon's surface
2. in the mid-1980s a particular form of dance, in which the dancer appears to be sliding on the spot, an effect perfected by pop star Michael Jackson.

MOR *abbrev.* [1970]
an acronym for Middle Of the Road: simple popular music of little lyrical or musical merit, but adequate and saleable fodder for the pop charts and radio stations.

moral majority *n.* [1978]
1. *in the UK*: those individuals within a society who espouse traditionally conservative moralistic views (generally based upon an uncritical view of the Bible) and wish to impose them upon society at large; their assumption is that the majority of the country (while less vocal than their liberal opponents) feels much the same
2. *in the US*: the term originated as a descendent of the earlier Silent Majority, and the Moral Majority movement is an association of fundamentalist Christians who wish to reverse what they see as the godless advance of liberal philosophies.

* *'As so much of the Reagan era symbolism slips away . . . President Bush has quietly sidled away from yet another of his predecessor's "moral majority" positions.'* (*The Independent*, 6 April 1990)

motormouth *n.* [1988]
anyone who speaks fast, loudly and continuously. A Saturday morning children's television programme in 1991 was called *Motormouth*.

Motown *n.* [1960]
an abbreviation for Motor Town: thus Detroit, known to Americans from its main product as the Motor City. Motown describes a type of black music, originated by Tamla-Motown Records, founded in 1960 by Berry Gordy Jr, which mixed a heavy beat and a strong gospel influence and featured such artistes as The Supremes and Smokey Robinson.

* *'Though Berry Gordy wrote Jackie's first few hits and was once a close friend, Wilson never benefited from Gordy's success at Motown.'* (*Rolling Stone Illustrated History of Rock & Roll*, 1976)

mountain *n.* [1969]
any of the massive surplus stockpiles of food produced by the ➪EC as a spinoff from the ➪Common Agricultural Policy, under which farmers are heavily subsidized and thus produce more than is actually required by the Community's consumers. Among such stockpiles, some of which are dumped (sold cheaply) to ➪Third World nations, are butter and beef mountains, and a wine lake.

* *'The US is attempting to cut a swathe through Europe's grain mountains.'* (*Independent on Sunday*, 3 June 1990)

mountain bicycle (*or* bike) *n.* [1986]
the most popular style of bicycle today; these tough, multi-geared machines were ostensibly designed for use on rough mountain tracks, but have become increasingly popular, with their sturdy frames and thick tyres, as the ideal way of dealing with the bumpy rides that face

the urban cyclist on pot-holed city streets.

✱ *'Mountain bikes, light and rugged, with bulbous tyres and numerous gears, sprang from the hedonistic culture of southern California.'* (*The Independent*, 31 March 1990)

mouse *n.* [1960]
in computing: a small wheeled box, attached to a computer and equipped with certain electronic controllers, which, when teamed with suitable ⇨software and graphics can improve on the performance of keyboard-only computers in the field of high-resolution graphics. Developed by Xerox in 1960, but not widely recognized until the last few years, the mouse is most commonly touted as the best way for non-typists to operate their machine.

✱ *'If you purchase a new device, like a mouse or a scanner, you generally will receive device driver software with that device.'* (*Microsoft MSDOS User's Guide and User's Reference*, 1988)

Movement, the *n.* [1966]
the general name for the mix of New Left and student protestors fighting against US involvement in Vietnam and on a wider level, the entire youth movement of the 1960s.

✱ *'One law of Movement dynamics is that the Movement is never contained by political events – it is propelled by them.'* (R. Neville, *Play Power*, 1970)

✱ *'Political unity 'nuff to warm the heart of any Movement stumper.'* (L. Bangs, *Psychotic Reactions and Carburetor Dung*, 1988)

movers and shakers *n.* [1986]
energetic active individuals who get things done and influence others to act with similar enthusiasm.

✱ *'Some movers and shakers objected that the project as merely a remake of Peter Brook's . . . black and white version.'* (*Independent on Sunday*, 24 June 1990)

Mr Clean *n.* [1971]
an emblematic figure who embodies moral rectitude, especially a politician or other allegedly incorruptible public figure.

Ms *abbrev.* [1970]
title that replaces Miss or Mrs; the abbreviation was initially proposed in 1952 but only gained mass usage in the 1970s, when it became the most easily assumed badge of feminist liberation. The point of 'Ms' was that like 'Mr' – and unlike 'Mrs' or 'Miss' – it described the sex of the person addressed, but made no statement as to their marital status.

✱ *'He was also doing some very serious thinking about his secretary Ms Murphy, whom he'd been avidly trying to seduce.'* (C. McFadden, *The Serial*, 1976)

MTV *abbrev.* [1984]
Music Television: the 24-hour per day rock station originated in the US and now available on a variety of the world's satellite and ⇨cable networks. Basically a showcase for a nonstop parade of rock videos, it has reduced the music to little more than audio-visual wallpaper.

✱ *'PS – what is this fucking "M.T.V." Thought for sure it was some new drug, but Rick says no it's not.'* (L. Bangs, *Psychotic Reactions and Carburetor Dung*, 1988)

muesli belt *n.* [1972]
on the pattern of the older scampi belt (1950s, UK) and Borscht belt (1930s, US): an area primarily occupied by the consumers of muesli,

thus health-conscious, probably leftwing and *Guardian*-reading, keen on feminism, the ➪New Man, environmentalism, and kindred concerns.

multicultural *adj.* [1970]
a society that is made up of a variety of cultural groups and which acknowledges and accommodates the interests of each of those groups.

✱ *'The development of this country as a multicultural institution does not depend on the English any more.'* (J. Green, *Them*, 1990)

multimedia *n., adj.* [1962]
any of a variety of media technologies – recording, encoding, and editing video; scanning, drawing, painting, and manipulating photos and graphics; capturing, editing, and digitizing motion video and animation; editing and index text – all of which can be amalgamated for a multimedia package.

✱ *'This "multimedia" system is here to stay and its only limitation is your imagination. It is the future.'* (ad for Informix software in the *Sunday Correspondent*, 8 April 1990)

✱ *'Software vendors have now pledged to develop Windows-based tools for putting together multimedia presentations.'* (*Byte*, May 1990)

multinational *n., adj.* [1962]
any large corporation which possesses offices, factories or branches in a variety of different countries.

✱ *'A multinational group involved in defence engineering and offshore engineering.'* (recruitment ad for Qubit UK Ltd in *Independent on Sunday*, 8 April 1990)

multi-occupation *n.* [1963]
any dwelling which is occupied by a number of individuals (other than a family group), or by a number of separate families who share a kitchen and a bathroom.

✱ *'Another idea is to extend the relief available to adults in multi-occupation beyond the present limit of two persons.'* (*Sunday Correspondent*, 8 April 1990)

multitask(ing) *n.* [1986]
in computing: the concurrent execution of a number of different tasks, either jobs or processes, by the same machine.

✱ *'It operates in OS/2's protected mode and can exploit such multitasking features as simultaneous communication from multiple ports, and interprocess communications.'* (*Byte*, May 1990)

Muppets *n.* [1970]
a collection of puppets created by the late Jim Henson and used first in the children's programme *Sesame Street* and since 1976 on the *Muppet Show*. They include Kermit the Frog, Miss Piggy, and Fozzie Bear.

murder room *n.* [1968]
a special room set up by a police force to act as the base for the investigation of a murder.

muscle shirt *n.* [1961]
a tight shirt that is specifically designed to set off the development of its wearer's musculature.

musicassette *n.* [1966]
a tape cassette containing pre-recorded music.

music centre *n.* [1974]
a stereo system, often in a single ➪box. It invariably offers a tape cassette and record

player, with the possible addition of a graphic equalizer and other ⇨high-tech accoutrements.

* *'A system that requires you to understand as much about electronics as the buyer of a music centre knows about hi-fi.'* (D. Jarrett, *The Good Computing Book for Beginners*, 1980)

muso *n.* [1980]
a colloquialism for a musician, usually one who plays rock 'n' roll.

mutual assured survival *n.* [1985]
see MAS.

MX *abbrev.* [1976]
Missile-Experimental: the most advanced, if controversial of America's ⇨ICBMs. MX has been designed to combine two important factors necessary in an ICBM: pinpoint accuracy on target and, when a suitable basing system is developed, ⇨survivability. Ostensibly a ⇨second-strike counterforce weapon which will ride out a hostile attack, then act as the spearhead of a counterattack, its very accuracy makes critics in the US and USSR suspect that its real destiny is as a ⇨first-strike weapon.

* *'The interim plan of putting 40 MX missiles in silos was also unsuccessful.'* (R.C. Aldridge, *First Strike!*, 1983)

NA *abbrev.* [1980]
Narcotics Anonymous: an organzation for drug addicts, founded on the basis of the older Alcoholics Anonymous, using the same quasi-religious terminology, and basing their counselling on regular 'meetings' at which former junkies are encouraged to stand up and retail the travails of their own drug addiction and its aftermath.

* *'The opening announcements and the reading of NA's 12 traditions and 12 steps, adapted from those of Alcoholics Anonymous.'* (*Sunday Correspondent*, 10 June 1990)

naked ape *n.* [1967]
homo sapiens, man; the synonym was popularized by anthrolopologist Dr Desmond Morris, who in 1967 published his best-selling book *The Naked Ape*.

name of the game *n.* [1966]
the essence of an action, the basics.

nanny state *n.* [1962]
the concept of the state as a form of domineering over-protective nursemaid; the image is of the traditional bombazine-clad, endlessly admonitory British nanny, most recently epitomized to many (both critics and supporters) by the former prime minister Margaret Thatcher.

* *'However, I wonder whether even the vile anti-rambler landowners . . . are not to be preferred to the nanny bureaucrats who would like to turn the countryside into a glorified theme-park.'* (*The Independent*, 6 October 1990)

nanosecond *n.* [1960]
one billionth of a second.

* *'Nanosecond: One billionth of a second. That's a US billion which, by the way, is the one we prefer.'* (D. Jarrett, *The Good Computing Book for Beginners*, 1980)

nanotechnology *n.* [1990]
technology that works on the nano- (millionth of a millimetre) level; posited in the 1990 book *Engines of Creation: the Coming Era of Nanotechnology* by K. Eric Drexler. The technology can, in theory, arrange atoms from scratch, and build everything from silicon chips through to space colonies. Working as it does on the level of molecules, it holds none of the dangers of nuclear technology, and it minimizes the chance of polluting by-products.

* *'Nanotechnology also moves from the tiny to the vast, but promises benefits where Chaos only attractively patterned incoherence.'* (*Sunday Correspondent*, 3 June 1990)

Nashville *adj.* [1963]
pertaining to American country and western music; Nashville, Tennessee, is the home of such music, holding the majority of Country's recording studios and record companies, as well as C&W's showcase auditorium, the Grand Ole Opry.

* *'Nashville cats, they're clean as country*

water/Nashville cats, they're pure as mountain dew.' (Lovin' Spoonful, 'Nashville Cats', 1969)

nasties *n.* [1970]
unpleasant circumstances.

* *'The Conservative backbenchers who cheered John Major for delivering them from the nasties.'* (*Independent on Sunday*, 25 March 1990)

national curriculum *n.* [1988]
the core proposition of the Conservative education reforms of the 1980s, the imposition on schools of a nationwide curriculum, high on the Three Rs, emphasizing vocational work over the purely cerebral concerns associated with the arts, and downgrading the classics, history, literature, and modern languages in favour of engineering and the sciences.

* *'At the present time, NCC is concerned primarily with the introduction of the National Curriculum and its work is therefore of national importance.'* (ad for National Curriculum Council in *The Independent*, 5 April 1990)

National Front *n.* [1967]
Britain's Nazi Party, a far-right group who from 1967 usurped the extremist banner from Oswald Mosley's British Union of Fascists of the 1930s and turned their attentions to the country's coloured immigrant population, rather than the Jews who had been targeted by the BUF.

* *'The real catalysts . . . which brought the National Front to birth in February 1967 were the general election of 1966 and the convergence of Labour and Tory policies on immigration.'* (M. Walker, *The National Front*, 1977)

native American *n., adj.* [1973]
an American Indian, or, as an adjective, pertaining to that culture.

* *'Native Americans, folk heroes, nature healers, writers from Thoreau to Annie Dillard.'* (ad for University of Chicago Press in *New York Review of Books*, 19 July 1990)

natural *n.* [1965]
a synonym for ⇨Afro.

* *'There's nothing wrong with having a natural. I have a natural and I like it, but power for the people doesn't grow out of the sleeves of a dashiki.'* (B. Seale, *Seize the Time*, 1968)

NCC *abbrev.* [1988]
see **national curriculum.**

necklace *n., v.* [1987]
a petrol-filled tyre put round the neck of a victim and set alight; the notorious weapon of South Africa's young black revolutionaries in the internecine feuding in the townships. The term can also be used as a transitive verb.

* *'A mob of Wararas waylaid him on his way home . . . and necklaced him – put a car tire around his neck, poured gasoline on him, and burned him alive.'* (R. Malan, *My Traitor's Heart*, 1990)
* *'In an age of necklace killings and township riots, it was rather comforting to hear singer Eve Boswell's evocation'.* (*Sunday Correspondent*, 3 June 1990)

NEDDY *abbrev.* [1962]
a colloquial rendering of the abbreviation NEDC, the National Economic Development Council, a governmental quango created to offer economic advice.

* *'The great significance of Neddy is that it is the first time in this country that a concerted effort has been made by the Government, management and the unions to set the country moving on a course which can be steadily sustained.'* (*The Times*, 11 June 1963)

needle time *n.* [1962]
that proportion of broadcasting time that is, by arrangement with the unions, devoted to recorded music.

Nehru jacket *n.* [1967]
a long, narrow jacket with a high stand-up collar, named for Jawaharlal Nehru (1889–1964), the former Prime Minister of India. Sometimes called a Mao jacket, because of a similar (although shorter) garment worn by Chairman Mao and his millions of imitators in China.

neighbourhood watch *n.* [1984]
also known as **home watch**: a voluntary group of neighbours who band together to augment the usual police patrols in their area, reporting suspicious occurrences and individuals to the local police station.

* *'Protecting your home and setting up as Neighbourhood Watch scheme, if you want one, is largely your own responsibility.'* (*Independent on Sunday*, 21 October 1990)

nelly *n., adj.* [1961]
a pejorative for a weak, ineffectual person, often a homosexual; presumably from the rhyming slang Nellie Duff, meaning puff, thus poof, homosexual.

neo-colonialism *n.* [1965]
the indirect maintainance of colonial power, often over countries that formerly formed part of a nation's colonial empire, by using political and economic ➲leverage. – **neo-colonial** *or* **neo-colonialist** *adj.*

neo-conservative *n.* [1960]
the term was coined in the early 1960s, but its current use refers to the right-wing resurgence in the US and UK, stressing a style of conservatism that rejects the extremes of liberal/socialist utopianism and continues to believe that democratic capitalism is the ideal method of government, while still allowing for a degree of welfare state interference – payments to the needy, health insurance, etc.

network *n.* [1973]
in computing: the linking together of a number of machines – often as terminals operating from a large central computer – to pool data, speed operation, and to enable many operators to gain a degree of access and computing power that they could not obtain working alone on a single machine.
Also: **network front end**: an extra processor or other system which is used specifically to connect a computer into a network which already has a central computer. The intention of the extra machine is to improve overall network performance.

* *'386 and 486 PCs can be found in all sorts of weird and wonderful networks'.* (*PC World*, April 1990)

network *n., v.* [1981]
in business: the creation, in an ➲upwardly-mobile world, of a 'new boy net', usually geared to City arrivistes and media professionals. Self-conscious aggrandisement for a new establishment in a hurry. Also used as an intransitive verb.

* *'With the studied lack of respect for the work ethic and the exaggerated importance attached to the college . . . go a deadly insistence on clubbiness, on getting on, on "networking".'* (*The Independent*, 5 April 1990)

network architecture *n.* [1973]
the design and construction of a communications ➪network with regard to the communication it performs and the physical connections of its components. Such ➪architecture deals directly with encoding and transmitting of information, control of the data flow and of any errors within it, techniques for addressing the various subscribers to the network and analysis of the network's overall performance.

neutron bomb *n.* [1961]
the general term for what its developers called the enhanced radiation weapon, a bomb that was designed, with its extra radiation, to wreak greater havoc on human beings than on buildings.

* *'The neutron bomb is shorthand for a family of nuclear weapons, the basic research on which started in the 1950s.'* (C. Campbell, *War Facts Now*, 1982)

New Age *n., adj.* [1970]
the new spirituality that emerged from the ➪counter-culture and the ➪alternative society of the 1960s and which developed into a number of cult religions, variations on traditional Oriental themes and a general move into the mystic. The New Age has also fostered a number of *New Age therapies*, such as ➪est, ➪Rolfing, etc.

* *'Diamonds may be forever, but the New Age rock is a quartz crystal.'* (*The Independent*, 31 March 1990)

New Age music *n.* [1987]
a style of music popular in the mid- to late 1980s, typified by a fusion of jazz and classical themes, played on a variety of electronic ➪synthesizers and similar ➪high-tech instruments.

new aristocracy *n.* [1964]
the meritocracy of the Swinging 1960s – models, photographers, rock stars – all supposedly self-created products of the gutter who were now strutting centre-stage, and replacing the tired old aristocracy of traditional fuddy-duddy England.

* *'Far from repulsing those who were creating a parallel elite ("the new aristocracy") everything would be democratically hunky-dory.'* (J. Meades, *Peter Knows What Dick Likes*, 1989)

new Commonwealth *n.* [1960]
an identifying catch-all used by UK bureaucrats and politicians for those immigrants arriving from states other than Canada, Australia, and New Zealand, i.e.: coloured immigrants. This euphemism is doubly otiose, since apart from its essential racism, it is not even chronologically accurate since India was hardly a 'new' member of the Empire on which the Commonwealth was based.

* *'The government may have dignified the coloured population with the euphemism "New Commonwealth" . . . but there are no bonds of kith and kin here.'* (J. Green, *Them*, 1990)

new establishment *n.* [1985]
the ➪upwardly mobile classes of the 1980s; self-made members of the lower middle classes who were seen, as encouraged by their spiritual (and political) leader Margaret Thatcher to have replaced the old liberal Oxbridge-cum-landed gentry establishment with for-

ward-looking, business and technology orientated entrepreneurial skills, replacing the tired complacency of ➪wet Conservatives and (probably) leftwing academics and media figures.

✱ *'Those of us at the sharp end of national life had formed what I called the "New Establishment".'* (T. Blacker, *Fixx*, 1989)

New Frontier *n.* [1960]
a slogan and a concept initially coined in the 1930s, but brought to prominence by President John F. Kennedy when he accepted the Democratic Party nomination in 1960: 'We stand together on the edge of a new frontier the frontier of the 1960s, a frontier of unknown opportunities and paths, a frontier of unfulfilled hopes and threats . . . [it] is not a set of promises, it is a set of challenges. It sums up not what I intend to offer the American people, but what I intend to ask of them.'

New Georgians *n.* [1986]
the architectural version of the ➪Young Fogey, an individual who lives in a renovated Georgian house, carefully restoring its original features and in extreme cases forsaking such modern conveniences as electric light and central heating, and using only period furniture, hanging period pictures, etc.

New History *n.* [1975]
known in France as the '*Annales* school' (from the journal that champions this style of history) the new historians have abandoned the traditional preoccupation with monarchs, governments, wars and treaties, for the minutiae of births, marriages and deaths and a wide range of day-to-day events as experienced by the mass of the population.

new journalism *n.* [1972]
a genre of involved, concerned (although not especially campaigning or 'investigative') journalism that emerged in the mid-1960s from such writers as Tom Wolfe, Gay Talese, Jimmy Breslin, Hunter S. Thompson, *et al.* Aiming to resurrect the 'social realism' of the 19th century, the new journalists rejected the traditional objective style of reporting in favour of a trumpeted personal viewpoint, unrestrained speculation on almost any aspect of the story, a lack of worry as to the absolute facts and other 'straight' aspects of writing.

✱ *'I doubt if many of the aces I will be extolling in this story went into journalism with the faintest notion of creating a "new" journalism, a "higher" journalism, or even a mildly improved variety.'* (T. Wolfe (ed.), *The New Journalism*, 1975)

New Left *n.* [1960]
coined as a description by US sociologist C. Wright Mills (1916–1962), the New Left were youthful radicals who rejected the traditions of the ➪Old Left and attempted to inject novelty and energy into what was, in the wake of McCarthy, Hungary, and similar attacks and disillusions, more a name than an active radical movement. At its height during the protests against the Vietnam War, the New Left barely survived the end of US involvement, the source, undoubtedly, of its main rallying point.

✱ *'Certainly some jabs will be taken here at my cousin revolutionaries, especially those identified in the mind of the public as the "New Left".'* (A. Hoffman, *Woodstock Nation*, 1969)

new man *n.* [1975]
the post-feminist man: caring, sharing, and

rejecting the traditional ➪macho stereotype.

* *'I feel the same kind of embarrassment today when I am forced to witness the antics of the new man.'* (*Independent on Sunday*, 17 June 1990)

New Math(s) *n.* [1960]
a system of teaching basic maths which rejects rote learning of tables for methods that concentrate on encouraging the child to discover things for themselves; such maths also includes the basic forms of ➪set theory, number system, and symbolic logic, none of which would have been included in a traditional syllabus. The system evolved in the US, thus the original spelling 'Math'.

new penny/pence [1971]
the basic unit of Britain's decimal currency, which replaced the old pounds, shillings and (240 old) pence with pounds and (one hundred) new pence on 15 February 1971.
See also **decimalize.**

new politics *n.* [1972]
a shortlived revolution in US presidential politics whereby a number of liberal candidates including George McGovern and, Eugene McCarthy, attempted to set aside the domination of the old party machine, and replace it with a new degree of voter participation.

new realism *n.* [1988]
a term used in the British Labour movement, both by the Labour party and by its associate trade unions, to describe the way in which a number of hitherto fundamental socialist beliefs have been abandoned in the face of triumphalist Thatcherism, and the concomitant need to create a programme that will appeal to voters. Notable victims of the new realism are mandatory nationalization ('clause four' socialism) and unilateralism. Leftwing critics of the new realism feel that such policies strip away Labour's socialist appeal, and render the party, and the unions little more than old-fashioned (pre-Thatcher) Conservatives.

New Right *n.* [1980]
a coalition of conservative groups, originating in the US but growing in the UK during the Thatcher era, whose political and social platform is essentially aimed to reverse the advances made in the 1960s as regarded capital punishment, abortion, gay and lesbian rights, censorship and similar issues.
See also **moral majority.**

* *'In the US the New Right's on-going crusade against abortion, homosexuality and pornography gained new momentum with the re-election of Ronald Reagan.'* (V. Burstyn (ed.) *Women Against Censorship*, 1985)

new romantics *n.* [1980]
members of a youth movement, based on their musical taste, elaborately smart clothes, makeup, and ultra-cool style, that flourished in the early 1980s. They were also known as the **Blitz Kids**, from the name of the night club they frequented.

news peg *n.* [1960]
a news story that forms the basis of an editorial, feature, cartoon, etc.

new therapies *n.* [1970]
a variety of modern quasi-psychiatric therapies, including ➪est, ➪transactional analysis (TA), rebirthing, ➪co-counselling, ➪primal

therapy, etc., which have become popular in the past decade, most of which can be traced back to easy simplifications of Freudian theory and practice and which, unlike Freud himself, aim to eliminate the lengthy learning processes of classical analysis, instead promising to provide all who can pay their fees with a speedy and almost miraculous 'cure'.

* *'Freud never seemed to have foreseen the crowning achievement embodied in the new therapies which is the final obliteration of the notion of original sin.'* (A. Clare & S. Thompson, *Let's Talk About Me*, 1981)

new thing *n.* [1966]
a development first in jazz and then black writing in the 1970s which emphasized original and aggressive playing and writing and reflected the developments in black consciousness of the time.

new wave *n., adj.* [1960]
1. (from the French *nouvelle vague*) originally applied to a trend in film-making that developed in France during the 1950s, epitomized in the work of such directors as Francois Truffaut and Jean-Luc Godard.
2. the term surfaced in rock music *c.* 1976, defining the 'punk' music of the period, epitomized in the work of such bands as the Sex Pistols, the Damned, the Clash, and the Jam. – **new wave,** *adj.*

* *'Presently the noise of the new wave could be heard as he blasted himself with his favourite songs.'* (G. Sams, *The Punk*, 1977).
* *'To hear new-wave bands on the radio (a treat for American ears) and find the Empire jumping again.'* (L. Bangs, *Psychotic Reactions and Carburetor Dung*, 1988)

new woman *n.* [1985]
the ⇨post-feminist woman, freed of the old stereotypes, and able to assert herself as a woman in her own right, rather than as the adjunct to the traditional male.

* *'The New Woman must relate to herself, to become truly self-sufficient, spiritually, emotionally.'* (T. Blacker, *Fixx*, 1989)

new world order *n.* [1990]
the theory, posited by US President George Bush, that in the wake of the thawing of the Cold War in late 1989, and the decline of the Soviet Union as a superpower comparable to the US, a 'new world order' of peace, stability and international cooperation might be created to ensure a better future for all. This theory, which seemed at best utopian against the most optimistic background (early 1990) seemed even less tenable in the face of the Gulf War. Consciously or otherwise, Bush's usage unfortunately echoed the last proponent of such a new order, Adolf Hitler.

* *'Bush's dream of a new world order hangs on the edge of a volcano, with burning lava already rumbling below. Nothing will be as it was, not the Middle East, North Africa, East or West, not Christianity nor Islam, not the United States nor the rest of the world.'* (*Ma'ariv* (Israel), 8 February 1991)

nexus *n.*
originally (1663) the bond or link between two or more things, the term is currently used as a synonym for that place where things come to a point.

niche market *n.* [1983]
a new market that fills a gap between other long-established markets. Such niches can

prove highly profitable. Thus 'niche marketing': the finding of such a market; 'niche ➪player': one who exploits such markets.

* *'The market is now maturing, major niche markets have been identified and served.'* (*PC World*, April 1990)
* *'Market share – being creative with technology – exploiting new niche opportunities – is going to be the key to challenging the Japanese.'* (*Independent on Sunday*, 8 April 1990)

nightmare scenario *n.* [1990]
the worst possible circumstance, usually used with reference to a speculative future. The term became widespread during the Gulf Crisis, when a variety of ➪scenarios – whether utopian or nightmare – fuelled the contemporary debate.

* *'The "nightmare scenario" is now a sign of hope.'* (*The Independent*, 16 February 1991)

-nik *suffix.* [1960]
on the pattern of the original beatnik, the suffix -nik has been added to a variety of combinations, all implying 'an adept of': *folknik; nogoodnik; peacenik;* etc.

* *'Kate, who confessed to being a neatnik, also found Harold a total slob.'* (C. McFadden, The Serial, 1976)

nimby *n.* [1988]
an acronym for not in my back yard – the 'I'm all right, Jack' of the environment, referring to those who are happy to sanction development, rail links, etc., but only when suitably distant from their own home. The term gained nationwide popularity when attached to the policies of the then Minister of the Environment Nicholas Ridley who was seen to sanction a new town (much against local opinion) but complain against possible developments near his own home.

* *'The Nimby syndrome . . . has been applied to military installations, nuclear power stations, landfill rubbish disposal, and even wild life parks.'* (*Longman/Guardian New Words*, 1986)

nine-to-five *adj.* [1960]
referring to the regular working day.

nine-to-fiver *n.* [1960]
one who restricts their interest in work to those set hours; the assumption is that the quality of the work does not deserve any greater commitment.

nitrogen narcosis *n.*
see **rapture of the deep**.

nitty-gritty *n.* [1963]
the essence, the basics.

* *'He's not afraid to get down to the nitty-gritty of unpleasant problems.'* (*New York Times*, 27 June 1967)

Nixon doctrine *n.* [1970]
a foreign policy created by President Richard Nixon whereby the US would henceforth avoid any form of military entanglement or treaty that would lead her into the same destructive situation as had been experienced in Vietnam.

* *'Nixon advanced the idea informally to reporters in July 1969 . . . and soon his publicists elevated the notion to a "doctrine".'* (S. Karnow, *Vietnam*, 1983)

nod *v.* [1968]
to fall asleep, or at least become highly

comatose, after injecting, snorting, or smoking heroin. The effect of heroin is to depress the central nervous system, making the user appear sleepy. Adverbially the term is found as 'on the nod', as well as in the synonymous verb, 'to nod out'.

no-frills *adj.* [1960]
plain and simple, unadorned, stripped to the bone.

* *'An aggressive investigatory policy combined with tight editing and a no-frills presentation.'* (*The Listener*, 27 March 1969)

no-go (area) *n.* [1971]
any area that is forbidden to specified persons or groups, e.g. the Catholic areas of the Falls Road in Belfast which for a period were impassable for Protestant policemen.

no-goodnik *n.* [1960]
on the pattern of the ⊳-nik suffix in beatnik and peacenik, an unpleasant, untrustworthy person.

no-knock (law) *n.* [1970]
a law that sanctioned US policemen to make searches of individual property without a prior warrant or without issuing any warning (literally knocking on the door before breaking it down).

nominal *adverb.* [1966]
a synonym for yes; taken from the space jargon where it means 'in order' and refers to everything 'answering to its name'.

non-aligned *adj.* [1960]
any country that has not aligned itself with either of the two superpowers, the US or USSR, or any other power bloc.

* *'In its external relations Indonesia has for a long time pursued a non-aligned foreign policy.'* (J.D. & I. Darbyshire, *Political System of the World*, 1989)

non-book *n.* [1961]
one of a variety of books created for the gift or novelty markets; such books have no literary value nor, since they are usually non-fiction, do they deal seriously with the topic in question.
See also **instant book; coffee-table book.**

non-dairy cream *n.*
synthetic cream that is lower in fat and cholesterols than is real cream. It was invented primarily for reasons of cost and as a useful adjunct to mass catering, but recently, in a more health-conscious climate, it has also been promoted directly at those who like to keep an eye on their intake of fats.

non-event *n.* [1962]
a highly promoted event, often presented especially for the delectation of the assembled media, which turns out to be tedious and unimportant.

non-judgmental *adj.* [1965]
unbiased, free of prejudice; the term is neutral enough in itself, but in contemporary usage is usually within education or sociology, and implies that a supposed authority-figure will not praise or condemn an individual (often a child) by suggesting that their behaviour is wrong or right simply on the basis of normal 'bourgeois' society.

non-proliferation *n.* [1965]
any activity that prevents the spread of nuclear

weapons; thus the Non-Proliferation Treaty signed in 1968 by the US, USSR, the UK and an open-ended list of non-nuclear powers (by 1983 there were 117 of these). This treaty sought to restrict the further growth of national possession of nuclear arms. It has three major provisions: (1) the commitment by those states that already possess nuclear weapons not to make them available to any country that does not have them. (2) A pledge by the non-nuclear countries not to seek nuclear arsenals and to accept the regulations and monitoring of the International Atomic Energy Agency as regards their 'peaceful' use of nuclear power; in return the advanced nations promised to offer their nuclear reactor expertise to their poorer fellows. (3) An obligation on behalf of the nations with nuclear weapons to start serious talks on arms control and nuclear disarmament.

For all its vaunted importance, the NPT lacked signatures from those vital countries – Israel, South Africa and India – whose own nuclear programmes were reaching completion as well as those of the smaller nuclear powers – China and France – neither of which chose to sign.

NORAD *abbrev.* [1966]

an acronym for North American Aerospace Defense Command: an elaborate network of complimentary and overlapping surveillance systems designed to warn of imminent nuclear attack. NORAD, buried one third of a mile beneath Mt Cheyenne, Colorado – was opened in 1966 as one of the three hardened US command posts (the others are SAC HQ at Offutt AFB and the War Room in the Pentagon).

* *'There are fifteen steel buildings in the cold, gloomy tunnels of NORAD's netherworld installation.'* (D. Ford, *The Button*, 1985)

North *n.* [1976]

the industrially advanced and technologically sophisticated countries of the world, the bulk of which lie north of the Equator.

See also South; Third World.

* *'Jonathan's chat with the North and the South – which he tended to complicate by referring to, say, the Western world.'* (*Independent on Sunday*, 27 May 1990)

northern soul *n.* [1986]

the mainstream soul music of the 1960s, recycled during the 1980s as a 'new' fashion by Mancunian and other northern disc jockeys.

nose job *n.* [1960]

a cosmetic operation to alter (and thus improve) the shape of one's nose.

* 'Chapter Four: *In which Esther gets a nose job.*' (T. Pynchon, *V*, 1963)
* *'Thousands of older men and women who flock down . . . to improve their features. Tummy tucks, nose jobs, boob jobs, butt jobs, fat suctions, face lifts, you name it.'* (C. Hiaasen, *Skin Tight*, 1989)

nosh *n., v.* [1963]

from the Yiddish *naschen*, to nibble or eat on the sly, it means food, especially a snack, or, as a verb, to eat a snack.

* *'To nosh is to "have a little bite to eat before dinner is ready" or to "have a little something between meals."'* (L. Rosten, *The Joys of Yiddish*, 1967)

not *adj.* [1979]

an all-purpose term that sprang from the

1970s television comedy show *Not the 9 o'Clock News* and was extended to a variety of programmes, publications, etc., including *Not the Times* (produced during the shutdown of *The Times* newspaper); *Not the Royal Wedding*, etc.

notebook *n.* [1990]
the smallest available portable, battery-driven ➪personal computer, as near as possible the size of an A4 notebook (if not smaller), and designed to fulfill the same functions as do its paper-based equivalents.
See also **laptop, luggable.**

✱ *'Surely notebooks started arriving half way through last year? Well yes they did. And opretty damn good they were too. the Sharp PC 6200 won our Best Portable award.'* (*PC World*, March 1991)

nouveau pauvre *n.* [1965]
on the model of nouveau riche, the genteel poor, who were once well-off but have been forced to suffer 'reduced circumstances'.

nouveau roman *n.* [1961]
a term coined by Alain Robbe-Grillet (*c.* 1955) and further expanded in a book of essays *Pour un nouveau roman* (1963). It arrived in English *c.* 1961. In essence, Robbe-Grillet rejected such traditional trappings of the novel as plot, narrative, character delineation, and analysis and replaced them with a novel concentrating on things, a systematized, analystical, and highly detailed record of objects – rooms, adorning people, etc. It was through such infinite accumulating of detail that the reader was to appreciate the mental state of those who in the book were experiencing or seeing these objects.

nouvelle cuisine *n.* [1975]
from the French meaning 'new cookery': a style of health-conscious cooking, which was created by a group of French chefs in the 1970s as a direct challenge to the long-held primacy of cholesterol-filled overly rich French cooking.
See also **cuisine minceur.**

✱ *'The twee delights of nouvelle cuisine, which nobody really enjoys (and which leaves you as hungry as you were before you embarked on the dishes involved).'* (*Independent on Sunday*, 19 August 1990)

NOW *abbrev.* [1966]
National Organization of Women: founded in 1966, this was one of the earliest organizations to promote the contemporary ➪Women's Liberation Movement.

no way! *exclamation.* [1966]
impossible! it can't be done!

now generation *n.* [1967]
the fashionable young people of the 1960s; a media coinage, it was never used by those young people themsleves, other than ironically.
See also **beautiful people; me generation.**

no-win (situation) *n.* [1962]
an impossible situation in which there can be no victor.

✱ *'Sarah's attitude these days gave new resonance to the term "no-win" situation.'* (T. Blacker, *Fixx*, 1989)

nuclear freeze *n.* [1982]
a nuclear freeze does not seek to reduce weapons or to promote disarmament, but

simply to ban any further production of weapons, either in their current forms or as new systems. A freeze would demand an end to the production of the fissionable material used in nuclear weapons; of the manufacture and testing of warheads, the production and deployment of missiles, and the testing of any new strategic bombers.

* *'Brezhnev's proposal in START was meant to coincide with the appeals in the US Congress for a bilateral freeze on nuclear weapons.'* (S. Talbott, *Deadly Gambits*, 1984)

nuclear threshold *n.* [1960]
the time when nuclear weapons are finally used for the first time.

nuclear umbrella *n.* [1976]
the concept that US nuclear weapons are to be used in the defence of European countries as well as of the continental US. Such a concept, given the relative paucity of European arsenals and the proximity of the Soviet threat (although this, it is hoped, has been permanently lowered by the thawing of the Cold War), gives the US a certain degree of ➲leverage over its ostensible allies.
See also **linkage**.

nuclear winter *n.* [1983]
the concept, originated by Carl Sagan and other scientists, that the multi-megaton explosions of a nuclear war would shroud Earth's atmosphere in floating debris, shutting out the sun and terminating all that remained of natural life. Thus: **nuclear autumn**: a less intense version of the 'winter', but still severely harmful.

* *'For the first time it is demonstrated that severe and prolonged low temperatures, the "nuclear winter", would follow a nuclear war.'* (P. Ehrlich, C. Sagan, *et al.*, *The Nuclear Winter*, 1983)

nuke *n.*, *v.* [1967]
an abbreviation for a nuclear weapon, and thus, as a verb, to destroy with nuclear weapons.

number *n.* [1969]
number was used in a variety of contexts and had vague connotations with number in its musical sense, meaning tune or song and thus implied the repetitive playing of a given theme; like **thing** it presumes a complicity between the speaker and those to whom he/she spoke, and panders to the deliberately fostered inarticulacy of those who wishd to demonstrate how words are as nothing in face of cosmic consciousness. A **heavy number** is a difficult situation, to **roll a number** meant to make a joint.

* *'Their first priority . . . was to restructure their marriage. It was a heavy number, for sure, but they could do it.'* (C. McFadden, *The Serial*, 1976)

number-cruncher *n.* [1966]
in computing: a computer that is specially designed to perform lengthy and complex mathematical calculations at speeds of several million operations per second, thus dealing with problems that would take humans whole lifetimes to attempt. – **number-crunching** *adj.* – **number-crunch** *v.*

* *'Cray described how his little company . . . had come to build what are generally acknowledged to be the fastest computers in the world, the quintessential number-crunchers.'* (T. Kidder, *The Soul of a New Machine*, 1981)

numero uno *n.* [1973]
literally, number one: the best (both of objects and persons).

nunchaku *n.* [1970]
a weapon used in the martial arts, made of two hardwood sticks linked by a chain.
* *'Michaelangelo master of the whirling nunchakus.'* (*Teenage Mutant Hero Turtles*, June 1990)

nuts and bolts *n., adj.* [1962]
the basic elements, the essentials. Often used as **nuts and bolts person**, meaning someone who is good at tracing and dealing with the essentials of a problem.
See also **nitty-gritty**.

oater *n.* [1968]
also known as **horse opera:** a Western film with cowboys and Indians, ranchers and farmers, etc.

object-orientated programming *n.* [1978]
see OOPS.

ocker *n.* [1971]
an uncultivated Australian, epitomized by the *Crocodile Dundee* character; the term succeeded 'Alf'. Originally a nickname for anyone called Stevens, it gained widespread popularity in 1975 when comedian Ron Frazer portrayed a character whose name and manners were both 'Ocker'.

* *'The dreadful consequences of ocker realpolitik could be seen in* Savage Indictment *(C4).'* (*Independent on Sunday*, 24 June 1990)

OCR *abbrev.* [1966]
Optical Character Recognition: a process whereby a machine 'reads' into its own memory (by scanning, recognizing, and encoding it) information printed or typed in alphanumeric characters. In its simplest form, light is beamed onto the character and the reflected light projected onto a matrix of photocells; the output of the matrix is scanned and the received signal read into a storage cell where it is compared with a set of stored character patterns. The original OCR devices, marketed *c.* 1955, were strictly limited as to those characters they could recognize; more recent developments can read and encode copy that appears in many of the most popular typewriter faces as well as handwritten material, pre-20th century typefaces, etc.

* *'Scanners: Panasonic RS505 Flatbed Inc I/F Card and OCR S/W.'* (ad for Compuscan in *PC World*, July 1990)

off *v.* [1968]
to kill; presumably an abbreviation of 'turn off'. The term appeared in the 1960s when it was equally popular among radicals, ('Off the pigs!') and soldiers in Vietnam.

* *'Come the revolution they don't get offed with Pappalardi and West and George Harrison and all them other cats.'* (L. Bangs, *Psychotic Reactions and Carburetor Dung*, 1988)

off-off-Broadway *adj.* [1967]
the most radical and experimental of New York theatre which exists outside the 'real' theatre and concentrates on the impromptu, the improvised and the extreme, often only marginally definable as 'theatre'.

* *'An off-off-Broadway play,* Che, *was notable for containing the first act of sexual intercourse performed on stage.'* (R. Neville, *Play Power*, 1970)

off-piste *adj.*
any form of skiing that takes place 'off the beaten track', i.e. off the piste on which the majority of skiers perform.

* *'I think he means skiing is fun. And off-piste skiing is even more fun than skiing on the crowded and constrained piste.'* (*Independent on Sunday*, 24 February 1991)

off-road *adj.* [1973]
referring to any vehicle, usually employing four-wheel drive, a strengthened chassis and various other extras, that is to be driven across rough terrain rather than on the regular roads and highways.

offshore *adj.* [1972]
as **offshore funds**: investments that are registered outside an individual or a company's home country and which are therefore liable to more advantageous tax positions than those registered at home, due to the deliberate choice of a country of registration with less stringent demands than the US or UK. Similarly **offshore banks** refer to banks that exist outside the restrictions of the US or UK.

off-the-wall *adv.* [1974]
unconventional, unusual, possibly from the image of a ball bouncing off a wall at an odd angle.

* *'Certain of the engineers now entered what West called "the first off-the-wall period".'* (T. Kidder, *The Soul of a New Machine*, 1981)

oi *adj.* [1982]
referring to a style of music that featured dedicatedly aggressive posturing, similar to that of the ➪skinhead bands of a decade earlier, with a noticeable right-wing flavour. Thus **oi bands**, and **oi music**. The 'oi' comes from the onomatopoeic word with which one attempts to catch another's attenion, e.g., 'Oi you! Come here!'

* *'Such behaviour shouldn't be confused with the out-and-out thuggism of the early Eighties "Oi" bands.'* (*The Independent*, February 1991)

oil spill *n.* [1971]
the accidental escape of oil, usually from a tanker into a body of water; this environmental disaster kills fish and birds and as well as polluting the sea, may well drift onto the shoreline.

oil weapon *n.* [1974]
the use of oil pricing by the oil-producing countries to gain political ➪leverage on the oil-consuming countries. The 'weapon' was initially brandished in the aftermath of the Yom Kippur War between Israel and its neighbours in October 1973. Prices rose sharply as OPEC demonstrated its displeasure with Western support for Israel; the West's economy, which depends on oil for its energy, suffered accordingly.

old left *n.* [1960]
the traditional restrained, socialist Left which preceded the more radical, melodramatic ➪New Left of the 1960s; on the whole its members accepted traditional Marxism and the Party's values and directives as sent from Moscow, but rarely considered the guerilla tactics of their youthful successors.
See also **New Left**.

ombudsman *n.* [1966]
an official appointed to investigate complaints against public bodies by members of the public. The ombudsman is a Swedish creation: first instituted there in 1809 to oversee the fair operation of the legal system. The office was introduced in Finland in 1919, Denmark in

1954, and Norway in 1962. England's first ombudsman, Sir Edmund Compton, was appointed in 1966.

✱ *'That is what seized the public confidence and made the term "ombudsman" a trusted one.'* (*The Independent*, 31 March 1990)

on camera *adv.* [1962]
within the range of a film or television camera, a synonym for 'in shot'.

one-hit wonder *n.* [1969]
originally with reference to a pop star who scored one big hit and then vanished without trace; now extended to similar eruptions in a variety of contexts.

✱ *'One-hit wonders are very much less common in the computer world than they are in the music industry.'* (*PC World*, May 1990)

one-night stand *n.* [1963]
casual sex, specifically a brief sexual encounter that lasts for a single night, often the result of a liaison begun at a party or a club.

✱ *'It was as memorable a night as a no future, loveless one-night stand can be.'* (T. Blacker, *Fixx*, 1989)

one of us *n.* [1979]
on our side, our supporters, a political version of the snobbish PLUpeople like us and as popularized by Margaret Thatcher a term of some menace, insofar as those who are not thus classified have learnt to fear for their stability, professional or otherwise; used by Hugo Young for the title of his 1989 study of a decade of Thatcherism.

✱ *'The word had gone out from No 10 that he and his brothers were to be treated as one of us.'* (*Private Eye*, 16 March 1990)

one-on-one *adv.* [1967]
in direct confrontation, a synonym for ➪mano a mano.

✱ *'A way to enter three-dimensional space in your computer and interact with it, one-on-one.'* (*Byte*, July 1990)

on-going *adv.* [1960]
continuing, happening contemporaneously; like its linguistic soulmate 'situation' on-going represents a popular strain of current speech – the attempt to infuse perfectly simple actions or events with a veneer of ➪high-tech jargon.

✱ *'A comprehensive guide to all the world's major on-going conflicts.'* (*Sunday Correspondent*, 1 April 1990)

on song *adv.* [1967]
performing well, often used of an engine or of a sportsman or woman performing at their peak.

on the blanket *adv.* [1972]
referring to the protests made by imprisoned IRA terrorists who refused to wear clothes, or use the normal prison facilities as long as they were denied the status of political prisoners; instead they covered themselves only with blankets, smeared excrement on the walls, etc.

✱ *'Prisoners "on the blanket" . . . and by extension the whole republican movement see themselves as part of an unimpeachable tradition, up against an implacable enemy and entirely justified in all their actions.'* (*The Indepedent*, 26 February 1991)

OOPS *abbrev.* [1978]
an acronym for Object-Oriented Programming System: the ➪state of the art programming

system favoured by many computer programmers. As opposed to traditional structured programming, where each object, e.g. a cow, required the writing of many lines of program to specify all the variables – brown, grass, munching – that made it up, OOPS wraps together all those variables in a cohesive structure, the object that signifies 'cow'. Thus the programmer can create libraries of reusable modules, rather than rewrite new sections of the program whenever it is required.

op art *n.* [1964]
an art movement of the 1960s which specialized in producing dramatic effects on the viewer's optical system by creating sharply painted abstract patterns whose colour and contrasts forced the eyes to deal with fluctuating images, a 'shimmer' and other visual illusions.

* *'It dazzles like an object of the Op epoch which is also the past but not yet ye olden days.'* (J. Meades, *Peter Knows What Dick Likes*, 1989)

OPEC *abbrev.* [1960]
an acronym for Organization of Petroleum Exporting Countries, formed in 1960.

* *'The Vietnam defeat; the OPEC challenge; the erosion of dominance over capitalist rivals.'* (R.C. Aldridge, *First Strike!*, 1983)

op-ed *abbrev.* [1970]
Opposite the Editorial (Page): that page, initially in US newspapers but subsequently in general use, which stands opposite the editorial page and which carries the paper's regular columnists, feature pieces, possibly readers' letters, etc.

open government *n.* [1968]
any government which give full access to public interest and encourages the voters to participate.

open classroom *n.* [1971]
a style of education, especially at primary school level, where children are not forced to stay at their desks, but enjoy unstructured education, centred on investigation and discussion, rather than on traditional formal instruction.

* *'These groups aim particularly to purge American schools of the open classroom, the new math and creative writing, asserting that such relatively unstructured academic approaches break down standards of right and wrong, encourage 'socialistic' non- competitiveness and thus promote rebellion, sexual promiscuity and crime.'* (J. Green, *Encylopedia of Censorship*, 1990)

open heart (surgery) *n.* [1967]
surgery that is performed on the interior of the heart; while the heart is thus engaged, its circulatory function is taken over by a heart–lung machine.

open marriage *n.* [1973]
any marriage in which the partners agree to abandon traditional monogamy for a number of extraneous relationships; the assumption is that both partners should be allowed to enter into these without guilt and with the complete agreement of the other.
See also **serial monogamy**.

* *'A new lifestyle system which had recently become popular . . . that of open marriage.'* (T. Blacker, *Fixx*, 1989)

open systems *n.* [1986]
internationally agreed computer standards which have been designed to make it possible for a variety of manufacturers to produce machines that, although different in detail, can still communicate with each other.

Open University *n.* [1969]
a university founded in Britain in 1969 to provide tertiary education for adult working people; there is no campus as such, and courses are available through the radio, television, and by correspondence. As such it was originally known as the 'University of the Air'.

* *'In fact, at first sight, it looks horribly as if the Open University has been taken over by the Socialist Workers party.'* (*The Independent*, 6 October 1990)

OPM *abbrev.* [1981]
Other People's Money: the ideal financing for a speculator. One obtains money from another person and uses it as seen fit; if the speculator profits, then so does the other person, if the speculator loses, then only the other person need suffer the loss.

opt out *v.* [1989]
in education: for a school to opt out of local government control and arrange their own finances.

* *'The two Milton Keynes comprehensives . . . which opted out of Tory-run Buckingham's control last week after a bitter controversy.'* (*The Independent*, 24 May 1990)

Oracle *n.* [1973]
an acronym for Optional Reception of Announcements by Coded Line Electronics: a form of teletext system which broadcasts a continuous public information service to suitably adapted televisions. The name was apparently thought up over a lunch table, referring simply to the oracles of classical myth; the impressive expansion into an acronym came later.
See also **Teletext**.

* *'As the head of Oracle's engineering department you will be responsible for coordinating the work of our team of highly skilled hardware and software engineers.'* (*Independent on Sunday*, 8 April 1990)

oral history *n.* [1970]
a form of history that is based on the tape-recording of witnesses to a given historical event. What it may lack, in the raw data stage and in analysis, is compensated for by its immediacy.

* *'His chosen form is the oral history pioneered by Studs Turkel in which cross-cut voices recount a shared experience or epoch.'* (*The Guardian*, October 1988)

organic *adj.* [1972]
food or drink that is produced without the use of pesticides, fertilizers, etc. Organic farming dates back to 1940, but the description of its products is a more recent coinage, encouraged by the new interest in health and the environment that emerged in the late 1960s.

* *'The recent focus on the environment and increasing concern about the use of pesticides in farming have meant that organic wines are attracting keen interest.'* (*Bibendum wine list*, October 1990)

OTT *abbrev.* [1980]
over the top: an expression of disgust, amazement, shock, delight, amusement, etc., vary-

ing as to context. It originated amongst TV crews, but has long since spread into general use.

* *'If Bennett neglects the tidy novelist's craft – and parts are dull, obscure, or just plain OTT.'* (*Independent on Sunday*, 22 April 1990)

out *v.* [1990]
to expose someone as a homosexual against their will, a speciality of the New York ⇨gay magazine *Outweek* and in particular its column 'Gossip Watch'. Celebrities thus assailed include Richard Chamberlain (Dr Kildare) and the late Malcolm Forbes. The practice is known as **outing**, and its converse is **inning**: when a celebrity is known to be gay but the gay/lesbian community finds them (or more likely their politics) so reprehensible that it denies the fact.

* *'He would himself never "out" a public figure, he says.'* (*Independent on Sunday*, 22 April 1990)

out front *adj., adv.* [1968]
honest, open, candid.

* *'There can be no hard feelings when one is dealing totally out front on the bus.'* (T. Wolfe, *The Electric Kool-Aid Acid Test*, 1969)

out-of-body experience *n.*
the experience, claimed by a large number of people, of 'dying' and then returning to life; such experiences, which often happen when the person is seriously ill and lying on a hospital operating table, have certain consistent strains: one ascends to the ceiling and can look down on the medical team working on one's body; one may then move down a tunnel, at the end of which is a bright light; there may well be people within that light – dead friends, relations – who ask you to stay with them, but those who resist this siren call, and retreat down the tunnel, return to their body and thus to life.

* *'I had these out-of-body experiences where something would slip out of my head and go up into the corner.'* (*Independent on Sunday*, 17 June 1990)

out of it *adv.* [1963]
intoxicated by drink or drugs.

* *'Carlin had been so out of it at rehearsals that week.'* (B. Woodward, *Wired*, 1984)

out of one's tiny mind *phrase.* [1965]
crazy, utterly mad, a more emphatic version of 'out of one's mind'; a more emphatic version yet is 'out of your tiny Chinese mind', the *locus classicus* for which was its use by Labour politician Denis Healey.

out of sight *adv.* [1968]
amazing, remarkable; an essential hippie phrase, taken, like so many of its peers, from black slang. The word is also found as 'outasite' and 'outasight'.

outreach *n.* [1968]
1. the extending of government or social services beyond their current or conventional limits; especially in a situation where the people at whom these services are aimed are seen to be uninterested in using them and it is deemed necessary to bring those services to them, whether they desire such aid or not. Those who are employed in such activities are **outreach workers**.
2. in *religious use*: referring to anything directed primarily at the non-believer.

out-take *n.* [1960]
a sequence or scene that is rejected by the editor or director at the cutting stage and not included in the final film; out-takes often involve unscheduled moments of humour, actors forgetting their lines, effects failing to work, etc.

out to lunch *adv.* [1970]
eccentric, crazy.

* *'You got that letter I gave you this morning, or are you permanently out to lunch?'* (C. McFadden, *The Serial*, 1976)

Oval Office *n.* [1969]
the formal office of the president of the United States, thus the heart of executive power. The Oval Office was built in 1935 for Franklin D. Roosevelt; it had been the White House's old drying yard. The use of the term to denote presidential power came later, under President Richard Nixon (1968–74).

* *'The alleged conspiracy is perceived by most of the public as a distant and even amateurish intrigue, far removed from the Oval Office.'* (*New York Times*, 19 October 1972)

oven-ready *adj.* [1960]
prepared food that can be put straight into the oven with no effort from the cook, other than removing its packaging.

oven-to-table *adj.* [1979]
ovenware that can be used on the table as well as in the oven.

overachiever *n.* [1960]
a pupil who attains higher standards than their IQ had indicated should be expected; rather than praise such efforts, teachers tend to attribute them to neurosis, parental pressure, and other deviations from a preferred norm. Similar are **nonachiever** (1972) and **underachiever** (1960).

overdub *v.* [1962]
to add extra sound tracks to a basic recording – more instruments, vocals, special effects, or whatever is desired.

overkill *n.* [1968]
1. in a nuclear war; the concept of being able to destroy a target more than once; a requirement that justifies the building of massive arsenals and the firing of many missiles, but has no useful military application.

* *'The goal of reductions would have to be sacrificed to the goal of maximum overkill in t he SIOP.'* (S. Talbott, *Deadly Gambits*, 1984)

2. by extension from 1. any action that is seen to go too far in attaining its goal.

* *'In a modernn, highly technological society, with its CIA, FBI, electronic surveillance, and cops armed and equipped for overkill.'* (B. Seale, *Seize the Time*, 1968)
* *'However, the fear of hitting the economy too hard – of overkill – suggests a perverse appreciation of the present balance of . . . risks.'* (*Independent on Sunday*, 25 March 1990)

over-react *v.* [1961]
to respond with excessive emotion or force to a given situation.

over the top *adv.* [1980]
see **OTT**.

overview *n.* [1975]
a general wide-ranging view; from the concept of making an 'aerial surveillance' of an abstract or concrete problem.

own brand (*or* label) *adj.* [1970]
any range of goods marked not with the manufacturer's but with the retailer's name; Marks and Spencer's 'St Michael' brandname was one of the pioneers of this form of corporate labelling.

own goal *n.* [1987]
1. *in sport*: scoring against one's own team.
2. by extension from 1. any blunder that results in personal embarrassment, loss, or disaster; in IRA parlance an 'own goal' is a bomb that kills one's own men.

* *'No matter that many other forms of public housing have a similar record of own goals.'* (J. Meades, *Peter Knows What Dick Likes*, 1989)

Oxfam *n.* [1963]
an abbreviation for Oxford Committee for Famine Relief: the Committee was established in 1942 (although its popular nickname did not emerge for 20 more years) to help those suffering the results of the Second World War; since then it has concentrated on collecting and distributing food, clothes, and other vital supplies to disaster areas and to poor countries.

ozone shield *n.* [1976]
a synonym for the ozone layer that surrounds the earth at between 20–40 miles above its surface and shields it from the effects of excessive ultra-violet radiation. **Ozone layer** was coined in 1951, but it has only entered the mass consciousness in the last decade.

* *'They must campaign to repair the ozone layer, halt the greenhouse effect, preserve soils and save the tropical rainforest.'* (*Daily Telegraph*, Student Extra, 1989)

p (new penny) *n.* [1971]
the base unit of Britain's decimal currency, introduced as a replacement for the d. or old penny (named for the Roman denarius) in 1971.

PACE *abbrev.* [1984]
an acronym for Police and Criminal Evidence Act: an act designed to reform the system of police investigation of a crime, laying down precisely what is and what is not permissable during the process of investigation.

* *'Although PACE gave the police some extra powers, it also restricted their freedom of action.'* (R. Chesshyre, *The Force*, 1989)

Pacific Rim *n.* [1980]
those countries situated around the edge of the Pacfic Ocean – Japan, SE Asia, the West Coast of America, and which are seen as the next great area of commercial growth.

* *'Cheap knock-off products from the Pacific Rim and a cutthroat sales climate make entry into this market tough.'* (*Byte*, July 1990)

packaging *n.* [1962]
1. the putting together by one company – the ⇨packager – of every aspect of book production, from writing to design and printing, and then the selling of the finished product to a second company, who deal with the distribution.
2. *a synonym for* merchandising, the way in which a product is 'packaged' for mass consumption.

'This is probably called packaging by association.' (J. Meades, *Peter Knows What Dick Likes*, 1989)

packager *n*
1. [1970] *in publishing*: a publisher, e.g. Mitchell Beasley, Marshall Cavendish, who produces all aspects of a book – text, illustrations, design – often aimed at the ⇨coffee table market, but sells the distribution rights to mainstream publishers.

* *'He was a first-class editor, a one-man fiction factory, and a packager of genius.'* (*The Independent*, 18 February 1991)

2. [*c.* 1960] independent US television production companies who created TV shows and then sold them to the networks for transmission.

packet-switching *n.* [1971]
the transfer of packets of data over a communications system, each unit of data restricted as to size and bearing a specific address.

pack shot *n.* [1960]
a close-up shot of the product for which the advertisement is being made; usually the final climactic shot of the film.

pacman *n.* [1980]
an early computer game in which a small electronic blip is guided round a maze, encountering and attempting to avoid or destroy a variety of other electronic blips, which have

been programmed to destroy the adventurer.

* *'Happy Eaters are . . . flagged by their greedy logo, strangely reminiscent of the computer game pacman.'* (*The Independent*, 31 March 1990)

pager *n.* [1968]
a radio device that emits a sound when activated by a telephone call. The pager's owner can then find a telephone and make the necessary return call.

* *'We're looking at all these computer users, people who use fax machines, pagers, mobile communications, telephones, and are examining how we can best automate these processes.'* (*PC World*, November 1990)

Page Three (girl) *n.* [1969]
a tabloid newspaper pinup girl; the first paper to make regular use of such girls was *The Sun*, who placed them on Page Three; other tabloids have opted for page five or page seven, while the 'Sport' newspapers, taking the concept to the edges of unabashed 'men's magazine' publication, have Page Three girls on every page.

* *'This, he said, ignored the real problem, which was pornography and Page Three girls.'* (*Independent on Sunday*, 13 May 1990)

page-turner *n.* [1974]
a best-selling book that keeps its readers fascinated until the end.

pain threshold *n.* [1962]
the degree of pain which will become unbearable; this differs as to the individual under consideration.

Paisleyite *n.* [1966]
a devotee of the Revd Ian Paisley MP, Ulster's most conspicuous Protestant hardliner, whose intransigence reflects that of his equally hardline constituency. Thus **Paisleyism**: the philosophies so promoted.

Pak(k)i *n.* [1964]
pejorative abbreviation for Pakistani. The term originated when the majority of Asian immigrants were indeed from Pakistan, but latterly those thus categorized may well be East African Asians or Bangladeshis. By extension, **Paki-bashing**: deliberate racist assaults on Pakistanis.

* *'Then another technician says of Datsuns: "Paki-taxis – that's all they're good for".'* (J. Meades, *Peter Knows What Dick Likes*, 1989)
* *'There's nothing like a good bit of Paki-bashin' they all agree.'* (N. Fury, *Agro*, 1971)

palimony *n.* [1979]
on the pattern of alimony, the money paid by one half of an unmarried partnership after the relationship collapses. The term was coined in 1979 when film star Lee Marvin was sued by his ex-girlfriend Michele Triola Marvin who claimed that she had abandoned her own career to support him.

* *'The former singer is suing Marvin for "palimony" of up to half of the £3.6 million he made while they were living together.'* (*Chronicle of the 20th Century*, 1988)

pancake roll *n.* [1967]
also known as a **spring roll**: a staple Chinese hors d'oeuvre: a pancake with savoury meat and/or vegetable fillings, rolled, sealed, and deep fried.

* *'Sesame oil can be recommended for use as a dip when serving and consuming spring rolls.'* (K. Lo, *Memories of China Cookbook*, 1982)

panda-car *n.* [1966]
a police car, introduced to replace the officer walking the beat, which was so named after the Giant Panda (a popular animal hero of the 1960s) because of the broad white stripe that was painted on it.

panda-crossing *n.* [1962]
a type of pedestrian crossing which was designed to supplement Britain's traditional zebra crossing; the difference was that while the zebra had parallel black and white lines, the panda had black and white chevrons. The pandas also operated differently: while the lights at a zebra operate continually, and motorists are obliged to give way to pedestrians, panda crossings were operated by a push-button and cars only stopped when the pedestrian pressed that button to activate the flashing signals.

pant-suit *n.* [1970]
a synonym for trouser suit: a woman's suit consisting of matching trousers and jackets, as opposed to the traditional woman's suit which substituted a skirt for the trousers.

paparazzo (*pl.* paparazzi) *n.* [1968]
a freelance photographer who specializes in taking pictures of celebrities, the less guarded the celebrity the better. The word – like the originators of the practice – is Italian.

paralegal *n., adj.* [1972]
anyone trained, but not fully qualified in the law and thus employed in a legal office as a trainee or apprentice. The term is also used as an adjective, e.g. *paralegal services.*

Paralympics *n.* [1965]
an international sports competition modelled on the Olympic Games and designed for competitors who are confined to wheelchairs; more popularly known as the 'Wheelchair Olympics'.

paramedic *n.* [1963]
1. *in medicine:* an auxiliary worker; from 'para-' meaning 'similar to but not an exact copy'. – **paramedical,** *adj.*
2. *in military use:* (a contraction of 'parachuting' and 'medic') a corpsman (a soldier trained in medical skills) who actually parachutes into the battle to tend the wounded.

* *'According to a paramedic quoted in the report, Israeli police stopped the ambulance for ten minutes, and a furious shouting match ensued.'* (*The Independent,* 1 November 1990)

parameter *n.* [1962]
a boundary, a limit, a basic factor, a framework: parameter has a number of highly specific, technical, and abstruse meanings in mathematics, none of which seem to have been appreciated by those in business, government, communications, media, etc., who have elevated it into one of the most widely used (and abused) of recent vogue words.

* *'Despite the fact that she and Harvey hadn't finalized the parameters of their own interface . . . they were just terrifically stable right now.'* (C. McFadden, *The Serial,* 1976)
* *'These parameters, or limits, excluded four particular areas from detailed report or discussion.'* (H. Young, *The Crossman Affair,* 1976)

paramilitary *n., adj.* [1973]
originally used for any force or organization

which has a function similar to that of a military force, but is not composed of professional miltary personnel; the current use (in the UK) refers most commonly to a number of armed Protestant factions in Northern Ireland – the UFF, the UVF, etc. The nominally Roman Catholic IRA are technically paramilitary too, but political considerations have them listed simply as 'terrorists'.

paraprofessional *n.* [1967]
anyone without full professional training, but with sufficient knowledge, to whom certain aspects of a professional task can be turned over.
See also **paralegal, paramedic.**

paraquat *n.* [1961]
the trade name for dimethyl sulphate: a quick-acting contact herbicide that is rendered inactive when it touches the soil.

parascending *n.* [1970]
a sport in which the participants wear open parachutes and are towed behind a vehicle until they have gained sufficient height to be released, at which point they drift back to earth, often towards a specific target zone. – parascend, *v.*

parascience *n.* [1965]
any science that concetrates on studying phenomena usually considered outside the scope of conventional scientific research, or for which no scientific explanation exists.

parasuicide *n.* [1990]
a form of attempted suicide which results more from a cry for help than any attempt at deliberate self-harm.

* *'Measurable parameters of psychic stress – parasuicide . . . and acute psychiatric admissions to hospital.'* (*Independent on Sunday*, 3 June 1990)

parenting *n.* [1963]
the act of being a parent. – **parent,** *v.*

* *'But she was glad she had a chance to parent all over again with Tamalpa, Gregor, and Che.'* (C. McFadden, *The Serial*, 1976)

parity *n.* [1965]
a situation in which two hostile nations can offer equal military capability; especially in the case of a conflict between the US and USSR.

parkway *n.* [1972]
a British Rail station sited in the countryside rather than in the traditional town or village. Such stations act as a magnet for local commuters and invariably feature outsize carparks.

partner *n.* [1986]
currently the most popular non-specific designation of one half of a couple; carefully neutral, it categorizes neither as to sexual orientation nor to marital status.
See also **Ms.**

* *'Your Partner. Surname. Mr/Mrs/Miss/Ms.'* (application form for Lloyds Bowmaker loan in *The Independent*, 13 March 1990)

part-work *n.* [1969]
any publication that appears in regular weekly parts; such publications are usually reference works, giving the purchaser a complete guide to gardening, do-it-yourself, adventurous sex, or whatever.

PASCAL *n.* [1968]
a computer language named for the French mathematician Blaise Pascal (1623–62); it is designed to enable the teaching of programming as a systematic discipline and as such was especially favoured by the scientific community.

* *'PASCAL is based on ALGOL, emphasizing aspects of structured programming, and extending ALGOL with . . . data structuring facilities.'* (Macmillan, *Dictionary of Data Communications*, 1985)

passive smoking *n.* [1975]
the inhalation of toxic, carcinogenic cigarette smoke by non-smokers; this has been proved to occur whenever one is in proximity to a smoker.

patrial *adj.* [1971]
referring to those who have the right to live in the UK; thus **non-patrial**: the opposite; in many cases the two words appear to stand for 'white' and 'non-white' as far as immigration practice is seen to work.

* *'Abandoning the old distinction between "aliens" and Commonwealth citizens, this focussed on the distinction between patrials (those persons born, adopted, naturalized or registered in the UK . . .) and non-patrials.'* (J. Green, *Them*, 1990)

pax Americana/pax Sovietica *n.* [1967, 1969]
the contemporary descendent of the 'pax Romana': the peace and stability that can be exercised by a superpower, whether imperial (as was Britain) or quasi-imperial, as is America.

* *'Saddam Hussein has provided the first challenge to the pax Americana. One day we may all be grateful to him.'* (*Independent on Sunday*, 19 August 1990)

payload *n.* [1965]
1. *in military use*: the bombs, warheads, etc., carried in a military aircraft; or the capsule, instruments, astronauts, etc., carried in a space vehicle.

* *'A ballistic missile consists of a rocket booster, a guidance system, and a payload (which may contain conventional, explosive or nuclear warheads).'* (M. Stephenson & J. Wheal, *Nuclear Dictionary*, 1985)

2. *in air travel*: that part of an airliner's load from which the company makes its money: the passengers, cargo, and possibly airmail.

payroll tax *n.*
see **SET**.

PCB *abbrev.* [1966]
polychlorinated biphenyl: one of a number of compounds derived from biphenyl (C_6H_5) which are used widely in industry especially as electrical insulators and in plastics; PCBs pollute massively and as such are among the leading environmental villains. PCB manufacture was discontinued in the US in 1976.

* *'PCBs don't break down in soils, water or air, but carry on accumulating. PCBs can kill birds, and sea mammals'.* (*Daily Telegraph*, Student Extra, 1989)

PCP *abbrev.* [1970]
phencyclidine: an animal tranquillizer which has been used as a recreational drug with hallucinogenic qualities.
See also **angel dust**.

* *'Police reported that the drug was PCP, a Parke-Davis product not sold for human medical*

purposes since 1963.' (*Las Vegas Review-Journal*, 1971)

Peace Corps *n.* [1960]
an organization set up by President John F. Kennedy to train and send US volunteers to foreign countries to help meet the lack in such countries of skilled manpower; the aim of the Peace Corps was that while its workers brought with them US expertise, they lived amongst the people with whom they worked, and accepted their lifestyle, rather than trying to impose external Western standards.

* *'That peripatetic child of the marriage between Baden-Powell and John F. Kennedy, the US Peace Corps, is entrenched throughout the Third World.'* (R. Neville, *Play Power*, 1970)

peace dividend *n.* [1990]
the idea that were the annual arms budget (of the US, UK, etc.) to be reduced (given the supposed end of superpower rivalry) the resultant increases in national economies could be used for improving the home economy, the lot of the poor, etc. Another version of beating swords into ploughshares.

* *'Those Westerners who are in such a hurry to dismantle Nato's defences and reap that imaginary "peace dividend" might do well to take the pompous marshal more seriously.'* (*Sunday Correspondent*, 13 May 1990)

peace-keeper *n.* [1961]
any organization dedicated to keeping the peace whether between nations or individual communities. The function of that organization is **peace-keeping**.

peacenik *n.* [1963]
patterned on the ➲-nik suffix first used in beatnik and thus carrying the same pejorative feel: any member of a pacifist movement, especially those young people who united in their opposition to the Vietnam War. The term has persisted, whether as a description of those who opposed the Gulf War, or in Israel, where it describes those who seek some form of accommodation with the Palestinians.

Peace People *n.* [1976]
a short-lived organization in Northern Ireland, founded by two Catholic women, Mairead Corrigan and Betty Williams, which for a while attracted support from both Catholic and Protestant communities before, borne down by the intractable problems of the province, it collapsed. The two women won the Nobel Peace Prize in 1977.

peace sign (*or* symbol) *n.* [1969]
two fingers are raised in a V and the the palm is turned outwards, the reverse of the traditional hostile 'V-sign' in which the palm is turned in.

peace studies *n.* [1972]
any course of studies that concentrates on the subject of peace among nations and the best means of achieving it; despite such ostensibly laudable aims, peace studies became the bête noire of the right wing, who saw them as barely disguised Marxist propaganda, propagated to innocent schoolchildren by hard-left products of 1960s polytechnics.

* *'Remember peace studies? They were the rage among teachers of a certain political persuasion in the early 1980s.'* (*Daily Telegraph*, Student Extra, 1989)

peak experience *n.* [1962]
coined by Abraham Maslow to describe the breakthrough moments of supreme emotional significance that transcend any other levels of perception that may hitherto have been achieved; the sensing of life's every nuance with one's entire being.

pedal steel (guitar) *n.* [1969]
an electric guitar that is fixed on a stand rather than held by the player, and which is attached to foot pedals which can alter the tension of individual strings and produce special glissando effects.

pedestrianize *v.* [1963]
to ban cars from a section of roadway and to turn it into a pedestrians-only area; such areas, e.g. London's Carnaby Street or Covent Garden, tend to be aimed at tourists and shoppers. The creation of these **pedestrian precincts** was first put forward in the Buchanan Report on Britain's traffic system, published in 1963.

penalty clause *n.* [1967]
any clause in a contract – particularly those involving building or manufacture – which states that if that contract is not fulfilled by the agreed date, the party who has thus failed to keep to the contract will suffer a financial penalty.

penalty shoot-out *n.* [1978]
a means of determining an otherwise drawn soccer match when no result has been obtained even after the playing of extra time. Five players are designated from each side to take penalties in turn. The side who score most win. If this also produces a draw, the players enter a sudden-death contest.

penetrate *v.* [1962]
in espionage (political or industrial): to infiltrate a rival government, organization, etc.

* *'He organized a train-wrecking group until it was penetrated and the survivors fled.'* (L. Deighton, *The Ipcress File*, 1962)

people-centred *adj.* [1968]
any organization, philosophy, or other mode of operation which concentrates on serving the needs of individual human beings rather than on larger political or economic entities.

people journalism *n.* [1979]
that style of journalism dedicated to the celebration of the famous, no matter how transitory and trivial is their success, taken from the social section of *Time* magazine, entitled 'People' and latterly from *People* magazine, which exists solely on celebrities.

people mover *n.* [1968]
any means of moving people from one place to another.

people sniffer *n.* [1965]
a device that can detect the presence of a person by analysing the chemical presences in the air around them. The equipment was originally developed for use by US troops, searching for Viet Cong in the Vietnam jungles.

PEP *abbrev.* [1986]
an acronym for Personal Equity Plan: a scheme launched by the Tory government in 1986 which made it possible for individuals to invest up to £2400 per annum in UK shares without having to pay capital gains tax or tax on dividend income.
See also **Tessa**.

* *'For investors, an in-house Pep scheme is likely to prove much cheaper than one run by investment managers as a profit generator.'* (*Independent on Sunday*, 8 April 1990)

Pepsi Generation *n.* [1969]
coined by writer Nik Cohn in *Queen* magazine *c.* 1968, and used to mock the advertisement 'It's the real thing: Coke'. The Pepsi generation, which like the eponymous drink was de facto not the 'real thing', was composed of a wide range of trendy posers, what Cohn has called 'the fashionable mock-hip movement'.

* *'He also wears a crutch and a sign saying "You're in the Pepsi Generation and I'm a pimply freak!"'* (T. Wolfe, *The Electric Kool-Aid Acid Test*, 1969)

perestroika *n.* [1987]
from the Russian meaning rebuilding, reconstruction, or reform. An attempt spearheaded by premier Mikhail Gorbachev to revolutionize the USSR by a complete radical overhaul of the nation's over-bureaucratized corrupt administrative and economic institutions.
See also **glasnost**.

* *'Mikhail Gorbachev served the Soviet forces notice last week that they, like the rest of the country, had to change and submit to perestroika and reform.'* (*Independent on Sunday*, 13 May 1990)

performance art *n.* [1971]
any form of 'artwork' which comprises a variety of forms: dancing, acting, music, film, video, etc. – all of which are intended to execute a prescribed course of actions before an audience.

* *'A non-theatrical theatre that, developing from the New York happenings, has become known as performance art.'* (R. Hewison, *Too Much*, 1986)

performance car *n.* [1976]
a top-ranking car which gives very good performance as regards speed, fuel consumption, braking, etc.

* *'In the past the design and construction of performance cars has rarely been influenced by nature. The dominating influence tended to be engine power.'* (ad for Honda cars in *The Independent*, 6 October 1990)

peripheral *n.* [1966]
equipment linked to the central processing unit of a computer which enhances and increases its basic functions: printers, extra disk drives, external ⇨hard disks, terminals that connect with other machines, etc.; peripherals may be ⇨**smart** – with some processing ability of their own – or, if bereft of such ability, ⇨**dumb**.

* *'We were the first company to sell peripherals and software exclusively for IBM personal computers.'* (ad for PC Connection in *Byte*, June 1990)

permissive society *n.* [1966]
a catch-all description (usually offered by those who deplored it) of the social revolution of the 1960s, both in the new attitudes to the arts (the Obscene Publications Act), abortion, homosexuality, and to capital punishment, as well as in the general loosening (if only for a while) of Britain's long-outdated adherence to ⇨Victorian values.

-person *suffix.* [1970]
in the decade and a half since the burgeoning of the women's liberation movement, the

attack on 'male' vocabulary – spokesman, chairman, etc. – has led to a widespread use of 'person' in a variety of neologisms – *spokesperson; chairperson*; etc. Despite the ostensible androgeneity of these usages, it can usually be assumed that in such awkward contexts, '-person' equals 'woman'.

See also **herstory; wimmin; woman-**.

* *'I've got this feeling. Like maybe Ms has a contract out on me or something, You wanna be the hitperson?'* (C. McFadden, *The Serial*, 1976)
* *'Twenty years we've been married . . . and a month after you split, you get it on with a handyperson.'* (C. McFadden, *The Serial*, 1976)

personal computer *n.* [1977]

any computer that was designed for use by an individual, whether in the office or the home; such computers were naturally smaller and initially slower than their cousins the machines used by the military, by scientific institutions and by business and industry, but within their limits they offered for the first time real computing power to a vast new section of society.

* *'Before the Dell System 325 was named the top 386 personal computer by the rest of the world, it had quite a following at home.'* (ad for Dell Computer Corporation in *Byte*, June, 1990)

personal organizer *n.* [1986]

a synonym for the ➪Filofax, a 7" x 5" ring binder stuffable with supposedly vital information, was a long-running merchandising hit. Filofax being a trademark, the many imitators – from Woolworths upwards – had to coin this lower-case generalization.

* *'Filofax Group, manufacturers of the eponymous personal organizer, is desperate to throw off "the wretched tag of being a yuppie product" according to chairman David Collischon.'* (*The Independent*, 6 April 1990)

PERT *abbrev.* [1964]

an acronym for Programme Evaluation and Review Technique: a method of controlling and monitoring the progress of long-term projects by analysing each successive step as it is taken, both on the basis of the step seen in isolation, and as it exists in relation to the rest of the project.

* *'PERT stands for Programme Evaluation and Review Technique. A Pert chart is a graphical representation of the relationship between activities.'* (*PC World*, October 1990)

Peter principle *n.* [1969]

coined in 1969 by Dr. Lawrence Peter: the concept that in a large organization every individual is promoted to one level above their actual competence.

petit suisse *n.* [1966]

a small round fresh cream cheese; petit suisse was developed in 1850 by a French farmer's wife; it only gravitated across the Channel, like so many other 'exotic' foodstuffs, in the 1960s.

* *'Express distribution of the cheese, which was called Petit Suisse, was done in Paris in yellow-wheeled cabriolets with bells.'* (P. Rance, *The French Cheese Book*, 1989)

petro- *prefix.* [1973]

various combinations using petro- existed briefly in 1970s, including *petrofunds; petropower;* and *petrocrat*, but the only commonly used survivor is **petrodollars**: surplus dollars that are accumulated by oil-exporting nations and which are used for investments in and loans to oil-importing countries. When based on UK currency they become **petro-sterling**.

PGM *abbrev.* [1975]
precision-guided munitions: mass-produced, often lightweight or hand-held armamaments such as anti-tank or anti-aircraft missiles; with increased destructive power and flexibility of use (from air, sea, or land), they have vastly increased the vulnerability of many formerly 'impregnable' targets.

phallocrat *n.* ([977]
from the French *phallocrate*: anyone who calls for, or already assumes the pre-eminence of the male within a male-dominated society; as such a target villain for feminists and their allies, liberated gays. Thus **phallocracy** (on the pattern of 'aristocracy'): those who espouse such a philosophy.

phone-in *n., adj.* [1967]
any radio programme which permits listeners to call in to the presenter and give their own point of view, quiz the guest speaker, and similarly participate in the show.

✱ *'There were the usual phone-ins and rap music (only the guys who service the car normally find that wavelength . . .).'* (*Independent on Sunday*)

phone phreak (*or* freak) *n.* [1971]
anyone who employs their knowledge of the telephone system to make free calls; by sending tones down the phone lines to obtain unlimited free long-distance calls. A number of those who later played a major part in developing the ⇨personal computer industry started life as phone phreaks, using their special 'blue boxes' to send the necessary pulses down the line.

✱ *'Draper was helped by discovering a network of phone phreaks with similar interests, many of whom were blind men who could easily identify the tones which could whizz one through the system.'* (S. Levy, *Hackers*, 1984)

photofit *n., adj.* [1970]
a development of the ⇨identikit, in which a picture of a suspect is built up by combining a number of photographs (rather than drawings) of discrete facial features, as suggested by an eye-witness.

photo opportunity *n.* [1976]
an offshoot of politics' move into show business – carefully concocted events destined to look good on the front page or in the television news. The verbal equivalent -the newsworthy oneliner – is the ⇨'sound bite'.

✱ *'Gorillas: photo-opportunities in the mist.'* (*Sunday Correspondent*, 25 March 1990)

pig *n.* [1968]
a popular description for the police in particular and members of the Establishment in general; coined as early as the 18th century (for policemen), revived by the 1960s radicals, and still popular in extremist circles.

✱ *'Chicago is the capital of PIG NATION. There the pigs don't wear bell-bottoms and peace symbols, they wear riot helmets and gas masks.'* (A. Hoffman, *Woodstock Nation*, 1969)

pill, the *n.* [1960]
a popular abbreviation for the oral contraceptive pill, the first version of which, Enovid, was put on sale to US women on 9 May 1960.

✱ *'We live with them, as we live with The Bomb, The Pill, Vietnam, and The Space Race.'*

(H. Davies, *The Beatles*, 1968)

* *'After the Pill arrived, it became de rigeur to scorn the condom. "Like having a bath with your socks on,' was the wisdom of many a teenage roue.'* (*Independent on Sunday*, 19 August 1990)

pina colada *n.* [1967]
from the Spanish meaning 'strained pineapple': an alcoholic drink made of pineapple juice, coconut, and rum.

pindown *n.* [1988]
an illegal system of discipline used in certain secure children's homes in Staffordshire and operated by the county's social services. Pindown, which came to light in a report published in 1991, was allegedly used only as a last resort tactic in dealing with consistently problematic children. It consisted in isolating the children in solitary confinement for indeterminate periods. During this time they were provided with only basic meals, often had to remove all clothes but their underwear, and received little or no communication from the outside world or workers in the home.

ping-pong diplomacy *n.* [1971]
those tentative attempts to re-establish diplomatic relations between the US and China which were initiated in 1971 with the sending of a US table-tennis team to the People's Republic.

Pinteresque *adj.* [1970]
characteristic of the works of the British playwright Harold Pinter (1930–); the term usually refers to meandering dialogue, often covering thinly veiled menace, which is filled with significant pauses between the words and sentences. The menace aside, such dialogue is supposed to represent the way many people actually converse, rather than in the well-turned *bons mots* of traditional theatre.

Pinyin *n.* [1963]
from the Chinese 'spell sound': a system of Romanized spelling for the representation of the Chinese language, originally introduced in China as a teaching aid in 1958, and gradually adopted in the West since the mid-1970s. Pinyin replaces the earlier Wade system (named for the British scholar and diplomat Sir Thomas Wade, who devised it in the mid-19th century). It is supposed to recreate more accurately the sound of spoken Chinese and has radically altered many common words, e.g. Beijing (Peking), Mao Zedong (Mao Tse-tung), and Zhou Enlai (Chou En-lai).

pipelining *n.* [1971]
the regulation of computing processes whereby one must be concluded before the next can be initiated; using special modules which can operate concurrently, these processes can be considerably speeded up, and thus vastly increase the operating efficiency of the whole system.

* *'Acting on its assumption it finds, fetches, and decodes instructions ahead of time. It "gets them in the pipeline".'* (T. Kidder, *The Soul of a New Machine*, 1981)

pirate radio *n.* [1964]
any form of radio that has not been licensed by the British government; the first pirate radios emerged in the mid-1960s – Radio London, Radio Caroline; a new group began broadcasting twenty years later, catering mainly to the young people of the inner cities.

* *'The thinner of the two was Ronan O'Rahilly, the founder of Pirate Radio in England.'* (R. DiLello, *The Longest Cocktail Party*, 1971)

pisshead *n.* [1961]
a drunk.

* *'He told me the beer at the university was grot – "I should know: professional pisshead".'* (J. Meades, *Peter Knows What Dick Likes*, 1989)

pixel *n.* [1969]
used as a noun, but actually an abbreviation of picture element: a discrete coded unit or element of the bit-map mosaic that represents the image area of a letter or other graphic form.

* *'Blistering pace. Pixel perfect passing. Superb tactical gameplay.'* (ad for Anco Software in *Ace*, February 1991)

planning blight *n.* [1962]
a description of the situation that arises when a property is rendered unsaleable (or only saleable at a disastrously lowered price) because of rumours of or actual plans for future development of the area.

plastic *adj.* [1963]
artificial, synthetic; *of persons* insincere.

* *'You can keep your plastic job and then come home at night and turn on and make love better and enjoy music better and enjoy your dinner better and enjoy your friends better.'* (*Berkeley Barb*, February 1969)
* *'The eighteen-year-old Safeway checker he was living with in that plastic condo in Greenbrae.'* (C. McFadden, *The Serial*, 1976)
* *'Adolph hated those people who seemed to him to be no more than a bunch of posers and "plastic" 'people.'* (G. Sams, *The Punk*, 1977)

plastic *n.* [1971]
an abbreviation for plastic money, thus credit cards, made from the ubiquitous substance.

plastic bullet *n.* [1969]
used for riot control in Northern Ireland (and in many other countries across the world); allegedly non-lethal, they have still caused a number of deaths.
See also **baton round; rubber bullet.**

* *'New and highly effective plastic bullets in Belfast.'* (T. Blacker, *Fixx*, 1989)

plate tectonics *n.* [1966]
a theory of the composition of the earth's surface based on concepts of moving plates.

platform shoe (*or* sole) *n.* [1973]
a shoe with a very thick sole, sometimes of several inches.

* *'Harvey could really groove on a skirt slit up to the waist and platform shoes.'* (C. McFadden, *The Serial*, 1976)

platinum *adj.* [1970]
in the record business: referring to records that sells a million copies; thus **to go platinum**: to sell one million copies; **double platinum** two million copies.

* *'The combination of harmony, melody and spontaneous Liverpudlian soul that distinguished their triple-platinum 1987 debut.'* (*The Times*, 6 October 1990)

play-book *n.* [1967]
the book compiled by football coaches and used as a strategic bible by the whole team, comprising all those various plays which a team will attempt to execute during a match.

player *n.* [1980]

1. a pimp
2. by extension from 1, anyone who uses brains and wit rather than sweat and strain to make a living, obtain women, drugs, etc.
3. *in business:* any major participant, either corporate or individual, in a given business situation. Often used in the context of trade wars, takeovers, mergers, etc.

* *'Last time it was the short-term players, like the American banks, who were financing the projects we turned down.'* (*Independent on Sunday*, 3 June 1990)

playgroup *n.* [1962]

a group of pre-school children, organized either by the local authory or spontaneously by a collection of like-minded parents, to provide supervised companionship for pre-school children.

playlist *n.* [1975]

a pre-specified list of records, usually the Top 40 plus a certain number of old favourites and a few possible contenders for future success, that make up all the music played in a given period, usually lasting a week, on a radio station.

plea-bargain *v.* [1969]

the process whereby a defendant, or more usually the defence lawyer can bargain with the court for a reduction of sentence if the defendant is willing to plead guilty on some charges, while others will be dropped, and thus help to speed up the legal calendar, albeit forfeiting the possible advantages of a general 'Not Guilty' plea in front of a jury. – **plea-bargain**, *n.*

PLO *abbrev.* [1964]

Palestine Liberation Organization: formed at a conference of Arab leaders held in Cairo in 1964; in 1974 it was recognized by many countries as the single legitimate representative of the Palestinian people.

* *'That is why the PLO is continuing the brutal, wretched tradition of the fanatical Palestinian leadership that brought down one calamity after another upon its people.'* (A. Oz, *The Slopes of Lebanon*, 1987)

plonker *n.* [1980]

1. originally (and currently) slang for a penis.
2. Idiot, or fool. Thanks to its use on BBC TV's sitcom *Only Fools and Horses*, the word has moved away from its original meaning and is used in the same way as **dork** and **prick**.

plumber *n.* [1972]

1. *in general:* anyone whose task it is to investigate and stop up 'leaks' in government information
2. *specifically:* that group of undercover operators chosen to perform that job, as well as to penetrate rival political organizations (including the national Democratic Party) by Richard Nixon's Republican Committee to Re-Elect the President in 1972.

* *'The Plumbers were Howard Hunt, Gordon Liddy . . . and Egil "Bud" Krogh. They investigated "leaks" to the news media and reported to John Ehrlichman.'* (B. Woodward & C. Bernstein, *All The President's Men*, 1974)

PMT *abbrev.* [1968]

for pre-menstrual tension (the term was coined *c.* 1954, the abbreviation appeared during the late 1960s): a severe nervous tension that overtakes some women prior to their menstrual period and which can cause changes in their behaviour, irritability, depression and other more or less severe reactions. PMT is also (in the US) known as PMS: premenstrual stress.

pocket calculator *n.* [1973]
a small mathematical and scientific calculator, usually operated by batteries, which can be carried in the pocket; such calculators, depending on microchip technology, were among the first flowerings of a revolution that is currently epitomized by the ➩personal computer.

✱ *'I totted up a few numbers on my pocket calculator.'* (T. Blacker, *Fixx*, 1989)

pogo *n., v.* [1977]
a dance popular during the ➩punk rock era of the late 1970s; it involved jumping up and down on the spot, creating a similar effect to riding a Pogo stick; given the packed conditions of punk's usually tiny clubs, a mass of pogoing fans tended to ricochet off each other, causing a number of fights – natural byproducts of the basic dance.

✱ *'The crowd at the front were pogoing about three feet into the air. Some punks were so enthusiastic that they jumped on each other's feet.'* (G. Sams, *The Punk*, 1977)

✱ *'I pushed my way down through the pogoing masses, right into the belly of the beast.'* (L. Bangs, *Psychotic Reactions and Carburetor Dung*, 1988)

pointy-head(ed) *n., adj.* [1968]
intellectual, highbrow; always used as a pejorative and ironically describing the physical antithesis of the other popular condemnation of the notably intelligent: 'egghead'.

poison pill *n.* [1986]
one of a number of strategies used by a company that has been targeted for a hostile takeover which are designed to make that takeover less appealing to the predator. These include the incurring of massive debts, the giving of special rights to existing shareholders, etc.

poke *n., v.* [1980]
in computing: an addition to a program, usually written by an interested ➩hacker, that modifies the operation of that program; pokes often take the form of interfering with game programs so as to offer the hacker extra lives, infinite power, etc.

✱ *'Pokes and cheats are generally accepted to be an everyday part of computer gaming.'* (*Ace*, August, 1990)

police procedural *n., adj.* [1975]
that form of crime fiction that concentrates on the details of police work; among the most popular are Ed McBain's *87th Precinct* books, and Maj Sjöwall and Per Wahlöo's *Martin Beck* series. Crime buffs often use the original French term *policier*.

✱ *'The Wahlöos' police procedural novels also depict Swedish society, though in terms of individuals, rather than movements.'* (C. Steinbrunner & O. Penzler, *Encyclopedia of Mystery and Detection*, 1976)

Polisario *abbrev.* [1975]
an acronym for Frente Popular para la Liberacion de Sagnia el-Hamra y Rio de Oro.

✱ *'Polisario stepped up its guerrilla attacks, concentrating on Mauretania as the weaker target.'* (D. Brogan, *World Conflicts*, 1989)

political football *n.* [1971]
an issue that is 'kicked around' by rival politicians; the implication is that what may be an important issue is reduced to a politically convenient object, and the human beings involved are rendered irrelevant cyphers.

poll tax *n.*
see **charge-cap, community charge.**

polymorphous perversity *n.* [1964]
coined in 1909 to describe the indiscriminate exploration of every aspect of the body's potential, usually ascribed to children, or to a childlike state, in which the taboos and prohibitoons of adulthood have yet to cut off vast areas of spontaneous feeling; it was offered to a non-specialist public by Norman Mailer, who used the term in a number of essays to describe what he saw as the whole 'sexual revolution' of the 1960s. – **polymorphous perverse,** *adv.*

* *'Here were morgue voices, encomia of junk, polymorphous perversity as the norm, the natural order on its uppers.'* (J. Meades, *Peter Knows What Dick Likes,* 1989)

polyocracy *n.* [1972]
on the pattern of aristocracy: a supposed elite of academics, teachers, social workers and local counsellors, all products of the new polytechnics of the 1960s, whose left-leaning politics and socially liberal philosophies are blamed for a wide range of contemporary evils and are as such excoriated by the ⇨neo-conservatives of the Thatcher era in Britain.

pong *n.* [1968]
one of the first electronic games, in which two players attempt to play a form of electronic ping-pong, using electronic 'paddles' to bat a blip backwards and forwards across a video screen.

* *'The chip turned out to contain a program to play the new video game – Pong – the new Atari firm was just beginning to put together.'* (S. Levy, *Hackers,* 1984)

pooper-scooper *n.* [1972]
a small dustpan, used specifically for scooping up dog excrement from the streets.

pop *v.* [1963]
to consume (usually a drug).

pop *adj.* [1963]
an abbreviation of popular; used in various combinations to refer to any discipline, e.g. psychology or sociology, that has been popularized, and presented in an easily accessible form.

pop art *n.* [1963]
the art movement that developed in the 1960s and drew its inspiration from every variety of mass popular culture, drawing heavily on the 'visual vocabulary' of that culture and its invariably commercial techniques. Subjects were treated impersonally, with no political or moral statements attached to them, and the art often echoed the mass production techniques of industry.

Thus: *pop architecture:*

1. buildings that are generally popular with the majority of the public.
2. buildings or structures that are symbolically styled, e.g.: a hamburger restaurant that is built to resemble a hamburger, etc.
3. buildings by professional architects which reflect their having been influenced by commercial designs as in **2**.

4. architectural plans for sculptural projects on a vast scale.

* *'The thing about these post-modernist exercises is that they are the architectural equivalent of pop art in painting.'* (J. Meades, *Peter Knows What Dick Likes*, 1989)

pop culture *n.* [1966]
culture that is based on popular rather than elite taste (high culture), disseminated widely and subject to mass-market commercial standards.

* *'It was the realisation of the elevation of pop music and allied pop culture by the Beatles which drew my interest . . .'* (A. Aldridge, (ed.), *The Beatles Illustrated Lyrics*, 1969)

pop festival *n.* [1967]
an outdoor concert, usually consisting of a number of acts and lasting two or three days; the best known of such festivals, the product of 1960s entrepreneurial enthusiasms, were those held at Woodstock and Altamont in the US and, in England, at the Isle of Wight and Shepton Mallet, near Bath.

* *'It's been the pop festival of the year. It has been wonderful.'* (*Daily Sketch*, 29 August 1967)

popper *n.* [1969]
a slang synonym for amyl nitrate: it comes in an ampoule which is 'popped' under the nose of the taker; used in medicine to boost the heart rate. Poppers are considered especially stimulating if taken during sex, preferably at the moment of orgasm.

* *'Mick Jagger sang about her in his little vignettes of clubs, poppers, disposable blondes and trash parties.'* (J. Meades, *Peter Knows What Dick Likes*, 1989)

Popperian *adj.* [1962]
from Sir Karl Popper (*b.* 1902) whose most widely known theory states that scientific laws are only justified by the extent of their resistance to falsification and who has constantly attacked those facets of Marxism that act to curtail individual freedom.

popular capitalism *n.* [1986]
the extension of capitalism to a wide range of the population, epitomized by a variety of recent Conservative measures, notably the share issues that have accompanied large ➪privatisations.

pop-up (book) *n.* [1963]
a type of book, originally designed for children but briefly best-selling among adults in the early 1980s, which features cut out sections and pictures that are so incorporated into the binding that when the book is opened they 'pop-up' and give the illusion of a three-dimensional illustration.

pop-up (menu) *n.* [1986]
see **menu.**

pop (*or* rock) video *n.* [1968]
a video film that has been made to accompany the promotion of a given rock record; rate in the 1960s and 1970s, they became a mandatory part of rock n roll merchandising in the 1980s.

* *'Serious players were honour-bound to stay up late drinking and dancing till the pop videos turned real.'* (*The Times*, 6 October 1990)

porn/porno *abbrev.* [1970]
pornography.

* *'Man Ray might have been a gay porno star as*

far as his knowledge extended.' (L. Bangs, *Psychotic Reactions and Carburetor Dung*, 1988)

port [1970]

1. *n., in computing*: any socket on a computer into which a variety of terminals and other ⇨peripherals can be plugged.

* *'The ports that are present are for an external 5.25 in floppy drive, a parallel printer, a VGA monitor, and a serial device.'* (*PC World*, May, 1990)

2. *v.*: to transfer data from one material to another via a cable linked to connecting ports.

portable *adj., n.* [1986]

in computing use: a computer that is sufficiently light to be moved around; not as small as a ⇨laptop, but more convenient than the heavier, larger ⇨luggable.

See also **notebook.**

* *'Our rugged laptops and portables let you work on the road, without compromise.'* (ad for Compaq in *Byte*, June 1990)

Portakabin *n.* [1963]

a proprietary name of a make of portable building, especially as found on building sites, as factory outbuildings, temporary classrooms, etc.

portapak *n.* [1974]

a lightweight portable system used by news crews and documentary makers, comprising a small TV camera and a videotape recorder.

poser *n.* [1977]

1. *in general*: one who poses, puts on artificial airs.

2. specifically those who put on such airs during the late 1970s punk era; a descendent of the ⇨plastic ⇨hippie of the 1960s, albeit with a completely different sensibility and style.

See also **new romantics.**

* *'Adolph hated those people who seemed to him to be no more than a bunch of posers and "plastic" people.'* (G. Sams, *The Punk*, 1977)
* *'Ridiculously trendy club run by ex-Westwood man Graham Ball and longtime poseur Cristos.'* (*The Independent*, 29 May 1990)

position *v.* [1976]

to create for a given product the required public perception of that product, e.g. as a 'brand leader', 'status symbol', etc. This is a basic part of advertising and marketing strategy and requires the deliberate targeting of a segment of the market and the emphasizing for that market that the product in question has special qualities that make it unique and as such irresistible. *Cf.* **niche marketing.**

position paper *n.* [1965]

a document prepared to illustrate the position of any national or interest group – government, unions, civil service, etc. – on a currently vital issue; a written statement of attitude and/or intention.

positive discrimination *n.* [1967]

any policy whereby a given group (or individual from that group) – often an ethnic or physically or economically disadvantaged minority – is given opportunities over and above their actual qualifications.

See also **affirmative action.**

* *'I suggest that there ought to be positive discrimination along the lines adopted twenty years ago in the United States.'* (R. Chesshyre, *The Force*, 1989)

posse *n.* [1987]

1. used by (mainly) Black youth to describe a teenage gang, whether or not actually criminal.

See also **crew**.

2. Originally Latin, meaning 'to be able', then coopted by the Wild West to describe the band of local vigilantes, led by the sheriff, who pursued a variety of outlaws and kindred badmen.

postcode *n.* [1967]

a series of letters and/or numbers which are allocated to postal areas to facilitate the sorting and delivery of post.

post-feminist *n., adj.* [1985]

that generation of women who, younger than the feminist activists of the late 1960s/1970s, have reaped the benefits and adopted some of the beliefs of feminism, but are less inclined to live by its ideological strictures. As such they are disdained by the 'traditional' feminists of the 1970s, who feel that these descendents have coopted the movement's external style, but none of its committed content. – **post-feminism**, *n.*

* *'Post-femininists, if you like, are the women who have "interesting" jobs but still wear make-up. They are the women in advertisements who don't really exist.'* (*Sunday Correspondent*, 22 April 1990)

post-modernism *n.* [1966]

any of the artistic and particularly design movements developed in deliberate reaction to modernism. The philosophy of modernism, what social historian Peter Gay has called 'a second Renaissance' in all the arts, dominated Western culture since *c.* 1850, but since the 1960s a variety of critics, claiming that the old ideology had run its course, proposed as its successor post-modernism. The new theory crosses many artistic boundaries, but is best seen in design, architectural or otherwise, where it abandons modernism's emphasis on the machine as a metaphor for that of the body, a return of the irrationality and emotionality of human beings, which is to be reflected in the buildings they occupy and the objects they use. – **post-modern**, *adj., n.*

* *'It is a sign of the cultural confusion of the late twentieth century that there is no one definition of the post-modern.'* (R. Hewison, *Future Tense: A New Art for the 1990s*, 1990)

post-natal depression *n.* [1973]

the feeling of often overwhelming misery that can take over a woman in the days following childbirth, typified by depression, fatigue, irritability, and fits of crying.

post-structuralism *n.* [1972]

see **deconstruction**.

post-traumatic stress disorder, also known as **post traumatic shock syndrome** *n.* [1973]

The current euphemisms for those stresses that engulf the mind of a soldier whose mind, in the long or short run, has been overwhelmed by the experiences of battle; the contemporary successor to 'shell shock' (the First World War) and 'battle fatigue' (the Second World War and Korea).

* *'The medical conditions . . . fall into three main categories. The first comes under the heading of post-traumatic shock syndrome (PTSS).'* (*Sunday Correspondent*, 10 June 1990)

posture *n.* [1962]
in military use: a nation's overall military strength and readiness as far as such factors effect its capacity to fight a war.

* *'Having done so you may select from three levels of aggression (or posture), pick your destination, launch your attack and observe the resulting battle.'* (*Ace*, December 1990)

pot *n.* [1965]
an abbreviation of the Mexican *potiguaya*: marijuana leaves. One of a number of drug-related words that predate the 1960s, but only really achieved popular use in and after that decade. *See also* **acapulco gold**.

* *'Pot is becoming as American as H. Rap Brown and apple pie.'* (*Esquire magazine*, August 1968)

poverty gap *n.* [1972]
the gap between the richest and poorest within one society/nation.

* *'Beware of the poverty gap trap.'* (*Sunday Correspondent*, 13 May 1990)

poverty level *n.* [1966]
a synonym for the earlier poverty line (1901): that level of income beneath which, statistically, one is considered to be officially impoverished.

poverty trap *n.* [1972]
the situation of poor families who receive benefits, whether means tested or not: when the main provider finds a job these benefits will probably be relinquished but in many cases the family's real income will then drop, since that provider is unable to qualify for a job that earns, after deductions, sufficiently more than the benefits already provided.

Powellite *n., adj.* [1965]
a follower of the political and social philosophies of J. Enoch Powell (1912–), popularly seen as the restriction of further coloured immigration into Britain.

* *'The NF [National Front] also had to guard against the erosion of its own members to the Powellite wing of the Conservatives.'* (M. Walker, *The National Front*, 1977)

power *adj.* [1981]
the use of power as an adjective emerged in the 1950s, in terms like *power drinking; power tennis; power politics* (a direct translation of the German *machtpolitik*); *power broking*, and *power base*. The term declined in the 1960s, although the **power shake** complex ritual of hand-slapping and grasping, was popular among the ideologically pure. The contemporary use, with its ➪yuppie overtones, has its roots both in these earlier coinages and, like so many vogue terms, in computing. **Power user** refers to those whose computer needs require many ➪megabytes of memory and storage, fast machines with ➪number-crunching capabilities.

* *'I'm no power user, so I can't determine whether it's a software or hardware problem.'* (*Byte*, June 1990)

Above all the word implies hard dedicated work, as do such phrases as *power breakfast* (or lunch), *power dressing* (usually indulged by ➪Filofax-wielding ➪post-feminists, but on offer to men too) and *power buying* (invariably with a gold ➪credit card).

* *'Exhaused by the efforts to maintain the well-honed power images of the 1980s, we are now given leave by designers to party through the 1990s.'* (*Sunday Correspondent*, 13 May 1990)
* *'Big Dolph flexes pecs in pacy B-pic; power*

dressing bimbo-fu and mind-boggling body count.' (*Sunday Correspondent*, 10 June 1990)

power broker *n.* [1961]
the modern king-maker, one who influences the distribution of political power, usually by backstairs plotting and intrigue.

power drill *n.* [1961]
an electrically powered drill, beloved of do-it-yourself home improvers as well as building trade professionals.

power-sharing *n.* [1970]
one of many political 'solutions' put forward in the face of the continuing impasse in Northern Ireland: a proposed governmental coalition between the Protestants and Roman Catholics.

power structure *n.* [1968]
a synonym for the Establishment: the political status quo, whether local, national, or international; the phrase was often used by 1960s' radicals to denote the system they wished to destroy.

prat *n.* [1968]
a fool, an idiot; from the earlier meaning: 'buttocks', 'posterior' and thus similar to other insults derived from parts of the body e.g. 'twat', 'dickhead', etc.

precision-guided munitions *n.* [1972]
any form of ⇨smart weapons, featuring computer or ⇨laser technology; especially those with built-in computers, variable radar frequencies, anti-jamming devices and similar means of homing in accurately on a target and eluding all the defences, electronic and conventional, that may be encountered.

pre-emptive strike *n.* [1966]
an attack launched on an enemy who has had no prior warning of its coming; a surprise attack. The implication is less of staging an ambush than of implementing the philosophy 'do it to them before they do it to you'.

prepple (*or* preppy) *adj.* [1970]
characteristic of the manners, vocabulary, dress and background of pupils in America's prep schools (the equivalent of British public schools). The preppie is the US equivalent of the ⇨Sloane Ranger and Lisa Bernbach's *Official Preppie Handbook* (1981) predated Ann Barr's equally popular *Sloane Ranger Handbook* (1982).

* *'Maybe all American preppy women with East Coast backgrounds and bank accounts were doomed to be dumb.'* (C. Blake, *Girl Talk*, 1990)

prequel *n.* [1973]
a book, film or television drama that is written as a result of the successful publication or programme, but rather than a sequel, which follows the characters' lives on into new adventures, the prequel attempts to look at their lives prior to their entering into the story that initially brought their popularity. A prequel may also be the only means of capitalizing on a success when the author has foolishly killed off the hero or heroine in the original story.

* *'Three more novels followed the strangely named Dollanganger offspring beyond the attic, while a "prequel" depicted them before the key turned.'* (*The Independent*, 16 February 1991)

press kit *n.* [1968]
a folder containing a variety of information sheets, pictures, and possibly audio or video tapes, designed to familiarize journalists with a given event or personality.

press the flesh *phrase.* [1975]
to shake hands, usually used of a politician or public figure, for whom such flesh-pressing is a necessary duty.

* *'Apparently he was off pressing the flesh at some luncheon, and that was more important than seeing us.'* (G. V. Higgins, *A Choice of Enemies*, 1983)

pressure point *n.* [1975]
anything that can be used to pressurize another person, whether a piece of blackmail, the kidnapping of a child, or something less melodramatic.

Prestel *n.* [1978]
originally called Viewdata, the proprietary name for the computerized information system operated by British Telecom; one dials the appropriate telephone number and the data required is displayed on a suitably adapted television screen.

pre-tax (profit) *n.* [1976]
gross earnings, assets, funds, etc., as assessed prior to the levying of tax.

pre-teen *n., adj.* [1960]
anyone under the age of thirteen, although the inference is of the year or so immediately preceding one's teenage.

* *'Even pre-teen boy's shoes were slated for obsoleting. They were being designed away from their "sexless" look.'* (V. Packard, *The Waste Makers*, 1960)

prevail *v.* [1983]
a euphemism for win: a concept that was created in an era (under President Reagan) where it was believed that a nuclear war could be fought and won, in the same way and using the same tactics as in any conventional war.

* *'American nuclear forces had to be able not only to fight a prolonged nuclear war, they had to be prepared to prevail.'* (P. Pringle & W. Arkin, *SIOP*, 1983)

price-conscious *adj.* [1961]
thrifty.

price-earnings ratio *n.* [1965]
the current price of a company's stock as expressed as a multiple of the company's earnings per share; it is computed by dividing the annual earnings per share into the market value of the stock.

priesthood *n.* [1963]
an elite, which, like the medieval clergy, renders itself powerful by keeping a strict guard on the knowledge and the rituals which it dispenses to the masses; especially as categorized in Nicholas Garnham's book *The New Priesthood*, an analysis of the 'new class' who had taken over the media in the early 1960s.

* *'In the mid '70s as the priesthood of numeracy was getting thoroughly hooked on silicon, a principled Gardner was still keeping hardware at bay.'* (*Byte*, December 1989)

primal therapy *n.* [1970]
a system of therapy developed by Arthur Janov and expounded in his book *The Primal Scream*; the basis of such therapy is the reliving of one's birth in **the primal**; rebirth is generally

accompanied by shouts, screams, yells of 'Mummy!' etc.
The system has also coined **primal pains**: 'The central and universal pains which reside in all neurotics', the evocation through pain and shouting of one;'s earliest infantile traumas, the source of all one's subsequent pain and thus central to the inner delvings that make up primal therapy.

* *'T-groups, encounter groups, sensitivity training, group gropes, psychodrama and primal scream therapies (this last an apt reflection of the clamorous 1960s).'* (R. D. Rosen, *Psychobabble*, 1977)

prime rib *n.* [1960]
one of the first two ribs in the forequarter of a butchered cow.

* *'To satisfy customers, butchers bone, trim and tie up secondary cuts of meat . . . and sell them at a small amount less than, say, sirloin or prime ribs.'* (E. David, *French Provincial Cooking*, 1960)

prime time *n., adj.* [1964]
the chief division of the TV day (known to marketing specialists as a 'daypart') which runs from early to mid-evening viewing and as such is considered the main viewing period in most households; programmes transmitted during prime time are usually low in taste and intellectual demands but highly successful; the advertising rates that accompany them are the most expensive.

* *'Michaels put together the rest of his comedy troupe – "The Not Ready for Prime Time Players" – with Laraine Newman, with whom he'd worked on a Lily Tomlin TV Special and Jane Curtin.'* (B. Woodward, *Wired*, 1984)

print journalism *n.* [1975]
writing for magazines or newspapers, rather than broadcasting on radio or television.

print media *n.* [1968]
magazines, newspapers, book publishing.

print-out *n.* [1965]
the printing out on paper of a ⇨hard copy version of whatever the operator has been working on with a given program – calculations, word-processing, etc.

prioritize *v.* [1973]
to make a given topic a priority for consideration.

prisoner of conscience *n.* [1961]
one who is detained or imprisoned because of their political, racial or religious beliefs.

* *'A Christmas card sent to a prisoner of conscience in Spain is returned by prison authorities marked "Return to sender as consignee is free".'* (Amnesty International, *Voices for Freedom*, 1986)

privatization *n.* [1969]
the hiving off by a government of formerly nationalized industries, either in whole or in part, and the returning of such industries into private ownership. – **privatize**, *v.*

* *'Rolls Royce is one of the most exciting of all the privatization stocks.'* (*Independent on Sunday*, 3 June 1990)

proactive *adj.* [1980]
originally used in psychology to describe the mental effect, left over from a previous activity, which has an effect on the performance of a subsequent activity, proactive is now in

general use as the opposite of reactive: setting things in motion, initiating activities, rather than simply responding.

* '*"They are extremely pro-active", says Mark Amundson . . . , "That means they don't sit around waiting for instructions: they initiate".*'. (*The Independent*, 31 March 1990)

probe *n.* [1962]
a small unmanned exploratory spacecraft sent into space, sometimes for a number of years, to collect and transmit back to earth a variety of information.

pro-celebrity *adj.* [1970]
any form of sport – usually golf – which is played between teams made up of partnerships between professional golfers (who may be celebrities) and professional celebrities (who may be able to play decent golf).

* '*Pro-Celebrity Golf: why sports programmers should imagine audiences are interested in substandard golf . . .*' (*The Independent*, 16 June 1990)

professional foul *n.*
a deliberate foul committed on an opponent by a defender who realizes that there is no more subtle or legal way of stopping him from scoring.

profile (keep a low) *phrase.* [1975]
to act discreetly, to keep oneself hidden from the public gaze.

* '*Due to orders from 39 Brigade, we are not allowed into the area for a few hours and must maintain a low profile.*' (A. F. N. Clarke, *Contact*, 1983)

program *n.*, *v.* [1965]
the instructions written by a programmer that are used to control the operations of a computer system along the lines desired by the individual who creates that program.

* '*In theory there are three phases to writing a program, and if you're going to try your hand at it you'd better get used to them.*' (D. Jarrett, *The Good Computing Book for Beginners*, 1980)

programme *v.* [1963]
to train a person to behave in a predetermined way.

pro-life(r) *n.* [1976]
also known as a ○**right-to-lifer** or **pro-choicer**: *euphamism for* an anti-abortion campaigner; such figures have apostrophized their oppenents as 'anti-lifers' and 'pro-deathers'.

* '*The pro-life group appears to have accepted defeat in the two key issues which the Commons voted on last week.*' (*The Independent*, 23 May 1990)
* '*Faye Nettleton, of the pro-choice lobbying group Planned Parenthood, said, "We cannot tolerate a nominee not making his position explicit".*' (*The Independent*, 25 July 1990)

promo *n.* [1963]
an abbreviation of promotion, but accepted as a noun in its own right: any kind of advertising or marketing designed to sell a new product: giveaways, free gifts, foreign trips, press lunches – a vast spectrum of persuasion from the most costly and unique to the cheapest and most obvious. Also used as an adjective, e.g. *promo shot*.

protest rally *n.* [1960]
a meeting to protest a given cause, e.g. nuclear weapons, the US in Vietnam, the UK Poll Tax, etc.

protest singer *n.* [1968]
a singer (usually of folk or folk-rock music) specializing in politically oriented songs. Thus the *protest song*, as performed by such singers.

provo *n.* [1965]
1. *in Holland*: a group of youthful anarchists who set out (successfully) to provoke the authorities in the 1960s; presumably from *provocateur*.

✱ *'Provo feels it must make a choice: desperate revolt or cowering defeat. Provo encourages rebellion wherever it can . . . Provo sees anarchism as a well of inspiration for the revolt.'* (*Provo* magazine leaflet, 25 May 1965)

2. *in Northern Ireland*: the Provisional IRA, which in 1971 broke from the Official IRA, whose policies they felt were overly acquiescent towards the British government.

pseud *n.* [1962]
an abbreviation for pseudo-intellectual, coined by *Private Eye* magazine and, in common with so many of the magazine's attitudes, plucked from the public school backkground of its editorial board. Pseud can be used as an adjective, but is also found as **pseudy**.

pseudo-event *n.* [1962]
an event created with no more justification than the desire of those concerned to have their names and pictures in the newspapers or, better still, on TV; often arranged by an advertising agency, public relations firm or even, for lack of anything better to fill their space, the media themselves.
See also **media event; photo opportunity; sound bite.**

psychedelic *adj.* [1963]
mind-expanding, hallucinogenic, pertaining to the drug ➪LSD and the experiences it creates, shorthand for the ➪hippie world of the 1960s. Psychedelic was coined in 1957 by Humphrey Osmond, who with Aldous Huxley was among the first non-medical experimenters to test out hallucinogenic drugs. He took it from two Greek words: *psyche* (mind) and *deloun* (manifesting), explaining to Huxley that he had chosen it 'because it is clear, euphonious and uncontaminated by other associations.' Like the drugs it described, psychedelic remained a specialist's preserve until the 1960s, when LSD permeated the world's consciousness, either as a utopian cure-all, or as a potential threat to civilization.

✱ *'If the psychedelic movement can be said to possess a nostalgic highpoint, it would probably be those weeks in Zihuatanejo in the summer of 1962'.* (Jay Stevens, *Storming Heaven*, 1988)

psychobabble *n.* [1976]
coined in 1976 by US writer R.D. Rosen in *New Times* magazine, and subsequently used in his book *Psychobabble: Fast Talk and Quick Cure in the Era of Feeling* (1977): 'institutionalised garrulousness', . . . psychological patter . . . this need to catalogue the ego's condition' – all by-products of the mass of ➪new therapies that offer easy cures for the various maladies that afflict the affluent Western young of the late 20th century.

✱ *'When I was composing a book review in 1975 the word "psychobabble" materialized on the page, and I suddenly I had a term to describe a particular cultural climate.'* (R. D. Rosen, *Psychobabble,* 1977)

psy ops *n.* [1968]
an abbreviation for psychological operations, psychological war: active propaganda that uses actions – some friendly, some frightening – rather than words to persuade those at whom it is aimed that it is better to support you than oppose you; further characterized during the Vietnam War as the euphemistic 'winning the hearts and minds' of the Vietnamese people.'

psych out *v.* [1963]
to gain a psychological advantage over, to intimidate or demoralize.

psych up *v.* [1968]
used as both an intransitive and transitive verb, meaning to excite, to become worked up (often before an important event in one's life).

✱ *'Some prisoners, like our host, are psyched up for an imminent release day.'* (*Sunday Correspondent,* 13 May 1990)

pub rock *n.* [1973]
a variety of country-influenced rock played in London pubs by such bands as Kilburn and the Highroads and Ducks Deluxe.

✱ *'A British beat stalwart from the mid-1970s pub rock era.'* (*Sunday Correspondent,* 10 June 1990)

public lending right *n.* [1969]
a royalty paid since 1984 to British authors, it is based on the number of times their books are taken out of lending libraries.

pull *n,. v.* [1969]
1. *in sexual terms:* as an abbreviation for 'pull a bird', to seduce and/or to have sexual intercourse.
2. *in police/criminal use:* like ➪tug, to arrest, or, as a noun, an arrest.

pull back *v.* [1976]
in sport: for one team or individual competitor to draw level after a period of being behind on goals, points, etc.

pull-down (menu) *n.* [1986]
see menu.

pulsar *n.* [1968]
a cosmic source of radio signals that pulsates with great regularity at intervals of a second or less; pulsars are believed to be rapdily rotating neutron stars.

pump iron *v.* [1976]
to work out with weights in a gymnasium.

punji stick *n.* [1966]
a popular Viet Cong weapon during the Vietnam war: a sharpened bamboo stick, its sharp end often covered with excrement, which is planted in a camouflaged hole in the ground; the soldier who steps into the hole will pierce his foot with the stick, wounding and possibly poisoning himself.

punk *n* [1976]
a devotee of ➪punk rock and the youth cult that grew up around it in the late 1970s.

✱ *'The other kid grabbed the punk's safety pin ear-*

ring and pulled it from his ear. Blood gushed out a a surprisingly fast rate.' (G. Sams, *The Punk*, 1977).

punk rock *v.* [1976]

the form of rock music that accompanied the rise to fame of the Sex Pistols in 1976. There had been punk music in the US in the late 1960s (and punk, meaning a young, probably disreputable person, dated back many years), but punk rock was very much an urban British working class phenomenon (even if some of its leading practitioners proved, embarrassingly, to have been university-educated and relatively middle class). In direct antithesis to the peace-loving ➪hippies of the 1960s (and the ➪glam-rock marionettes that followed them) punk concentrated on filth, whether verbal as in the lyrics, or actual, as in the rabid, ripped clothes and harshly spiked hair sported by the bands and their followers. Other than the bands themslves, punk owed much to its Svengali Malcolm McClaren, a former art student and fringe member of the 1960s cultural anarchists, the ➪Situationists.

See also **pogo**.

* *'The kind of reports we get . . . about your punk rock scene had led me to expect seething audiences of rabid little miscreants.'* (L. Bangs, *Psychotic Reactions and Carburetor Dung*, 1988)

purple heart *n.* [1961]

a slang term for dexamphetamine, marketed as Drinamyl: the most popular of the 'pep-pills' of the early 1960s, particularly as ingested by the youthful ➪Mods as an adjunct to dancing all night.

* *'They found the answer in pills like Drinamyl (blues or purple hearts), combinations of amphetamine and barbiturate'.* (M. Farren, *Watch Out Kids*, 1972)

push (out) the envelope *phrase.* [1979]

to go to the limit; the term is an extension of its original use, meaning the same thing, but within the jargon of US test-pilots who 'pushed out the envelope' as they put new machines through their paces.

* *'Add protected-mode Windows applications running in extended memory with access to virtual memory, and you're really pushing the envelope.'* (*Byte*, June 1990)

pussy-whipped *adj.* [1975]

dominated by a woman, usually a wife or girlfriend.

* *'Richie liked the idea, the guy thinking he was mean but actually he was pussy-whipped. Yes, dear. Whatever you say, dear.'* (E. Leonard, *Trust*, 1989)

put-down *n.* [1962]

a verbal attack, a snub. – **put down.**

* *'These are good-natured put-downs, though some recidivists make teacher cross.'* (*Independent on Sunday*, 17 June 1990)

PWA *abbrev.* [1983]

Person With AIDS: the ideologically (and medically) correct name for those who have been diagnosed with ➪AIDS; ➪gays feel that terms like 'victim' and 'sufferer' are insufficiently neutral and have campaigned, successfully in most areas of the media, to replace such supposed pejoratives – implying weakness and dependency – with PWA.

* *'Second, the trust has campaigned only reactively for the rights of PWAs (Persons with AIDS), whose benefits have been severely reduced.'* (*The Independent*, 4 September 1990)

pyramid selling *n.* [1964]
the extension of a franchise by the selling not of the product involved, but of further franchises, and these new franchise holders then sell further franchises in their turn, thus creating a hollow 'pyramid' in which there is very little merchandising, but only a great many outlets with no commodities to offer; such 'pyramids' are illegal in the UK.

Quaaludes
see methaqualone.

quadraphonic *adj.* [1969]
a sound system that uses four signal sources and four or more loudspeakers; quadraphonic systems, introduced in 1969, were supposed to replace the two-way stereophonic systems, but despite a good deal of promotion they remained a minority interest.

* *'They'd rapped about saunas vs Japanese hot tubs, whether anyone really needs quadraphonic stereo.'* (C. McFadden, *The Serial* 1976)

qualipop *n.* [1980]
quality + popular: a description of any newspaper title that supposedly falls between the quality (*The Times, The Independent*) and the unashamedly popular (*Daily Mirror, Sun*)

quality *n. adj.* [1970]
➲upmarket broadsheet newspapers, e.g. *The Times, Daily Telegraph, The Guardian, The Independent* (and their Sunday equivalents).

* *'The spectacle . . . was far beyond entrapment in the grey review pages of the quality Sundays.'* (R. Neville, *Play Power*, 1970)
* *'The editor of another quality Sunday newspaper has come straight from work and, in his business suit, is sitting uncomfortably on a teeny chair.'* (*Independent on Sunday*, 21 October 1990)

quality time *n.* [1988]
any period of time spent with one's family, unimpeded by such externals as business worries, professional problems, etc.

* *'The quality time I devoted quite often during the evening to the child Jennifer.'* (T. Blacker, *Fixx*, 1989)

quango *n.* [1967]
an acronym for Quasi-Autonomous Non-Governmental Organization: a government body which acts outside the usual Civil Service departments as an ostensibly public organization, but which in fact is funded by the Exchequer. Quangos can be created and staffed as sweepingly and quickly as there emerge topics on which there might need to be discussion and subsequent administration.

* *'He sat on various reasonably influential quangos.'* (T. Blacker, *Fixx*, 1989)

quantum leap *n.* [1970]
a sudden large advance; from quantum, used in physics to describe the sudden leap of an electron or other particle from one energy level to another.

quark *n.* [1965]
coined in 1961 by US physicist Murray Gell-Mann: the proposition that all subatomic particles are composed of combinations of three fundamental particles: the quarks, named for 'Three quarks for Muster Mark' in James Joyce's *Finnegans Wake* (1939). The three

types were called 'flavours', notably the **down quark**, **up quark** and **strange quark**. Subsequent research has revealed three further quarks: the **charmed quark** (or charm), the **bottom quark** (or beauty) and the **top quark** (or truth). Other theories claim that there may be as many as 18 quarks altogether.

quasar *n.* [1964]
synonym for quasi-stellar object: any of a class of celestial objects that give off a star-like image on a photograph; probably the most powerful and most far-off objects in the universe.

quick and dirty *phrase.* [1977]
anything – usually a piece of work or solution to a problem – that is cheap, easy, and fast, but in the end proves to be second rate, even if it has disposed of a necessary task.

- *'Asked for a translation, he smiled and said, "If you can do a quick and dirty job and it works, do it".'* (T. Kidder, *The Soul of a New Machine*, 1981)

quick-fix *adj.* [1976]
an easy solution for a difficult problem, usually implying that corners have been cut and major compromises made.

- *'It's a quick fix chance at revival for ailing Polish industries, and a new export market for Western ones.'* (*Independent on Sunday*, 3 June 1990)

quirk *n.* [1961]
an eccentricity, a strange habit. Thus **quirky**, *adj.* (1960) unpredictable, eccentric, bizarre.

Rachmanism *n.* [1963]
exploitation of slum tenants by unscrupulous landlords; named for Peter Rachman (1919–62) who, if he did not pioneer the practice, was linked (via the Profumo Affair of 1963) most notoriously to it.

✱ *'What Harold Wilson described as the disease of "Rachmanism" (thereby coining the term that has entered the* Concise Oxford Dictionary*).'* S. Green, *Rachman*, 1979)

rack-mounted *adj.* [1965]
anything that is mounted on standardized racks, typically telephonic, electronic or computing equipment.

rack up *v.* [1961]
to score, to achieve, to chalk up. The original use referred to snooker or pool scoring, but has spread into the general vocabulary.

RAD *abbrev.* [1987]
see **reflex anal dilation.**

radial (ply tyre) *n.* [1964]
a tyre in which the layers of fabric that compose it are laid with the cords running at right angles to the circumference of the tyre; the tread is further strengthened by more layers of fabric running round its circumference.

rad(ical) *adj.* [1986]
extreme, usually in a positive sense; one of a number of words (e.g. ⇨wicked, ⇨safe, etc.) that have been borrowed from standard English and put to work as contemporary teenage slang.

✱ *'So many of you cool dudes were unable to get all the first three editions of this totally rad new comic.'* (*Teenage Mutant Hero Turtles*, June 1990)

radical chic *n.* [1970]
a synonym for ⇨limousine liberal and ⇨champagne socialist coined by Tom Wolfe in his eponymous essay: anyone who affects – through guilt, a desire to join a fashionable political group, or even plain sincerity – to espouse radical (usually left radical) politics. Radical chic had its heyday in the late 1960s and early 1970, but its essential conceit differed little from the reverse posturings of the affectedly right wing ⇨young fogeys of the 1980s.

✱ *'Deny it if you wish to, but these are the* pensées metaphysiques *that rush through one's head on these Radical Chic evenings just now in New York.'* (T. Wolfe, *Radical Chic & Mau-Mauing the Flak-Catchers*, 1970)

Radio One/Two/Three/Four *n.* [1967]
the four national radio stations set up by the BBC on 30 September 1967; they replaced (respectively) the Light Programme (which was split into Radios One (pop and Two (easy listening)), the Third Programme, and the Home Service.

radio-paging *n.* [1960, 1968]
see abbrev. **pager.**

R and D *abbrev.* [1965]
Research and Development.

* *'From now on they would not be engaged in anything like research and development but in work that was 1 per cent R and 99 per cent D.'* (T. Kidder, *The Soul of a New Machine,* 1981)

RAF *abbrev.* [1977]
Rote Armee Fraktion (Red Army Unit), a German urban guerrilla group founded on 2 April 1968 (their first attack), active in the 1970s and (though much depleted) in the 1980s; it was also known, in its first incarnation, as the 'Baader-Meinhof' gang, named for its leaders Andreas Baader and Ulrike Meinhof.

* *'A former member of the anarchist revolutionary Red Army Fraction.'* (*Sunday Correspondent,* 17 June 1990)

rag-roll *v.*
an interior decoration style, particularly popular in the mid-1980s, which, by rolling on paint with a rag rather than the conventional paintbrush, produces an effect similar to that of crushed velvet.

rail link *n.* [1975]
a railway service that joins two established transport systems.

rainbow (coalition) *n.* [1984]
a broad coalition of like-minded opinions, especially in a political context.

* *'By the early 1980s this "Rainbow Coalition" of peace activists, women, blacks, gay people, and trade unionists were venting their anger inside the Labour Party.'* M. Hollingsworth, *The Press and Political Dissent* 1986)

rallycross *n.* [1967]
a form of motorracing which combines rallying and autocross (in which battered 'old bangers' are driven around mud-covered hills).

RAM *abbrev.* [1977]
an acronym for Random Access Memory: that memory within a machine that allows data to be stored or retrieved in a random fashion in a short time; that part of the machine into which one loads programs and where they are held as long as the operator is using them. *See also* **ROM.**

* *'All you need is a 286/386 computer with 2 megabytes of random access memory. Also known as RAM.'* (ad for Microsoft products in *Byte,* May 1990)

Rambo *n.* [1982]
1. originally the character played by Sylvester Stallone in a number of movies (the first of which was *Rambo: First Blood,* 1982, a ridiculously ⇨macho figure who appealed to the less intelligent teenage boy. **2.** used figuratively to denote any form of macho posturings, especially as indulged by nations and their leaders.

* *'The US government represented us as a bunch of Rambos and mercenaries, who ignored warnings . . . to get out of Beirut.'* (*Sunday Correspondent,* 10 June 1990)

ranch-style *adj.* [1961]
a single storey or split-level house; briefly fashionable in the 1960s, such houses (usually found on suburban housing estates) were

supposed to conjure up life in the American West.

rap/rapping *n.* [1967, 1985]

1. **a slang term** for speech or conversation; adoped during the 1960s by the ⇨hippies, drawing as they did so often on black slang.

* *'Roy Seburn's lights washing past every head, Cassady rapping, Paul Foster handing people weird little things out of his Eccentric Bag.' (T. Wolfe, The Electric Kool-Aid Acid Test,* 1969)

2. used in a variety of ⇨new therapies to mean conversations, especially, as in ⇨encounter groups, in a structured situation in which one's feelings are laid out, analyzed, supported, or criticized. Such therapy-based conversations are also known as **rap sessions**, and the group as a **rap group**. All the terms were used by a number of ⇨New Left political groups to describe meetings in which they planned their activities.

* *'When the Pigs left we had a heavy rap session about self-defense, land, and whether or not the chickens barbecuing on the open fire were done yet.'* (A. Hoffman, *Woodstock Nation,* 1969)

3. in the 1980s the term reverted to its black roots, and was used in ⇨hip-hop music to describe singing or chanting the lyrics of a rap song against the heavy bass line, usually produced by a drum machine or ⇨synthesizer.

* *'Eye-opening for those who associate rap only with the questionable attitudes of Niggers With Attitude.'* (*Independent on Sunday* 3 June 1990)

rap group *n.* [1967]

see **rap**.

rap session *n.* [1967]

see **rap**.

rapture of the deep *n.* [1966]

also known as nitrogen narcosis, bends, uglies: a dazed or light-headed sensation that comes from breathing in heavily nitrogenized compressed air.

rare groove *n.* [1987]

vintage soul records of the 1960s and 1970s, known to their revivalists as rare groove.

* *'Norman Jay, the Godfather of rare groove, is very much the DJ's DJ.'* (*The Independent,* 29 May 1990)

rasta/rastaman *n., adj.* [1969]

a follower of Rastafarianism, a sect that developed in Jamaica in the 1950s and emerged in the UK in the 1960s, believing that blacks are the chosen people, that Ethiopia is the promised land and that its late emperor Haile Selassie (1892–1975) was the saviour. The name comes from Ras Tafari, by which Haile Selassie was known from 1916 to 1930, when he ascended his throne.

* *'Adolph . . . thumbed through a pile of records. Most of them were new wave, but there were some rasta records. Adolph picked out Bob Marley.'* (G. Sams, *The Punk,* 1977)

* *'And did what any other righteously upstandin Rasta woulda done: slunk downstairs 'n' drunk muhsef tuh nullhood.'* (L. Bangs, *Psychotic Reactions and Carburetor Dung,* 1988)

rat fink *n.* [1964]

a general pejorative denoting an obnoxious person with the specific implication, from 'fink' meaning informer, of traitorous behaviour.

raunchy *adj.* [1967]
sexy, provocative, with implications of sleaziness; raunchy, meaning simply physically dirty, predates the sexual use and was used in the US the Second World War.

rave *n.* [1960]
in the early 1960s, a party, also **rave-up**; those enjoying such parties were known as **ravers**; the terms were revived in the 1980s, with much the same meaning, although the parties concerned were often held in clubs or, in the case of the notorious ⇨acid house parties, in disused warehouses, hangars and so on.

* *'Seven thousand ravers at a guinea a head turned up to record their newfound spontaneity for handy randy BBC cameras.'* (R. Neville, *Play Power*, 1970)
* *'London's most successful club promoter, Nicky Holloway (Do at the Zoo, Alphabet City, and countless other raves).'* (*The Independent*, 29 May 1990)

rave-up *n.* [1960]
see **rave**.

razor cut *n.* [1965]
a haircut that is done with a straight (cut-throat) razor rather than the usual scissors.

reaction shot *n.* [1966]
in film and television: a shot that shows how a person who is seeing or hearing a given statement or circumstance reacts. When these shots are used in a TV interview, they may well be taken after the conversation is over and, given that they often depict the interviewer nodding his or her silent assent, are known professionally as 'noddies'.

reader-response criticism *n.* [1979]
criticism that is concerned not with the text itself as an autonomous isolated object, but with its relation to those that read it.

readout *n.* [1963]
the output, transmission, or display of data from a computer; thus **to read out**: to output data.

Reaganism *n.* [1966]
the policies and principles (especially the economic ones, hence **Reaganomics**) advocated by Ronald Reagan, governor of California 1967–75 and US President 1980–88.

* *'Given these dour possibilities, it is hardly surprising that the nation is rooting for Reaganomics to win.'* (*Newsweek*, 16 February 1981)

real ale *n.* [1972]
draught beer that has been brewed and stored in a traditional manner, as opposed to the mass-produced 'top pressure' beers that are marketed by the major brewers; real ale, championed by CAMRA (the Campaign for Real Ale), is also stronger and (to its fans) more flavoursome. In the wake of real ale, the 'real' tag was also added (although with markedly less success) to such comestibles as bread, cheese, etc.

* *'The beers worshipped by the campaigners for real ale . . . are, simply, richer, better, more satisfying than the Skols of this world.'* (*Independent on Sunday*, 19 August 1990)

real time *n.* [1965]
the actual time in which something takes place; any activities that the computer performs in combination with another entity,

usually its human operator, which force the computer to restrict the speed of its actions to those of the other party, e.g. recognizing the keystrokes at the typist's speed, rather than being able to deal with the electronic impulses at its own infinitely faster speeds.

* '"*Not so much a CPU as a chip to deal with real-time, continuous I/O," said Garth Hillman.*' (*Byte*, July 1990)

real world *n.* [1963]
the world of work, as opposed to that of academe. – **real-world,** *adj.*

* '*A good degree and real-world experience prior to consulting are taken for granted.*' (ad for Kinsley Lord management consultants in *Independent on Sunday*, 3 June 1990)

reception (class) *n.* [1972]
the first compulsory school class that children – usually aged around five years – attend. Thus, this is the lowest class in an infant school.

recombinant DNA *n.* [1976]
the basis of genetic engineering and also known as **gene-splicing** and **gene transplantation**: the methods and procedures whereby DNA fragments from different organisms may be recombined in a laboratory to create new or altered genes which can then be inserted into host cells to produce specific genetic functions.

recording engineer *n.* [1962]
the engineer who supervises the technical aspects of a recording session, as opposed to the producer who deals with the musical aesthetics.

recreational drug use *n.* [1970]
the use of drugs for pleasure rather than for health reasons: such drugs include cannabis, amphetamines, narcotics, etc.; although the user's concept of 'pleasure' may be somewhat idiosyncratic.

recycling *n.* [1960]
the reusing or reclamation of waste or discarded material: the word is by no means new, but it is one of many that have taken on a new and fashionable life in recent years, in this case thanks to the ⇨green revolution.

recycle, *v.*

* '*What you ecology-minded ladies don't realise is that before a bottle can be recycled it has to be emptied.*' (*New Yorker*, 16 October 1971)

Red Army *n.* [1972]
a group of hard-left Japanese ⇨urban guerrillas, linked to such organizations as the Red Army Fraktion (⇨RAF) in Germany and the ⇨PLO in the Middle East; they emerged in 1970 when they hijacked a Japanese Airlines plane to North Korea, but scored their most devastating attack in May 1972, when they killed 28 tourists at Israel's Lod airport.

* '*The right to decide their nations' future with the bomb and the gun verged on dementia (and the Japanese Red Army, clearly, was altogether demented).*' (P. Brogan, *World Conflicts*, 1989)

Red Brigades *n.* [1973]
a group of Italian ⇨urban guerrillas; the *Brigate Rosse* grew from the bourgeois ⇨drop-outs, infatuated with the suffering masses, who spearheaded the demonstrations of the late 1960s. Their major coup (1978) was the kidnapping and (on 10 May) assassination of the Italian premier Aldo Moro.

* *'Like the RAF and Action Directe, the Red Brigades are now a shadow of their former selves, thanks to successful police work.'* (D. Brogan, *World Conflicts*, 1989)

red card *n.* [1976]
a card shown by a soccer referee to a player who persistently or maliciously breaks one or more rules. Typical would be a deliberate injurious foul. The player must leave the field. *See also* **yellow card**.

* *'Taylor will ensure that the rash of red cards caused by the FIFA initiative has a prominent place on the agenda.'* (*The Independent*, 21 February 1991)

red/green channel *n.* [1968]
the two 'channels' through which arriving passengers are processed by the customs authorities of most countries; the red channel denotes 'something to declare' for customs duty, the green denotes 'nothing (other than the permitted duty-free goods) to declare'.

red-eye *n, adj.* [1968]
a flight that takes off late at night and arrives very early in the morning, its passengers emerge with eyes red from lack of sleep; especially used of certain internal US routes.

* *'Into the arrivals lounge they wandered, off the red-eye charters from London.'* (*Independent on Sunday*, 24 June 1990)

Red Guards *n.* [1966]
activist, propagandized students and schoolchildren who were used by Chairman Mao to spearhead the assault on the supposedly revisionist Old Guard of the Chinese revolution who were rooted out with violence and humiliation, and in the long run at the cost of setting back Chinese development for many years, during the ⇨Cultural Revolution of 1966–72.

* *'The seizure of power in the two papers is a question of national significance, and it is necessary to support their rebellion. Our newspapers must reproduce articles by the Red Guards. These are very well written, while ours are too rigid.'* (Speech by Chairman Mao Tse Tung, 9 January 1967)

redial *v.* [1961]
to dial again.

redline *v.* [1973]
the practice among loan firms and building societies of drawing a real or an imaginary red line around certain urban areas – usually the impoverished ⇨inner city – to signify that no credit will be allowed to any individual living in those areas, irrespective of actual creditworthiness, personal records, etc. The result of such redlining is to accelerate the decline of these areas, thus preparing them for lucrative development plans which may well enrich the redliners.

reds *n.* [1967]
a slang term for barbiturates.

* *'Suburban high school kids freaked out on reds and puberty and fantasies of nihilistic apocalypses.'* (L. Bangs, *Psychotic Reactions and Carburetor Dung*, 1988)

red (*or* warning) triangle *n.* [1969]
a triangular warning sign placed on the road to mark the presence of a broken-down vehicle; optional in the UK, such signs are compulsory in various European countries, notably France.

* *'All vehicles temporarily imported into France with the exception of two-wheelers must be equipped with either a warning triangle or hazard warning lights.'* (AA, *Travellers' Guide to France*, 1987)

re-education *n.* [1975]
the attempt by a political authority (usually in a totalitarian state) to remodel the minds of its former opponents by an intensive period of lecturing, indoctrination, and hard labour.

* *'The policy of "re-education" in these circumstances was introduced in an attempt to achieve national reconciliation instead of seeking vengeance.'* (Amnesty International, *Voices for Freedom*, 1986)

re-education camp *n.* [1975]
special camps in which a country's political authorities attempt to implant what they see as ideological purity within the minds of their opponents. Such camps are in effect prison camps, where the normal diet of harsh treatment is intensified by this brainwashing.

* *'Unexpected security considerations have arisen . . . which have made it impossible to release all detainees in re-education camps within the time period first envisaged.'* (Amnesty International, *Voices for Freedom*, 1986).

reel-to-reel *adj.* [1966]
any tape recorder that works by passing a tape between two reels which are mounted separately on the machine; the opposite of the ➪cassette machine.

re-escalation *n.* [1965]
the intensifying of a situation that had begun to calm.
See also **de-escalation; escalation**.

reflex anal dilation *n.* [1987]
a means of assessing the possibility of abuse by inspection of the anus: if it dilates involuntarily on inspection a doctor may have reason to suspect that there has been abuse. The use of RAD was at the centre of the furore that emerged in 1987 when out of a sample of 102 children examined in Cleveland, Dr Marietta Higgs claimed that, on the basis of RAD tests, 78 had been abused. As a result of this, RAD by itself is now considered inadequate as the sole test of abuse, and other evidence is considered necessary for a definite proof.

reflexology *n.* [1976]
a technique for relaxing nervous tension by massaging the feet.

refuge *n.* [1976]
any establishment that offers shelter to a battered wife, ie. a woman who suffers repeated physical violence from her husband or boyfriend.

refusenik *n.* [1975]
1. a Soviet Jew who wishes to emigrate to Israel but has been refused permission to do so.
2. by extension from 1 (but with a twist on the original meaning of 'being refused' to actively 'refusing') anyone who actively refuses to co-operate in a given scheme or plan.
See also **-nik**.

reggae *n.* [1968]
a type of West Indian music characterized by 'predominant and repetitive bass riffs and regular notes or chords played by an amplified rhythm guitar on the off beat with an upward stroke of the plucking hand' (T. Hibbert,

Rockspeak, 1983). Reggae is often infused with references to Rastafarianism, especially as sung by its most celebrated performer, the late Bob Marley.

* *'He would have preferred some reggae, ska or bluebeat, but then they never put anything decent in Juke-boxes.'* (N. Fury, *Agro*, 1971)

regulator *n.* [1961]
a means of manipulating the economy between budgets whereby the Chancellor of the Exchequer may alter the going rate of taxation.

rehash *n. v.* [1965]
a reworking.

rejectionist *n.* [1976]
referring to any Arab who refuses to recognize the state of Israel; thus **Rejectionist Front**: those Arab states that subscribe to this view.

relate *v.* [1970]
to approve of, to support.
See also **get behind**.

* *'Anita nodded, smiling sweetly. "Could you relate to a carrot?" she asked him.'* (C. McFadden, *The Serial*, 1976)

relational database *n.* [1983]
any computer ⇨database which makes it possible to access the data by a variety of different routes, either used individually, or simultaneously.

* *'Pure Magic: Computer aided programming application generator and relational database.'* (ad for MSE software in *Byte*, July 1990)

relationship *n.* [1974]
relationship, neither a new word nor concept, gained its specifically sexual overtones in the 1970s when the discussion of one's 'relationships' became an essential part of progressive ⇨discourse.

relaunch *n.* [1970]
the process of launching a product for the second time after the original launch is considered to have failed, or made insufficient impact; especially of a business, a newspaper, etc.

reliability *n.* [1965]
the predicted percentage of missiles that will reach their target after they have been launched. The reliability of US missiles varies between 75–80%; Soviet missiles vary between 65–75%.

remaster *v.* [1967]
to issue a new recording using the original master disc.

remit *n. v.* [1963]
a method used at Trade Union conferences and meetings of burying a resolution without even bothering to vote on it: such resolutions, for whatever reason, are **remitted**, i.e. referred to the Conference Executive for an unspecified 'future'.

remortgage *v., n.* [1960]
to take out a second mortgage on one's property or to change the first mortgage to obtain more money.

renewal *n.* [1965]
usually as in **urban renewal**: the development of urban areas, implying that old and/or slum areas have first been demolished.

rent-a *prefix.* [1961]
a widely-used prefix that denotes a lack of faith in the sincerity of the individual or individuals concerned. The assumption is that their presence or opinions are, metaphorically if not actually, up for sale to the highest bidder.
See also **rent-a-crowd; rent-a-quote.**

rent-a-crowd *n.* [1961]
a derisory description of the crowds of youthful demonstrators (usually from the leftwing, or at least chanting leftwing slogans, and holding concomitant banners) who can be found protesting a variety of (predictable) causes and issues.
See **rent-a.**

rent-a-quote *adj.* [1980]
a description, usually of MPs, who are available – indeed keen – to offer their opinions on any potentially controversial topic at the behest of the media. Although rent-a-quote MPs are available from all parties, the term generally indicates those hard-right post-Thatcherites whom the media know can always be relied on to outrage more liberal sensibilities.

rent boy *n.* [1969]
a young, male homosexual prostitute who can be 'rented' for one's enjoyment.

* *'Dennis is a runaway, rape victim, former rent boy and petty thief.'* (*The Independent*, 14 June 1990)

repeat fee *n.* [1969]
an additional fee (usually 75% of the original) paid to performers on radio or televison when the programme in which they initially appeared gets a second or subsequent broadcast.

reprogram *v.* [1963]
to ➪program differently, to suppply with a new program.

reprographic *n. adj.* [1961]
an omnibus word that covers a wide range of processes and methods used to produce printed documents.

rerun *n., v.* [1962]
a repeat showing of a given film, radio or television broadcast; *a synonym for* repeat.

re-sale (value) *n.* [1960]
second-hand value; the term is generally found in the second-hand car market.

reschedule *v.* [1966]
1. (1966) *in media use*: to move to a new schedule, often of business plans, radio or television broadcasts, etc.
2. (1968) *in economics*: to arrange a new scheme of repayments of an international debt with the aim of lessening the financial burden on the debtor country.

residency *n.* [1966]
of a musician or band: having a regular (weekly, nightly) date to perform at a given club or similar venue.

* *'Before moving into the band's first big-time residency, Lambert decided he needed a slogan. He came up with "Maximum R & B".'* (D. Marsh, *Before I Get Old*, 1983)

resident *n.* [1963]
an intelligence agent (of the KGB) who works in a foreign country and is attached to the local Soviet embassy, invariably disguised under some anodyne title; thus **residentura**:

the intelligence establishment maintained by the KGB in a foreign country.

residual *n.* [1965]
any payments made to performers, writers, directors, etc. for the repeat of a play, TV programme, commercial, etc.

responaut *n.* [1964]
in medicine a patient who depends upon any sort of artificial breathing aid.

retaliation *n.* [1960]
a nuclear attack launched by one nation as a reply to an earlier attack by another, i.e. a ◇second strike. Whether or not they espouse the concept of limited winnable nuclear wars, most nuclear strategists are determined that if the other side starts the battle, then their forces must retain the capability of retaliation.

retread *n.* [1985]
from its original meaning of a tyre that has been reprocessed with a new tread, to extend its practical life, the current slang meaning denotes anything old that has been trotted out for a new lease of life, specifically of anyone who has been retrained for a new job.

retro *n., adj.* [1975]
an abbreviation for retrogressive: clothing styles that look to the past rather than developing towards the future; harking back to the 'looks' of earlier eras.

* *'Think retro. Think 1960s. Think Jackie O.'* (*The Independent*, 14 June 1990)

Recently the term as been used in more general sense.

* *'By the mid-1960s they began, with Camus, to appear retro, even romantic.'* (*Independent on Sunday*, 10 June 1990)

retrofire *v.* [1962]
to ignite or fire a retro-rocket, which gives a backwards thrust to the engine.

retrofit *n.* [1969]
any modification made to a product (usually an aircraft) which takes in changes that have been made to later more sophisticated models.

retrovirus *n.* [1976]
from Reverse Transcriptase: an ◇RNA virus of the family *Retroviridae*, characterized by oncogeneity (the creation of cancerous tumours) and the possession of reverse transcriptase (the ability to synthesize DNA on an RNA template, rather than the usual reverse process).

returner *n.* [1989]
a woman who resumes her career after a period of retirement, probably to have and bring up her children.

reverb *n.* [1961]
an abbreviation for reverberation: a distant echoing sound effect used by a number of musicians and singers.

reverse discrimination *n.* [1971]
the deliberate discrimination against members of a dominant group (usually the White Anglo-Saxon Protestants) in order to compensate for previous discrimination against minorities, especially in the allotment of jobs, college places, etc., to members of such minorities over the claims of (sometimes better-qualified) ◇WASPs.

* *'I hated Carol's guts when she was straight. Now I'm supposed to love her because she's gay? Isn't that, like, reverse discrimination or something?'* (*C. McFadden*, The Serial, 1976)

reverse engineering *n.*
the pirating or copying of a given machine by stripping it right down to its components and reproducing both its plan and parts in perfect detail.

* *'It's difficult but possible . . . to create a functionally equivalent copy of the machine. Reverse engineering is the name of that art.'* (T. Kidder, *The Soul of a New Machine*, 1981)

revolving door *n.* [1966]
any form of constantly recurring or repetitive activity; an automatic cycle. The term often refers to the legal system, where, for instance, a prostitute is arrested and fined for picking up paying customers; but only by taking on more paying customers can she pay the fine, which lays her open to new arrest, and so on.

rig *n.* [1964]
slang for the penis.

* *'There are rigs in them, there are scraps of tackle, pines and valseuses.'* (J. Meades, *Peter Knows What Dick Likes*, 1989)

right-on *exclamation, adj.* [1966]
1. as an exhortatory exclamation, 'Right on!' became a *sine qua non* of any 1960s' leftwing political meeting; like so much of the 1960s language, its origins were in the black community.

* *'The brothers said, "Right on Bobby, right on. We understand".'* (B. Seale, *Seize the Time*, 1968)
* *'We had a lotta zingy lingo when I was a lad – sharp riffs like "Right on!" and "Peace, brother!"'"* (L. Bangs, *Psychotic Reactions and Carburetor Dung*, 1988)

2. politically sound, ideologically pure; from the exclamation.

* *'It is one of the many unanswered questions of an afternoon spent behind bars in the company of England's most right-on singer-songwriter.'* (*Sunday Correspondent*, 13 May 1990)

right-to-die *adj.* [1975]
permitting or supporting the right of an incurably ill or injured patient to have all life support systems withdrawn; the patient can then die, as far as is possible, in peace and dignity, unencumbered by the impotent paraphernalia of high-tech medicine.

right-to-lifer *n.* [1976]
anyone who rejects the right of a woman to exercise her rights in having an abortion if she wishes, and who campaigns to reverse the laws that permit it. The term, in the same way as many right-wing causes, adopts neutral or even deceitful names (e.g. the Freedom Association), and often simply disguises the extreme anti-abortion stance of its supporters.

* *'Also plaguing Carter at every step were the "right-to-lifers", protesting his opposition to a constitutional amendment banning abortion.'* (*The People's Almanac*, February, 1978)

right-to-work *adj.* [1970]
relating to a worker's right to hold a job, whether or not he or she belongs to a union; also to the belief, voiced particularly during periods of high unemployment, that within a capitalist system which demands that everyone works, then everyone should have the opportunity to do so.

ringpull *n.* [1970]
the metal ring, attached to a specially perforated section of a can's top, that when pulled facilitates the opening of the can.

ringway *n.* [1969]
any circular system of major roads that surrounds a large town or city.

riot shield *n.* [1967]
any purpose-built shield used by police or troops in situations when they are combating riots.

rip-and-read *n.* [1973]
material that is transmitted over a wire service teletype; thus **rip-and-reader**: a newsreader; from the tearing off of sheets from wire service machines and Telexes.

rip off [1967]
1. *n.* a fraud, a swindle, a racket, plagiarism.
* *'The song titles looked promising too: aside from two rip offs from the Who, they were all originals.'* (L. Bangs, *Psychotic Reactions and Carburetor Dung*, 1988)

2. *v.* to steal, to betray, to plagiarize.
* *'Where . . . was the last place the Las Vegas police would look for a drug addled fraud fugitive who had just ripped off a downtown hotel?'* H.S. Thompson, *Fear and Loathing in Las Vegas*, 1971)

ripped (to the tits) *adj.* [1971]
extremely intoxicated, either on alcohol or drugs.
* *'Two good old boys in a fireapple red convertible . . . stoned, ripped twisted . . . Good People.'* (H.S. Thompson, *Fear and Loathing in Las Vegas*, 1971)

RISC *abbrev.* [1986]
an acronym for reduced intruction set computer: a computer in which the instruction set (those instructions that are necessary to make the machine work) has been cut down to a bare minimum; such paring down creates a faster, cheaper machine.
* *'Expect to see this RISC chipset in true low-cost desktop machines within three years.'* (*PC World*, April 1990

rising *adj.* [1975]
of schoolchildren's ages; usually found as *rising fives* (nearly five), *rising seven* (nearly seven), or whatever. The use of 'rising' to mean 'nearly' in this way goes back to the 19th century, but its use in the educational context is much more recent.

risk analysis *n.* [1964]
the systematic analysis and forecasting of possible risks in a business enterprise.

RNA *abbrev.* [1962]
genetic code *also known as* **ribonucleic acid**: any of the nucleic acids that yields ribose on hydrolysis; they occur mainly in the cytoplasm of certain cells, where they direct the synthesis of proteins, and in some viruses, where they store genetic information.
* *'The blueprint is the genetic code, the two nucleic acids – the long, intertwined duplicating chains of DNA and the controlling regulation of RNA.'* (T. Leary, *The Politics of Ecstasy*, 1968)

roach *n.* [1968]
the butt-end of a marijuana cigarette. While English ➩joints are usually made with a cardboard filter, their US cousins are simply a roll-

up cigarette containing pure marijuana, which gets hot as it reaches the last half inch or so; thus **roach clip**: a small metal appliance, often resembling a pair of tiny tweezers, used to hold the hot roach, which would otherwise burn one's fingers.

* *'The reefer butt is called a "roach" because it resembles a cockroach.'* (H.S. Thompson, *Fear and Loathing in Las Vegas*, 1971)

road crew *n.* [1968]
see **roadie**.

roadie *n.* [1969]
an abbreviation for road manager: a member of the team of assistants – the road crew – who maintain and manhandle the instruments, amplification, lights, and allied equipment required by a rock band for their on-stage performances.

* *'A muscular roadie with a bicycle pump was never going to be a serious serious option.'* (*The Independent*, 15 June 1990

road movie *n.* [1969]
1. modern road movies began with *Easy Rider* (1969) and included such classics as *Two-Lane Blacktop* (1971); the 'road' was the highways and lesser thoroughfares (almost invariably of America) down which the heroes (and occasional heroines) made their tortured way. 2. The first 'road movies' referred specifically to the Dorothy Lamour/Bob Hope/Bing Crosby vehicles, starting with *Road to Singapore* in 1940. Here the 'road' referred to the title.

road rash *n.* [1976]
used by skateboarders to refer to the bumps, bruises, and general wounds accumulated in falling off the skateboard.

rock *n.* [1988]
a synonym for crack.

* *'Keep smoking that rock and my pocket's getting bigger.'* (N.W.A., *'Dopeman', 1988)*

rock *n. adj. v.* [1966]
abbreviation for rock music, itself taken from the 'rock 'n' roll' of the 1950s: the general term for the majority of modern popular music. Rock can be used as noun, or as a multipurpose adjective as in *rock star, rock concert, rock critic*, etc.

* *'Rock is revolutionary. Usually the performers and promoters are not, at least consciously.'* (R. Neville, *Play Power, 1970)*
* *'Writing about them and getting them in free to rock concerts.'* (N. Fury, *Agro*, 1971)
* *'What we need are more rock "stars" willing to make fools of themselves.'* (L. Bangs, *Psychotic Reactions and Carburetor Dung, 1988)*
* *'You may, however, wonder how such an album . . . could be sold . . . by said record company to the "hard rock" consumers of America.'* (L. Bangs, *Psychotic Reactions and Carburetor Dung*, 1988)
* *'Bread's middle of the road pop, Queen's British pomp rock, and the Stooges' rabid proto-rock.'* (*Independent on Sunday*, 21 October 1990)

rocker *n.* [1963]
the antithesis of a ⇨Mod: a member of a youth cult which wore leather jackets, rode motorcycles, and danced to 1950s rock n roll music.

* *'After the Baths had let us out for the night, groups of Mods and Rockers used to gang up round the bus stop waiting for the bus home. There were a few little fights.'* (J. Mandelkau, *Buttons*, 1971)

rocksteady *n., adj.* [1969]
a style of popular music from Jamaica, it has a slow tempo and a stressed off-beat.
See also **ska; bluebeat.**

* *'Late in the sixties the ska, bluebeat, rocksteady tradition moved into today's reggae.'* (J. Green (ed.), *Bob Marley & the Wailers,* 1976)

rock video *n.* [1968]
see **pop video.**

role playing games (*or* **role-gaming)** *n.* [1985]
computer or board games in which the player takes on the role of a given character – usually a hero or villain plucked from the staple castlist of Tolkienesque sword and sorcery – and sets off adventuring around a fantasy universe.
See also **Dungeons and Dragons.**

* *'The ultimate role playing game. Sixteen thousand objects, two hunded and fifty characters, unlimited encounters.'* (*Ace,* August 1990)

rolfing *n.* [1972]
from Ida P. Rolf (1897–1979) who developed a therapy based on 'deep massage', which was intended to relax mental tensions by dealing with muscular, physical ones.

* *'So what is Rolfing, according to the physiologist-turned-body therapist who "discovered" it?'* (A. Clare & S. Thompson, *Let's Talk About Me,* 1981)

roller disco *n.* [1978]
the amalgamation of disco music and roller-skating, briefly fashionable in the late 1970s.

ROM *abbrev.* [1966]
acronym for Read Only Memory: a permanent store of information within the computer which can only be changed by a particular user, by particular operating conditions or by a particular external process, but not by conventional write processes, i.e. simply adding new data. ROM is used to store permanent procedures in the machine, e.g. the operating system.
See also **RAM.**

* *'Software, including a spreadsheet, a word processor and a very powerful BASIC compiler, is in ROM.'* (*Byte,* June 1990)

roof tax *n.* [1990]
the Labour Party's proposed alternative to the much-vilified ➪Community Charge or Poll Tax: it would be levied on houses (similarly to the rates, but on a sliding scale depending on the size of the 'roof') rather than on the number of individuals who occupy them.

roots man *n.* [1969]
a Rastafarian (➪**rasta**), who goes back to his black African roots. The term can be found as an adjective, **rootsy,** referring to the qualities of the person or object (often a record) in question.

* *'If you're black, there's worries. Especially if you're a cultural person, a roots man, it's just terrible.'* (J. Green, *Them,* 1990)

RORO ship *n.* [1969]
acronym for roll-on roll-off ship or ferry: a merchant ship so designed that tourist or commercial traffic can drive on at the embarkation point and drive off again at the ship's destination.

ROSLA *abbrev.* [1970]
raising of the school leaving age. The school leaving age in the UK was raised from 15 to 16 as from 1 September 1973.

rough mix *n.* [1977]
the first basic mixing together of the various recorded tracks to be incorporated in a song or piece of music.

roundeye *n.* [1967]
1. a Westerner, who has round eyes, as opposed to the 'slant' eyes of an Oriental; used by both races.
2. *a slang term* for the anus.

round trip *n.* [1974]
in the stock market: used to describe the practice of earning profits by borrowing on one's overdraft and using the money to lend out at interest on the money markets. Those who practice this **round-tripping** are **round-trippers**.

round-the-table (talks) *n.* [1963]
any talks that are held by a number of rival interest groups – from international diplomacy to local industrial relations – at which all those concerned sit down together to work out an agreement.

routier *n.* [1961]
from the French word meaning a long-distance lorry driver, the small cafes and restaurants frequented by such drivers. Such cafes are listed in the *Guide des Relais Routiers*.

RSI *abbrev.* [1987]
repetitive stress injury: a variety of injuries that afflict those who perform repetitive jobs, especially the operation of computer keyboards, when acute pains, similar to "tennis elbow" can strike an individual.

* *'Never mind RSI – repetitive stress injury – the real perils of 20th century designer living . . . are express coffee maker's wrist and choking.'* (*The Independent*, 22 June 1990)

rubber bullet *n.* [1971]
hard rubber ammunition used for riot control and supposedly non-lethal, although the large bullets, about nine inches long and two in diameter, are sufficiently solid to kill if they hit their target in a vulnerable area of the head or body.
See also **baton round; plastic bullet**.

* *'A loud report and the rubber bullet thwacks into a teenage boy, catching him between the legs.'* (A.F.N. Clarke, *Contact*, 1983)

rubbish *v.* [1972]
to attack, to decry (*see also* **put down**); the term was originated in Australia but has become colloquial in English since the 1970s.

* *'Teachers in schools have been rubbished by the Government for the last ten years.'* (*Independent on Sunday*, 3 June 1990)

Rubik's cube *n.* [1975]
a puzzle designed and patented by E. Rubik, a Hungarian teacher, and distributed with great success throughout the world; the cube consists of 27 smaller cubes, linked together and given a different colour on each of their six faces. These cubes can be rotated on their own plane. The point of the puzzle is to rotate these cubes until each of the nine smaller cubes that make up one side of the larger cubes is showing the same colour.

rude boy (or rudie) *n.* [1967]
a poor Jamaican tearaway who flourished in the 1960s; the rude boy was seen as a criminal hooligan by his opponents, and as a cool daring role model by his peers. His apotheosis

came in the the film *The Harder They Come* (1971).

rumpy-pumpy *n.* [1972]
sexual intercourse.

✱ *'Cor! I envy the chick that gets a piece of your rumpy-pumpy action tonight, you saucy sex-machine! Hubba, hubba!'* (*Cheap Thrills* magazine, August 1990)

run a game (on) *phrase.* [1967]
to obtain money by deceit or trickery (originally black usage only).

run (it) down *v.* [1964]
to describe a situation.

✱ *'I ran it all down to them about Bobby Hutton. And you know what? Those people really applauded at what I had told them.'* (B. Seale, *Seize the Time*, 1968)

run out of road *phrase.* [1961]
to crash one's vehicle when, instead of turning a corner, one keeps going straight, and thus off the road into a wall, ditch or similar obstacle.

run out of steam *phrase.* [1961]
to reach one's limit, to become exhausted; the image is of a steam engine gradually losing its impetus.

runs *n.* [1962]
diarrhoea.

run scared *v.* [1960]
to be frightened or apprehensive.

run (something) by *v.* [1965]
similar to the older 'run it up the flagpole and we'll see who salutes', 'run by' means to test out, to put up for criticism.

✱ *'"Martha," he said when she'd finished, "run that one by me again slowly, will you".'* (C. McFadden, *The Serial*, 1976)

run time *n.* [1965]
1. the time at or during which a computing task is executed.
2. the time taken to execute a task. Often as **run time version**: a cut down version of a programe, which is distributed possibly as a demonstration or to accompany another programe which requires only some of the first program's features.

run with *v.* [1980]
to go along with, to encourage, to back up.

rush-release *v. n.* [1966]
to produce and market a product (usually a record or a film) in the shortest possible time.

Sabatier (knife) *n.*
a range of kitchen knives produced by the Sabatier company of France; supposedly the best of their type, and increasingly popular in the 1960s and 1970s as gourmet cooking (with gourmet equipment) became fashionable in the UK and America.
See **cookware.**

sack(ed) *v., adj.* [1969]
in US football: to tackle the quarterback while he is retreating behind the line of scrimmage and still preparing to pass the ball.

SAD *abbrev.* [1987]
an acronym for seasonal affectiveness disorder: the phenomenon whereby some people have serious physiological and (more often) psychological changes in direct relation to the changing seasons; usually this means that the winter, with its long nights and cold days, has a notably adverse effect.

safari park *n.* [1969]
an area of parkland, often surrounding a British stately home fallen on the need to make money for its upkeep, which has been populated with wild animals; the animals are allowed to roam free and visitors can drive past them in their cars.

safari suit *n.* [1967]
a style of suit that supposedly mimics those worn in Africa by white hunters on safari. *Also* **safari shirt.**

* *'One of these big rancher king motheroos with the broad belly and the $70 lisle Safari shirt.'* (T. Wolfe, *The Mid-Atlantic Man,* 1968)

safe *adj.* [1988]
an all-purpose term of approval used to describe clothes, records, etc. by US and then UK teenagers. The term has arrived via two borrowings: the first from standard English by black Americans, and subsequently by the white young from their black counterparts.
See also **rad, wicked.**

safe! [1989]
a popular greeting among British youth, especially black youth, in the late 1980s.
See also **rad; wicked.**

safe house *n.* [1963]
a building used for housing defectors or other sensitive individuals, or for meetings during clandestine operations to give instructions to or to debrief an agent; also used by secret police for the imprisonment and/or torture of their victims.

safe sex *n.* [1986]
non-penetrative sex in various permutations, a by-product of the spread of ➪AIDS. Safe sex also implies the use of condoms, caps, and other forms of contraception.

* *'Perhaps de Monchaux feels it is fallacious to be dabbling in vagina dentata in an era of safe sex.'* (*Sunday Correspondent*, 13 May 1990)

safing *n.* [1972]
the reducing of (nuclear) weapons from a state of immediate readiness to fire back to a safe condition, once the emergency that caused their arming has passed.

sail wing *n.* [1962]
the sail of a hang-glider, usually a fabric envelope that resembles a large-scale paper dart made of aluminium spars and nylon cloth.

salads *n.* [1988]
an acronym for the Social and Liberal Democratic Party, the party formed of the old Liberal Party and that part of the SDP that chose to reject the leadership of Dr David Owen.

salsa *n.* [1975]
a type of South American dance music, and the dance that is performed to it.

SALT I/II/III *abbrev.* [1968/72]
an acronym for the Strategic Arms Limitation Talks, three sets of talks that were held between the two superpowers. They included:
1. SALT I talks between the superpowers that lasted from 1969 to the signature in 1972 of the Anti-Ballistic Missile Treaty (⇨ABM). Like all such talks, national strategic interest ensured that little real progress in reducing the arms race could be achieved but the feeling in 1972 was that the world was a safer place. SALT I stands in retrospect as the peak achievement of ⇨detente.

* *'Although SALT I was partly the result of other countries' pressure for superpower strategic arms limitation, there was already some unease among European NATO allies.'* (A. Wilson *The Disarmer's Handbook*, 1983)

2. SALT II a series of ultimately inconclusive negotiations that began in Vladivostock in 1974 and ran on to Vienna in 1979. While President Carter and General Secretary Brezhnev signed a document which provided for some very broad restrictions on the arms that can be held by each superpower, the US Congress refused to ratify the treaty and it remained in suspension. In effect the two powers have held to SALT II, but neither side has felt constrained in any way to restrict their research and development of new and more devastating weapons.

* *'Under the terms of the SALT II agreement, the Soviets are permitted to develop one new ICBM . . . but they were not permitted the option of dropping it and trying an alternative model.'* (A. Cockburn *The Threat*, 1983)

3. SALT III the round of arms talks that were scheduled to follow on from the SALT II talks that had ended with the unratified agreement of 1979. These talks were intended, *inter alia*, to consider the problem of intermediate-range weapons based in the European theatre. Although President Reagan promised in 1980 to prepare for new arms negotiations, there were no immediate developments. In the event SALT III as such never materialized. Instead the abortive ⇨INF and ⇨START talks were commenced, neither of which managed to achieve any real progress.

* *'It was almost certainly the proposal that the Soviets had intended to make in SALT III. It would have been an improvement . . . insofar as there would have been fewer Soviet MIRVed ICBMs.'* (S. Talbott, *Deadly Gambits*, 1984)

SAM *abbrev.* [1975]
an acronym for surface-to-air missile; a prefix generally restricted to descriptions of Soviet anti-aircraft missiles.

* *'The only way to avoid a SAM was to dive for the deck. The SAM's own G-forces were so great that they couldn't make the loop and come back down.'* (T. Wolfe, *Mauve Gloves and Madmen*, 1976)

samizdat *n.* [1970]
from Russian 'self-publishing': the dissident 'underground press' that works to copy and disseminate otherwise forbidden literature, criticism, and other works that are banned in the USSR and its satellites.

* *'The word samizdat describes those literary works, political writings, newsletters, petitions, open letters, trial transcripts, and allied materials . . . that are disseminated outside the official channels in the Soviet Union.'* (J. Green, *Encyclopedia of Censorship*, 1990)

samosa *n.* [1960]
a savoury meat or vegetable pasty, a staple of Indian cooking.

sample *v., n.* [1987]
the taking of extracts from a number of other songs, sound effects, film sound tracks, etc., and combining them to make up a new song; particularly popular in the production of dance music records since the late 1980s.

* *'The . . . two chips allow the 1040 STE to replay high-quality sampled sounds, in stereo, without burdening the CPU.'* (ad for Atari Corporation in *Ace*, August 1990)

sampler *n.* [1970]
an album made up of single tracks from a variety of other albums, demonstrating the range of a record company's artistes.

* *'Robert Moog's synthesizer (the analogue precursor of the sampler)'.* (*Sunday Correspondent*, 3 June 1990)

sanctions-buster (*or* **-breaker**) *n.* [1970]
any individual, company, or country that deliberately sets out to break the sanctions applied to a given country.

Sandinista *n., adj.* [1962]
a member of the leftwing military and political organization that took power in Nicaragua after the fall of the dicator Luis Somoza in 1979. The name comes from Augusto Sandino, a Nicaraguan nationalist hero, who was murdered, allegedly on the instructions of Somoza's father, Anastasio, in 1934.

* *'The Sandinistas . . . argued that the previous regimes had failed to achieve the political, social and economic ends for which governments are instituted.'* (P. Brogan, *World Conflicts*, 1989)

S and M *abbrev.* [1965]
sadism and masochism.

* *'Their bodies are caricatures of women; specifically they recall the dominatrices of S&M magazines.'* (J. Meades, *Peter Knows What Dick Likes*, 1989)

sanitize *v.* [1966]
1. to remove any embarrassing, incriminating, or classified material from documents that are revealed to the public – as under the US Freedom of Information Act – or circulated within government departments where they may be read by 'insecure' people.

2. by extension from 1. the general word in government/political circles for the keeping of such 'dirt' away from the public or the media.

* *'However much the generals try to sanitize the strategy with talk of destroying Iraqi equipment, they know, and we know, that death on a large scale will be involved.'* (*Independent on Sunday*, 10 February 1991)

sanpaku *n.* [1963]
a situation when the white of the eye is visible below the pupil; supposedly the unhealthy condition that follows a failure to follow a ◇macrobiotic diet.

* *'Her eyes, still sanpaku, were sunken in their sockets. She could barely sit up. She could not have weighed more than 80 pounds.'* (R. Christgau, *Beth Ann and Macrobioticism* 1965)

sarney (*or* sarnie) *n.* [1961]
a slang term for sandwich.

* *'Do you want a bacon sarney, boss? There's a bit of bread.'* (A.F.N. Clarke, *Contact*, 1983)

SAT *abbrev.* [1988]
an acronym for standard assessment test: the term has been used for some time in the US, but has only emerged in British education in the last few years, coupled to the emergence of a ◇national curriculum.

* *'For the past three weeks, 2 per cent of seven year-olds have been doing pilot tests, or Standard Assessment Tests.'* (*Independent on Sunday*, 27 May 1990)

satellite television *n.* [1966]
any form of television that is beamed to individual homes via an orbiting satellite; two satellite broadcasters – SKY and BSB – were launched in the 1980s, and were amalgamated in 1989 as BSkyB.

satisfaction note *n.* [1971]
in insurance, an acknowledgment by an individual claiming repayment from an insurance company that the repairs made to his car after a crash are satisfactory.

saucy *n.* [1962]
a popular synonym for smutty or risqué; usually found in conjunction with 'postcard'.

SAVAK *abbrev.* [1967]
an acronym for of Sazman-i-Attalat Va Amniyat-i-Keshvar (National Security and Intelligence Organization): Iran's secret intelligence organization, whose brutal methods were largely responsible for maintaining the Shah in power.

* *'The Shah . . . had a 400,000-man army, a large and effective police force, and a sinisterly effective secret police, Savak.'* (P. Brogan, *World Conflicts*, 1989)

scag *n.* [1967]
a slang term for heroin.

* *'"The truth is," he said, "we're going to Las Vegas to croak a scag baron named Savage Henry".'* (H.S. Thompson *Fear and Loathing in Las Vegas*, 1971)

* *'Who just last week graduated from Rocky Horror Show lines to scag-dabblings and now stumble around Max's.'* (L. Bangs, *Psychotic Reactions and Carburetor Dung*, 1988)

scam *n.* [1963]
any form of trick, swindle, racket or confidence game; especially a large-scale scheme

for the importation and selling of illegal drugs.

* *'Assigned to help Capaldi crack a takeover scam is a conservative crown prosecutor* (Robert Pugh).' (*The Independent*)

scare story *n.* [1960]
a news story that is deliberately played up as frightening in order to push through an otherwise unacceptable policy.

scare tactics *n.* [1967]
any strategem of disinformation that sets out to manipulate public worries in order to achieve a given aim, which might not be possible were the public to give it rational consideration.

scattershot *adj.*
wide ranging, on the analogy of a shotgun charge, which scatters small pellets over a wide arc of fire.
See also **broadbrush**.

scattersite *adj.* [1972]
referring to government-sponsored housing that is intended to break up the concentration of the poor in inner-city ghettoes by spreading such projects throughout all areas of the city.

scenario *n.* [1962]
originally movie jargon, describing the script from which the film will actually be shot, with the dialogue, the camera angles and all other technical directions included; thence corrupted to provide a spuriously sophisticated synonym for any course of action, description of an event, circumstance, happening, etc.

* *'A range of forecasts on Britain's future CO_2 emissions . . . based on a "business as usual" scenario in which nothing is done to reduce them.'* (*The Independent* 24 May 1990)

schools television *n.* [1971]
educational television programmes, aimed at schools and broadcast during school hours; such television is usually accompanied by a variety of written and visual material, sent to teachers and pupils to accompany the televised course.

schtick (*or* **schtik)** *n.* [1961]
from the Yiddish, the essence of a comedy performance; a piece of carefully contrived 'business'.

* *'Allen's schtick was a development of the story of the Princess and the Pea, only there was no mattress anywhere soft enough to sooth him.'* (*The Independent* 26 July 1990)

scientific notation *n.* [1961]
also known as **floating point**: the handling of very large numbers in a machine that has only limited computational space by moving the decimal point and performing the calculations with each number expressed as a factor of 10.

score *v., n.* [1961]
1. *a slang term* that essentially means buy, and generally refers either to obtaining sex (whether commercial, in which it is literally a purchase, or otherwise, in which it means seduction), or to buy drugs.
2. in a more general, usually criminal/police sense; to carry out a robbery.

* *'The punters knew where to score, the school authorities were untroubled by messy scandals.'* (T. Blacker, *Fixx 1989*)
* *'Glowing A-Zs of marijuana, growing your*

own, how to roll a joint, how to score, market reports on prices and quality.' (R. Neville, *Play Power* 1970)

Scot(s) Nat *n.* [1974]
an abbreviation for the Scottish Nationalist Party.

scratch pad *n.* [1965]
an area of a machine's memory reserved for short-term working with, or storage of material that can then be erased; a small fast and reusable memory.

* *'The beautiful and, to me, inscrutable language of the microelectronic era: hexaddresses, default redix, floating point mantissas, swapbites, sys log, sim dot, scratch pad.'* (T. Kidder, *The Soul of a New Machine*, 1981)

screwdriver job *n.* [1987]
production of commodities that consists simply in the final assembly of parts manufactured elsewhere and delivered to a factory; often the practice of multinational corporations who maximize profits out of such divisions of labour. The factories that carry out this type of work are known as **screwdriver plants or screwdriver factories.**

SCSI *abbrev.* [1982]
Small Computer System Interface (pronounced scuzzy): a microcomputer-oriented serial interface, first proposed in 1982; SCSI interfaces improve the overall performance of hard disks, linking a number of otherwise disparate devices together and generally improving compatibility and thus speed.

* *'An i486 motherboard, a caching SCSI disk drive controller, an Ethernet adaptor, and a prototype TIGA graphics co-processor.'* (*Byte*, April 1990)

Scud (missile) *n.* [1965]
the Soviet SS-1B/C surface-to-surface missile, which gained international prominence during the Gulf War of 1991. 'Scud' is the name allotted it by NATO analysts of Soviet weapons systems. First deployed in 1965 the Scud, carried on a wheeled launcher, had a maximum range of 110 miles when equipped with a nhuclear warhead, and of 170 miles with a conventional warhead. An inaccurate weapon, it could guarantee hitting at best within 1 km of a target. The Scuds used in the Gulf had been modified by the Iraqis, and were capable of reaching Israel and Saudi Arabia, giving them a range of *c.* 300 miles.

* *'There were 30 Scud surface-to-surface missiles with a 180 mile range that could pass over the Golan heights.'* (R.W. Howe, *Weapons*, 1980)

scumbag *n.* [1967/71]
a slang term for condom, and by extension a general pejorative for an unpleasant person.

scungy *adj.* [1966]
unpleasant, disgusting, a mixture of 'grungy' and 'scummy'

scut work *n.* [1960]
all the trivial and/or unpleasant chores – either dirty, tedious or both – that have to be performed in a hospital. Extended to general use.

scuzzy *adj.* [1968]
dirty, grimy, murky, generally unpleasant.

* *'The scuzzy slide guitar encrusted "You Can't Tell How Much Suffering (On A Face That's Always Smiling)".'* (*The Independent*, 8 June 1990)

SDI *abbrev.* [1983]
Strategic Defence Initiative: a research programme for a non-nuclear global defence 'umbrella' (⇨nuclear umbrella), proposed by President Reagan in 1983, probably based on powerful satellite based laser weaponry and intelligence systems. The initiative is more generally known, after the 1974 hit film, as **Star Wars**. Despite the overwhelming criticisms from a broad spectrum of US expert opinion, and the almost inconceivable advances in science required, the demands of national pride, coupled with the keenness of the military-industrial-academic complex to capitalize on the vast sums of cash (the basic research costs will top $30 billion) available will probably ensure that the SDI will become a centrepiece of the arms race for many years. The rundown of the Cold War should have put paid to SDI, but there has yet to be an official cancellation, and the Gulf War – notably in its deployment of the anti-missile Patriot missiles – may well give further ammunition to its supporters.

* *'Serious critics of the SDI, such as . . . George W. Ball, who has called the scheme "one of the most irresponsible acts by any head of state in modern times".'* (J. Green, *The A-Z of Nuclear Jargon*, 1986)

SDLP *abbrev.* [1970]
Social Democratic and Labour Party: the equivalent of the mainland Labour Party in Northern Ireland.

SDP *abbrev.* [1981]
Social Democratic Party: formed by four breakaway Labour MPs – Roy Jenkins, David Owen, Shirley Williams and Bill Rodgers – who rejected what they saw as the Party's drift towards the doctrinaire left.
See also **salads**.

* *'The SDP, free from rigid adherence to any familiar party programme, seemed an influential force in British politics during the early months of 1982.'* (A. Palmer, *Penguin Dictionary of 20th Century History*, 1990)

SDR *abbrev.* [1967]
special drawing rights: an additional drawing right allotted to members of the International Monetary Fund (IMF) which gives them the powers to draw extra foreign currency from the Fund, with which they can increase their foreign currency reserves.

SDS *abbrev.* [1961]
1. Students for a Democratic Society: the earliest of the radical US student organizations campaigning first for student rights and latterly for a variety of causes, notably the ending of US involvement in Vietnam; founded in 1961 the original SDS had split by the end of the 1960s into a number of factions, whose members formed groups ranging from the anarcho-hippie ⇨Yippies to the ⇨urban guerillas of ⇨Weatherman, all of which could loosely be bracketed as the ⇨New Left.

* *'To succeed, SDS had to reaffirm the tradition of native American radicalism . . . without losing the sense of worldwide revolution that had driven people into the streets in the first place.'* (H. Jacobs (ed.), *Weatherman*, 1970)

2. a parallel SDS, espousing much the same ends and like some elements of the US model moving on to radical urban terrorism, existed in Germany.

* *'You've screwed SDS and now they're shocked, so they scream for democracy – as if you'd ever*

stick to the rules of the game.' (Berlin Kommune 1, *An Application*, 1 June 1967)

Sealed Knot, The *n.* [1971]
an organization of military and historical devotees, incorporated in 1971, which re-enacts battles of the English Civil War.

SEAQ *abbrev.* [1986]
Stock Exchange Automated Quotations: the computerized system of displaying share prices and recording share dealings that underlies the computerization of the City since the ➪Big Bang of 1986.

search and destroy *v, adj., n.* [1966]
a military strategy developed for US troops during the Vietnam War: an area would be designated and the troops would move through it, searching out hostile forces and destroying them and their supplies and equipment. As events proved, search and destroy missions were rarely so selective, and could lead to a high level of generalized destruction.

* *'Search and Destroy, more a gestalt than a tactic, brought up alive and steaming from the Command psyche.'* (M. Herr, *Dispatches*, 1977)

second strike *n., adj.* [1960]
the retaliatory attack by whichever of the superpowers has already been hit by a first (and possibly ➪pre-emptive) ➪first strike. Thus **second strike capability**: the ability of a military power to launch a retaliatory attack on its enemy, after surviving a hostile first strike; **second strike counterforce capability**: the ability to launch a retaliatory strike, after suffering a first strike against the enemy's forces; essentially a more specific version of a general second strike and one which, given its supposed 'sparing' of hostile populations, would not be used. Once one side had suffered the effect of a full nuclear attack, the questions of where one sent one's retaliation, were it feasible, would probably be academic.

* *'Even without Minuteman, our surviving second strike capability would remain large.'* (US Department of Defence, *Annual Report*, 1980)

Second World *n.* [1974]
all the nations of the developed world, with the exception of the superpowers themselves.

secular humanism *n.* [1981]
a term developed by America's ultra-fundamentalists to categorize any book or teaching method that denies the primacy of absolute values, refuses to base its central tenets on religion and is thus rendered unacceptable.

* *'The fundamentalist lobby . . . attempts to show that teenage prostitution, pornography, and murder are all a result of secular humanism in the schools.'* (J. Green, *Encyclopedia of Censorship*, 1990)

security blanket *n.* [1971]
any form of totem that gives its owner a sense of security and reassurance; from the blanket, piece of cloth, or similar item carried around by many small children.

security dilemma *n.* [1963]
the driving force behind the arms race: since one power fears the weapons of the other it adds to its own arsenal, believing that only by this attempt to gain the advantage, which the first power promotes as a purely defensive measure, can it maintain its own security. The

second power can only see this increase in weapons as offensive, and thus reverses the situation, pulling ahead once more in the arms race, once again, claiming that its new systems are purely defensive. The first power, seeing this, chooses to believe that its opponent is really building up for an attack and then reinforces its already modernized arsenal.

self-starter *n.* [1960]
an executive who provides his/her own motivation and ideas for the job in hand. Those who achieve this are known to **self-start**.

* '*The president, de Castro, liked "self-starters", it was said. Initiative was welcomed at Data General.*' (T. Kidder, *The Soul of a New Machine*, 1981)

sell-by (date) *n.* [1965]
a date, stamped on a variety of perishable goods, by which time the item must be sold or removed from the shelves and (presumably) discarded; therefore the mid-1980s' slang **past his** (*or her*) **sell-by date**: out of date, over the hill, 'past it'.

sell-out *v.* [1968]
1. to abandon one's beliefs, especially political ones, and enter the mainstream (often after being lured by the seduction of financial gain).
2. Also used to describe the person who acts in this way. The term goes back to the mid-19th century, but came into wider use during the radical activism of the 1960s. – **sell-out**, *n.*

semantics *n.*
an ⇨upmarket version of the plain English 'playing with words'; thus 'It's all semantics to me'. The original use, the study of relationships between linguistic symbols and their meanings, dates back to the 1890s.

semiotics (*or* **semiology**) *n.* [1973]
the study of signs and, in sociology, the means of analysing messages, both written and visual. Semiotics uses three concepts: the signifier, the signified and the sign – which last denotes the relationship between the first two. It is possible to go beyond the immediate impact of the sign and ask questions concerning the wider meanings and social functions of the codes and myths that such signs prompt. The term semiology was coined by Ferdinand de Saussure in 1915, although its current use springs more immediately from the work of the US philosopher C.S. Peirce and from the author Umberto Eco's book *A Theory of Semiotics* (1976).

* '*Saussure's work provided the foundation for the methodological analysis of sign systems (semiotics).*' (M. Wynne-Davies (ed.), *The Bloomsbury Guide to English Literature*, 1989)

Sendero Luminoso *n.*
see **Shining Path**.

send up *v.* [1962]

sensurround *n., adj.* [1974]
a short-lived innovation in the cinema, designed literally to surround the audience with sound, thus projecting them right into the middle of the filmic action, rather than relying on the traditional speakers mounted to either side of the screen.

* '*Sensurround: A system evolved in 1975 for Earthquake, this dispensible gimmick involved the augmentation of violent action on screen by*

intense waves of high decibel sound.' (L. Halliwell, *Filmgoer's Companion*, 8th edn,. 1984)

serial killer *n.* [1970]
a multiple murderer who kills a series of victims (usually of a similar type and using a similar method of killing) over an extended period. The practice is as old as humanity, the term is more recent and gained wide usage through a number of crimes committed in the 1960s and 1970s.

* *'She is adored by the hideously disfigured Englund ("composer by day, serial killer by night").'* (*The Independent*, 14 June 1990)

serial monogamy *n.* [1972]
short-lived monogamous relationships that follow one another in succession, the term is often used of those who undergo multiple divorces, swapping one partner for a new one, albeit remaining faithful for the duration of the relationship.
See also **open marriage**.

serious *adj.* [1982]
an all-purpose descriptor of anything, but usually money, e.g. salaries, house prices, that are worthy of respect; the implication is of hushed tones.

* *'Morton said that "TML came looking for serious money and has not got it." TML, incandescent, demanded his resignation.'* (*Independent on Sunday*, 13 May 1990)

SERPS *abbrev.*
an acronym for State Earnings-Related Pension Scheme.

service industry *n.* [1970]
catering, entertainment, computer maintenance – a whole world of ancillary trades that have sprung up to replace the heavy industries of yore. Unlike pig-iron, of course, they don't do much for the balance of trade. Such industries make up the **service sector**.

* *'Some twenty years before Great Britain Limited followed my example, I abandoned product in favour of the service industries.'* (T. Blacker, *Fixx*, 1989)

Thus: **service millionaires**: lawyers, distributors, managers, etc., whose earnings are geared to the percentage they take out of the earnings of or generated by the big stars.

* *'Madonna's lawyers are "service millionaires" of the sort Phillips wants people to get angry about.'* (*New York Review of Books*, 19 July 1990)

services *n.* [1963]
as used by architects, electricity, waste disposal, heating and similar provisions for domestic use.

SET *abbrev.* [1966]
an acronym for Selective Employment Tax: also known popularly as the **payroll tax**, which was paid by employers to the government on the basis of the wages they paid out to their workers.

* *'At eleven o'clock we gathered to be told the budget secrets, and SET was revealed to us.'* (R. Crossman, *Diary*, 2 May 1966)

set and setting *n.* [1968]
the immediate environment as considered as a modifier of behaviour and experience; used specifically in respect of the taking of ⇨LSD trips; the drug is best experienced, according to such gurus as Timothy Leary, in a quiet room, surrounded by friends, in an atmos-

phere of serenity, possibly with soothing music playing and appealing pictures on the walls. Such a view was not universal among other LSD proselytizers such Ken Kesey, the name of whose acolytes, the 'Merry Pranksters', summed up a more rumbustious attitude to the consumption of hallucinogens.

* *'If the set and setting are supportive and spiritual, then from 40–90 percent of the experiences will be revelatory and mystico-religious.'* (T. Leary, *The Politics of Ecstasy*, 1968)

set theory *n.* [1960]
a branch of mathematics that deals with sets without regard to the nature of their individual constituents.

set-up *n.* [1968]
a synonym for the older 'frame-up': a situation in which a criminal has been tricked into betraying himself (and his companions) by the police.

Seven Sisters *n.* [1962]
the seven largest international oil companies: British Petroleum, Exxon, Gulf, Mobil, Royal Dutch Shell, Standard Oil of California, and Texaco (as in 1979).

sex aid *n.* [1977]
known in the trade as 'toys', any item that enhances sexual pleasure or makes it possible for those in some way handicapped, to lead a more active sex life.

sex and shopping *adj.* [1980]
see **shopping and fucking**.

sex-bomb *n.* [1963]
an overtly sexy woman, often a film-star or pin-up girl who is actively promoted as such.

sex-change *n. adj.* [1960]
the physical changing of one's sex by a surgical operation; dictated by anatomy, this invariably deals with men who become women.

* *'I promised you that if you died in a plane-crash I'd have a sex-change operation, so at least you'd be laughing on the way down.'* (C. Blake, *Girl Talk*, 1990)

sexism *n.* [1968]
discrimination and prejudice based on sex, usually biased against women; the stereotyping of women into 'mother', 'mistress', 'typist', etc.

* *'He's just another trafficker in cheap nihilism with all that it includes – cheap racism, sexism, etc.'* (L. Bangs, *Psychotic Reactions and Carburetor Dung*, 1988)

sexist *adj.* [1965)]
offering discrimination and/or prejudice based on one's sex (usually of men towards women).

* *'I'm not being sexist, women are just as ready with their pens as men.'* (J. Meades, *Peter Knows What Dick Likes*, 1989)

sex manual *n.* [1975]
any form of manual created to instruct its reader in sexual techniques and the general enhancement of their sex life.

sex object *n.* [1963]
anyone – male or more likely female – regarded purely and simply as an object of sexual desire and possible gratification.

sexploitation *adj.*
descriptive of any film, though not necessarily hard- or softcore pornography, that depends

for its audience appeal on the maker's unashamed and deliberate exploitation of its sexual content, and the alleged sexiness of its (female) star.

See also **blaxploitation.**

✱ *'Rat, like the underground papers, was feeling the squeeze of the new sexploitation mags that were crowding them off the newsstands.'* (A. Hoffman, *Woodstock Nation*, 1969)

sex-shop *n.* [1970]
any shop, often advertising itself (in England at least) as a 'Book Shop' that sells pornography (visual and written, hard and softcore) and a range of sex aids.

sex surrogate *n.* [1969]
a person employed as a sexual partner for an individual who is undergoing sex therapy. The term surrogate is also found as an adjective.

✱ *'Masters and Johnson researchers . . . also provided "surrogate wives" as sex partners for dysfunctional men.'* (G. Talese, *Thy Neighbor's Wife*, 1980)

sex therapy *n.* [1970]
the treatment by counselling, psychotherapy and other disciplines of various sexual problems, such as impotence or frigidity. Those who conduct such treatment are **sex therapists** (1976).

sex tourism *n.* [1983]
a form of tourism that concentrates on visiting those areas of the world – Hamburg, Bangkok – where commercial sex of every variety (much of it, such as intercourse with child prostitutes, impossible to obtain legally in the West) is available without hindrance.

✱ *'Sex tourism may be morally reprehensible but there's no denying it's a great way to meet girls.* (*Arena*, July–August 1990)

sexual discrimination *n.* [1964]
discrimination (usually in employment) that is based on excluding one sex (usually women) to the benefit of the other.

sexual politics *n.* [1970]
the term originates in feminist Kate Millet's book *Sexual Politics* (1970) in which she proposed the theory that any form of interaction between people was, ultimately, a form of sexual politics. This has been developed in the last twenty years to refer to any form of politics – feminism, gay liberation – that is based on the relationship between the sexes, whether men and women, or homosexuals and heterosexuals.

✱ *'Among the early members were several for whom homosexuality was a crusade. Sexual politics mixed with genuine concern.'* (*The Independent*, 4 September 1990)

sexy *adj.* [1964]
in print and broadcast media; any newsworthy events, especially those involving war, disaster, death or anything suitably violent and/or shocking; coined by the *Sunday Times* 'Insight' team in the early 1960s.

✱ *'What I am interested in is why disasters have suddenly become sexy?'* (*The Independent*, 2 May 1990)

✱ *'Yuppoid soap where the friends are all in sexy employment – advertising, photography, law, etc.'* (*The Independent*, 16 June 1990)

shag *n. adj.* [1972]
a razor-cut hairstyle in which the hair was sculpted into shaggy layers; ➲rock stars such as

Rod Stewart and Ron Wood were its first proponents, although it survives among a variety of ⇨heavy metal bands.

* *'Hey, baby! Here I come with my shag haircut and my big Wazoo.'* (L. Bangs, *Psychotic Reactions and Carburetor Dung*, 1988)

share *v.* [1970]
see **sharing**.

shareowner *n.* [1987]
a person who owns shares; referring to those who have bought shares in the various privatizations of the last decade, rather than the traditional shareholders whose dealings have always fuelled the Stock Exchange.

shareware *n.* [1985]
a system of ⇨software design and distribution whereby copies of a ⇨program are sent out to certain selected individuals who are then encouraged to make copies and give them out. Satisfied users – who receive basic instructions on the disk – can then send a set fee to the program's author, who will then send a proper manual, updates, etc.

* *'Shareware. The best of memory-resident management utilities.'* (*PC World*, May 1990)

sharing *n.*
telling one another one's troubles in the hope that such exchanges will provide mutual benefit and support. – **share**, *v.*

* *'Yuppoid soap where the friends are all in sexy employment . . . and enjoy "sharing" and "talking it out".'* (*The Independent*, 16 June 1990)

Sharon *n.* [1986]
a derogatory term to describe any working-class girl who is considered slightly tarty and devoid of chic taste; her male counterpart is ⇨Kevin.

* *'Now you can get a built-in grass skirt on your swimsuit to match the parasols at Club 18–30. Sharon and Tracey are going to love it.'* (*Independent on Sunday*, 22 April 1990)

sharp end, at the *adv.* [1976]
in the front line, at the heart; from the prow of a ship which, for forging through the water, is sharp.

shell *n.* [1987]
any means of masking the complexities of a computer's operating system, usually by replacing the command line (which has to be typed onto the screen) by some form of visually-based alternative.
See also **front-end**; **GUI**.

* *'I'm no fan of DOS shells; the ones I've tried feel like straitjackets.'* (*Byte*, June 1990)

shell (company) *n.* [1964]
1. a company which exists on paper but not in fact and is used for illegal reasons, e.g. tax avoidance, rather than for actual legitimate trading.
2. a company that is registered for the purpose of its name, and then made available for sale to anyone who requires a ready-made company.

* *'They allowed their names to be used on the notepaper of the particular shell company we were using at the time.'* (T. Blacker, *Fixx*, 1989)

shia (*or* **shi'ite) (muslim)** *n., adj.* [1978]
both these terms, which have gained common currency with the Iranian revolution of 1978,

date back to the foundation of Islam in the 7th century. The Shia sect broke away from the orthodox Sunni Muslims, claiming that Ali (the prophet Muhammad's cousin and son-in-law) was the first true successor to the prophet; they deny the legitimacy of the first three Sunni caliphs.

* *'The key country is Iran, patron of the Shi'ite clans who hold the hostages.'* (*Sunday Correspondent*, 10 June 1990)

Shining Path *n.* [1980]
from the Spanish *Sendero Luminoso*: The Communist Party of Peru for the Shining Path of Jose Carlos Mariategui: Peru's radical Maoist guerrillas, formed in 1980 and agents of a continuing civil war within the country which has claimed up to 15,000 lives.

* *'Sendero Luminoso (the Shining Path) is the most secretive and vicious of Latin American terrorist organizations.'* (P. Brogan, *World Conflicts*, 1989)

shirtlifter *n.* [1966]
a homosexual. – **shirtlift,** *v.*

* *'Squaddies hate: Ruperts and Hugos, shirt-lifting arsebandit foreign nationals, closing time, nouvelle cuisine.'* (*Sunday Correspondent*, 19 August 1990

shithead *n.* [1961]
idiot, fool, incompetent.

shit-hot *adj.* [1961]
excellent, first-rate, (of people) highly enthusiastic.

shitkicker *n.* [1966]
a peasant; originally used in the US, it arrived in Britain in the 1960s.

shitwork *n.* [1968]
any unrewarding laborious probably dirty work.
See also **scut work.**

shoah *n.* [1986]
from the Hebrew: the Holocaust or mass destruction of the Jews during the Second World War. The term gained wide use (if temporarily) with the release of film director Claude Lanzmann's epic study of the Holocaust, which he called *Shoah.*

* *'Claude Lanzmann's film Shoah: An Oral History of the Holocaust (1985) is the most powerful film I have ever seen. It is a creation that transforms the viewer.'* (A. Oz, *The Slopes of Lebanon*, 1987)

shock-horror *adj.* [1977]
facetious exclamation or adjective implying a supposed level of shock or horror which might not be felt with quite the same degree of sincerity as it appears, usually as a highly sensational newspaper feature.

shoe-box *n.* [1968]
any building that resembles a shoebox, usually a plain multi-storey office block, typical of 1960s architecture.

* *'Leeds hasn't changed much. There are a few changes. Some of those glass shoeboxes have been plonked down at random in the city centre.'* (*The Listener*, 1 August 1968)

shoot'em-up *n.* [1988]
originally denoting a film Western, with plenty of gunplay and attendant drama; now a form of computer game, similarly replete with synthetic violence, in which the sole object is for the player to shoot, bomb or otherwise destroy

a series of on-screen 'enemies'. A synonym for the simplest and least intellectually demanding of computer games.

✱ *'Now the leading . . . software developer has set its sights on the shoot'em-up player looking for something special.'* (*Ace*, August 1990)

shopping and fucking *adj.* [1984]
a type of blockbusting novel, developed during the materialist 1980s, in which the normal ingredient of a certain type of best-seller – 'procrastinated rape' – is boosted by regular excursions into the world's ➪upmarket shopping malls in search of lovingly delineated ➪designer-labelled garments and other consumables. When bowdlerized the term is found as **sex and shopping**.

✱ *'Sentimental and escapist, but gutsy and even sage, this is sex and shopping rendered wholesome.'* (*Independent on Sunday*, 21 October 1990)

shopping mall *n.* [1967]
the modern version of the traditional marketplace: a large covered area (pioneered in the US) in which a variety of leading stores have their branches; carefully landscaped, with greenery and fountains and probably piped music and a creche for the young, the mall provides safe, clean shopping, bereft of traffic noise and fumes and with little to distract one from the business of consumption.

✱ *'It was as if an army had been turned loose on the nation's shopping malls.'* (*Newsweek*, 12 December 1983)

short-life *adj.* [1966]
any commodity that has a short storage capacity.
See also **sell-by date**.

show house/flat *n.* [1962]
a fully furnished, but unoccupied, house or flat that is displayed to potential purchasers by the builders of a new estate or block of flats.

shrink *n.* [1966]
an abbreviation of the slang headshrinker, and thus a psychiatrist, a psychoanalyst, or any form of psychotherapist.

✱ *'Might that explain why Mr Reed decided to eschew the waiting shrink in favour of giving a press conference to a most grateful international press corps?'* (*Sunday Correspondent* 13 May 1990)

shrinkage n. [1961]
a retail trade euphemism for shoplifting; many stores assume an annual level of shrinkage and if this drops it may as well reflect an overall decline in trade as it does an increase in security operations.

shrink-wrap *v.* [1961]
to wrap an item, often but not invariably a perishable, in cling-film in order to preserve its freshness. Thus **shrink-wrapped**: an item so packaged.

shtup *v.* [1969]
to have sexual intercourse; from the Yiddish, meaning the same thing.

✱ *'Shtup is vulgar and obscene. I caution finicky readers: Read no further, worse is yet to come!'* (L. Rosten, *Hooray for Yiddish*, 1983)

shuttle diplomacy *n.* [1974]
negotiations between two or more countries conducted by a mediator who flies frequently back and forth between the various parties to the dispute; first highlighted by the efforts of

Dr. Henry Kissinger to unravel the Middle Eastern imbroglio (*c.* 1974).

SIB *abbrev.* [1986]
an acronym for Securities and Investment Board: that body which since the ➩Big Bang of 1987 has been responsible for policing the investment business of the City of London.

sickbag *n.* [1962]
a bag provided on an aircraft into which those who suffer from airsickness may vomit.

sick building syndrome *n.* [1980]
the prevalence of illnesses created by modern hi-tech office blocks, the fabric of which creates a sub-lethal habitat in which toxins in the recycled air, lack of natural light, and the mental and physical stress of working in front of a ➩VDU all combine to create a variety of illnesses that attack an alleged 80% of office workers.

* *'Sick building syndrome is a disease of our time. Largely unidentified until 1980, it is now rampant.'* (*Independent on Sunday* 25 March 1990)

SIDS *abbrev.* [1970]
an acronym for sudden infant death syndrome: generally known as ➩**cot death** and referring to the still unexplained, but massively theorized sudden deaths of very young children who are found dead in their cots.

sigint *abbrev.* [1969]
signals intelligence: intelligence derived from the processing of electronic intelligence and communications intelligence sources.

* *'I, as the MI5 SIGINT expert, pointed out to the management at the meeting that the evidence MI5 had was not sufficient to prove even the intention to communicate secrets to a foreign power.'* (P. Wright, *Spycatcher*, 1987)

signifier *n.* [1960]
from the French *signifiant*: in the linguistic science of ➩semiotics a physical object, a word or picture which performs the act of giving out a message, as opposed to the sign (French *signifié*), which is the message actually given out. The two terms were coined by Ferdinand de Saussure, the originator of ➩semiotics.

* *'I am convinced that when we . . . read a map we do not automatically translate signifier into signified.'* (J. Meades, *Peter Knows What Dick Likes*, 1989)

silent majority *n.* [1970]
the politically silent, but invariably conservative majority of a country's voters; originally a synonym for Middle America, the idea of a passive group of voters – overlooked because of their lack of vocal involvement in the political process – has spread into general use. The term originated in President Richard Nixon's speech of 3 November 1969: 'And so – to you, the great silent majority of my fellow Americans – I ask for your support.'

* *'The suffering silent majority who . . . were making their own way in the world as . . . average housewives.'* (T. Blacker *Fixx*, 1989)
* *'And the silent majority will be able to sleep peacefully in their beds again.'* (N. Fury, *Agro*, 1971)

silicon *n., adj.* [1974]
the base element of the ➩microchip revolution, a non-metallic chemical element which has to date offered the best material for the construction of semiconductor circuits.

Silicon can also be used metaphorically, e.g. **go to silicon**: to move off the drawing board and start making an actual circuit.
See also **Silicon Valley**.

✱ *'Ion Implantation Equipment is used in several key steps during the manufacture of Semiconductors of "Silicon Chips".'* (*Independent on Sunday*, 22 April 1990)

✱ *'Dick Tracy is obviously going to hit silicon, and so will Duck Tales and Rescue Rangers.'* (*Ace*, August 1990)

Silicon Valley *n.* [1974]
the US computer industry; from that area of California, the Santa Clara Valley, south of San Francisco, where so many of the state's leading computer firms are located. Scotland's homegrown equivalent is known as **Silicon Glen**.

✱ *'Silicon Valley's 'computer cops' are using the latest high-tech tools to track down the growing number of criminals who plan to kidnap children.'* (*Sunday Correspondent*, 22 April 22 1990)

sim *abbrev.* [1988]
simulation: a variety of computer games which base their appeal on simulating (as accurately as possible) a jet fighter, a submarine, a tank, etc.

✱ *'It's not a simulation, it's an experience . . . Ocean's first flight sim is the best out!'* (*Zzap*, July 1990)

single *n., adj.* [1969]
unmarried, unattached; the term was particularly popular in the early 1970s, usually as in **swinging single**, a promiscuous unattached person, or in **singles bar**, a bar where such individuals could meet with the express intention of picking each other up for (usually) casual sex.

✱ *No more female ad agency executives telling me how they make men want to get into their pants at singles bars!* (R.D. Rosen, *Psychobabble*, 1977)

single-issue *adj.* [1986]
in politics: denoting any debate, law, individual, concerned only with one issue, e.g. ➪battered wives, the poll tax, etc., rather than with overall strategy.

single market *n* [1989]
the tariff-free European market that is to come on stream in 1992, as stated under the Single European Act.

✱ *'If you want to be more competitive in the single market, write to Jim Cotton-Betteridge, Commercial Manager, Royal Mail International.'* (ad for Royal Mail International in the *Sunday Correspondent*, 8 April 1990)

single parent *n.* [1969]
an unmarried or divorced mother or father who bears the sole responsibility for the rearing of a child or children; thus the **single parent family**: a family unit headed by such a parent.

✱ *'Henry liked the idea of being a single-parent family. There would be programmes about him on the television.'* (N. Williams, *The Wimbledon Poisoner*, 1990)

single-union agreement *n.* [1987]
a trade union agreement between management and the union whereby only one union represents all the workers (irrespective of traditional interests and demarcation lines) in a single factory.

✱ *'Ford blamed a row between the TGWU and the AEU over a single-union deal for its decision to shelve plans for a new factory.'* (*Independent on Sunday*, 8 April 1990)

sink (school) *n.* [1972]
a school situated in a deprived area – the ⇨inner city, a rundown council estate – and which is seen to suffer accordingly both in the teaching provided and the standard of pupils enrolled.

sink tidy *n.* [1972]
a small perforated container placed on or next to the sink, which holds the brushes, cloths, etc., used for washing up.

sinsemilla *n.* [1975]
from the Spanish 'without seeds': a form of particularly strong marijuana, tests have shown its strength to be approximately five times that of common or garden Mexican marijuana.

SIOP *abbrev.* [1960]
an acronym for Single Integrated Operational Plan: the top secret range of interlocking contingency plans under which the US and the UK would fight a nuclear war. The first SIOP was issued in 1960, an amalgam of the various strategic bombing plans evolved in the 1950s, and has been modified continually since.

✱ *'By December 1960 the first Single Integrated Operational Plan (SIOP) was drawn up. The SIOP is probably the Pentagon's most secret document.'* (R.C. Aldridge, *First Strike!*, 1983)

sissy bar *n.* [1969]
a metal loop attached to a motorcycle; this bar is supposed to protect the allegedly 'sissy' (cowardly) rider from harm.

sister *n.* [1968]
a feminist adoption of the earlier black use to mean another woman; in this context the sister is presumably a fellow feminist.

sisterhood *n.* [1968]
a member of the women's movement.

✱ *'I thought the whole point of your women's group was, you know, sisterhood.'* (C. McFadden, *The Serial*, 1976)

✱ *'Those quieter members of the sisterhood, the suffering silent majority.'* (T. Blacker, *Fixx*, 1989)

sitcom *n.* [1964]
an abbreviation for situation comedy.

✱ *'10.05 Not With A Bang. Roll the drums . . . it's a new sitcom.'* (*Independent on Sunday*, 25 March 1990)

sit-in *n.*[(1960]
a public protest that takes the form of occupying a given area by sitting down in it. Other varieties of '-in' include **read-ins**, **kneel-ins**, and **swim-ins**. – **sit in**, *v.*

✱ *'People turn on and fuck everywhere, naked swim-ins in the gym pool, a black dorm, nice woods, co-ed dorms.'* (A. Hoffman, *Woodstock Nation*, 1969)

✱ *'As early as January 1967 a series of disruptions and sit-ins had taken place at the London School of Economics.'* (M. Farren, *Watch Out Kids*, 1972)

situation *n.* [1972]
a redundant term, similar to and popularized at the same time as ⇨ongoing, which is used to

confer upon a simple statement a degree of spurious 'technological' jargon.

✱ *'An officer rang with information that a riot situation may occur in the chapel tomorrow – 1 April.'* (*The Independent*, 6 April 1990)

situationism *n.* [1964]
a set of revolutionary beliefs proposed and espoused by members of the French movement Situationist International and its followers from the 1950s to 1970s. These beliefs centred on a fight against a modern society in which the rise of technology and science had reduced the individual to one more commodity, subject to massive cultural repression and impotent in the face of the all-embracing industrial world. Thus **situationists**: those who chose to attack that world, especially in its faceless bureaucracy and international homogeneity. Situationist philosophy underpinned much of the ideology that emerged in the 'Evenements' of 1968.

✱ *'The Situationist revolution was the revolution of everyday life . . . this naturally fitted together with the hippie thing, except they couldn't stand hippies.'* (J. Green, *Days in the Life*, 1988)

Six Day War *n.* [1967]
the Middle East war fought between Israel and its Arab neighbours from 5–10 June 1967.

✱ *'There have not been many occasions since 1945 when military action was wholly justified. The Six Day War was one of them.'* (P. Brogan, *World Conflicts*, 1989)

six-pack *n.* [1961]
a pack of six bottles or, more recently, cans of beer, linked together by some form of plastic or paper wrapping.

sixth form college *n.* [1965]
a college designed for pupils of 16-plus, teaching A-level courses.

ska *n.* [1964]
a form of Jamaican dance music popular in the 1960s; characterized by a fast beat and emphasis on the off-beat.
See also **bluebeat; reggae**.

✱ *'He would have preferred some reggae, ska, or bluebeat, but then they never put anything decent in Juke-boxes.'* (N. Fury, *Agro*, 1971)

skag *n.* [1967]
see **scag**.

skateboard *n.*, *v.* [1964]
a narrow platform mounted on four roller-skate type wheels on which the user can ride and, if sufficiently skilled, perform tricks. Thus **skateboarding**: the sport developed by the surfers of California as an on-shore substitute for the waves. Those who perform the sport are **skateboarders**.

✱ *'Skateboards – I've almost made them respectable'.* (J. Jackson, 'I'm a Man', 1980)

ski bob *n.* [1966]
a vehicle that resembles a bicycle, but is equipped with skis rather than wheels, and which moves swiftly over snow.

ski bum *n.* [1960]
a skiing enthusiast who takes a variety of casual jobs in a ski resort, with which he or she earns enough to pay for a season's skiing.

✱ *'The story concerns two rival bands of ski bums which vie for control of a mountain resort.'* (*The Independent*, 14 June 1990)

skill centre *n.* [1963]
a centre for the training of vocational rather than academic skills. Such centres are often sponsored by the government in an attempt to reduce unemployment statistics.
See also **job centre.**

skim *v.* [1966]
the retention of a portion of the profits of a casino from being declared to the tax authorities; this money is sent out of the country to foreign banks which will ⇨launder it before it is returned to the country of origin; thus the practice of **skimming**.

skin-flick *n.* [1968]
a pornographic film which depends for its appeal on the exposure of a good deal of unclothed skin.

* *'His latest film . . . looks like the bastard offspring of Cola Advert and Skin Flick.'* (J. Meades, *Peter Knows What Dick Likes*, 1989)

skinhead (*or* **skin)** *n.* [1969]
a member of a working-class youth cult that developed in the late 1960s and has been revived regularly (especially during the resurgence of the quasi-Nazi ⇨National Front in the mid-1970s) ever since. Skinheads, as the name implies, have shaved heads, and deliberately celebrate ugliness and aggression and the fear it inspires in others. The original skins threw off a subgroup, the **suedeheads**, whose hair was slightly longer, but whose manners and politics were equally hostile.

* *'When the Skins leave Edward's flat, they feel as elated as the day they bought their first boots.'* (N. Fury, *Agro*, 1971)
* *'Police detained four skinheads in connection with the attack on Wednesday, but released one after questioning.'* (*Independent on Sunday*, 13 May, 1990)

skinny-dip *v.* [1966]
to bath naked. – **skinny-dipping**, *n.*

skinny-rib sweater *n.* [1973]
a tight sweater that derives its name from being knitted in rib stitch – which makes for greater elasticity – and thus fits tightly over the figure.

skoob *n.* [1963]
an artistic term that comes from reversing the word 'books'; it is a quantity of books assembled deliberately for subsequent 'public' burning. Such burnings were created by the artist John Latham, who concentrated on art books, as a statement against what he considered was an excessive proliferation of and respect for the printed word.

skull/gourd, out of (one's) *phrase.* [1967]
extremely intoxicated, whether on alcohol or, more usually, drugs.

* *'"Stoned out of their skulls," he opines to himself and sniffs with a jerk of his head.'* (N. Fury, *Agro*, 1971)
* *'Joan climbed in with some difficulty, because she was still stoned out of her gourd.'* (C. McFadden, *The Serial*, 1976)

skydiving *n.* [1965]
a sport in which one jumps from an aeroplane and freefalls (often while performing acrobatics in mid-air) for a long distance before finally opening one's parachute.

skyjack *v.* [1961]
to hijack an aeroplane.

Skylab *n.* [1970]
a space laboratory launched by the US in May 1973.

Skytrain *n.* [1971]
the tradename of airline entrepreneur Freddie Laker's attempt to run a cheap service between London and New York. Skytrain took off from London on 26 September 1977, offering the normal £186 single fare for £59. The service lasted until 7 February 1982, when the company was wound up

* *'Cheap travel between the UK and USA is easier since the Skytrain service began.'* (*The Flier's Handbook*, 1978)

SLA *abbrev.* [1974]
Symbionese Liberation Army: a group of ⇨urban guerrillas who flourished in California in the late 1970s; the SLA won worldwide notoriety when they kidnapped media heiress Patty Hearst in 1974, and a grimmer fame when six members died in a fiery shootout with California police.

* *'17 May 1974: 6 SLA terrorists killed in gun battle with Los Angeles police.'* (D. Brogan, *World Conflicts*, 1989)

slag (off) *v.* [1971]
to vilify, to denigrate; from slag: an unpleasant person.

* *'He was doing a good job of bad-mouthing and slagging me to a number of the Angels.'* (J. Mandelkau, *Buttons*, 1971)

slam dance *n., v.* [1980]
a form of violent dancing in which the dancers jump up and down and deliberately slam into each other.
See also **pogo**.

* *'Several dozen skinheads . . . were invited to slam dance on stage during the songs.'* (B. Woodward, *Wired*, 1984)

slam-dunk *n.* [1976]
a basketball shot that is made by leaping up and slamming the ball down through the net.

slasher *n., adj.* [1985]
a particularly gory horror film, depending for its appeal on the liberal graphically depicted shedding of blood, usually of a teenage girl (or girls).

SLBM *abbrev.* [1967]
Submarine-Launched Ballistic Missile: the submarine version of the heavyweight silo-based ⇨ICBM. These long-range missiles include the Polaris, Poseidon, and Trident C-4. Given the elusiveness of the submarine, SLBMs and the submarines on which they are carried, represent the most potent examples of destructive nuclear power.

* *'The Soviets . . . were just beginning to increase the number of submarine-launched ballistic missiles (SLBMs).'* (R.C. Aldridge, *First Strike!* 1983)

SLCM *abbrev.* [1969]
Sea-Launched Cruise Missile: a variety of the Tomahawk ⇨cruise missile – the BGM-109 – that can be used aboard both surface ships and submarines. Highly accurate, with a range of 2500 km, the SLCM has been deployed since 1983.

* *'General Dynamics' sea-launched version*

(SLCM), the Tomahawk . . . can be fired not only from surface vessels but also, theoretically, from torpedo tubes.' (R.W. Howe, *Weapons*, 1980)

SLD *abbrev.* [1988]
Social and Liberal Democrats: a political party formed in 1988 from members of the old Liberal Party and the rump of the Social Democratic Party (founded in 1981 by the ⇨Gang of Four).
See also **salads**

* *'These were generally regarded as the five main candidates – although both the SDP and the SLD would tell you there were four.'* (*The Independent*, 31 March 1990)

sleaze *n.* [1967]
seediness, dilapidation, squalor. Thus **sleazy** *adj.*, sordid, squalid, etc.

* *'The atmosphere of the whole town is electric. The sleaze and the hype just get to you.'* (*The Times*, 6 October 1990)

sleazo *n.* [1967]
a sordid disreputable person; from ⇨sleaze, which itself can be used to describe a person.

sledge *v.* [1977]
an abbreviation for sledgehammer: from the phrase 'subtle as a sledgehammer' – the practice in cricket, especially prevalent in Australia, of the fielding side aiming continuous and aggressive insults at the batsmen during the match; the intent is intimidation or the provoking of a loss of concentration.

sleeping policeman *n.* [1974]
an artificial bump in the road intended to slow down a car and keep speeds at a low level; first introduced after the passage of the Road Traffic Act, 1974.

slimline *adj.* [1973]
spare, sparse, slimmed down. Specifically, slimline predated ⇨diet on the labels of soft drinks to denote a version of the basic product that contained less sugar/sweetener than usual, e.g. 'Schweppes Slimline Tonic'.
See also **lite.**

sling-bag *n.* **[1965]**
a bag with a long strap which is usually carried slung from the shoulder.

Sloane Ranger *n.* [1975]
a pun on the television cowboy, the Lone Ranger, and on Sloane Square, London SW1: coined by journalist Ann Barr and market researcher Peter York in a piece in *Harpers/Queen* magazine in 1975 to characterize the personality and style of a fashionable, but strictly conventional upper-class young woman.

When used as an adjective the 'Ranger' is usually dropped, leaving simply 'Sloane', e.g. 'The Duchess of York and her gang of Sloane pals.'

* *'Sloane Ranger clothes exactly reflect regimental values and solid background – solid and reassuring.'* (*The Official Sloane Ranger Handbook*, 1982)

SLR *abbrev.* [1964]
single lens reflex: the most popular type of professionally used 35mm camera

slurb *n.* [1962]
from slum + suburb: an area of unplanned suburban development.

smack *n.* [1960]
from the Yiddish *schmeck* meaning sniff: heroin.
* *'Goddamit, I'm serious. I want to sell you some pure fuckin' smack!'* (H.S. Thompson, *Fear and Loathing in Las Vegas*, 1971)

small is beautiful *phr.* [1973]
a phrase originated by E.F. Schumacher in 1973, when he used it as a book title, denoting his belief that small-scale institutions and systems are preferable to the large-scale ones that were increasingly dominating the contemporary world.

smart *adj.* [1972]
referring to any technology that involves the use of computers, thus **smart weapons**: any form of ⇨precision guided munitions

smart-ass (*or* smart-arse) *n., adj.* [1960]
one who is smugly clever, a know-it-all, glib, boastful.

smart card *n.* [1987]
any form of plastic card that has been programmed (through a magnetic strip) to operate a variety of machines – door locks, cash dispensers, etc.

smartiboots *n.* [1962]
see **smart ass.**

smart terminal *n.* [1972]
see **dumb terminal.**

smashed *adj.* [1962]
intoxicated on either drugs or alcohol.
* *'It was like being smashed out of your mind on beer – loose but mobile.'* (B. Woodward, *Wired*, 1984)

smokestack industry *n.*
traditional manufacturing industry, whose factories tended to feature large smokestacks, pouring tons of polluting waste into the atmosphere.
* *'Industry itself has changed from mass-production smokestack factories to more technical and service jobs.'* (*Christian Science Monitor*, 18 October 1982)

Smokey (the) Bear *n.* [1974]
used by ⇨Citizens' Band radio enthusiasts as a slang term for a state policeman, so-called for the wide-brimmed hat worn by many such officers, and taken in turn from the character 'Smokey the Bear' who is used in US fire prevention advertising.

smoking gun *n.* [1974]
undeniable evidence; from the image of a murder suspect being caught standing over the fresh corpse, holding a still-smoking gun. The term gained its popularity during the Watergate Affair (1972–4) when a tape recording, made in the Oval Office, that linked President Nixon absolutely to the coverup was known as 'the smoking gun'.

snake *n.* [1972]
a system of jointly floated currencies established in 1972 by the then member countries of the Common Market (EEC), and whose exchange rates are allowed to fluctuate against each other as well as, within a wider margin, against those of non-EEC countries. *See also* **ERM.**

snatch-squad *n.* [1970]
a group of police or soldiers used in crowd control: the squad works as a unit, rushing

into the crowd and extracting targetted leaders or trouble-makers.

✱ *'A snatch squad would detach itself, now and then, from the lines of police on foot and charge into the crowd.'* (M. Farren, *Watch Out Kids*, 1972)

SNCC *abbrev.* [1960]
an acronym for Student Non-violent Coordinating Committee (pronounced 'snick'): a black civil rights movement in the US, popular on the campuses and proliferating into the overall ➪New Left Movement.

✱ *'Eldridge and I went down to the SNCC office later that night. We talked to a lot of different organizations.'* (B. Seale, *Seize the Time*, 1968)

✱ *'But SNCC, while it set up a few draft counselling programmes for young men, did not generally focus organizational energy on the anti-war movement.'* (R. Fraser, *1968*, 1988)

SNOBOL *abbrev.* [1964]
an acronym for String Orientated Symbolic Language: a programming language created specifically for dealing with complex strings of symbols.

snooze button *n.* [1974]
a button on a bedside clock which temporarily turns off the alarm, giving the sleeper time for a short snooze prior to facing the day.

snort-and-tell *n., adj.* [1989]
see **kiss and tell**.

snowmobile *n.* [1967]
a tracked vehicle designed to travel over snow, when normal wheeled vehicles are unable to move.

snuff *v., adj.* [1975]
to kill, to murder; thus **snuff movies** or **snuff films**: the hardest core pornography, in which (or so it is made to appear) one or more of the participants are actually murdered as part of the script.

✱ *'After Kent State, Manson, Altamont, Jimi and Janis getting snuffed . . .'* (N. Fury, *Agro*, 1971)

✱ *'A long-rumoured but never proven ring of murderous pornographers producing snuff films for private distribution.'* (*Sunday Correspondent*, 22 April 1990)

soaraway *adj.* [1969]
mounting and leaping towards excellence; usually found in *The Sun*'s efforts to publicize itself.

✱ *'The soaraway success of the Japanese economy in recent years.'* (*Sunday Correspondent*, 22 April 1990)

soca *n.* [1986]
a style of popular music, originated in Trinidad, which blends soul and calypso.

social contract *n.* [1967]
an agreement entered into by the Labour Party (then in opposition) and the trade unions in 1973, under which the unions promised to back measures designed to curb inflation, while the Party, were it to take power, would abolish the Tory Industrial Relations Act of 1971 and any statutory controls on pay rises.

✱ *'When national officials were asked to deliver their side of the social contract they couldn't.'* (*Independent on Sunday*, 8 April 1990)

social drinker *n.* [1969]
a drinker who drinks regularly – at parties, over dinner or lunch – but is not seen as an alcoholic. – **social drinking,** *n.*

social fund *n.* [1988]
created under the Social Security Act of 1988, the social fund is a set amount of money reserved for paying out to those in need who require such basics as furniture or clothing.

social ownership *n.* [1986]
a synonym for nationalization: devised by the Labour Party to counteract the general unpopularity of that term: the ownership of a business or industry by a national government.

sociologese *n.* [1963]
the language of the professional sociologist, heavily larded with jargon, such as 'core institutional framework', 'de-skilling', 'deviancy amplification', etc.

Sod's law *n.* [1970]
like the veteran Murphy's Law, one of those 'natural laws' that, while never codified in statute, seems to permeate daily life: the belief that whatever might be the most inconvenient occurrence in a given situation will certainly happen.

* *'Sod's Law: the degree of failure is in direct proportion to the effort expended and to the need for success.'* (P. Dickson, *The Official Rules,* 1978)

soft *adj.* [1961]
undefended; specifically, lacking the special hardening measures that, to an increasingly limited extent, can shield installations, individuals and weapons systems from nuclear attack. The term **soft-skinned** is also used of lightly armed military vehicles.
See also **hard.**

softcore (*or* soft porn) *n., adj.* [1966]
mild pornography, typically that available in the wide range of 'men's magazines' available in the corner newsagent, rather than the harder material on offer beneath the counter of the ⇨dedicated sex shop.
See also **hardcore.**

* *'There was nothing to watch on the TV. All the in-house movies were soft porn.'* (*Independent on Sunday,* 27 May 1990)

soft drugs *n.* [1960]
such drugs as cannabis, the minor tranquillizers, and amphetamine, all of which are considered milder than the ⇨hard drugs such as heroin and cocaine.

softly softly *adv.* [1967]
from the term 'softly-softly catchee monkee': a form of policing that depends on subtlety and stealth, rather than talking loudly and wielding a big truncheon.

* *'Police last night were adopting a softly softly approach in the hope that the . . . weather would persuade the inmates to surrender.'* (*Sunday Correspondent,* 8 April 1990)

soft rock *n.* [1969]
middle of the road rock music, aimed less at the rebellious young than at their elder siblings or, possibly, their parents.
See also **AOR; MOR.**

software *n., adj.* [1960]
in computing. 1. the programs which give instructions to the ⇨hardware and which actu-

ally make it work, without which the machine is still effectively a ➩dumb, albeit immensely complex collection of electronics.

2. packages that have been worked out in advance to take advantage of the ability of the machine to perform a wide variety of tasks – ➩word processing, calculations, ➩spreadsheets, ➩database management, etc.

✱ *'The most free software is public domain, which means the author explicitly relinquishes the copyright.'* (*Byte*, June 1990)

software piracy *n.* [1983]

the illegal copying of computer programs and their distribution to other users, whether for free or for a small charge.

✱ *'Revenues will go up as software piracy and multiple usage are prevented.'* (ad for Fast Electronic GmbH in *Byte*, June 1990)

SOGAT *abbrev.* [1966]

an acronym for Society of Graphical and Allied Trades: the print-workers' trade union, formed in 1966 by the amalgamation of the National Union of Printing, Bookbinding, and Paper Workers and the National Society of Operative Printers and Assistants. In 1982 SOGAT further amalgamated with the National Society of Operative Printers, Graphical, and Media Personnel to form **SOGAT 82**.

SoHo *abbrev.* [1972]

an acronym for South of Houston Street: an area of New York, formerly devoted to warehousing and light industry. Colonized initially by impoverished artists who used its large cheap lofts (warehouse floors) as studios, the area developed into New York's second art centre, a rival to the uptown upmarket galleries of Madison Avenue.

See also **Tribeca**.

solarium *n.* [1960]

originally a room designed to catch the maximum of sunlight, its modern descendant is a room, often within a health centre or gymnasium, which is equipped with sun lamps and sunbeds, designed for creating an artificial tan.

solar power energy *n.* [1974]

any form of power that is directly derived from the natural energy emanating from the Sun.

✱ *'A couple were discussing solar energy, the military-industrial-complex and education.'* (T. Kidder, *The Soul of a New Machine*, 1981)

solar wind *n.* [1961]

the stream of ions and electrons which are constantly exuded by the Sun and which permeates the whole solar system.

soldier *n.* [1963]

the lowest echelon of Mafia member, the 'other ranks' who serve the 'don' and his 'caporegimes'.

Solidarity *n.* [1980]

Poland's independent trade union, established in September 1980; Solidarity pushed forward a new atmosphere of reform in Poland, before it was banned in 1982, and its continued agitation, despite efforts to suppress its aims, led directly to the collapse of Poland's communist government in 1989.

✱ *'Solidarity demanded that it be legalized before it would open formal "round table" talks with the regime.'* (P. Brogan, *World Conflicts*, 1989)

solid-state *adj.* [1963]
relating to solid-state physics, thus using the conductive and other properties of solid materials; typical solid-state devices are transistors and other semi-conductor valves.

solvent abuse *n.* [1977]
the sniffing of glue and other solvent substances.

-something *suffix.* [1988]
the contemporary equivalent of '-ish', usually referring to an age, or a generation. Derived from the television series *thirtysomething*, which dealt with the lives of a group of men and women in their thirties.

- ✱ *'Certain of the defendents are, like Grob, sixty-something.'* (*Private Eye*, 16 March 1990)
- ✱ *'Class rock stations . . . are as popular with teenagers as with thirty-somethingers.'* (Charles Shaar Murray, *Crosstown Traffic*, 1989)

soul brother/sister *n.* [1967]
a fellow black person.

soul food *n.* [1964]
the traditional food of US blacks, typically chitterlings, pig's feet, and turnip greens.

- ✱ *'This tradition is different from Soul Food . . . It's . . . not as greasy and you don't cook it as long. Of course, there's no denying that Soul Food is a kissin' cousin.'* (E.M. Mickler, *White Trash Cooking*, 1986)

soul kiss *n.* [1960]
a synonym for French kiss; a deep kiss.

soul music *n.* [1961]
a type of black music, typically performed by such stars as Aretha Franklin, Otis Redding, and Ray Charles, in which the lyrics and the music are seen as epitomizing the essential aspects of the American black culture.

- ✱ *'Soul music approaches folk music in its lack of self-consciousness. And it is art, even though the artist may not seek to do anything beyond entertain.'* (J. Miller (ed.), *The Rolling Stone Illustrated History of Rock & Roll*, 1976)

sound archive *n.* [1962]
a 'library' of sound recordings, both musical and spoken word; typically that held by the BBC in Broadcasting House, London.

sound bite *n.* [1976]
a brief audio segment inserted into a filmed report used on the television news; nothing new in itself, the sound bite (like the ⇨photo opportunity) has become central to the planning of increasingly orchestrated electoral campaigns in the UK and US. Politicians, once by necessity more or less accomplished orators, now concentrate not on the whole speech, but on the three or four punchy sentences that will guarantee them media exposure.
See also **media event**.

- ✱ *'I have heard Brits who speak like books, but Mr Kinnock talks like a speech. In the land of the sound bite this leaves you dead from hunger.'* (*The Independent*, 19 July 1990)

sounds *n.* [1969]
the all-purpose hippie term for music, usually as heard on record or tape.

- ✱ *'Diggin' sounds after hours and smokin' your bamalam and walking down the street stark noble savage naked to the world.'* (L. Bangs,

Psychotic Reactions and Carburetor Dung, 1988)

sound system *n.* [1970]
a system for the playing of records in public, using turntables and large speakers, which originated in Jamaica and has been exported to the UK. Rival system attract their own groups of followers, all of whom are best seen at such events as the annual Notting Hill Carnival

source *v.* [1960]
1. to obtain goods and/or components from a specific source.
2. to locate a given manufacturing activity in a specific place.

South *n.* [1975]
those nations of the world which are generally seen as less wealthy and less developed than the average and which tend to be found in the Southern hemisphere.

* *'The residual South, holding more of the world's population and with little immediate hope of overcoming poverty and despair, will command less and less attention.'* (*New York Review of Books,* 7 March 1991)

space *n.* [1976]
1. used in architecture as an abbreviation for living space, and thence, more recently to describe a given room: 'That's a beautiful space', etc.
2. one's personal mental environment, 'where one is at'; the boundaries of an area which is devoted to one's own spiritual well-being.

* *'But Leonard had a lot going for him and Kate liked the space he was in.'* (C. McFadden, *The Serial,* 1976).
* *'The same ritual est phrases . . . about having created the space in which to experience herself and about wanting to assist me in my understanding.'* (R.D. Rosen, *Psychobabble,* 1977)
* *'The friends . . . enjoy sharing and talking it out when they don't need their own space.'* (*The Independent,* 16 June 1990)

space blanket *n.* [1972]
a light metal-coated sheet designed to retain heat.

* *'I had this sleeping bag which my mother had made from a space blanket, which was brilliant, and I'd carried it for two years.'* (J. Green, *Them,* 1990)

spaced (out) *adv.* [1968]
1. experiencing the effects of drugs, especially of ➲LSD, where one's physical perceptions (as well as all other perceptions) are radically altered.

* *'Spaced: he was sitting on the floor by the air conditioner with his back against the wall trying to watch the sweat running down from his hairling.'* (M. Herr, *Dispatches,* 1977)

2. by extension from 1, any situation in which one is radically disorientated. The active verb **to space (out)** (1967) means to disorientate.

* *'There one could dig the whole spaced-out scene and dine on California grapes and champagne.'* (A. Hoffman, *Woodstock Nation,* 1969)

Spacey, when referring to people, implies someone who gives off the air of being permanently under the influence of some hallucinogen.

* *'She spotted Martha's ex-husband-once-removed with his spacey new old lady.'* (C. McFadden, *The Serial,* 1976)

space industry *n.* [1962]
the industry that revolves around the exploration of space, manufacturing all the necessary goods and materials.

Space Invaders *n.* [1979]
the first mass-popular computer game, in which the player defends him or herself against successive waves of 'invaders' who appear at the top of the screen and move inexorably downwards.

✱ *'Games-linked crimes (stealing to sustain a Space Invaders habit, for example).'* (*Sunday Correspondent*, 25 March 1990

spacelab *n.* [1969]
a scientific laboratory in space; specifically Spacelab which was launched in 1969.
See also **Skylab**.

spaceship earth *n.* [1966]
popularized by engineer R. Buckminster Fuller in his book entitled *Operating Manual, Spaceship Earth* (1969), the idea of the earth as a spaceship floating in the universe, on which, as on any other spaceship, resources are limited and should not be taken for granted nor allowed to run out.

space walk n. [1966]
any form of physical activity taken outside a spacecraft by one of its crew.

spag bol *n.* [1968]
an abbreviation for spaghetti bolognese.

spaghetti n. [1960]
1.the complex masses of electrical, hydraulic, and other cables running through an aircraft. **2.** the coloured piping that is slipped over wires and serves to identify one from another. **3.** the mass of wires that connect the various parts of a stereo system or computer.

spaghetti junction *n.* [1966]
1. the Gravelly Hill motorway interchange on the M6 outside Birmingham. **2.** by extension from 1. any complex motorway intersection.

✱ *'Anyone witnessing the growth of a huge fireball over Spaghetti Junction might believe the end of the world had come.'* (P. Goodwin, *Nuclear War: The Facts*, 1981)

spaghetti strap *n.* [1972]
very thin, almost string-like shoulder straps on a woman's dress.

spaghetti western *n.* [1969]
a variety of cowboy film, the product mainly of the 1960s, made by Italians (especially the director Sergio Leone) which is long on 'atmosphere' and minimal on dialogue; often starring US actors, notably Clint Eastwood and Lee Van Cleef; similiar films, but shot in Spain rather than in Italy, have been called **paella westerns**.

✱ *'Spaghetti western: a dismissive name for the blood-spattered Italian imitations of American westerns which became popular in the 1960s.'* (L. Halliwell, *Filmgoer's Companion*, 8th edn., 1985)

spart *n.* [1970]
a doctrinaire leftwinger, usually young, polytechnic-educated and presumably a founder member of the ➪Loony Left. The term was coined in *Private Eye* magazine, which based it on the Spartacists, a German revolutionary group who attempted to recreate the Russian Revolution in Berlin in 1919, and whose leaders Karl Liebknecht and Rosa Luxem-

bourg were summarily executed for their pains.

spasm war *n.* [1965]
a conflict in which both sides abandon themselves to uncontrolled reflex attacks; goals, aims, plans and any other modifications are rendered irrelevant in the gut-directed mania; the final rung on nuclear theorist Herman Kahn's ➪escalation ladder.

-speak *suffix.*
an all-pupose suffix that when applied to a given noun (usually describing an occupation) indicates the jargon used by that job. The word is based on George Orwell's **Newspeak**, which he created in 1948 for his novel 1984; there are a wide variety of -speaks, all of which pertain to a given profession or interest group.

* *'But at least I had BBC training in fixing and airlinespeak.'* (*Independent on Sunday*, 25 March 1990)
* *'"There is no basic problem of affordability among potential purchasers . . ." the firm says in glorious agentspeak.'* (*The Independent*, 31 March 1990)
* *'It it as if he had written a script in despised standard English, and had then crudely translated into cabbie-speak.'* (J. Meades, *Peter Knows What Dick Likes*, 1989)

speciesism *n.* [1975]
the discrimination by man against other species – animals, fish, etc., on account of humanity's supposed superiority. – **specialist**, *n. adj.*

* *'Well, without wishing to appear speciesist, the patronising agonies of the liberal conscience . . . strike me as pale alternatives.'* (*Sunday Correspondent*, 17 June 1990)

speed *n.* [1966]
slang for amphetamine. Thus the **Frisco speedball**: a mixture of heroin, cocaine (the 'speed' in this case) and ➪LSD.

* *'While the god Speed sizzles like a short-order French fry in the gut of some guy who doesn't even stop talking to breathe.'* (T. Wolfe, *The Electric Kool-Aid Acid Test*, 1969)
* *'His range was extensive – beginning with New Jersey pot and ending with something called a 'Frisco Speedball', a concoction of heroin and cocaine, with a touch of acid ("gives it a little colour").'* (T. Southern, *Red-Dirt Marijuana*, 1973)

speedfreak *n., adj.* [1967]
an enthusiast of amphetamine or methedrine.

* *'With a blocked sensory perception, frenetic speedfreak energy and a sophisticated pattern of status and consumption, mod society spread.'* (M. Farren, *Watch Out Kids*, 1972)

speed metal *n.*
see **thrash**.

speed-read *v.* [1960]
a method of reading very rapidly by absorbing not single words but whole phrases or even sentences at once. Speed-reading became briefly popular when President John F. Kennedy announced that he was a devotee.

spell-checker *n.* [1988]
a built in electronic dictionary that is supplied with a number of ➪word processing programs. Such checkers can be used to point out misspellings (or words that are not in their vocabulary) and, when used in conjunction with an electronic thesaurus, offer the opportunity to vary one's writing.

✱ *'They can't use the spell-checker or the thesaurus, or even the on-line help – there simply isn't room on the disk.'* (*PC World*, March 1991)

spend *n.* [1988]

a synonym for budget: how much there is to spend, or how much has been spent on a particular project, usually the marketing or advertising of a given product.

sperm bank *n.* [1963]

a store of sperm, taken from voluntary donors, which is kept for use in artificial insemination.

SPG *abbrev.* [1980]

Special Patrol Group: a specially trained unit of uniformed policeman who are not attached to any specific area, but are on call for special duties, especially as riot squads and any other intensive policing.

spike [1965]

1. *n.* a hypodermic needle, used for injecting a variety of ➪hard drugs.

✱ *'When I put a spike into my vein . . .'* (L. Reed, 'Heroin', 1966)

2. *v.t.* to adulterate with a drug, usually ➪LSD.

✱ *'He laughed and held me very close and told me that the Kool-Aid had been "spiked".'* (T. Wolfe, *The Electric Kool-Aid Acid Test*, 1969)

spin *n.* [1984]

a particular interpretation or slant given to a piece of information, a news story or similar statement, especially when offered by a politician. The image is of a snooker player imparting spin to a ball as a means of directing it in the required direction.

✱ *'Microsoft puts new spin on Windows, OS/2.'* (*Byte*, July, 1990)

Thus the **spin-doctor**: one charged with creating 'spin'.

✱ *'The spin-doctors who try to put a gloss on truth are already hard at work on the Eastbourne by-election, pretending that it was really not that bad.'* (*Sunday Correspondent*, 21 October 1990)

spin-off *n., adj.* [1963]

a by-product, or an added effect. Used as an adjective in such phrases as *spin-off products'.*

✱ *'The research could have an important spin-off for human flying machines.'* (*Sunday Correspondent*, 8 April 1990)

splatter movie *n.* [1974]

a genre of ultra-violent films, coined as a name by director George Romero; typical of such is the *Texas Chainsaw Massacre* in which the main action/appeal is the covering of the screen in blood.

splendid first strike *n.* [1972]

a ➪pre-emptive ➪first strike that destroys the enemy's forces before he can activate them and should thus provide the aggressor with an outright victory.

split *v.* [1968]

to leave, to depart.

✱ *'Haul ass, Kesey. Move. Scram. Split flee hide vanish disintegrate. Like run.'* (T. Wolfe, *The Electric Kool-Aid Acid Test*, 1969)

spoiler *n.* [1963]

1. in cars: a structure placed on a motor vehicle which is intended to reduce lift and thus increase the pressure on the wheels when the vehicle is moving at speed; originally seen only on racing cars, which achieve speeds requiring such a modification, but now a component of family saloons as well.

2. in journalism and broadcasting: a story run in one paper or on one channel as a deliberate attempt to ruin a rival's much touted scoop.

* *'This was a spoiler in the best traditions of the tabloid press – not as thoroughly prepared as the original, but stealing its thunder by getting in first.'* (*The Independent*, 20 February 1991)

spokesperson *n.* [1972]

the non-sexist gender-neutral form of the traditional spokesman.

See also **Ms**; **-person**.

sponsored walk *n.* [1966]

a form of charity fund-raising whereby the participants volunteer to walk a given distance, for which walk they obtain sponsorship from supporters, based on the distance walked.

spook *n.* [1961]

1. a member of an intelligence agency, specifically the CIA. The term comes from the original recruits to the pre-CIA OSS (the Office of Strategic Services: a Second World War security group) who, like their opposite numbers in the UK, were primarily recruited from the Establishment – in the case of many OSS men, from Yale University's 'Skull and Bones' club, an exclusive secret student club.

2. *in US slang*: a black person – from the idea that they are invisible to the white majority.

Both meanings were nicely combined in Sam Greenlee's novel of a black CIA man, *The Spook Who Sat By The Door* (1969).

sports medicine *n.* [1961]

that branch of medicine dedicated to dealing with sport, both as to physical fitness and dealing with injuries.

spot-reducing *n., adj.* [1960]

a form of weight reduction in which fat on certain specified parts of the body is removed.

spreadsheet *n.* [1982]

a ⇨program that allows any part of a rectangular array of positions (usually known as 'cells') to de displayed on a computer screen; each cell can be specified either independently or in the context of the other cells. Spreadsheets, which can perform within microseconds mass calculations and projections that would have taken the traditional adding machine-wielding accountant infinitely longer to perform are, alongside ⇨word processors, the staple of today's business ⇨software.

* *'Full Impact 2.0 is considerably improved, and it faces a more open spreadsheet market than previously.'* (*Byte*, June 1990)

spring roll *n.*

see **pancake roll**.

spritzer *n.* [1961]

a drink made of white wine and soda water.

spy in the cab *n.* [1968]

a colloquial synonym for the tachograph, a device placed by law in lorry cabs to measure the distance travelled by each driver and to ensure that he does not exceed what are set out as safe hours at the wheel without taking a rest.

spy in the sky *n.* [1960]
any form of ➪spyplane or ➪spy satellite that uses its very powerful cameras and other sensing equipment to spy on activities on the earth below.

spy movie *n.* [1969]
a film, originally featuring such popular secret agents as Ian Fleming's 'James Bond' or Len Deighton's 'Harry Palmer' (as his otherwise anonymous spy was christened for the films), that takes international espionage as its theme. Such films were especially popular in the 1960s.

spy-plane *n.* [1960]
a high-flying plane, e.g. the American U2 of the early 1960s or the later Blackbird of the 1980s, which overflies hostile territory, into which it would be hard to infiltrate human agents, and takes pictures of activities on earth, which can then be analysed in the security of the home base.

spy-satellite *n.* [1960]
a satellite that performs the same surveillance function as does the ➪spy plane.

SQL *abbrev.* [1986]
Structured Query Language: the latest form of query language used in ➪relational databases to extract the relevant data.

square *adj., n.* [1960]
conventional, law-abiding, dull.

* *'She had a boyfriend who – well, he probably thought of himself as a "beatnik" in his square hip way.'* (T. Wolfe, *The Electric Kool-Aid Acid Test*, 1969])

square-eyes *n.* [1964]
a slang description of anyone who, through watching what is seen as an excess of television, develops square eyes – mimicking the square dimensions of the television screen. Possibly an extension of **four-eyes**: someone who wears glasses.

squarial *n.* [1988]
the small rectangular aerial designed for use with BSB (British Satellite Broadcasting), the second of the two satellite television systems to be made available in the UK. The squarial will presumably vanish with the absorption of BSB by Sky, its satellite TV rival, and the creation of the new BSkyB company.

* *'Having emphasised the technical and environmental qualities of its small flat squarial, the thing did not work.'* (*Independent on Sunday*, 25 March 1990)

squat *n., v.* [1975]
the illegal occupation of an uninhabitated building, usually organized by a group of homeless people. Thus, the actual house or flat that is being used by **squatters**. The practice of squatting long predates the 20th century, but it gained both popularity and notoriety towards the end of the 1960s, especially during the occupation of 144 Piccadilly in July 1969, and with the proliferation of squatters movements during the early 1970s.

* *'Inspired by the success of the squatters' movements, Jim Haynes finally broke into the condemned hotel at which he had "stared stupidly" for two years.'* (R. Neville, *Play Power*, 1970)
* *'What was she up to in that squat of hers? Who were her friends?'* (T. Blacker, *Fixx*, 1989)

Sri Lanka *n.* [1972]
the current name of the former British colony,

Ceylon; the name comes from *Sri*, an honorary prefix, and *Lanka*, meaning island in Singhalese.

✱ *'Ceylon, which changed its name to Sri Lanka in 1972, instead became a case study in the dynamics of national dissolution.'* (P. Brogan, *World Conflicts*, 1989)

SRO *abbrev.* [1986]

for self-regulatory organization: any of a number of regulatory bodies that work under the ⇨SIB to regulate affairs in the City of London.

stack system *n.*

a fullsized stereo system, in which a number of modules – amplifier, tape deck, graphical equalizer, etc. – are placed one above the other, as opposed to older systems where the modules were placed side by side, taking up much more space.

stadium gig (*or* **concert)** *n.* [1975)

any large-scale rock music performance played in a sports stadium, such as the Wembley Stadium outside London. Stadium concerts tend to host 'stadium rock', typified by such bands as Queen.

stag film *n.* [1968]

a pornographic film; from the US slang 'stag' (1905), meaning an unattached, bachelor male and, more recently, such terms as **stag night**: a bridegroom's pre-wedding party.

stand-alone *n., adj.* [1966]

1. a piece of a computing system that can stand alone and perform its tasks without needing to be linked in to any other machine.

✱ *'If run as a stand-alone system, applications typically run on the system will be the X Server . . . a windows manager . . . multiple DOS applications and multiple X clients.'* (*DESQview/X booklet*, November 1990)

2. By extension from 1. implying independent operation, often in a figurative sense.

✱ *'The Head of Contracts Services . . . will coordinate and control all aspects within the newly created "stand-alone" DSO.'* (recruitment ad for Borough of Spelthorne (Surrey) in the *Independent on Sunday*, 3 June 1990)

stand-by *adj.* [1963]

referring to the airlines' practice of offering pasengers who have not booked in advance the opportunity of 'standing by' to see if there are any last minute cancellations on a given flight, thus making seats available.

See also **bump**.

standing ovation n. [1969]

a round of applause that is delivered by an audience who, to show the extent of their appreciation, rise to their feet to deliver it.

stand-up (comedian) *n.* [1966]

a comedian who stands up on stage, bereft of props or partner, and delivers a comic monologue.

✱ *'The stand-up comic is our hero . . . a waspish or laconic or outrageous commentator.'* (J. Fisher, *Funny Way To Be A Hero*, 1976)

START *abbrev.* [1981]

an acronym for Strategic Arms Reduction Talks: the arms talks with which the US and USSR replaced the series of ⇨SALT meetings between 1981 and 1983. Nothing practical came of the talks, which foundered on the superpowers' inability to accept each other's terms of reference; a continuing series of propaganda announcements and the fact that the Reagan Administration could not overcome its fundamental reservations about negotiations *per se.* The talks were further undermined by the appearance of the Strategic Defence Initiative and collapsed in late 1983.

* *'In late June 1982, well over a quarter of the way into the Reagan presidency, the START negotiations (Strategic Arms Reduction Talks) began.'* (M. Dando & P. Rogers, *The Death of Deterrence,* 1984)

starter *n.* [1966]
a dish eaten at the beginning of a meal, a synonym for first course or, possibly, *hors d'oeuvres.*

starter home *n.* [1976]
in *the property market:* a basic house with few amenities but a reasonably low price, the first house a young couple are likely to buy.

* *'They still have value as cheap housing, providing one- or two-bedroom starter homes at around £30,000.'* (*Independent on Sunday,* 3 June 1990)

starter pack *n.* [1976]
the basic equipment required for its user to start work; usually used of a basic computer system.
See also **entry-level.**

start-up *n. adj.* [1960]
1. in ⇨venture capital investment, the first stage at which finance will be injected into a new venture.
2. by extension from the company that is launching itself on the basis of that investment.

* *'Special work including raising finance, start-ups and computer consultancy.'* (ad for Maidment Penney Quick accountants in the *Independent on Sunday,* 3 June 1990)

star wars *n.* [1983]
see **SDI.**

* *'An undertaking that received full Presidential sanction in Mr Reagan's "Star Wars" speech of 23 March, 1983.'* (D. Ford, *The Button,* 1985)

stash *n. v.* [1965]
1. a hiding place for drugs; to hide drugs.
2. to put away.

* *'The Black Room became the stash box for all the bits and pieces of life that one could accumulate.'* (R. DiLello, *The Longest Cocktail Party,* 1971)
* *'So, aside from stashing the stamps, I would read each of these shit-pile mss. very carefully.'* (T. Southern, *Red-Dirt Marijuana,* 1973)

state of play *n.* [1966]
the current situation.

state of the art *n. adj.* [1960]
originally the description of a current level of scientific or technological advance; now simply a merchandiser's synonym for 'latest'.

* *'A masterful implementation of a classical object-orientated programming language and a state of the art graphical user interface.'* (ad for Smalltalk/V in *Byte,* April 1990)

state terrorism *n.* [1986]
aggressive activities either performed by a single state or, more often sponsored by them; if such activities were performed by a single guerrilla group they would be termed terrorism.

statusful *adj.* [1975]
possessing or conferring high status or distinction.

statutory *adj.* [1968]
a synonym for ⇨token: required by law, obligatory, only for the sake of appearance.
* *'I've noticed that most committees nowadays have a statutory woman on them.'* (*The Guardian*, 1 May 1977)

steady state theory *n.* [1966]
in astronomy: the theory that at any time the universe, when considered on a large scale, is essentially unchanging; thus a **steady-stater** refers to one who espouses the theory. *Cf.* **big bang theory**.

stealth *n., adj.* [1977]
1. a development programme which is attempting to create a new technology that will enable military ships, submarines, and aeroplanes to avoid hostile radar scanners.
2. the Advanced Technology Bomber (ATB): based on stealth technology, this aircraft, which operated to great effect in the Gulf War, has a redesigned tail, high-mounted engines, heat- suppression devices, and a carefully shaped airframe, in which radar-reflecting 'corners' are eliminated as far as possible, thus deflecting radar beams to the side rather than sending them straight back to their source.
* *'Some critics say the Pentagon is downplaying stealth to keep the B1-B in work.'* (R.C. Aldridge, *First Strike!* 1983)

steaming *n.* [1977]
mass theft by gangs who run through crowds (e.g. the Notting Hill Carnival) or captive audiences (e.g. a tube carriage) stealing and menacing as they go. A more violent (American) version is **wilding**.

stew *n.* [1970]
an abbreviation for stewardess.
* *'Little old Linda the Stew was certainly a must, we decided, after she had danced by and stopped and had another brief chat with us.'* (D. Jenkins, *Semi Tough*, 1972)

stick-and-carrot *adj.* [1963]
a negotiating technique characterized by on the one hand the offering of rewards and on the other hand the threat of punishment.

Stickle *n.* [1972]
in Northern Ireland: the official branch of the Irish Republican Army (as opposed to the Provisionals); from the sticky backs of the Easter seals that are used by Catholics.

stick shift *n.* [1960]
a gear lever or gear stick.

stir-fry *v., n., adj.* [1960]
from the Chinese *chow* (or *ch'ao*), a cooking method (one of the 40 basic methods of heating food) in which the food to be cooked is pre-cut into uniform strips or small pieces and then cooked in a wok with a small amount of very hot oil; the pieces are 'stirred' with a pair of chopsticks or a slotted spoon and kept in almost continual motion for the two or three minutes it requires to make the dish.
* *'Harold said he didn't stir-fry, he chowed. Furthermore he chowed on cold-pressed safflower oil.'* (C. McFadden, *The Serial*, 1976)

stitch up *v., n.* [1970]
for the police, as regarded through criminal

eyes, to fabricate evidence which is produced in court to ensure a conviction.
See also **set up**.

stockbroker belt *n.* [1960]
that area of the Home Counties – Surrey, Hertfordshire, Buckinghamshire – in which wealthy stockbrokers are supposed to live; thus a general description of the affluent areas near the metropolis.

stock cube *n.* [1965]
a cube of concentrated dehydrated stock – originally beef only, but now available as chicken stock, fish stock and vegetarian stock – which can be mixed with water and used in stews, soups, etc.

Stockholm syndrome *n.* [1973]
the phenomenon noticed in kidnaps, hijacks or any other situation in which hostages are taken and held for some time: after a certain period the hostage, rather than hating or fearing his/her captor, starts to ally with them and even feels some degree of affection, in the face of the police/army or other authorities who are waiting for them to give up. The phenomenon was first noted in a bank robbery in Stockholm in 1973.

* *'As soon as my debriefers heard what I was saying they started to say that I had Stockholm syndrome.'* (*Sunday Correspondent*, 10 June 1990)

stocking mask *n.* [1966]
a form of mask adopted by many bank robbers and other criminals who wish to maintain their anonymity; it employs a woman's nylon stocking, or half a pair of tights, pulled down over the hair and face.

* *'As we ran, a piercing shriek rang out from the next road; a man in a stocking mask was battering a woman over the head.'* (R. Chesshyre, *The Force*, 1989)

STOL (*or* v/stol) *abbrev.* [1966]
an acronym for short take-off and landing or vertical/short take-off and landing aircraft. The best known of such aircraft is the Harrier jump-jet used to such effect during the Falklands War of 1982.

stomach upset *n.* [1973]
a general term that covers food-poisoning, or any form of non-specific pain experienced in the stomach.

stoned *adj.* [1967]
originally reserved for alcoholic intoxication, stoned moved into the drug area once recreational drug use became widespread in the 1960s.
See also **ripped; wasted**.

* *'Coming up over the Blue Ridge Mountains everybody was stoned on acid, Cassady included.'* (T. Wolfe, *Electric Kool-Aid Acid Test*, 1969)

stonewall *v.* [1964]
to stand fast, to refuse to compromise; from the idea of erecting a stone wall against all opposition and from the nickname of the US Civil War General 'Stonewall' Jackson.

stop-and-search *n., adj.* [1974]
the police procedure whereby officers can stop any individual walking down the street and search them for illegal weapons, drugs, etc. This procedure has led to much public opposition, especially from black and Asian

groups, who see their young people as being unfairly targetted by officers who see all coloured minority groups as *de facto* criminals.

stop-go *adj.* [1962]
referring to a British economic policy that alternates economic expansion and contraction; generally considered a bad one, since the continuous changes never allow the economy to establish itself properly.

storage heater *n.* [1961]
an economical form of home heating whereby an electric heater stores up heat during the night (when consumption charges are cheaper) and releases it during the day.

STP *abbrev.* [1967]
Scientifically Treated Petroleum: the tradename for 2,5-dimethoxy-4-methylamphetamine: one of a number of derivatives from the hallucingen ⇨LSD; chemically related to amphetamine it compressed the normal eight-hour ⇨trip into some 20 minutes and on these grounds was known as the 'businessman's trip'.

straight *adj.* [1960]
conventional, specifically not ⇨gay, or not drug-using.
See also **square.**

* *'The straight world outside, it seems, is made up of millions of people involved, trapped, in games they aren't even aware of.'* (T. Wolfe, *The Electric Kool-Aid Acid Test*, 1969)
* *'I hated Carol's guts when she was straight. Now I'm supposed to love her because she's gay?'* (C. McFadden, *The Serial*, 1976)

straight *n.* [1967]
a normal factory-manufactured cigarette, rather than a joint, made of a cannabis-and-tobacco mixture.

strange particle *n.* [1965]
the third ⇨quark, so called because the particles within it were seen to act in a strange way; such quarks possess the property of **strangeness.**

Strategic Arms Limitation Talks *n.* [1968]
see **SALT I/II/III.**

strategic coupling
see **coupling.**

strategic superiority *n.* [1978]

* *'the ability to control a process of deliberate escalation in pursuit of acceptable terms for war termination. The United States would have a politically relevant measure of strategic superiority if it could escalate out of a gathering military disaster in Europe, reasonably confident that the Soviet Union would be unable or unwilling to match or overmatch the American escalation. It follows that the United States has a fundamental foreign policy requirement that its strategic nuclear forces provide credible limited first strike options.'* (Colin S. Gray, Director of National Security Studies at the Hudson Institute, 1978).

strategic triad *n.* [1970]
the three-way mix of weapons and forces which determines the military planning and strategy of both superpowers. The US triad, in order of precedence, comprises the Navy's missiles, the USAF's missiles, and the USAF fleet of strategic bombers. The Soviet triad is dominated by the Strategic Rocket Forces, whose 1398 silo-based missiles total some 75% of the total USSR strategic strength (US

➲ICBMs represent only 25% of the national forces).

✱ *'Understanding the strategic triad as it is called, is a first step in comprehending the aggressiveness of the new weapons which are being developed.'* (R.C. Aldridge, *First Strike!* 1983)

streaker *n.* [1973]
a devotee of **streaking**: a short-lived fad of the early 1970s (although regular revivals still occur at such events as Test Matches and similar sporting occasions) which called upon its adherents to strip off their clothes and run naked across a rugby pitch or similar open space, to the delight or shock of the assembled audience. – **streak**, *v.*

street cred *n. adj.* [1977]
from street credibility: a popular phrase used originally in the rock business and now popular in any of the industries that cater for the young consumer, including rock, magazine publishing, fashion and clothing, etc.; a contemporary variation on the adoration of youth as youth in the 1960s, the belief that the 'artist' must relate genuinely to the 'people', i.e. the working class youth of the streets and housing estates who are the consumers of such goods and whose tastes must be monitored and as far as possible satisfied.

✱ *'This was a group called Crass, one of the most "street credible" (that is, obscene and unlistenable) punk outfits.'* (*The Independent*, 26 May 1990)

street crime *n.* [1973]
any form of crime that takes place in the street, rather than as an attack on private property, especially mugging and assault.
See also **steaming, wilding**.

street jewellery *n.* [1978]
painted enamel plates, dating from before the Second World War and earlier, which are considered to be collectors' items.

street legal *adj.* [1976]
a car or motorcycle which can be driven or ridden on the public streets and roads; the opposite of specially tuned and augmented racing cars.

street people *n.* [1967]
1. homeless or vagrant people who live in the streets, sometimes as a calculated protest against the values of conventional society.

✱ *'A lot of street kids would come to me with problems they were having with pimps.'* (*The Independent*, 14 June 1990)

2. the petty criminals who deal in a variety of street crime, especially in the sale of drugs.

✱ *'He knew the street people, he was one with them, and they wouldn't let him down.'* (B. Woodward, *Wired*, 1984)

streetwise *adv., adj.* [1965]
from street (the non-establishment world) + wise: the ability to function in the tough world of the urban environment. The 'street' originates in US criminal slang (*c.* 1900) when it meant the whole world outside prison. This developed into the modern idea of the 'mean streets' where one could only survive by using one's 'street smarts'. By 1970 down-and-out ➲hippies, begging for a living and with little interest in love and peace, were known as ➲street people. The punk movement emphasized the importance of the street and for musicians and fans alike what mattered was ➲street cred, often requiring careful denial of

a middle-class upbringing or a university education.

✱ *'Streetwise teams to form front line against dealers.'* headline in the *Sunday Correspondent*, 8 April 8 1990)

stretcher (off) *v.* [1976]
to remove a badly injured player from a sports arena (usually a football or rugby pitch) by means of a stretcher.

stretch (limousine) *n.* [1971]
an outsized limousine which appears, given its many doors and more seats, to have been stretched beyond the normal dimensions of such vehicles.

✱ *'He has eschewed his normal form of transport – the stretch limousine – and is travelling to and from court by subway.'* (*Sunday Correspondent*, 8 April 1990)

stretch marks *n.* [1960]
horizontal lines on the stomach or thighs which are caused by pregnancy or obesity.

✱ *'The more potent topical steroids can cause . . . permanent stretch marks, skin pigment loss, and increased skin fragility.'* (N.L Novick, *Super Skin*, 1988)

string, the *n.* [1974]
a minuscule bikini, which resembles little more than the G-string, of which the name is presumably an abbreviation.

strip cell *n.* [1971]
a bare cell, used for the punishment of recalcitrant prisoners, which lacks even the basic amenities.

strippagram *n.*
see **kissagram.**

strip search *n. v.* [1970]
a search that is carried out, usually by police or Customs officers, when the subject has been forced to remove most or all of their clothes.

stroke *v.* [1964]
a term used by certain schools of popular (Californian-originated) psychiatry to describe the way one can reassure and comfort another individual; the negative aspect of stroking is using the same techniques in a fraudulent manner, to flatter, to persuade, and to manipulate.
See also **est**; **Rolfing**; **TA**.

strong it *v.* [1964]
to overemphasize, to push too far, to inflate.

✱ *'Amanda certainly hasn't got where she is today by overestimating the taste of pubescent boppers, but this is stronging it a bit, isn't it?'* (J. Meades, *Peter Knows What Dick Likes*, 1989)

structuralism *n.* [1968]
1. a sociological perspective based on the concept of social structure and the view that society comes before individuals.
2. for those sociologists who follow the school of Levi-Strauss (1908–), the theory that there are a set of social structures which are unobservable but which generate observable social phenomena.
3. *in linguistics*: any approach to the analysis of language that considers the text in terms of its structures and systems. This form of analysis is heavily influenced by Levi-Strauss (*see* **2.**), and by Ferdinand de Saussure (1857–1913), one the most important pioneers of ⇨semiotics).

✱ *'The contribution of this notion in linguistics is*

apparent in the more general concept of structuralism, especially as formulated in the work of . . . Claude Levi-Strauss.' (D. Crystal, *A First Dictionary of Linguistics*, 1983)

structural unemployment *n.* [1961]
unemployment that results from changes in the structure of the economy: new technology, population shifts, foreign economic influences, etc.

student card *n.* [1973]
a card that identifies its holder as a student, thus rendering them eligible for various reductions – on travel, theatre tickets, etc.

student protest *n.* [1965]
the protest movement of the 1960s which took off in universities across the world and created alied terms such as **student power** and **student politics**.

stun grenade *n.* [1977]
a grenade that does not wound, but explodes with a blinding flash and a very loud noise, thus stunning those around the explosion and, theoretically, giving attackers time to take advantage of the confusion. As did the ⇨Exocet missile in the Falklands War, the stun grenade reached a non-military audience through the siege of the Iranian Embassy in London in 1980.

* *'Who dares wins: black track-suited members of the SAS toss stun grenades as they enter the embassy.'* (*Chronicle of the 20th Century*, 1988)

stun gun *n.* [1971]
a gun that fires shot which stuns but does not cause serious injury.

* *'A father of two was brutally tortured with a stun gun while his family were imprisoned in another room by mad gunmen.'* (*South London Press*, 1988)

stunnah (*or* stunner) *n.* [1985]
a synonym for ⇨Page Three Girl: an attractive pinup, usually devoid of most of her clothes; usually spelt 'stunnah' and much used by the tabloid press. The term is vintage slang – and had possibly become somewhat antique – but was resuscitated with the pinup boom, especially in the *Sun* and the *Sport* in the 1980s.

* *'Sometimes we have a reader's wife type who's not that attractive, and sometimes we have an exceedingly attractive young stunner.'* (*Independent on Sunday*, 27 May 1990)

-style *suffix.*
a marketing euphemism for fake or synthetic, thus *Bordeaux-style wine* and similar usages.

style counsellor *n.* [1982]
see **style guru**.

style guru *n.* [1982]
also known as style counsellor: the modern *arbiter elegentiae* who rose to prominence during the style-conscious 1980s; US writer Tom Wolfe remains the doyen of the type, with such imitators as Robert Elms and Peter York offering their own advice in the UK.

* *'That curious modern beast, the style writer. You have read Peter York, you have read Lloyd Grossman, you have read Robert Elms.'* (J. Meades, *Peter Knows What Dick Likes*, 1989)

subset/superset *n.* [1980]
a pair of mathematical terms, which date back

to the early 20th century, which are now used in a wider sense meaning either a cut down or expanded version of an original theory.

✱ *'He came up with a really elegant subset of those ideas – simple, sweet, elegant, cheap, efficient, clean.'* (T. Kidder, *The Soul of a New Machine*, 1981)

subtext *n.* [1960]
the secondary hidden meaning, which is either implicit, or which has been imparted either consciously or unconsciously by a writer or speaker.

✱ *Two subtexts have emerged in the argument.'* (*Sunday Correspondent*, 1 April 1990)

sudser *n.* [1968]
a slang synonym for a soap opera.
See also **actioner**; **oater**.

suite *n.* [1967]
in computing: descriptive of a collection of related ⇨programs which can be run one after another without interruption.

sulphate *n.* [1970]
an abbreviation for amphetamine sulphate; a strong long-lasting amphetamine, which comes in powder form and is often sold to the gullible as cocaine.

✱ *'The band themselves have admitted to favouring sulphate, widely available at £5 a kick.'* (*Independent on Sunday*, 10 June 1990)

Sunbelt *n., adj.* [1972]
the southern region of the United States, running from Virginia west to California.

sunrise industry *n.* [1983]
the new successful styles of manufacturing industries, upon which the economic sun is supposedly rising: the manufacture and use of ⇨high-technology electronics, using robots, ⇨microchips, and sophisticated automation. The term is a direct development of the earlier ⇨sunset industry.

sunset industry *n.* [1980]
the old staple industries of the 19th century Industrial Revolution upon which, in their accelerating decline, the economic sun is setting. They include steel, shipbuilding, textiles and other traditional trades. The decline in such trades – or their increasing monopolization by the lower-paid workers of the ⇨Third World – is creating massive unemployment and many Western governments have been forced to invest in them against all economic sense, both to sustain jobs and maintain electoral support.

sunshine *n.* [1967]
in drug use, a proprietary name for a type of ⇨LSD, mainly available in orange tablets.

✱ *'But here's this. Your half of the sunshine blotter. Just chew it up like baseball gum.'* (H.S. Thompson, *Fear and Loathing in Las Vegas*, 1971)

sunshine law *n.* [1972]
a law that requires all US government agencies, commissions and programmes to undergo a regular re-assessment to check on their continuing usefulness and efficiency.

superbike *n.* [1970]
a large speedy motorbicycle, carrying an engine of at least 750cc capacity.

Super Bowl *n.* [1967]
the annual contest of the rival champions of US football's twin leagues, the AFC and NFC, played every January.

supercomputer *n.* [1968]
a class of extremely powerful computers, capable of in excess of 10 megaflops (➪FLOPS) and thus used for massive mathematical calculations requiring this high speed and substantial storage capacity.

* *'Two researchers discover supercomputer power that's free for the taking, and we discover a staff member's hidden past.'* (*Byte*, May 1990)

supercontinent *n.* [1963]
one of the large masses of land that are thought to have existed in the distant past and which, when they broke up, created today's continental landmasses.

superfly *n.* [1971]
1. *a black slang term* for first rate cocaine.
2. by extension from **1.** anything first rate. The term was widely popularized by the film *Superfly* (1972) which featured a New York cocaine dealer.

super-glue *n.* [1977]
the proprietary name of an extremely strong adhesive.

supergrass *n.* [1978]
a police informer hoping for lenient treatment in return for turning in other villains; supergrasses were usually enmeshed in the higher echelons of the underworld and thus were able to clear up large numbers of crimes, and betray some of the country's leading villains. The supergrass system was extended to Northern Ireland, but foundered when a number of cases based on such evidence were thrown out of court. The word **grass** is well established rhyming slang, from grasshopper which rhymes with shopper, which in turn comes from shop (inform to the police).

supergroup *n.* [1969]
a rock group formed from the leading members of a number of other groups; the first supergroup was Blind Faith, formed in 1969; others included Emerson, Lake and Palmer and Beck, Bogert, and Appice. The phenomenon, very typical of rock's growing self-importance in the early 1970s, did not catch on, nor did it survive.

* *'Stoking reds at the mere utterance of certain magic incantations like supergroup and superstar.'* (L. Bangs, *Psychotic Reactions and Carburetor Dung*, 1988)

superloo *n.* [1960]
a public convenience, first installed in a number of British Rail termini, which offered a wide range of washing facilities, in addition to the normal lavatory and washbasin.

supermini (computer) *n.* [1972]
a range of fast computers that falls between the extremely powerful ➪supercomputer and the less powerful ➪minicomputers (which in turn outpace the ➪workstation and the ➪personal or ➪desktop computer).

* *'Into the world of the minicomputer a new thing had been born, a class of computer known as a 32-bit supermini.'* (T. Kidder, *The Soul of a New Machine*, 1981)

super-rat *n.* [1974]
a strain of rat that is impervious to the otherwise deadly coagulent pesticides such as Warfarin.

superset *n.* [1984]
see **subset**.

superstore *n.* [1965]
a synonym for ⇨hypermarket.

supertanker *n.* [1974]
the largest type of oil tankers, carrying in excess of 200,000 tons of crude oil.
See also **ULCC**; **VLCC**.

✱ *'Spawned by the relentless economics of oil, the gargantuan crude carriers called supertankers are today plying the seas in ever growing numbers.'* (N. Mostert, *Supership*, 1974)

super Tuesday *n.* [1988]
that Tuesday, usually in March, on which a large number of primary elections take place during a US presidential campaign; the results that come in on Super Tuesday are used by experts and commentators to help their predictions as to the outcome of the coming Party Conventions, which select the final presidential candidates.

superwoman *n.* [1975]
the post-feminist ideal as delineated in the eponymous book by Shirley Conran: a wife, a mother, and a successful career woman, all rolled into one.

supply-side *adj.* [1976]
the economic standpoint that advocates monetary restraint, reduction of the role of the government in the economy, and a cut in the tax rate to stimulate investment and increase the production of goods and services; claimed as new, but its roots can be seen in the early 18th century French and Italian physiocrats who attempted to create tax structures that would liberate business enterprise, and later by Jean-Baptiste Say who claimed 'Supply creates its own demand'.

✱ *'Supply-side economics was supposed to promote savings, investment, and entrepreneurial creativity.'* (*New York Review of Books*, 19 July 1990)

supply teacher *n.* [1963]
a teacher supplied by a local education authority to fill a (temporary) vacancy at a given school.

support group *n.* [1969]
any of the groups playing at a rock concert positioned lower down the bill than the main attraction; such bands are rarely famous and often receive a less than enthusiastic response from the fans.

support stocking *n.* [1970]
stockings or tights that have been reinforced with elastic yarn to give added support to the leg.

surface-to-air missile *n.* [1975]
see **SAM**.

surf and turf *n.* [1976]
a restaurant specializing in meals of lobster (surf) and steak (turf), or dishes that comprise the two foods.

✱ *'When distinguished visitors from the States visited the generals' compind, the usual fare was surf 'n' turf, that peculiarly American combi-*

nation of lobster and steak.' (R. Atkinson, *The Long Gray Line*, 1989)

surgical (strike) *n.* [1965]
an attack, often without a declaration of war or even a prior warning, that is made to deal with a specific target, e.g. the Israeli destruction of Iraq's nuclear plant in 1981.

✱ *'Mr Bush is said to be considering a surgical pre-emptive strike.*' (*The Independent*, 4 September 1990)

surrogate mother *n.* [1975]
a woman who volunteers to undergo pregnancy for another woman who is unable to have children herself; a fertilized egg is implanted in the surrogate's womb, and at full term a child duly appears and is handed over to the 'mother'.

surrogate wife *n.* [1978]
see **sex surrogate**.

survivability *n.* [1964]
the ability to survive a full-scale attack or war, especially one involving nuclear weapons.

survivalist *n.* [1987]
anyone whose hobby is in the collection of guns, uniforms, and any other items of weaponry and military hardware; such collections are supposed to be used for 'surviving' some unspecified disaster, but sometimes – as in the case of the mass killer Michael Ryan, a self-professed survivalist – are amassed simply to provide a lethal arsenal for potentially unstable individuals.

survivor syndrome *n.* [1968]
a delayed reaction to being a survivor, especially of some appalling experience such as a concentration camp or a major natural disaster; the individual concerned suffers guilt, tension, nightmares, and a general emotional breakdown.

sus (law) *n.* [1970]
a law under which the police may stop and arrest anyone they claim to suspect of having committed or being about to commit a crime. The law, which originated in the Vagrancy Act of 1824, was abandoned after substantial public pressure, in 1981.

✱ *'Traffic violations or possession of cannabis or petty theft or "sus".*' (J. Meades, *Peter Knows What Dick Likes*, 1989)

sus (*or* suss) (it) out *v.* [1966]
to understand, to work out.

✱ *'When chicks came round I enjoyed sussing them out, and trying to guess which one would last and which one would be dropped.*' (J. Fabian & J. Byrne, *Groupie*, 1969)

✱ *'He can sus out the best places, get the electricity on, square it with the local pigs.*' (T. Blacker, *Fixx*, 1989)

suspenser *n.* [1968]
on the same pattern as ⇨oater or ⇨sudser, a suspense film or television drama.

swap-meet *n.* [1973]
a gathering at which people get together to discuss, exchange, or trade items in which they are all interested.

swap shop *n.* [1976]
an agency which puts individuals who wish to barter their possessions in touch with one another.

SWAT *abbrev.* [1968]
an acronym for Special Weapons and Tactics: the name of a number of special police squads employed by US cities. The term is also used in the UK.
See also **SPG**.
* *'Many of these teams live up to the televised image of SWAT teams, in a phrase, shoot first and ask questions later – if you ask questions at all.'* (J. McClure, *Cop World*, 1984)
* *'In real situations his own instructors . . . act as SWAT (Special Weapons and Tactics) squads, sometimes alone, sometimes in conjunction with Scotland Yard's firearms branch.'* (R. Chesshyre, *The Force*, 1989)

sweat equity *n.* [1968]
a share or interest in a building that is earned by a tenant who makes a contribution to its maintenance or renovation.

sweep *v.* [1968]
to use electronic instruments to check that a building or room contains no clandestine eavesdropping devices or bombs.

sweeper *n.* [1964]
in soccer. a player who acts as the last line of defence other than the goalkeeper, especially in 'sweeping up' long balls hit forward by the opposition.

sweetheart (neckline) *n.* [1965]
a dress neckline that is cut in two almost semicircular curves, resembling a stylized heart.

swing *v.* [1964]
1. to indulge in random sexual promiscuity.
2. specifically to engage in (organized) partner-swapping.
See also **swinging**.

swinging *n.* [1964]
1. in general, random sexual promiscuity.
2. *a synonym for* wife-swapping or ⇨group sex. – **swinger**, *n.*
* *'Don't worry. Miriam's easy. She swings either way.'* (C. McFadden, *The Serial*, 1976)
* *'Sam always agreed with her that Harvey's single-swinger number was just terrifically immature.'* (C. McFadden, *The Serial*, 1976)

swinging *adj.* [1962]
fashionable, exciting, chic; especially popular as 'Swinging London', a term that originated in a *Time* magazine article published in 1965.
* *'It was I who stoked the coals within her that later set Swinging London on fire.'* (T. Blacker, *Fixx*, 1989)
* *'Swinging 1960s' film, with trendy photography by Christopher Challis.'* (*Independent on Sunday*, 21 October 1990)

swing voter *n.* [1964]
a voter who has no particular party allegiance and is just as likely to prefer a personality to a policy; such voters often provide the real imponderables in an election and can swing the result one way or the other.

switched-on *adv.* [1964]
aware, au fait, up to the minute.

switch-hitter *n.* [1970]
1. a batter whose batting stance varies as to the pitcher he faces; e.g. one who bats left-handed

against a right-handed pitcher and vice versa. **2.** by extension from **1.** a bisexual.
See also **AC/DC**.

synergistic *adj.* [1970]
referring to the belief that backs many takeovers and mergers: that the new combined version of the two firms will create a more perfect commercial entity than they could achieve as individual companies. From **synergetics**: the culminating concept of the design philosophy of R. Buckminster Fuller: 'the behaviour of the whole system unpredicted by the behaviour of their parts taken separately'.

synthesizer *n.* [1969]
an electronic musical instrument, most notably that invented by US engineer R.A. Moog, on which could be produced the full range of instrumental sounds, plus many that were beyond normal instruments played by humans.

system (building) *n., adj.* [1962]
a method of modular building that was popular in the 1960s and involved the assembly of large structures such as ⇨tower blocks by putting together a number of pre-designed, prefabricated components.

* *'Most system built (i.e. industrially prefabricated) architecture looks just like that.'* (J. Meades, *Peter Knows What Dick Likes*, 1989)

systems analysis *n.* [1966]
the analysis (often using mathematics) of complex situations and processes which is used as an aid to decision making in commerce and industry.

systems bargaining *n.* [1965]
the preservation, during an ⇨escalation towards nuclear war, of precedents that reduce the likelihood of further escalation, and which place thresholds in the way of an eruption into war.

TA *abbrev.* [1972]
transactional analysis: a form of psychotherapy, created by Eric Berne and Thomas Harris, which concentrates on analysing individual episodes of social interaction by breaking down each individual into a tripartite entity containing (1) the Parent, (2) the Child, and (3) the Adult (as in Freud's superego, id and ego).
See also **est**; **Rolfing**.

✱ *'Look at the way he'd baited her TA instructor at the Brennan's the other night. "You are not OK", he had told him loudly.'* (C. McFadden, *The Serial*, 1976)

tab *n.* [1961]
an abbreviation for tablet: any drug that comes in tablet form.

✱ *'It might have been the green tab, the red one, the blue, the Dravon, four joints, no food, hash, no sleep for five days.'* (A. Hoffman, *Woodstock Nation*, 1969)

tab *n.* [1963]
see **ring-pull**.

tabloid television *n.* [1988]
television programmes that offer as little depth and intellectual stimulus as does the tabloid press: such television, which is increasingly dominant in the US and the staple of Britain's satellite network BSkyB, offers game shows, gossipy ⇨chat shows (especially when larded with true life horror stories *à la* Oprah Winfrey), ⇨rock videos, etc.

tae kwon do *n.* [1967]
from the Korean *tae* (fist), *kwon* (art), and *do* (method or way). The Korean version of the Japanese martial art karate.

tag *n.* [1987]
used by graffiti artists to describe the writing of their own name, which will be individually created in lovingly designed colours and shapes to stamp the artist's personality on his or her work.

t'ai chi *n.* [1962]
from the Chinese meaning 'extreme limit': a Chinese martial art, supposedly devised by a taoist priest of the Sung dynasty (960–1279); it promotes inner calm as well as physical proficiency.

✱ *'Brian was also deeply into body personality awareness and spent long hours doing Tai chi on the deck.'* (C. McFadden, *The Serial*, 1976)

tailback *n.* [1977]
a long line of vehicles, brought to a halt, or at best an extremely slow speed, by a bottleneck on a road or (usually) motorway.

take *n.* [1973]
feeling, perception; often as

✱ *'My take on this is . . . '*

takeaway *n., adj.* [1964]
also known as a **take-out** (1970): any food that

can be bought in a restaurant and taken home to be eaten there. Thus the restaurant that provides such food is also a takeaway. The Scottish equivalent is 'carry out'.

talk a good/great game *phrase.* [1972]
to speak persuasively, to have 'the gift of the gab'; the assumption is that the words may be impressive, but the actions may well not match up.

* *'When he felt he had mastered enough of the jargon to talk a good game . . . he talked his way into a job at RCA.'* (T. Kidder, *The Soul of a New Machine*, 1981)

talking *v.* [1980]
the contemporary use of 'talking' as a transitive verb, with the word 'about' unstated, implying not so much person-to-person communication, but as a way of emphasizing the importance and immediacy of the topic in hand, comes from Hollywood, where studio jargon tends to the hyperbolic. 'We're talking telephone numbers' means simply 'This will be a very large sum of money'. The implication is often one of slight reproof, i.e. don't forget, we are not discussing any old topic/sum of money/success/failure, but something quite exceptional/startling.

* *'The name of the flick is Mad Monkey Kung Fu. We're talking serious chopsocky here. We're talking Hong Kong direct.'* (J.B. Briggs, *Joe Bob Goes to the Drive-In*, 1987)

talking head *n.* [1968]
in the media, anyone seen talking, rather than moving, usually in a head and shoulders close-up shot; talking heads programmes tend to ignore the dynamic visual opportunities of the medium and remain static and often didactic.

talk show *n.* [1965]
see **chat show.**

tank top *n.* [1968]
a sleeveless garment with a round neck and deep armholes, worn by either sex it looks most like the top of a bathing suit.

* *'Everybody's dressed to the fillings in all kinda chains and whatnot, taco tanktopping it with frappe de Yardley on the side.'* (L. Bangs, *Psychotic Reactions and Carburetor Dung*, 1988)

Tanzania *n.* [1964]
the East African republic formed in 1964 from the old colonial countries of Zanzibar and Tanganyika.

* *'In September 1978, possibly to distract them, possibly out of mere blind folly, Amin invaded Tanzania.'* (P. Brogan, *World Conlicts*, 1989)

tapas (bar) *n.* [1988]
a variety of savoury snacks and hors d'oeuvres traditionally served in Spanish bars and exported, along with the bars, to Britain during the 1980s.

tape cartridge *n.* [1961]
see **cassette.**

tape cassette *n.* [1972]
see **cassette.**

target *v.* [1966]
to select for action, to single out, to identify.

task *v.* [1965]
to entrust an individual with a specific job or task.

taste *n.* [1965]
a sample of drugs, usually heroin.

* *'He's got the works/Gives you sweet taste/Then you've got to split/'Cos you've got no time to waste.'* (L. Reed, 'I'm Waiting for my Man', 1966)

tasty *adj.* [1979]
1. very attractive, appealing; originally restricted to sexual references, the term is in general use.
2. in police use: suitable for arrest.

tax bracket *n.* [1975]
the level of tax that an individual pays, calculated on the basis of their annual income: the basic rate or a succession of higher 'brackets' – 40% of earnings, 50%, etc.

* *'Some PCs were said to be earning up to £2000 a month in overtime. "They were in the supertax bracket," said an inspector.'* (R. Chesshyre, *The Force*, 1989)

tax break *n.* [1968]
any form of concession on one's taxes that is permitted by a government.

tax dodge *n.* [1962]
any method of tax avoidance; such dodges are technically legal, but usually frowned upon as 'cheating'.

tax exile *n.* [1969]
a successful individual whose high earnings are taxed so heavily in his or her country of domicile that they choose to live elsewhere and pay concomitantly lower rates in another country.

tax haven *n.* [1960]
any country that attracts either businesses or wealthy individuals (often ⇨tax exiles) because of its low rates of taxation.

tax shelter *n.* [1961]
an opportunity for an individual to offset some of their income – in investment, donations to charity and similar tailor-made schemes – and thus lessen the amount that falls subject to income tax.

* *'Wealth . . . became staggeringly non-productive in the Reagan era. It was diverted into shelters. It was shuffled through paper deals . . .'* (*New York Review of Books*, 19 July 1990

tax threshold *n.* [1976]
the level of income at which one starts to pay income tax.

TCB *abbrev.* [1969]
take care of business, a slang term meaning to act prudently, efficiently, and even selfishly, putting oneself first, irrespective of the situation.

* *''Cause this was a no-jive, take-care-of-business band (few of the spawn in its wake have been so starkly pure).'* (L. Bangs, *Psychotic Reactions and Carburetor Dung*, 1988)

teach-in *n.* [1965]
an informal symposium, often held at some academic institution, but operating outside the established academic curriculum; the first teach-ins were held in the US in the mid-1960s, and concerned themselves with the Vietnam War.
See also **-in**).

* *'We now experience simultaneously the dropout and the teach-in. The two forms are correlative.'* (M. McLuhan, *The Medium is the Message*, 1967)

techie (*or* tekkie) *n.* [1980]
a computer enthusiast who derives the maximum pleasure from tinkering with the technology of the machine, rather than actually using it for its applications.

* *'The manual attempts to make up for some of its shortcomings with small sidebars entitled "Techie Tidbits". I don't consider myself a "Techie" but I still found a lot of out of context information.'* (*PC World*, November 1990)

technofear *n.* [1965]
also known as technophobia: the (unnatural) fear of the advances in or the complexities of technology, e.g. the inability of many individuals to break down a personal barrier against the use of computers.

technofreak *n.* [1965]
an enthusiast, probably a fanatic, for the latest advances in technology, either in general or as regards a specific discipline or piece of machinery.

technomania *n.* [1969]
an obsession with all things technical, especially as relating to the use of computers.

technopolis *n.* [1965]
a society dominated by technology.

technostructure *n.* [1967]
those individuals in a society who control its technology; coined by economist John Kenneth Galbraith.

* *'These men of the technostructure are the new and universal priesthood. Their religion is business success; their test of virtue is growth and profit. Their bible is the computer printout; their communion bench is the committee room.'* (J. K. Galbraith, *The Age of Uncertainty*, 1977)

teenybopper *n.* [1966]
a young pop fan, usually female, who consumes, uncritically and enthusiastically, everything the merchandisers can push their way. Even younger versions are known as **microboppers**.

* *'Teenybopper – originally a teenage girl hip to rock and turned on by rock bands, latterly applied to both sexes, with implications of pre- or proto-hippie.'* (T. Del Renzio, *The Flower Children* 1968)
* *'He'd grind like a cement mixer and the microbops loved every last dirty word of him.'* (N. Cohn, *Awopbopaloobopalopbamboom*, 1970)

teeth-to-tail ratio *n.* [1961]
the ratio of actual combat troops (teeth) to those required in support (tail); the closer one is fighting to one's home territory the smaller this ratio need be.

tele-banking n. [1981]
a variety of banking transactions – deposit, withdrawal, delivery of statements – that can be achieved through electronic means, rather than actually needing to go into the bank. Similar constructions, dependent on the same electronic facility, include *teleshopping*, *telemessaging* and *telemarketing*.

* *'If it does, it risks incurring the regulatory wrath of Oftel and could lose its telemarketing license.'* (*Independent on Sunday* 25 March 1990)

telecommuting *n.* [1974]
working from home, using an array of elec-

tronic aids – a ⇨fax machine, a personal computer, a ⇨modem, etc.
See telecottage.

teleconferencing n. [1973]
an electronic conference that is held by a number of individuals in disparate locations, all linked by a variety of telecommunications devices – telephones, computer screens, etc.

* *'These . . . include teleconferencing, publishing, library services and office paperwork filing and distribution.'* (*Educom*, fall issue, 1971)

telecopier *n.* [1967]
the original name for the ⇨fax (facsimile) machine.

telecottage *n.*
a country home, not necessarily a cottage, in which ⇨high tech equipment (computers, ⇨faxes, etc.) is used to communicate with a city office and thus permit the combination of urban work with a rural lifestyle.

* *'But all is not well at the telecottage.'* (*Independent on Sunday*, 25 March 1990)

Teletext *n.* [1974]
the BBC equivalent of ⇨Oracle, a system whereby a suitably adapted televison can be used to access a number of 'pages' of information.

* *'A knowledge of, or interest in Teletext services is also desirable.'* (*Independent on Sunday*, 8 April 1990)

telethon *n.* [1980]
a method of mass-appeal fund-raising, which uses the television – and a variety of its amenable celebrities – to spread the charitable word. The first telethon was broadcast in the US in 1949, and comprised a day-long ⇨phone-in, with non-stop television entertainment being used to encourage pledges to a number of charities. The format, which had previously been seen as overly vulgar, eventually arrived in the UK in the 1980s.
See -athon.

televangelist *n.*
one of the many US preachers – Billy Graham, Jim and Tammy Bakker, Oral Roberts, Pat Robertson, etc. – who have taken the old-style 'tent-show' and put it on television. Such televangelists offer all the old staples: healing the sick, confessions of sin, and constant appeals for cash donations.

telint *abbrev.* [1969]
telemetry intelligence: all information gathered through tracking and listening in to foreign missile tests.

tell it like it is *phrase.* [1964]
to be honest, to be candid, to reject any form of subterfuge. The confessional attitude thus encouraged stems from the attitude supposed to emerge from the analyst's couch.

* *'He is the author of a paperback book titled Marijuana which – according to the cover – "tells it like it is".'* (H.S. Thompson, *Fear and Loathing in Las Vegas*, 1971)

Telstar *n.* [1962]
the world's first telecommunications satellite, built by AT&T and launched by the US on 10 July 1962.

* *'Telstar is the forerunner of satellites designed to make round the world television possible.'* (*Chronicle of the 20th Century*, 1988)

temp *n., v.* [1967]
an abbreviation for temporary, and, when spelt out, invariably bracketed with secretary: a self-employed secretary, usually attached to an agency, who works as, when and where she is required.

ten-four (10–4) *interjection* [1962]
message understood; the best-known number of the 'ten-code', a system of call signs, all prefixed by the number '10-', which is used widely by US police forces and by ⇨Citizens' Band radio enthusiasts.

tendency *n.* [1974]
a political grouping; as a political term it comes from the French, *tendence* – thus the graffito of the Evenements of 1968: *Je suis Marxiste, tendence Groucho* – and is most widely known in the UK when bracketed with the left-wing group ⇨Militant, who emerged in 1977. *See also* **entryism**.

* *'In your extensive coverage of the community charge (11 March) your reporter linked me with Terry Fields . . . as being one of the "Militant tendency MPs".'* (*Independent on Sunday*, 25 March 1990)

tenure-track *n.* [1981]
an employment structure (found primarily in the US and usually in the academic world) whereby it is guaranteed that the holder of a post will, at a stated future time, be considered for eventual tenure, i.e. a permanent post from which he or she cannot (other than under exceptional circumstances) be dismissed. The term is an extension of tenure, coined in the 1950s, which means security of employment.

tequila sunrise *n.* [1965]
a mix of tequila and grenadine, the flushed red and orange colours of which supposedly resemble a sunrise; it became the fashionable drink of the late 1960s/early 1970s, prior to which it was virtually unknown in the UK, although it can be found in the US as early as 1954, e.g. in Jim Thompson's hard-boiled detective novel *The Golden Gizmo*.

* *'Give me a Harvey Wallbanger and a Tequila Sunrise please and could you try and get us a table.'* (G. Sams, *The Punk*, 1977)

teriyaki n. [1962]
a Japanese dish, consisting of fish or meat marinated in soy (*shoyu*) sauce, arranged on skewers, and charcoal-grilled.

* *'Teriyaki refers to the cooking process of marinating foods in soy sauce, mirin and sake, and then grilling them preferably over charcoal.'* (P. & J. Martin, *Japanese Cooking*, 1970)

terminate (with extreme prejudice) *v.* [1975]
to kill, usually as an assassin; the popular euphemism used (certainly in spy novels) by members of US intelligence agencies, particularly the CIA.

* *'That bastard Reality (who ought to be terminated with extreme prejudice) set in.'* (L. Bangs, *Psychotic Reactions and Carburetor Dung*, 1988)

TESSA *abbrev.* [1989]
am acronym for Tax Exempt Special Savings Account: an account held in a bank or building society on the interest from which no tax falls due unless the capital is withdrawn before five years have passed.

test-tube baby *n.* [1974]
a baby conceived through artificial insemination, or a baby that has developed from an egg that has been fertilized outside the mother's body.

✱ *'It was announced that the world's first test-tube baby . . . had been delivered by Caesarian operation at Oldham District General Hospital.'* (*Chronicle of the 20th Century*, 1987)

textured vegetable protein *n.* [1978]
see TVP.

thalidomide baby (*or* child) *n.* [1962]
one of the more than 450 children born to mothers who took the drug Thalidomide (marketed as Distaval, a non-barbiturate sedative and hypnotic) during pregnancy. Thalidomide was given to a number of mothers in the early months of their pregnancy and was found, too late, to cause serious malformations in the growing foetus. Children were born either without limbs or with severe malformations.

✱ *'The erratic nature of the interest in the Thalidomide children was also a reflection of the way in which newspapers and television news programmes work.'* (H. Evans, *Good Times, Bad Times*, 1983)

Thatcherism *n.* [1979]
policies advocated and carried through by UK Prime Minister Margaret Thatcher (1923–). The word dates back to the 1970s, but the 1980s celebrated its apotheosis: which might be expressed as the philosophy that all Britons are equal, but the entrepreneur deserves to be more equal that others. It was possibly originated by professor Stuart Hall.

✱ *'After 10 years of being left at the post by the thoroughbreds of Thatcherism, trade union leaders are busy grooming the workers' movement for a grand national role again.'* (*Independent on Sunday*, 8 April 1990)

Thatcherite *adj., n.* [1979]
pertaining to the policies carried out by the government of and epitomized in the person of Prime Minister Margaret Thatcher; devotee of such policies.

✱ *'Mr Hicks measures its approval in a very Thatcherite way – by the amount of money deposited in the donation boxes.'* (*The Independent*, 31 March 1990)

THC *abbrev.* [1968]
delta-9-tetrahydrocannabinol, the active ingredient of cannabis, which helps the smoker get 'high'.

✱ *'Marijuana grown in Mississippi from high-quality Mexican seed proved to contain much more of the psychoactive substance (THC) than marijuana from domestic seed grown on the same plot.'* (E.M. Brecher, *Licit and Illicit Drugs*, 1972)

theatre (weapons) *n.* [1977]
short-range armaments, both nuclear and conventional, that are designed for use by troops engaged in a short-range battle.

✱ *'In military jargon "theater" refers to the zone of combat and communications involved in a war, extending to the larger area that may be directly affected by the fighting.'* (S. Talbott, *Deadly Gambits*, 1984)

theme *adj.* [1960]
any environment, usually designed for entertainment or recreation which is arranged around a single unifying idea.

Typical of such creations is the **theme park** (1960): amusement parks such as Disneyland in the US, Alton Towers in the UK or Parc Asterix in France. Themed environments have been extended beyond parks, and the concept of theming underlies much of 1980s merchandising and marketing, with **theme pubs** (1983) and **theme restaurants** (1983) springing up in profusion.
See also **heritage**.

- ✱ *'BSB with its themed channels, sport, movies, Galaxy, Now and Powerstation.'* (*Sunday Correspondent*, 10 June 1990)
- ✱ *'The impression I got was of a theme park or open air museum devoted to the "alternative lifestyle" of a decade and a half hitherto.'* (J. Meades, *Peter Knows What Dick Likes*, 1989)

theme park *n.* [1960]
see **theme**.

theme pub *n.* [1983]
see **theme**.

theme restaurant *n.* [1983]
see **theme**.

thingism *n.* [1961]
from the French *chosisme*: the dominant style of such ⇨new wave writers as A. Robbe-Grillet, in which there are minutely detailed descriptions of every 'thing' in a given scene.

third market *n.* [1986]
the market in listed stocks which are not traded on a stock exchange.

Third World *n.* [1966]
those nations whose territories, if not their politics, do not form part of the industrially developed world. The term was coined by French diplomat Georges Balandier in 1956 and then referred specifically to the 29 African and Asian nations who met at the Bandung Conference in April 1955. This conference, despite a number of inevitable differences regarding the various political and cultural groupings, passed a number of motions supporting cultural and economic cooperation, self-determination and the opposition to colonialism. Although it has been challenged as a description by the concept of ⇨'developing nations' and the new term 'The ⇨South', the phrase, which gained far greater currency during the last two decades, is still generally popular.

- ✱ *'Black Power means that black people see themselves as part of a new force, sometimes called the "Third World".'* (S. Carmichael & C. Hamilton, *Black Power*, 1967)

thong *n.* [1967]
an open sandal, originated in Australia, and similar to a ⇨flip-flop.

thrash *n., adj.* [1987]
also known as **thrashcore, thrash metal** and **speed metal**: a mix of ⇨heavy metal and ⇨punk, low on melody, high on noise.

- ✱ *'So are drag fans thrash metal enthusiasts? Not, it would seem, on the evidence of the music played.'* (*Independent on Sunday*, 22 April 1990)

threshold *n.* [1967]
when combined with wage or price, a predetermined level at which wage or price increases become obligatory.

through-ball *n.* [1969]
in soccer: a forward pass which cuts through the

opponents' defence and, if perfectly timed, should land at the feet of one's advancing striker.

throw-weight *n.* [1969]
the total weight of what can be carried by a missile over a particular range; the weight of the 'business end' of a rocket, including its armaments and the guidance system that will deliver them on target. In older missiles, the throw-weight was merely the warhead itself; modern ➪MIRVed missiles create a throw-weight that includes all the warheads, the post-boost vehicle (the 'bus'), plus all necessary guidance systems and electronic counter-measures and any other propulsion or penetration aids.

✱ *'Deep cuts focussed by a formula which combines throw-weight (of missiles) and warhead numbers.'* (M. Dando & P. Rogers, *The Death of Deterrence*, 1984)

thrust *n.* [1962]
the salient or intending meaning of a statement, an argument or piece of writing.

thruster *n.* [1962]
a small rocket engine attached to a spacecraft and which can be manipulated by the astronaut to modify the craft's flightpath.

ticky tacky *n.* [1962]
inferior, cheap, second-rate building material.

✱ *'And they're all made out of ticky-tacky/And they all look just the same.'* (M. Reynolds, 'Little Boxes', 1964)

tie-break *n.* [1970]
a means of deciding the winner out of two contestants who have tied every regular game or round of a competition but who must be separated for the overall competition to continue or (if a final) to end; usually found in tennis where the normal method of scoring (15-Love, etc.) is replaced by a single point series of serves, where the 'break' goes to the first player to score 7 points.

tie-dye *adj.* [1968]
referring to garments that have been tied into knots and then dipped into a variety of dyes; when the garment is dry and the knots untied these can form attractive patterns, although, since few of those that tied the knots had much design ability, such excellence is rare. Tie-dye, like flared trousers (➪flares) regained youthful approval – much to the surprise of its original fans – in the early 1990s.

✱ *'They were dazed, they wore tie-dye shirts and they were under 25! Simon Garfield witnessed a northern phenomenon.'* (*Independent on Sunday*, 3 June 1990)

tie-in *n. adj.* [1962]
a book, film or (increasingly) toy or series of toys, that is marketed to exploit the appearance of the same work or characters in a different medium. Thus the worldwide merchandising in 1990 of Teenage Mutant Ninja Turtles, originally a comic magazine, but available as a film, a TV series, a computer game, and an infinity of mugs, masks, weapons, plastic toys, and much more.

time-expired *adj.* [1972]
used in the retail trade to refer to perishable goods that are no longer fit for sale.
See also **sell-by date**.

timeframe *n.* [1969]
currently used by businessmen, who have borrowed it from technology, to mean no more than 'length of time'.

time-release *adj.* [1977]
a form of pill, usually containing a painkiller or cold cure, which is constructed so as to release its active chemicals over a period of time, rather than immediately on consumption.

time-share *n., adj.* [1976]
a system of joint ownership of a holiday home, under which the owners take turns in using the property at pre-arranged times.

* *'Yet time-share, despite its unsavoury image, is the fastest growing sector of the UK leisure industry.'* (*Sunday Correspondent*, 22 April, 1990)

time-slice *n.* [1965]
a predefined period of time, the quantum, which is allotted to a specific task in a time-share system. All tasks receive slices in rotation until they are completed, thus ensuring that all users have a fair share of the machine.

time slot *n.* [1962]
the time allocated to a given radio or television programme, or to a transmission via satellite. Among broadcasters, the mandatory period allotted to religious programmes on Sunday evenings is the **God-slot**.

TINA *abbrev.* [1979]
an acronym for There is no alternative, supposedly Margaret Thatcher's favourite acronym; her ministers tended to echo it as their justification for unpalatable policies aimed at intractable events.

tin parachute *n.* [1981]
a less than generous payment offered to a sacked employee which does not really 'let them down gently'. The opposite of **golden parachute**.

tired and emotional *adj.* [1965]
coined in *Private Eye* magazine as a euphemism (on the lines of 'confirmed bachelor' for homosexual) for extremely drunk. *See also* **Uganda, talking about**.

tissue-typing *n.* [1965]
the assessment of tissue for the purpose of working out whether or not it will prove compatible with other tissue; used particularly when planning a transplant operation.

tit mag *n.* [1969]
a colloquialism for a softcore pornographic magazine, usually euphemized as a 'men's magazine'.

* *'But socially Hefner is still a man who runs a tit magazine and a string of clubs that recall the parlor floor of a red-flock whorehouse.'* (T. Wolfe, *The Mid-Atlantic Man*, 1968)

TLC *abbrev.* [1970]
tender loving care: optimum attention, especial solicitude; the image is of the care given out by the ideal nurse.

TM *abbrev.* [1967]
transcendental meditation: a method of relaxation and meditatation based generally on yoga and popularized in the West during the late 1960s by the Maharishi Mahesh Yogi, whose fashionable devotees included the Beatles, Rolling Stones and other ⇨rock bands. *See also* **est; Rolfing; TA**.

✱ *'Shrinks, sex therapists, est alumni, Kate's TA and TM instructors; vegetarians, masseurs.'* (C. McFadden, *The Serial*, 1976)

toasting *n.* [1976]
the practice of West Indian disk jockeys who add their own lyrics, often witty and/or relevant to current affairs, to a background of the bass line of a ⇨reggae song that can be found with its own different set of lyrics; toasting is the predecessor of ⇨hip-hop. Thus **toaster**: a DJ who performs this style. – **toast**, *v.*

together *adv., adj.* [1969]
in a state of calmness, efficiency, self-awareness, mental and emotional stability.

✱ *'Jerry smiled and nodded knowingly. "Sure you've been together, Harv, but in this really fragmented way".'* (C. McFadden, *The Serial*, 1976)

toggle *v.* [1982]
in computing: descriptive of any command that works first one way and then another, e.g. to turn on a function and, the next time it is used, then to turn it off.

toke *n., v.* [1968]
a puff of a marijuana or hashish cigarette.

✱ *'He and the boys took a few tokes on a joint and the Hell's Angels were on the bus.'* (T. Wolfe, *The Electric Kool-Aid Acid Test*, 1969)

token *adj.* [1972]
usually used with 'woman', 'gay', or 'black', and denoting an individual who has been included in a situation not so much on merit (although coincidentally that may be there), but because it is necessary to have a representative member of the given social or ethnic group.

See also **statutory**; **tokenism**.

✱ *'By the standards of . . . promising young black lawyers forgoing what they could make as token niggers in big white law firms, forty, fifty grand a year seems pretty generous.'* (G. Higgins, *A Choice of Enemies*, 1983)

✱ *'Just now he is, by his own admission, taken up as the "token youth".'* (J. Meades, *Peter Knows What Dick Likes*, 1989)

tokenism *n.* [1962]
the use by governments, the media, business, and many other areas of essentially white male society of a few blacks, women, members of minority or handicapped groups for cosmetic ⇨token purposes; such variations on the ⇨visible negro pander to a growing agitation, but do little or nothing to alter the continuing realities of the status quo.

See also **statutory**.

✱ *'"You've got me all wrong, you know? I've been working for Margaret Azevedo." "Tokenism," Julie said. "Big deal".'* (C. McFadden, *The Serial*, 1976)

Tonton Macoute *n.* [1962]
the militia formed by François 'Papa Doc' Duvalier, the Haitian dictator; thugs in uniform, wearing their inevitable dark glasses, the Tontons were known for their arbitrary savage brutality.

ton-up *adj.* [1961]
1. a motorcycle that will 'do the ton', i.e. travel at 100 miles per hour.
2. A rider (*ton up boy, ton-up girl*) who rides at that speed.

toon *n.* [1989]
an abbreviation for cartoon: thus an animated

cartoon; the word was coined for the film *Who Killed Roger Rabbit?* (1987), which mixed animation and normal live action.

toot *n.* [1977]
1. a sniff of cocaine.
2. a gadget, usually made of glass tubing, through which one could take a toot. (sense 1.)

top gun *n.* [1987]
from the nickname for the leading pilots at the USAF fighter school: a star, a leader, a ➪macho man. The term entered non-military use with the release of the eponymous film in 1987.

topless *adj.* [1964]
naked from the waist up; used invariably of women and usually in such combinations as *topless dancer, topless bar, topless beach*, etc. Possibly the most exotic combination of the word is in **topless radio**: radio programmes in which listeners are invited to call in and chat about their personal sexual proclivities and problems to a studio host and one or two experts – sex therapists, doctors, newspaper advice columnists, etc.

✱ *'Go-go dancer, topless waitress, massage parlor, call girl . . . it all boiled down to the same thing.'* (L. Bangs, *Psychotic Reactions and Carburetor Dung*, 1988)

top of the line *n.* [1963]
the brand leader, a position gained either through cost, efficiency, sales appeal, or any other outstanding characteristic.

top out *v.* [1961]
to finish a building, by putting on its roof (the top). On particularly large or important buildings there may well be a **topping out** ceremony to mark the conclusion of construction.

top table, at the *adv.* [1964]
privy to the leadership, in a position of influence and power.

touch base (with) *v.* [1976]
to communicate with, to meet.

✱ *'Sergeant Juarez is still out touching bases, as he calls it, when dusk comes to the barrio.'* (J. McClure, *Cop World*, 1984)

touch-tone (phone) *n.* [1962]
any form of telephone which uses press-buttons rather than the traditional dial.

tower block *n.* [1966]
a highrise building designed for residential rather than office use; tower blocks tended to be built in the 1960s by local government housing authorities for their tenants whose old homes had been torn down as inadequate for modern housing.

✱ *'Of these, 150,000 were built after the Second World War, including numerous concrete tower blocks in the 1960s.'* (*The Independent*, 23 May 1990)

tower system *n.*
1. *in stereo use:* the equivalent of the ➪stack system.
2. *in computing:* an arrangement of the usual three parts of the system – the screen, the keyboard, and system box – whereby a larger than average box is placed vertically on the floor (what would be a 'side' on the desk becoming the bottom on the floor) leaving the desk to hold the screen and keyboard only.

✱ *'The FlexCache 25386DT Model 40 from ALR is a redesign of the company's 386/25 tower system.'* (*Byte*, May 1990)

town house *n.* [1965]
originally the London ('town') home of a wealthy landowner whose principal home was on his country estate; now used by estate agents and speculative builders to describe a modern row of terraced houses, often designed in a stylish or novel manner.

toy library *n.*
a collection of toys, usually housed in some public facility like a nursery or playgroup, which can be borrowed by the children who attend it.

✱ *'We may look hardbitten but within us beat the hearts of toy librarians and playgroup counsellors.'* (J. Meades, *Peter Knows What Dick Likes*, 1989)

toyboy *n.* [1984]
what the ➪bimbo is to the older richer man, so is the toyboy to the 'woman of a certain age'; popularized by the amours of such as Britt Ekland and Joan Collins.

✱ *'Five novels peopled by posh dross – conmen and pornographers and fascists and toyboys and tarts.'* (J. Meades, *Peter Knows What Dick Likes*, 1989)

toys *n.* [1977]
see **sex aids**.

track record *n.* [1965]
from the sporting use, one's previous performance or one's background (usually professional); used as a guide for future potential.

✱ *'An excellent track record in a sales/marketing position in an environment close to that of Locstar.'* (ad for Locstar in the (*Independent on Sunday*, 3 June 1990)

track-lighting *n.* [1972]
lighting which is fitted onto tracks and can thus be moved up and down those tracks, varying the lighting within a room.

trackball *n.* [1969]
in computing: touted as a popular (and improved) alternative to the ➪mouse, the trackball is a small ball which is rotated inside a fixed holder and, connected to the computer, moves the cursor on the screen.

✱ *'And since the trackball gives you direct finger-tip control, there's never any mouse cursor creep.'* (*Byte*, June 1990)

tradecraft *n.* [1961]
in espionage: the various methods whereby a spy conducts his or her profession.

✱ *'He was suddenly alert . . . Was it the latent skill of his own tradecraft which informed him?'* (J. Le Carré, *Call for the Dead*, 1961)

trade mission *n.* [1973]
a mission that is sent to another country in order to promote trade.

trade-off *n., v.* [1962]
a bargain, a compromise.
See also **bargaining chip**.

trainer *n.* [1978]
a training shoe; originally used for sport, with the boom in ➪leisure wear trainers (often sold at grossly inflated prices) have become the basic footwear of contemporary society.

✱ *'Suddenly trainers and hi-tech tennis racquets*

became public property.' (*The Independent*, 31 March 1990)

trank *n.* [1967]
slang abbreviation for tranquillizer.

tranny (*or* trannie) *n.* [1969]
1. *a colloquial abbreviation for* transistor (radio).
* *'Three men in jeans were watching a fourth dig a hole to the strains of a tranny.'* (D. Raymond, *He Died With His Eyes Open*, 1984)

2. *an abbreviation for* (35 mm film) transparency. It is also used, although less widely, as an abbreviation of (35 mm film) transparency.

transcendental meditation *n.* [1966]
see TM.

transit lounge *n.* [1962]
that part of an airport terminal which is set aside for passsengers who are in transit from one flight to another. The transit lounge is technically stateless, since such passengers have not passed through the host country's customs.

transmission electron microscope *n.* [1969]
an electron microscope in which the electrons are detected after they pass through the specimen.

transmit button *n.* [1968]
a button on a person-to-person radio which activates transmission by one of the speakers.

transparent *adj.* [1962]
in computing. descriptive of any process or procedure which occurs during the operation of a program although the user will not be actively aware of its existence.

transplant *n.* [1967]
any organ that has been taken from the body of one individual (the donor) and placed in the body of another (the recipient). A variety of transplants had been achieved during the century, but the term entered wide use with the first heart transplant operation, performed by Dr Christian Barnard in South Africa in 1967.

transputer *n.* [1978]
from transistor + computer, and colloquially known as the 'computer on a chip'; a single ⇨microchip on which are incorporated all the functions of an entire ⇨microprocessor, including the memory. The potential of this miniaturization is to multiply to a vast extent the power of the machine in which such chips are installed. The term transputer originated in 1978, but the first transputer chips did not appear until 1985 when the Inmos company began manufacturing them.
* *'Inmos' vision of the future of computing encompasses the concept of networks of "transputers"; multi-processing communicating machines based on VLSI technology and using concurrent processing to achieve much greater performance than today's devices.'* (*Soft* magazine, June 1983)

trapdoor *n.* [1976]
in computing. a means of entering a system by using the identity and password of a legitimate user and then accessing, altering, or even destroying files. Once within the system, the illegal user can create a new, and *de facto* legiti-

mate identity which can be used for infinite entries into the system in the future.

trash *v.* [1970]
to destroy, to render useless, to turn into rubbish; the original use of trash in this context (it simply means rubbish in the US) was by a variety of US revolutionary groups of the late 1960s, notably ⇨Weatherman, whose attacks on public property were known as **trashing**.

* *'Resist actively, sabotage, jam the computer, hijack planes, trash every lethal machine in the land.'* (*San Francisco Good Times*, 18 September 1970)
* *'I would take up arms and march on the media centres of Merrie Olde . . . and trash them beyond recognition.'* (L. Bangs, *Psychotic Reactions and Carburetor Dung*, 1988)
* *'Which means there's no need to trash any of your existing code.'* (*Byte*, July 1990)

trawl *v.* [1971]
to meet a number of people, whether socially or in formal interviews, to select a candidate for a job appointment.
See also **milk round; networking.**

Trekkie *n.* [1976]
a dedicated (even obsessive) fan of Star Trek, the 1960s' science fiction series, revived with a new cast in 1990.

trendiness *n.* [1966]
the slavish following of short-lived trends and briefly fashionable fads.
See also **trendy**.

trend-setter *n.* [1960]
anyone who is perceived as laying down a new fashion, in whatever field they may operate. *See also* **style guru.** – **trend-setting,** *n.*

* *'As Lao-tzu, Freud, Erhard and other trend-setters know, knowledge alone will get you nowhere.'* (R.D. Rosen, *Psychobabble*, 1977)

trend-spotter *n.* [1965]
one who observes and predicts (when possible) the changing modes of what is and might become fashionable.
See also **style guru.**

trendy [1962]
1. *adj.* fashionable, albeit ephemeral, the ⇨flavour of the month.
2. *n.* one who indulges in such pursuits.

* *'At first it was hyped as being yuppie and trendy but now it's more for ordinary families.'* (*Sunday Correspondent*, 8 April 1990
* *'A crystal chandelier hung from the ceiling through a hole in the bedspread which was patterned in exotic Eastern colours. Blooming trendies, thought Adolph to himself.'* (G. Sams, *The Punk*, 1977)

Triads *n.* [1960]
Chinese secret societies; originally restricted to the Far East, these societies have accompanied the Chinese migration to the West.

trial by television *n.* [1960]
1. the subjection of a public figure to a depth interview during a television programme; originated by those who complained that John Freeman's *Face to Face* interviews for the BBC, lacking the usual sycophancy were therefore unacceptably hostile.

* *'"But it's trial by television, everyone knows that," he wailed as he paced up and down.'* (T. Blacker, *Fixx*, 1989)

2. extension from 1. used by the Thatcher

government, whose leader popularized the term, to cover any programme that questioned the truth of the government line.

trialist *n.* [1960]
anyone involved in a sporting trial for selection for a major event, e.g. the Olympic trials.

Tribeca *n.* [1975]
an area of New York City that lies on Manhattan Island. *an acronym for* Triangle Below Canal Street.
See also SoHo.

tricyclic antidepressants *n.* [1966]
any of a group of antidepressant drugs that have in common a molecular structure based on three interlocking rings.

trigger price *n.* [1978]
the keeping open of old and obsolete facilities, e.g. steel plants, that offer employment but are in fact economically useless, by holding the price of their products well above what would be charged were they produced in new cost-efficient facilities.

trilateral commission *n.* [1973]
a New York based policy group created in 1973 by Nelson Rockefeller to create alternatives to President Nixon's nationalistic economic foreign policy, which was seen as hostile by a number of US allies.

Trimphone *n.* [1965]
a proprietary name for a design of telephone, with a high-pitched warbling ringing tone, which was made available by the Post Office from 1965.

trip *n.* [1966]
1. originally used of drugs: the experience of taking a hallucinogenic drug, particularly ⇨LSD.

✱ *'Someone whispered in my ear that Lucy in the Sky with Diamonds was a song about an LSD trip.'* (A. Aldridge (ed). *The Beatles Illustrated Lyrics*, (1969)

2. by extension from 1. *a synonym for* experience.

✱ *'West rarely lent his enthusiasm to someone else's trip, Alsing noted.'* (T. Kidder, *The Soul of a New Machine*, 1981)

trip out *v.* [1966]
to take ⇨LSD and to experience its effects.

trippy *adj.* [1969]
bizarre, disorientating, similar in effect to the experience of an ⇨LSD ⇨trip.

tripwire force *n.* [1960]
those troops who are stationed on a hostile border as the first line of defence; such troops are deemed expendable and their role is not to stop an invasion, merely to hold it up long enough for the major part of the defences to be activated. Thus **tripwire position**, the area – usually on a border with a hostile power – in which tripwire forces are stationed.

triumphalism *n.* [1964]
in religious use. descriptive of that sense of pride (and even ostentation) that certain of the devout feel in the achievements, and particularly the moral rightness of their church.

Trivial Pursuit *n.* [1985]
the proprietary name of a popular board game released in the mid-1980s; players were

faced with a series of general knowledge questions, their progress around the board, during which they aimed to collect a number of tokens, depending on how well they managed to answer these.

- ✱ *'But the truth about Trivial Pursuit sales in Britain is that they have gone from 1.5m in the glorious heyday of 1987 to 400,000 last year.'* (*Sunday Correspondent*, 8 April 1990)

Trojan horse *n.* [1986]
in computing. 1. used to describe an entry point placed in a computer system by an invader of that system. The regular users of the system will be unaware of the entry which can be used to break down data security, destroy or alter files, or for computer fraud and theft.
2. the description of an unexpected or malicious side-effect of a program that usually works as required.
See also **logic bomb**; **virus**.

- ✱ *'A Trojan Horse is any bug inserted into a computer program that takes advantage of the trusted status of its host by surreptitiously performing unintended functions.'* (*PC World*, July 1990)

Trot *n.* [1962]
an abbreviation for Trotskyite. Thus: **Trotslot** (on the analogy of God-slot, *see* **time slot**): any programme, usually of current affairs, that attacks the prevailing Establishment position and is thus considered, perhaps ironically, to be fomenting red revolution.

truck *n.* [1976]
in ➪skateboarding, one of a pair of axles that support the board's wheels.

trucker *n.* [1961]
the US equivalent of a lorry-driver, and as such increasingly adopted today by UK drivers.

trucking, keep on *phrase.* [1967]
a popular exhortation of the ➪hippie years (apostrophized in a celebrated illustration by ➪underground cartoonist Robert Crumb), calling upon the individual so addressed not to give up, to persist in what they're doing.

truck stop *n.* [1961]
a roadside restaurant or cafe which is frequented primarily by truckdrivers; a garage selling petrol may be attached.

- ✱ *'Wake up in the middle of the night in a truck stop/Stumble in a restaurant, wonder why I don't stop.'* (S. Earle, 'Guitar Town', 1988)

truth *n.* [1977]
a synonym for top ➪quark, and the opposite of ➪beauty.
See also **charm**.

tube (beer) *n.* [1965]
originally Australian slang for a bottle or can of beer, the term is now used wherever Australian (or any other) lager is consumed. It was popularized in the UK with the publication of the 'Barry McKenzie' strip in the magazine *Private Eye*.

- ✱ *'Shit a brick. I reckon this is going to be a bit of solid yakka . . . Right now I wouldn't say no to a few tubes of the old frosty fluid.'* (B. Humphries, *The Wonderful World of Barry McKenzie*, 1968)

tube sock *n.* [1976]
an elasticized sock which has no special shaping for the heel.

tubes, go down the *phrase.* [1963]
to fail, often used of commercial endeavours; the tubes in question are presumably those that lead to the sewers.

tufted carpet *n.* [1960]
a type of carpet that consists of a pile yarn of tufts or loops which is inserted into a prewoven backing and secured by means of a bonding material.

tug-of-love *adj.* [1973]
usually found as *tug-of-love baby* or *tug-of-love child*: a child whose divorced or separated parents both claim custody, and are neither of them willing to relinquish the infant. The term is possibly linked to Israel Zangwill's play *The Tug of Love* (1907).

tummler *n.* [1966]
from the Yiddish, meaning noisy commotion, tumult: the paid social director of those resorts in the Catskill mountains known, through their predominantly Jewish clientele, as the 'Borscht belt'.

* *'The tummler is a noise-maker, a fun-generator, a hilarity-organizer and overall buffoon.'* (L. Rosten, *The Joys of Yiddish*, 1968)

tunnel-vision *n.* [1967]
1. literally, a defect in one's vision which reduces it to a narrrow 'tunnel' of sight.
2. by extension from 1. a narrowness of sight and thus of mind, the inability to see any but a single point of view.

Tupamaros *n.* [1969]
a guerrilla group operating in Uruguay since 1970.

* *Tupamaros kidnap British ambassador to Uruguay, Geoffrey Jackson; keep him in a box for eight months.'* (P. Brogan, *World Conflicts*, 1989)

turbo *adj.* [1986]
1. *an abbreviation for* turbocharged: used originally by the automobile industry to denote engines that, powered by gas turbine engines, could run at faster than average speeds.
2. in computing: used by computer manufacturers to describe any fast machine.

turf *n.* [1970]
a US synonym for the UK 'patch' or 'manor': that area of a town or city that is considered the personal fiefdom of either a criminal or a detective; also used figuratively.

* *'Samuels, president of New York's new Off-Track Betting Corporation, was trying to muscle in on his turf.'* (*Newsweek, 14 June 1971*)

Turkish pollen *n.* [1968]
see **Acapulco gold.**

turned-on *adv.* [1967]
excited, enthused, fascinated.

turnkey system *n.* [1979]
1. *in general use:* (as such dating back to 1958), referring to any piece of technology or manufacturing that is delivered to a customer ready for use; the maker or seller has provided a stock system or unit, the client takes his recommendation at face value and merely accepts delivery of the product, requiring only to 'turn a key' to set things in motion; turnkey deals extend from an entire office-block or factory through to a single piece of equipment.
2. *in computing:* a system which has been

designed, assembled, and checked by its manufacturer, and double-checked by the retailer and which is then turned over to the user who needs only to turn a real or metaphorical key for the system to be ready for immediate use.

* *'Turnkey operation: The delivery and installation of a complete computer system plus application programs so that the system can be placed into immediate operation.'* (*Sphere Dictionary of Computing*, 1983)

turn-off *n.* [1966]
the opposite of turn-on: anything or anyone seen as unpleasant or distasteful.

turn on *v.* [1966]
1. originally to light up a drugged cigarette and get high or to give drugs to someone else.
2. To enthuse others with one's own interests or pleasures; as noun a **turn-on** implies anything pleasurable, interesting or exciting.

* *'If you can't turn your parents on . . . turn on them.'* (IT, 12 December 1966)
* *'The Beatles are a religion: they turn people on by what they say and by what they represent.'* (A. Aldridge (ed.), *The Beatles Illustrated Lyrics*, 1969)

turnover *n.* [1969]
in US football: for one side to lose possession of the ball and turn it over to their opponents.

turn (round) *v.* [1966]
for an intelligence agency to persuade the agent of a hostile power to start working for those upon whom he or she was initially deputed to spy; such 'turned' agents then become 'double-agents'.

turnround *n.* [1963]
the reversal of a trend, especially in the success or failure of a commercial enterprise.

* *'There is a growing feeling in market quarters that . . . the end of an upswing is in sight and a turnround may be near.'* (*The Times*, 29 January 1963)

TV dinner *n.* [1970]
a frozen meal, designed to be eaten in front of the television, that needs only be heated up for instant consumption.

TVP *abbrev.* [1968]
textured vegetable protein: the basis of a number of foods which are constructed so as to resemble meat (in both texture and flavour) but which are actually made of synthetic vegetable-based products.

twelve inch (*or* **12-inch)** *n., adj.* [1977]
a twelve-inch diameter record – usually that of an album, which has only one track (albeit extended) and which is played at the single's speed of 45rpm, rather than the album's 33rpm.

* *'You'd never see Jimmy coming home from town without a new album or a 12-inch or at least a 7-inch single.'* (Roddy Doyle, *The Commitments*, 1987)

twilight areas (*or* **zones)** *n.* [1960]
a synonym for ➪inner city: a declining area of the town or city where the housing stock is dilapidated and the shops rundown or closed.

twin-tub *n., adj.* [1962]
a washing machine that has two separate top-loading drums, one for washing and one for spin-drying.

twist *n. v.* [1961]
a popular dance that originated in New York's Peppermint Lounge in 1961 and spread rapidly through the Western world, popularized both by socialites and the mass teeenage market.

* *'One week in October 1961, a few socialites . . . discovered the Peppermint Lounge and by the next week all of Jet Set New York was discovering the Twist, after the manner of the first 19900 decorators who ever laid hands on an African mask.'* (T. Wolfe, *The Kandy-Kolored Tangerine Flake Streamline Baby*, 1966)

twisted *adj.* [1966]
in drug use, heavily under the influence of drugs, probably hallucinogenic, given the 'mind-bending' propensities of such drugs.

* *'They would be tough miles. very soon, I knew, we would both be completely twisted.'* (H.S. Thompson, *Fear and Loathing in Las Vegas*, 1971)

twister *n.* [1961]
one who performs the ⇨twist.

twofer *n.* [1977]
from 'two for the price of one': a political term referring to the appointment of a black woman to office – the use of two 'oppressed' groups embodied in one individual is meant to satisfy both the racial and sexual equality lobbies.
See also **statutory**; **tokenism**.

two-pence (piece) *n.* [1972]
a bronze coin, the second lowest denomination in the UK decimal system, first introduced in 1972.

two-way mirror *n.* [1967]
a mirror which, by letting a certain amount of light filter through, permits an observer at one side to watch activities on the other, although those observed cannot tell that they are being watched.

UB40 *abbrev.*
Unemployment Benefit form 40.

UEFA *abbrev.* [1963]
an acronym for Union of European Football Associations: this organization is responsible for the annual UEFA Cup.

Uganda, talking about *phrase.* [1972]
also known as **Ugandan discussions**, popularized by *Private Eye* magazine as a euphemism for sexual intercourse: widely believed to have derived from the alleged discovery, *in flagrante delicto*, of Uganda's then female Minister of Foreign Affairs in an airport lavatory (and thus underwritten by the *Eye*); this theory was latterly repudiated by the writer Corinna Adam who, in a letter to *The Times* in September 1983, claimed that in 1971 a passionate literary critic, caught in a similar situation, was the first to offer this excuse.

uglies *n.*
see **rapture of the deep.**

UHT milk *abbrev.* [1968]
ultra heat treated milk: a form of ➪longlife milk.

Uhuru *n.* [1961]
from the Swahili, meaning freedom. The term came to refer to the national independence struggle of a number of African countries.

ujamaa *n.* [1962]
from the Swahili *jamaa* (family), thus brotherhood: the form of socialism introduced into Tanzania in the 1960s by President Nyrere which was centred on village cooperatives based on equality of opportunity and self-help.

ULCC *abbrev.* [1973]
Ultra-Large Crude Carrier: an ocean-going oil tanker of more than 300,000 metric tons deadweight.

unacceptable damage *n.* [1966]
the concept that the damage one's own nation might suffer in a possible hostile ➪second strike might be too great for the launching of one's own ➪first strike against the enemy.
See also **assured destruction; collateral damage.**

unbundle *v.* [1969]
to the breaking down (often after a takeover) the various assets of a conglomerate into their component parts and return them to individual use: retail stores, factories, ➪R and D, etc. – **unbundling,** *n.*

✱ *'Meanwhile the dogged BAT chairman has set in train the unbundling of the tobacco conglomerate.'* (*Independent on Sunday*, 25 March 1990)

underachiever *n.* [1960]
a pupil who attains lower standards than his/her IQ had indicated should be expected.

Frowned on by teachers and parents, the children are often less perturbed: in 1990 so popular was a T shirt which aped the catchphrase of television's cartoon character 'Bart Simpson' – 'Underachiever and proud of it' – that concerned authorities banned it. – **underactive**, *v.*

* *'Michael finds the school setting difficult and is, therefore, underachieving.'* (*The Independent*, 31 March 1990)
* *'A new Calvinist fad called the underachiever program: young men whose brains seemed much better than their grades were expelled for a year, so that they might improve their characters.'* (T. Kidder, *The Soul of a New Machine*, 1981)

under-age *adj.* [1978]
referring to young people below the legal age of consent.

* *'He would, he said . . . make a report to the CID about possible, unlawful under-age sex.'* (R. Chesshyre, *The Force*, 1989)

underclass *n.* [1986]
the very lowest rung of the social ladder, characterized by poor housing, poor education, social instability, a low level of ambition and aspiration, and a propensity to crime.

* *'Kate Muir and Anna Blundy talked to some of Britain's hidden underclass whose anger boiled over in London's well-heeled West End.'* (*Sunday Correspondent*, 8 April 1990)

underground *n.* [1969]
a synonym for the ⇨counter culture and the ⇨alternative society. The term was often found in such combinations as *underground press* and *underground movie*.

* *'For the underground press is the molder and chronicler of that amorphous body of young freaks you see sticking their tongues out at you in the TV news.'* (A. Hoffman, *Woodstock Nation*, 1969)
* *'That unpopular label, Underground, embraces hippies, beats, madmen, mystics, freaks, yippies, crazies, crackpots, communards.'* (R. Neville, *Play Power*, 1970)

underuse *v.* [1960]
to make insufficient use of.

Unification Church *n.* [1973]
see **Moonie**.

union baron *n.* [1974]
a union leader, whose power and influence (especially during the 1970s, led to comparisons (rarely flattering) with the great medieval barons whose independence of and influence upon the King was seen as paralleled in the unions' relations with the Labour Party.

union-bashing *n.* [1977]
governmental (and right-wing media) attacks on the unions.

Union Corse *n.* [1963]
the Corsican equivalent of Sicily's Mafia.

unipolar *adj.* [1991]
usually found as 'unipolar world' and referring to the re-alignment of the international power balance in the post-Cold War world. Rather than as in the old 'bipolar' world, where there were two superpowers – the US and USSR – the perceived weakening of the USSR has left the US (especially as seen after its Gulf War victory) as the world's sole superpower.

✱ *'The successful prosecution of the war under the leadershiop of President Bush has encouraged the view that with the decline of the Soviet Union we are entering a "unipolar" world.'* (*The Independent*, 1 March 1991)

unisex *adj.* [1968]
pertaining to, or characterized by a style–dress, appearance, facilities – that is equally applicable to either sex. A phenomenon of the ⇨swinging 1960s, with its short-haired girls and long-haired boys, the unisex concept embraced boutiques, hairdressers, and similar fashion outlets.

Unita *abbrev.* [1967]
an acronym for Uniao Nacional para la Independencia Total de Angola; a guerrilla group who were formed to free Angola from its Portuguese rulers. Based on the Ovimbundu tribe, Unita was backed by South Africa and the US in its fight against Angola's postcolonial leftwing rulers.

✱ *'When the FNLA disintegrated, Jonas Savimbi and Unita retreated in good order into the bush to continue the war.'* (P. Brogan, *World Conflicts*, 1989)

Unix *n.* [1971]
a computer operating system introduced by Bell Laboratories for the DEC PDP-11 ⇨minicomputer. Unix was the first operating system to provide a ⇨networking facility, making it possible for a number of users to collaborate on a single system. Originally seen as exclusively orientated towards ⇨minicomputers, Unix (in a variety of versions) is becoming increasingly popular among ⇨microcomputer users, for the flexibility of its operation (despite what remains a more daunting operating system than most users of personal computers find acceptable today) and its ⇨multitasking facilities.

✱ *'Developing the Unix benchmarks was interesting for Ben because he enjoys pulling together ideas and code . . . into an integrated system'.* (*Byte*, **3**, 1990)

unliberated *adj.* [1970]
referring to women who have resisted the feminist ideology of ⇨Women's Liberation.

untogether *adv., adj.* [1969]
inefficient, unstable, emotionally inadequate. *See also* **together.**

✱ *'Something approaching an Underground, flabby and untogether, but going in one direction . . .'* (N. Cohn, *Awopbopaloobopalopbamboom*, 1970)

unwaged *adv., adj.*[1971]
the current euphemism for unemployed. *See also* **waged.**

UPC *abbrev.* [1974]
universal product code: more widely known as the ⇨**bar-code**: a pattern of lines and numbers by which information about a product may be encoded for automatic scanning; such codes can contain price information, stock and inventory numbers, and similar facts.

update *n., v.* [1966]
new information or a new version; to revise on the basis of new information.

upfront *adv.* [1967]
candid, honest, unguarded.

✱ *'She just flashed on it: for once in her life she ought to put her own needs right up front and then get behind them.'* (C. McFadden, *The Serial*, 1976)

* *'For example, honesty or being up front is generally a good policy, but it can also become a nervous habit.'* (R.D. Rosen, *Psychobabble*, 1977)

upfront *adj.* [1972]
usually used of money, meaning in advance, on deposit; often in such combinations as *upfront payment* or *upfront cash*.

up-market *adj.* [1972]
1. *in commerce*: aimed at the more expensive end of the market; the opposite of ⇨down market.
2. in general terms, high quality, or at least aimed at such quality.

* *'For the last four years the up-market Picador imprint's editorial director'.* (Private Eye, 16 March 1990)
* *'Their advertisements now include step-by-step lessons in the island's new up-market sensibility.'* (*The Times*, 6 October 1990)

upper *n.* [1966]
a slang term for amphetamine.
See also **downer; speed.**

* *'A whole galaxy of multi-coloured uppers, downers, screamers, laughers . . . '* (H.S. Thompson, *Fear and Loathing in Las Vegas*, 1971)

up quark *n.* [1976]
a ⇨quark which supposedly possesses an 'upward spin'.
See also **charm; beauty; truth.**

upscale/downscale *v.* [1966]
to make larger/smaller; in advertising, it refers to a higher/lower income, or at least one that is higher/lower than that previously mentioned.

upside *n.* [1961]
originally used in the City to refer to an upward movement of share prices, now more generally as a synonym for 'the future'.

* *'The upside should again be approximate yield parity with the equity market.'* (*The Times*, 18 June 1984)

upstairs-downstairs *adj* [1971]
the social contrast between the employer and the employed, specifically in the great houses of earlier years when a small number of those 'upstairs' were tended by legions of servants 'downstairs'. The term became widespread with the immensely popular eponymous television series of the 1970s.

up there (with) *adv.* [1970]
on a level with, equal to, the equivalent of.

uptick *n.* [1970]
an upswing in business or trading.

uptight *adj.* [1966]
tense, nervous, depressed, suffering a varying degree of emotional instability.

* *'Uptight . . . although trad was nowhere as solid as Elvis or Jerry Lee or Little Richard, it did at least bop along in a jolly manner, and . . . nobody got uptight.'* (M. Farren, *Watch Out Kids*, 1972)
* *'Uptight . . . a word used to describe an individual experiencing anything from mild uneasiness to a clinical depression.'* (R.D. Rosen, *Psychobabble*, 1977)

upward/downward compatibility *n.* [1964]
a pair of terms used in the computer industry to categorize the relations of a given piece of ⇨hardware or ⇨software with its previous and subsequent versions. **Upward**: said of a machine that can do anything that the subsequent model of its type can do. **Downward**: of the latest machine – it can do everything its predecessors did, plus some exciting extras.

* *'Moreover the designers had made the Eclipse upwardly compatible with NOVAs. This meant that . . . old programs written for NOVAs would work on Eclipses.'* (T. Kidder, *The Soul of a New Machine*, 1981)

upwardly mobile *adj.* [1964]
moving upwards through the strata of society; the impression the term carries is that the person so depicted is very keen to make this rise. *See also* **downwardly mobile**.

* *'The upwardly mobile socialite, arriviste about town . . . that sort of thing.'* (T. Blacker, *Fixx*, 1989)

urban guerrilla *n.* [1967]
a member of one of many groups of revolutionaries – usually recruited from the ideologically leftwing middle classes and emerging primarily in the late 1960s – such as Germany's Baader-Meinhof gang or Japan's ⇨Red Army.

* *'Obviously she doesn't dig London's number one urban guerrilla too much.'* (N. Fury, *Agro*, 1971)

urban legends *n.* [1983]
modern folk tales, which have evolved without any specific provenance, and which are widely believed in the same way as traditional folk myths were believed. Such stories, invariably, have been experienced by a relative or close friend. Typical of such legends – equally prevalent on both sides of the Atlantic – is that of the alligators dwelling in the Manhattan sewers, or the baby-sitter who stuffed the baby in the microwave.

* *'Urban legends belong to the subclass of folk narratives, legends that – unlike fairy tales – are believed, or at least believable.'* (J.H. Brunvand, *The Vanishing Hitchhiker*, 1983)

user-friendly *adj.* [1979]
designed with the needs of users in mind: a term coined in 1979 by Harlan Crowder to represent the ease, or lack of ease, the lay user encountered in running a computer system. Its growth parallelled the emergence of the ⇨microcomputer in the early 1980s and it has spread, like a number of other computer terms. *See also* **down; hands-on**) into more general use. Also *user-definable, user-assigned, user interface*, etc.

* *'The program it works from is user-friendly insofar as the commands are based on initials such as CV for "centre vertically" and FD for "forms design".* (*New Scientist*, 30 September 1982)
* *'Advertising is more user-friendly in Britain; you have to woo people. In America you can still jump into bed without saying please.'* (*The Times*, 6 October 1990)

USM *abbrev.* [1979]
unlisted securities market: a market for securities in small companies admitted for trading on the Stock Exchange but not bound to comply with the rules that exist for listed securities.

U-turn *n.* [1961]

a political reversal; the concept gained especial notoriety after Mrs Thatcher's speech on government economic policy at the Tory Conference of 1980 when, faced by media suggestions that she should moderate her economic policy, given its deleterious effect on much of the country, her reply gave no sign of weakness. 'To those waiting with baited breath for that favourite media catchphrase, the U-turn, I have only one thing to say: you turn if you want to. The lady's not for turning.' Her last phrase also puns on Christopher Fry's play of 1948, set in the year 1400. The 'lady' in question, Jennet Jourdemayne, is accused of turning the local rag and bone man into a dog.

* *'The Prime Minister was yesterday accused in the Commons of performing a "humiliating U-turn" in agreeing to Britain's entry into the Exchange Rate Mechanism.'* (*The Independent*, 16 October 1990)

Uzi *n.* [1966]

a type of sub-machinegun, designed and manufactured in Israel and named for an army officer, Uziel Gal. The Uzi has become the automatic weapon of choice for America's rival ➪crack pedlars.

* *'He'd . . . seen pickpockets and parasol salesmen, vagabonds and drunks, druggies and God freaks all melting aside, swimming away from the path of his uniform, of Tad with the Uzi clasped loose at his side.'* (P. Davies, *Dollarville*,1990)

vacuum aspiration *n.* [1967]
a method of abortion, performed before the twelfth week of pregnancy, in which a specially designed tube is inserted into the uterus to draw out the contents by suction.

Valley girl *n.* [1982]
teenage Californian girls, specifically the daughters of the affluent middle classes living in the Los Angeles area; the term was coined *c.*1980 by Moon Unit, daughter of rock star Frank Zappa; the Valley girls were much feted for their supposed 'new' vocabulary **Valley-speak**, but the bulk of their terminology: 'grody', 'to the max', etc., was far from new, but a recycled mix of surfer, drug, and general US teen slang.

vanilla *adj.* [1984]
standard, run of the mill.
See also **bog standard**; **boilerplate**.

- *'How it fits into the spectrum that starts at vanilla DOS and ends with 32-bit OS/2.'* (*Byte*, July 1990)

vanity plate *n.* [1967]
a car licence plate that bears the owner's initials or some other reference to their identity or profession.

vapourware *n.* [1987]
see **-ware**.

VAT abbrev. [1966]
an acronym for Value Added Tax: a tax levied on the value added to an article or the raw material that forms it at each stage during its production or distribution; thus **VATman**: a collector of VAT; **VAT-able**: liable to VAT.

- *'A sealed envelope costs £10 including VAT with Lloyds and the TSB.'* (*Independent on Sunday* 10 June 1990)

Vatican roulette *n.* [1962]
a colloquial term for the rhythm method of contraception, proscribed for religious Roman Catholics by the Pope.

- *'As his thesis awaits its birth in the British Museum, his wife studies the thermometer at home. But it seems that "Vatican Roulette" has failed them again and a fourth little faithful is on the way.'* (blurb for D. Lodge, *The British Museum Is Falling Down*, 1965)

VC *abbrev.* [1966]
Viet Cong: the North Vietnamese guerrilla movement, direct successors to the Viet Minh, who fought during the 1960s and 1970s during the war against the South and its ally America. Another popular slang term, the military code for VC was 'Victor Charlie'.

- *'The Mission was always telling us about VC units being engaged and wiped out, and then reappearing a month later in full strength.'* (M. Herr, *Dispatches*, 1977)
- *'Charlie don't relax, just when you get good and comfortable is when he comes over and*

takes a giant shit on you.' (M. Herr, *Dispatches*, 1977)

VCR *abbrev.* [1971]

Video Cassette Recorder.

* *'The UK public caught onto the idea of renting VCRs and televisions together rather than buying, and VHS happened to be preferred by the leading shops.'* (*Sunday Correspondent*, 13 May 1990)

VDQS *abbrev.* [1962]

Vin Delimité De Qualité Superieure: a classification of wine that falls beneath the standards that would qualify it as Appellation Controllé, but is superior to simple vin ordinaire.

* *'The cadet branch, as it were . . . is known as VDQS. VDQS wines are often seen in France, but so far the initials have made little impact abroad.'* (H. Johnson, *Wine*, 1974)

VDU *abbrev.* [1968]

video display unit: the screen on which a computer user can see ⇨word processing, ⇨spread sheets, calculations, graphics, and other visual displays of the ⇨program that is being run.

* *'The visual display unit or VDU is the classic example. It actually comprises two separate devices.'* (D. Jarrett, *The Good Computing Book for Beginners* 1980)

Velcro *n.* [1960]

from the French *velours croche*, meaning hooked velvet: a proprietary name for a fabric fastener made into two complementary strips: one has a series of tiny hooks, the other equally tiny loops; when pressed together the two strips lock until they are pulled apart again.

velvet revolution *n.* [1989]

the bloodless overthrow of Communism in Czechoslovakia that took place in late 1989.

* *'Last year's velvet revolution may have made him a household name (and potent box-office draw).'* (*The Independent*, 8 June 1990)

venture capital/capitalism *n.* [1971]

1. the investment of long-term capital in ventures that are particularly prone to risk; such ventures are usually involve new ideas, relatively untried individuals and their business ideas, etc. Those who make such investments are **venture capitalists**.

2. spec the provision by persons other than the proprietors of the financial backing for a new undertaking.

* *'In the late 1960s, the period memorialized in John Brooks's The Go-Go Years, venture capital (among other things) abounded.'* (T. Kidder, *The Soul of a New Machine*, 1981)

verification *n.* [1972]

the checking by one partner in a treaty that the other partner is keeping to the terms of that treaty. As far as nuclear arms control is considered, verification is carried out by the spy satellites of each superpower. Verification is vital to the continued success of deterrence: a statement by the Arms Control and Disarmament Agency in 1980 noted 'the deterrent value of verification depends to a considerable extent upon the potential violator being ignorant of the exact capability of the intelligence techniques used to monitor his compliance with an agreement', but did add that 'verification contributes to mutual trust among the parties.' – **verify**, *v.*

* *'The main reason had to do with verification: one side could, with relative ease and certainty,*

keep track of the other side's launchers.' (S. Talbott, *Deadly Gambits*, 1984)

vertical *adj.* [1975]
involving or pertaining to different levels of a hierarchy; the opposite of ➪**horizontal**, which deals with the same levels. Often found in such combinations as *vertical divestiture* (the abandoning of assets on a number of levels of the hierarchy of the same organization), *vertical integration* (the linking of the various levels of the same organization), etc.

vertical proliferation *n.* [1966]
the upward spread of the numbers of nuclear weapons held by those nations who already have some degree of nuclear arsenal.

VHS *abbrev.* [1982]
Video Home System: one of the two rival formats for use on ➪VCRs and the one preferred by the majority of British users.
See also **betamax**.

vibes [1968]
1. *an abbreviation for* vibrations: one's instinctive feelings and senses, usually combined (as originated in the 1960s) as *good vibes* or *bad vibes*.

✱ *'After less that three months on air, bad vibes have broken out at Manchester's funky spunky Sunset Radio.'* (*Private Eye*, 16 March 1990)

2. *v.* to experience vibes, or as **vibe out**: to treat in hostile manner (often by exerting wordless emotional pressure).

✱ *'He's sitting there vibing away in his black T-shirt and shades.'* (L. Bangs, *Psychotic Reactions and Carburetor Dung*, 1988)

vibrations *n.* [1968]
see **vibes**.

✱ *'A lot of meditating with your legs crossed, chanting, eating rice, feeling vibrations, walking softly over the forest floor and thinking big.'* (T. Wolfe, *The Electric Kool-Aid Acid Test*, 1969)

Victor Charlie *n.* [1966]
see VC.

Victorian values n. [1965]
the fantasy, much beloved of Mrs Thatcher and her government, of a golden age of conservative moral absolutes and laisser-faire capitalism, supposedly coincident with the later years of the reign of Queen Victoria.

✱ *'Victorian values, after all, are as much a myth as the most zany hippie fantasy.'* (J. Green, *Days in the Life*, 1988)

video *n.* [1980]
an abbreviation for rock or pop video: a promotional film designed to accompany and promote the release of a given record. These videos, once rare, developed through the 1980s as a vital adjunct to any record industry promotion.

videocassette *n.* [1970]
a cassette or videotape, whether in ➪VHS or ➪betamax format, that is used in a ➪VCR.

videofit *n.*
the video version of the older ➪identikit: a number of discrete videotaped images are combined together, on the instructions of one or more eyewitnesses to a crime, to create a likeness of a criminal suspect.

video game *n.* [1976]
an electronic game played either in an arcade or on a television or computer screen.

* *'Video games zap the minds of a generation.'* (headline in *the Sunday Correspondent*, 25 March 1990)

video nasty *n.* [1983]
a horror film, usually with overtones of sadistic sex, available on a video. Video nasties – epitomized in the much-berated *Nightmares in a Damaged Brain* – took on for the 1980s the same role as had US horror comics in the 1950s, exciting the right-wing and censorious far more effectively than they did their alleged 'victims', the young and impressionable.

* *'A horror highlight from a video nasty? No. A scene from an Elizabethan drama written 400 years ago: Shakespeare's Titus Andronicus.'* (M. Barker, *The Video Nasties*, 1984)

video piracy *n.* [1980]
the illegal copying of pre-recorded videotapes (usually of first-run movies) and the distribution, for money, of the resulting copies.

video porn *n.* [1979]
a pornographic film released on videotape, either for sale or rental.

video-record *v.* [1960]
to record on videotape.

video-recorder *n.* [1960]
see VCR.

video rental *n.*
a film that has been copied onto videotape and is available for rental from ⇨video stores.

* *'The video rental release starts about the time you read this.'* (*Ace*, August 1990)

video store/shop *n.*
a shop that sells and rents out pre-recorded videotapes, usually of films.

* *'Along the perimeter fence of the base is a seedy array of brothels, tattoo shops, video stores and cheap car yards.'* (*The Independent*, 16 October 1990)

videotext *n.* [1980]
any information system in which a television is used to display data to a viewer.

Vietnik *n.* [1965]
a pejorative term to describe an opponent of the US involvement in Vietnam; the suffix ⇨-nik has overtones both of an antisocial group, the beatniks, and in its 'Russian' style, of America's enemy.

Viewdata *n.* [1975]
an interactive information and retrieval system: the viewer's television set displays a variety of data taken from a computer ⇨database, while the viewer is able to maintain communication via a telephone link.
See also **Ceefax; Oracle.**

viff *v.* [1972]
to vector in flight: to change direction abruptly as a result of a change in the direction of the engine thrust.

-ville *suffix.* [1962]
a synonym for -city: its use as a suffix turns descriptive abstract adjectives into concrete 'places'.

* *"What's Dimension X Like?" "It's grimsville,*

man".' (*Teenage Mutant Hero Turtles,* June 1990)

✱ *'An' we thought this place was dullsville! But this is a blast!'* (*Teenage Mutant Hero Turtles,* June 1990)

virtual memory *n.* [1966]
a system designed to overcome the limitations of a machine's actual ⇨hardware by temporarily redefining the memory to accept ⇨programs that, usually, would require computers of infinitely greater power; the distinction between the internal memory and the disk drive is set aside, the computer then 'reads' the large program as a number of small, and thus accessible, segments; it runs the program by taking on such segments as it can handle and then, after use, replaces them with the next one required. The concept, if not the term, was originated in 1960 by Honeywell and IBM.

✱ *'No doubt this is a side effect of using the disk as a virtual memory.'* (*Which Computer?* April 1985)

virtual reality *n.* [1989]
the creation, through high-speed computer graphics and a variety of ⇨dedicated ⇨programmes, of a hypothetical 'world' generally known as 'cyberspace'. While this world does not actually exist, it is possible to interact with it, whether using special goggles, fibre-optic gloves or other purpose-built devices. While VR, as it is known, is still at its most primitive stage and its most immediate uses may lie within computer games, it has limitless potential – an imaginary world is limited only by the imagination (and the power of the computers involved).

virus *n.* [1985]
unlike a 'bug', or simple error, the electronic virus is a program deliberately inserted into a computer system to create maximum damage; dependent on their character, viruses include such as the ⇨Trojan horse and the ⇨logic bomb. Continuing the medical metaphor, a program designed to counteract the virus is known as a 'vaccine'.

✱ *'While that doesn't guarantee that you won't get a virus attack . . . it means that you can at least decide to be responsible for your own safety.'* (*Byte,* June 1990)

visible *adj.* [1977]
1. referring to any public figure who occupies th' limelight.
2. as in such combinations as *visible negro* and *visible woman: a synonym for* ⇨statutory or ⇨token.

visiting rights *n.* [1971]
the right of one parent of a divorced or separated couple to visit their mutual child when that child is living with the other estranged parent. The term stems from its older use in the context of a prison or similar institution.

visitor centre *n.* [1964]
a (usually) purpose-built building constructed at a tourist site in which the visitor may gain an introduction (possibly through slides, films, and leaflets) to the site in question, and (very often) purchase a variety of souvenirs.

✱ *'Another quibble is that the new visitor centre (though it will be completely invisible from the floor of the valley) will generate too much noise.'* (*Architectural Review,* February 1988)

VLCC *abbrev.* [1968]
very large crude (oil) carrier: an ocean going oil tanker of 200,000 to 300,000 metric tons deadweight.
See also **ULCC**.

✱ *'The 236,000 ton Japanese VLCC Showa Maru grounded in the Malacca Straits near Singapore harbour five months later.'* (N. Mostert, *Supership*, 1974)

VLSI *abbrev.* [1978]
very large scale integrated circuits: this advance in micro-electronics engineering, which places more electronic circuits than ever before – in excess of 1000 – on a single silicon ➪chip, is currently central to commercial electronics developments.
See also **transputer**.

✱ *'Very Large Scale Integration (VLSI) is what we've seen so far and what we'll see more of: the cramming of ever more electronic circuitry into ever smaller spaces.'* (D. Ford, *The Button*, 1985)

voice print *n.* [1962]
the aural equivalent of fingerprints, the identification of an individual based on a tape of their voice, using the ten words most commonly used in telephone conversations.

voucher system *n.* [1980]
a system proposed for British education whereby an individual is issued with some form of document which entitles them to receive schooling or university education for their child.

✱ *'The row over education vouchers is not encouraging. It suggests that Mrs Thatcher is still locked in the ideological battles of the 1970s, rather than committed to the simple goal of improving education.'* (*Sunday Correspondent*, 21 October 1990)

vox pop *n.* [1964]
from Latin *vox populi* (the voice of the people): interviews conducted with men and women in the street in order to elicit their views on whatever topic the broadcaster may care to throw at them.

✱ *'Vox pop joins battle for Paternoster Square'.* (headline in the *Sunday Correspondent*, 25 March 1990)

VSO *abbrev.* [1960]
Voluntary Service Overseas: an organization promoting voluntary service by young people in developing countries.

✱ *'The researcher understood how the police felt; he had been to Ghana on VSO and had looked on those six months as the most important and exciting of his life.'* (R. Chesshyre, *The Force*, 1989)

V/STOL (aircraft) *n.* (1961)
see **STP**.

Vuitton (luggage) *n.* [1975]
proprietary name for the luxury luggage produced by the French firm of Louis Vuitton.

Wabenzi *n.* [1967]
literally, the 'Mercedes Benz tribe' (on the pattern of the central African tribe Watusi, etc.): Africa's black politicians, businessmen and other successful figures whose badge of office is the ownership of a Mercedes Benz.

wack *n.* [1963]
pal or mate: a familiar term of address in Liverpool and as such popularized by the Beatles and the Liverpudlian cult that accompanied their rise to stardom.

wack *adj.* [1988]
in ➪*hip-hop use*: useless, second-rate.

✱ *'What do you call a crew that can rap like that?/Yo! NWA call the motherfuckers wack.'* (N.W.A., *Compton's In The House*, 1988)

wacko *n., adj.* [1977]
crazy, mad, eccentric.

wad *n.* [1987]
see **wedge**.

waged *adv., adj.* [1971]
the current euphemism for 'employed'. *See also* **unwaged**.

wah-wah pedal *n.* [1969]
a pedal that is attached to an electric guitar so as to modify the output from the amplifier. The noise so produced is roughly rendered as 'wah-wah'.

waitnik *n.* [1989]
on the pattern of ➪refusenik, a Russian Jew who is awaiting final permission to leave the Soviet Union.
See also **-nik**.

waitress service *n.* [1960]
service by waitresses in a restaurant; the opposite of self-service.

walk *v.* [1960]
in cricket: for a batsman against whom the fielding side have appealed to leave the field of his own volition before the umpire has actually given him out.

walkabout *n.* [1970]
used to describe the way in which members of the Royal Family, forsaking the protection of their bodyguards, walk through a crowd, shaking hands and greeting their well-wishers. The term can be applied to heads of state, movie stars, and similar figures.

walker *n.* [1980]
a man who accompanies a single or widowed woman on shopping trips, and to restaurants, concerts, and similar outings; their relationship is platonic, and his role is that of escort and confidant rather than that of a lover.

✱ *'The Fairchild influence extends to another area of international fashion – the inner circle: the customer, her husband, her walker, and sometimes, her lover.'* (*The Observer*, 10 February 1991)

Walkman *n.* [1981]
a small portable tape recorder, plus its integral headphones, which was created by the Sony Corporation in 1981 and is used worldwide by walkers, joggers, cyclists, and travellers of all sorts (as well as those who prefer to stay in one place) to listen to pre-recorded tapes.

* *'I was unconsoled even by the Walkman which could not entirely drown the shrieks and gurgles of animals we'd certainly not been introduced to.'* (*Independent on Sunday,* 25 March 1990)

wall-to-wall *adj.* [1977]
complete, all-encompassing; from the idea of a wall-to-wall carpet.

wally *n.* [1969]
suitably late for its coinage (the 1960s), wally became an all-purpose putdown of the unfashionable and ineffectual in the early 1980s. Its etymology remains debatable, and it has been usurped by ⇨plonker.

* *'They learn . . . about how anyone can do anything, about the wallies who run television, about the spuriousness of the notion of originality.'* (J. Meades, *Peter Knows What Dick Likes,* 1989)

Wankel engine *n.* [1961]
a form of rotary internal combustion engine designed by and named for the German engineer Felix Wankel; an approximately triangular, eccentrically pivoted shaft rotates continuously in a chamber with its corners touching the walls; this forms three combustion spaces that vary in volume as the shaft rotates.

wannabee *n., adj.* [1985]
a mimic, especially of a pop star; pop has always thrown up its hordes of acolytes, lookalike pubescents aping their gods. The singer Madonna's ascent gave them a name: 'I wanna be . . . like Madonna'.

* *'Christopher Reeve can play Clark Kent, mild-mannered nerd wannabee in real life as well as on film.'* (*Sky* magazine, December 1989)

-ware *suffix.*
in computing: an all-purpose suffix; orthodox versions are ⇨**hardware** (the machine), ⇨**software** (its ⇨program), both of which have gravitated into mainstream speech; less well known are **wetware** (the human brain), **bogusware** (electronic viruses); **vapourware** (computer products that are announced and much-hyped, but never seem to materialize); **firmware** (neither hard-nor software); and **liveware** (the personnel involved in computer work [1966] although liveware has also been defined [*PC World,* July 1990] as a 'benign ⇨virus').

* *'Smalltalk/V PM. It helps stop the natural drift toward vaporware so common in software development today.'* (in *Byte,* ad for Smalltalk/V 4, 1990)

war-fighting *adj.* [1965]
usually as 'nuclear war-fighting capability': the actual launching of an attack and fighting of the subsequent war, rather than merely rattling (nuclear) sabres.

* *'It is a dubious proposition to allow such powerful war-fighting machines to remain at sea without greater positive control over what they can do.'* (D. Ford, *The Button,* [1985]

wargame *v., n.* [1970]
to experiment with a variety of putative bat-

tles, attacks, nuclear strikes, etc., with the intention of developing a strategy that might have to be tested in a real war. War games had existed for some time, but the use of the noun as a verb is a more recent coinage.

* *'The merits of this policy are supposedly demonstrated in war games, exercises that simulate the possible circumstances that could lead to nuclear war.'* (D. Ford, *The Button*, 1985)

washer-drier *n.* [1968]
early washer-driers were machines that first washed clothes and then rinsed and part-dried them; modern versions incorporate a tumble-drier which dries the washed clothes completely.

WASP *abbrev.* [1962]
an acronym for White Anglo-Saxon Protestant: shorthand for the American Protestant upper class, descendants of the first 17th century colonists of New England.

* *'Ask questions, be polite, be a good WASP, always slightly distant from the fray. Above it.'* (C. Blake, *Girl Talk*, 1990)

wasted *adj.* [1970]
intoxicated, possibly to the point of collapse, through drink or drugs.
See also **ripped**; **twisted**.

* *'Enough of your drinking, Stop. You can't handle it. I don't want you to get wasted.'* (L. Bangs, *Psychotic Reactions and Carburetor Dung*, 1988)

waste disposal unit *n.* [1967]
an electrically operated mechanical device for reducing kitchen into fragments small enough to be flushed into the drainage system.

-watcher *suffix.* [1966]
an all-purpose suffix that is used of any professional analyst who specializes in a given speciality, e.g. China, Russia, the Middle East, etc. The word 'watcher' is also found in the novels of John le Carré as a jargon term meaning surveillance experts.

* *'Detroit-watchers say Mr Stempel's unspoken challenge is not to break even . . . but to keep losses down.'* (*Sunday Correspondent*, 8 April 1990)

waterbed *n.* [1969]
a type of bed, very popular in the late 1960s/early 1970s (and still surviving in massage parlours and similar environs), which was a large heavy-duty plastic sack which could be filled with water, set in a wooden frame and then, suitably draped in bedding, slept on.

* *'He had run a hose from the bathtub and filled the Innerspace waterbed that signaled his emergence as a liberated man.'* (C. McFadden, *The Serial*, 1976)

Watergate *n.* [1972]
shorthand for the Watergate Affair, the scandal that brought down President Richard M. Nixon in August 1974 when it was revealed that he had been instrumental in covering up the illegal activities of members of the Committee to Re-Elect the President (CREEP), a semi-clandestine group created to boost the Republican election campaign of 1972.

* *'The word Watergate has come to stand for the whole gamut of crime, scandal, and rumour that adds up to the most serious domestic political crisis in America since the Civil War.'* (C. McCrystal, L. Chester, *et al.*, *Watergate: The Full Inside Story*, 1973)

water-pik *n.* [1963]
a device for cleaning the teeth by directing a jet of water at them.

way out *adj.* [1966]
bizarre, eccentric.
See also **far out**.
* *'Kings Road clothes get way-out as you get way up.'* (J. Aitken, *The Young Meteors*, 1967)

wealth creation/creators *n.* [1985]
the practice of making money, and those that carry it out. The theory of those that believe in the practice is that one must encourage the wealth creator because the success that he or she generates will eventually trickle down to those who are less adept; in the event such pieties remain no more than theory – wealth creators certainly create wealth, but only for themselves.
* *'He was bored with his boat construction business . . . wealth creation, he had heard, was back in fashion.'* (T. Blacker, *Fixx*, 1989)

weaponize *v.* [1969]
to equip with military weapons.

weapons-delivery (system) *n.* [1963]
military jargon for an aircraft capable of bombing or firing missiles.

weapons grade (uranium) *n.* [1961]
that grade of uranium-235 that is suitable for processing into the raw material of nuclear bombs.

Weatherman *n.* [1970]
also known as the **Weatherpeople** and the **Weather Underground**: a group of American ⇨urban guerrillas who flourished in the late 1960s. Like many of their European peers Weatherman was drawn from the educated children of the successful middle classes, whose ideology demanded that they use violence in the promotion of a mass revolution. The name was taken from Bob Dylan's line 'You don't need a weatherman to tell which way the wind blows'.
* *'Weatherman has led extremely militant street demonstrations and taken credit for bombings against major capitalist institutions.'* (H. Jacobs (ed.), *Weatherman*, 1970)

wedge *n.* [1979]
once lumps of silver melted down by 18th century coiners, wedge has arrived, via television's *Minder*, at meaning simply money, though usually a good deal of it. Britain's equivalent to the US 'roll'.

weenybopper *n.* [1972]
a younger (pre-teen) version of the ⇨teenybopper.

weight *n.* [1971]
in drug use: one pound weight.
* *'Avoid carrying weight late at night.'* (*Frendz* magazine, 21 May 1971)

Weight Watcher(s) *n.* [1961]
the proprietary name of Weight Watchers International Incorporated, a group of slimming clubs, who offer special diets to their paying membership.

welfare benefits *n.* [1977]
any form of benefit provided by the state for those in need.

welfare capitalism *n.* [1960]
a capitalist system that combines the traditional desire to make profits with an active concern for the welfare of those who work to provide those profits.

welfare hotel *n.* [1971]
in the US: a hotel where people living on welfare are housed temporarily until more permanent quarters can be found for them.

well *adj.* [1979]
well is an all-purpose intensifier, best translated as 'very'. It dates back to the 19th century, but its current use came, with a number of other slang terms, with the popularity of the television series *Minder* in the late 1970s. Usually found in combination such as *well hard, well sus;* etc.

* *'As we drove off, Tony said with sarcastic satisfaction, "He's well hard; I wonder if he's got any more carol-singing to do".'* (R. Chesshyre, *The Force,* 1989)

well-behaved *adj.* [1984]
in computing: referring to computer ⇨programs which will work on the operating systems of a variety of machines. Thus the opposite, ill-behaved.

* *'Applications that use the DOS and BIOS routines are termed well-behaved and others that write directly to the video area are ill-behaved. Typically graphical applications are ill-behaved, text applications may be either.'* (*DESQview booklet,* November 1990)

wellie, give (it) some *phrase.* [1977]
to hit hard, to accelerate (of a car), to put in more effort and energy; the image in all uses is of giving something a kick with a wellington-booted foot.

West Bank *n. adj.* [1967]
that area on the West Bank of the river Jordan which, since the Six Days' War of 1967, has been occupied by Israel and which, to Israeli rightwingers, is known by the Biblical names of Judea and Samaria. Also used as an adjective, e.g. West Bank Arabs.

* *'I was in Israel visiting my brother. Henry Zuckerman. Hanoch. He's at an ulpan on the West Bank.'* (P. Roth, *The Counterlife,* 1986)

wet *n., adj.* [1980]
used by the former Prime Minister Margaret Thatcher to mean feeble, liable to take the easy option, devoid of mental and political toughness, specifically in refusing to take harsh economic measures; a traditional public-school putdown, hijacked by a meritocratic prime minister.

* *'He was the nephew of Jim Prior, discredited wet and early Thatcher sackee'.* (*The Independent,* 31 March 1990)

wet look *n., adj.* [1970]
a shiny synthetic material, used for clothing, which made garments look as if they were shiny with rain.

* *'Really neat lightweight trousers and a waisted wet-look leather jacket.'* (N. Fury, *Agro,* 1971)

wetware *n.* [1975]
any organic intelligence involved with a computer, notably the human brain, which is neither hardware not software.
See also **-ware**.

whacked out *adj.* [1969]
exhausted, tired out; the transitive verb to whack out also exists, meaning to kill, to murder.

whack out *v.* [1969]
to kill, to murder.

wham, bam, thank-you ma'am *phrase.* [1971]
anything quick and forceful; often used of quick emotionless sexual intercourse.

* *'The MC5 might have put you flat on your back with nipple stiffeners and wham bam thank you ma'am jams.'* (L. Bangs, *Psychotic Reactions and Carburetor Dung*, 1988)

what-for, show (him/her) *v.* [1960]
to impress upon, to point out.

what-if *adj.* [1973]
hypothetical, involving speculation as to what might have happened.

wheeler-dealer *n.* [1960]
a shrewd bargainer, an entrepreneur (usually carrying negative overtones as to dishonesty and sharp practice). – **wheel and deal** *v.* (1961).

* *'The teenage pharamaceutical tycoons . . . who wheel and deal and graft and burn anyone they can.'* (N. Fury, *Agro*, 1971)

wheelie *n.* [1966]
a motorcycle stunt in which the rider revs up his bike, while keeping the brake on, until, when he finally takes the brake off, the front wheel rises into the air and the machine moves off on its back wheel only.

* *'Tramp, Sergeant-at-Arms, doing a wheelie on his chopper.'* (J. Mandelkau, *Buttons*, 1971)
* *'Her favourite is "r", which she rolls with the exhibitionist relish of a Hell's Angel revving up for a super-wheelie down the main drag.'* (*The Independent*, 18 April 1990)

wheel in/on/out *v.* [1970]
to bring in, to take out, etc.

whip-pan *n.* [1960]
a very fast side-to-side (panning) movement of a film or television camera which causes a blurred picture.

whiskey mac *n.* [1960]
a drink made of whiskey and ginger wine.

whistleblower *n.* [1970]
a government employee who is unable to bear the evidence of duplicity, incompetence, corruption or mismanagement that he or she sees and therefore decides to inform the press and thus the public of what he or she has hitherto managed to accept.

white backlash/whitelash *n.* [1964]
the counter-reaction by white racists to black civil rights militancy.

Whitehall warrior *n.* [1973]
a member of the services who has been seconded to the civil service (Whitehall) rather than performing his or her military duties.

white knight *n.* [1970]
in City use: when one firm is attempting to launch a hostile takeover of a second, a third firm, more acceptable to the one under threat of takeover, who is encouraged by that firm to challenge the original raider:

* *'A white knight, a third firm that was willing to pay an even higher price for the stock and thus rescue ESB.'* (D. Halberstam, *The Reckoning*, 1986)

white knuckle (ride) *n.* [1988]
a particularly terrifying ride at a ⇨theme park; riders will presumably grip with their fists until their knuckles whiten under the strain.

whiteout *n.* [1975]
zero visibility caused by fog or heavy snow.

white out *v.* [1975]
to cover up or obscure typewritten errors with some form of proprietary white liquid, typically Tippex.

white room *n.* [1961]
in aerospace and computing: a special room, often called a 'clean room', kept surgically clean and purged of all dust and foreign bodies used for the assembly of those delicate mechanisms that are used in spaceflight, computer construction etc.

* *'The functionality of microchips is appreciated by many people, but they may not be aware that the actual production is a complex, clean-room chemical/physical process.'* (*PC World*, October 1990)

whites *n.* [1970]
a slang term for amphetamines.
See also **blues; reds.**

* *'Tim was back to his old regimen of reds and whites.'* (L. Bangs, *Psychotic Reactions and Carburetor Dung*, 1988)

whizkid *n.* [1960]
a synonym for ⇨high flier: a bright young man seen as a future leader of his firm, government department, academic faculty, etc. The term comes from the original Whiz Kids, a team of exceptionally talented young men recruited by the automobile manufacturer General Motors, such as the later US Secretary of Defence Robert McNamara.

* *'The Whiz Kids were the forerunner of the new class in American business. Their knowledge was not concrete, about a product, but about systems – systems that could, if used properly, govern any company.'* (D. Halberstam, *The Reckoning*, 1987)

whole *adj.* [1975]
the complete self, as understood when one 'gets in touch with oneself'.

* *'Talk about the whole person and feeling whole may actually repressed or uncultivated.'* (R.D. Rosen, *Psychobabble*, 1977)

whole earther *n.* [1975]
an environmentalist and conservationist, concerned about the state of all of the earth's living things.

wholefood *n., adj.* [1960]
a synonym for health food: unrefined food that has not been adulterated with any form of artificial additive.

wicked *adj.* [1985]
an all-purpose term of approval used by US and then UK teenagers. The term has arrived via two borrowings: the first from standard English by black Americans, and subsequently by the white young from their black counterparts.
See also **rad; safe.**

wide-bodied jet *n.* [1970]
any civilian airliner that has a wide fuselage, specifically the Boeing 747 ⇨jumbo jet.

wild card *n., adj.* [1976]
1. *in sport*: a player or team drawn for inclusion in a competition after the regular places have all been allotted.
2. *in computing*: the wild card refers to the signs ? and * which, in data searches, refer respectively to any single letter or number, or any combination of letters and/or numbers.

✱ *'The wildcard characters are the asterisk (*) and the question mark (?). They are useful in MS-DOS command lines.'* (*Microsoft MS-DOS User's Guide*, 1987)

wild child *n.* [1985]
a fashionable if wayward teenager (usually an attractive girl), the supposed excitements of whose life (invariably drugs and sex) are charted in prurient detail by the tabloid press.

✱ *'Presenters are Terry Christian, a radio DJ from the inevitable Manchester, and the former Chelsea wild child Amanda de Cadanet.'* (*Sunday Corresponmdent*, 19 August 1990)

wildlife park *n.* [1965]
see **safari park**.

wimmin *n.* [1983]
the ideologically correct spelling of the word women by those feminists who feel that the full range of phallocentric ⇨sexism can only be eliminated if the language, as well as individual attitudes, is thoroughly purged and recreated.
See also **herstory**.

✱ *Wimmin might be universally applauded as a clever piece of spelling reform, had it not become associated with the unpopular extremism of the women's movement.'* (J. Mills, *Womanwords*, 1989)

WIMP *abbrev.* [1981]
in computing: *an acronym for* Windows, ⇨Icons, ⇨Mouse, and Pointers: the earlier name for today's ⇨GUIs, any form of visual ⇨interface, operating by pointing at visual icons with the mouse, which is supposed to make it easier for the user to operate the computer system.

✱ *'The system puts up a small window (which you can move just as you would any other WIMP window).'* (*Ace*, August 1990)

wimp *n.* [1967]
a coward, from Wellington Wimpy, the coward in *Popeye* strips.

✱ *'Alright you chickenshit wimps! You pansies! When this goddam, light flips green I'm gonna . . . blow every one of you gutless punks off the road.'* (H.S. Thompson, *Fear and Loathing in Las Vegas*, 1971)

wimp out *v.* [1987]
to act in a cowardly manner, to back down; from ⇨wimp.

win *n.* [1976]
success, victory. *See also* **spend**.

✱ *'The win was the object of all this sport, and the big win was something that could be achieved by maximizing the smaller one.'* (T. Kidder, *The Soul of a New Machine*, 1981)

Winchester *n.* [1973]
in computing: the ⇨hard disk memory, capable of holding millions of ⇨bytes (megabytes) of information and offering concurrently faster retrieval times than floppies (⇨floppy disk);

from the IBM 3030 computer, nicknamed for the Winchester 3030 gauge rifle, which it resembled in speed and accuracy.

* *'There are five main reasons for a small-system builder to look at Winchesters – access speed, reliability, cheapness, compact size, and quiet operation.'* (D. Jarrett, *The Good Computing Book for Beginners*, 1980)

wind down *v.* [1969]
to terminate, to diminish, to finish off.

Windies *n.* [1965]
an abbreviation for the West Indies: specifically the national cricket team.

wind of change *n.* [1960]
used figuratively to describe the growing determination of Africa's former colonies to attain independence from their erstwhile masters; the phrase, a somewhat flowery image for change, originated around 1905, but it took on this specific meaning after a speech on the topic delivered by then Prime Minister Harold Macmillan to the South African Parliament on 3 Febrary 1960: 'The most striking of all impressions I have formed since I left London a month ago is of the strength of this African national consciousness. In different places it may take different forms but it is happening everywhere. The wind of change is blowing through this continent. Whether we like it or not, this growth of political consciousness is a political fact.'

window *n.* [1974]
a rectangular area on a ⇨VDU inside which part of an image or file can be displayed. A screen can incorporate a number of windows revealing a number of files or images simultaneously. Windows can expand or contract and 'move' about the screen. Data can be moved from one window to another. Among the best-selling ⇨GUI systems is Microsoft's 'Windows 3.0'.

* *'Most programs you run in DESQview display only a single window on the screen. However programs written expressly for DESQview may display multiple windows.'* (*DESQview manual*, 1987)

window of opportunity *n.* [1980]
any situation, often temporary and spontaneously created, which can be used for one's own benefit. One side's window of opportunity often coincides with another's ⇨window of vulnerability.

window of vulnerability *n.* [1980]
a situation in which one is vulnerable to attack. The term was coined by Edward Rowney, the Joint Chiefs of Staff representative at the ⇨SALT II talks in 1980, who felt that the agreement reached between Carter and Brezhnev which set constraints on armaments left the Russians with an approximate 5:2 advantage in nuclear missiles. To the general, this meant an unacceptable strategic imbalance and potential vulnerability for the US through which 'window' the Soviets could and would take devastating advantage. This 'window', a descendant of various 'gaps' (bomber, missile, etc.) has been used to justify much US weapons development.

* *'The military buildup is declared as necessary . . . to close the window of vulnerability.'* (R.C. Aldridge, *First Strike!* 1983)

windsurfer *n.* [1969]
1. *a synonym for* sailboard: a surfboard on which is mounted a triangular sail. 2. the indi-

vidual who rides one, standing on the board and blown along the water by the wind filling the sail. – **windsurf**, *v.*

* *'When I'm windsurfing I always wear shorts and a singlet as protection.'* (*Independent on Sunday*, 10 June 1990)

wind up *v. n.* [1978]
to tease, to aggravate deliberately; also used as a noun.

* *'They have a propensity to wind people up, which can easily be misunderstood.'* (R. Chesshyre, *The Force*, 1989)

wine and cheese party *n.* [1961]
a party at which wine and cheese is served, very popular in the early 1960s.

wine-buff *n.* [1976]
an expert in wine; the original use of buff to mean enthusiast (dating from 1900) came from the volunteer firemen of New York's Fire Service, who wore buff uniforms.

wine bar *n.* [1971]
popularized in the early 1970s, the wine bar – which sold various wines but no beers or spirits – provided the first real rival to Britain's traditional public house, especially as regarded the ⇨upwardly mobile young.

* *'There is a bookshop with a very few hardbacks, there is a wine-bar (more misspellings, I'm afraid), there is an old-fashioned game dealer.'* (J. Meades, *Peter Knows What Dick Likes*, 1989)

wine lake *n.* [1974]
on the pattern of the butter ⇨mountain, the surplus of wine that has been produced by EC farmers, whose production is subsidized, whether or not their products are actually required.

wine writer *n.* [1975]
a journalist who specializes in writing about wine.

winklepicker(s) *n.* [1960]
a shoe with a long pointed toe, often worn by Teddy Boys.

Winnebago *n.* [1966]
a specially designed van or truck with customized living space built into the back; named for the Winnebago tribe of American Indians, whose name originally meant 'person of dirty water', a reference to the muddy Fox River near Lake Winnebago, which became clogged with dead fish during the hot summers.

winner-takes-all *adj.* [1969]
referring to a competition in which only the winner gains a reward.

winter of discontent *n.* [1979]
the winter of 1978–79 when Britain was beset by a wave of strikes – affecting both private and public sectors – and which led first to a vote of no confidence in James Callaghan's Labour government, and in the General Election which followed in May, to the election of the Conservatives under Margaret Thatcher. In the broader view, the Winter brought to an end the post-war system of consensus politics in Britain, and replaced it with the very different form of government apostrophized as ⇨Thatcherism. The term itself was coined by the political columnist Peter Jenkins (who

claimed the coinage in a column in *The Independent* on 17 January 1979).

* *'The Winter of Discontent put the finishing touches to the destruction of the Post-War Settlement. It made a fitting obituary to the Old Order.'* (P. Jenkins, *Mrs Thatcher's Revolution*, 1987)

wired *adj.* [1969]
high on drugs, especially, with its image of a taut wire, on some form of amphetamine or ➪'speed'.

* *'Wired is told with the same narrative style that Woodward employed so effectively in All The President's Men.'* (*Chicago Tribune*, 1984)

-wise *suffix.*
relevant to, referring to.

* *'The world . . . provided him with a crash course in the facts of life power-wise, woman-wise, money-wise.'* (T. Blacker, *Fixx*, 1989)
* *'Kate filled Ginger in on the whole scene . . . "It's all been good, experiencewise," she said.'* (C. McFadden, *The Serial*, 1976)

wishlist *n.* [1972]
a list of desired objects or occurrences.

* *'It had a presently confidential wishlist of programmes it would like to see abandoned.'* (*The Times*, 30 May 1972)

with-it *adj.* [1962]
fashionable, chic, trendy.

wobbly, throw a *v.* [1984]
to act in an unstable manner, to lose one's temper, to have a fit or nervous breakdown.

* *'Then again, she was unbalanced enough to . . . throw yet another wobbly.'* (T. Blacker, *Fixx*, 1989)

wogbox
see **ghetto blaster**.

woman- prefix. [1969]
combinations of the prefix woman- include a variety of terms created in the wake of the feminist movement; on the whole they simply replace 'man' in familiar phrases such as woman-hours, woman-year, womanfully (although this was actually coined as early as 1821 – with no apparent feminist overtones at that stage).
See also **herstory**; **-person**; **wimmin**.

Wombles *n.* [1968]
a tribe of imaginary animals, whose habitat is Wimbledon Common (hence the name which is an abbreviation for Wombledon) and whose main occupation is cleaning up the litter that less public-minded individuals persist in depositing there.

women's lib *n.* [1966]
a popular abbreviation for ➪*women's liberation.*

* *'Women's Lib would be literally following them around to commandeer the stage.'* (L. Bangs, *Psychotic Reactions and Carburetor Dung*, 1988)

women's libber *n.* [1969]
a popular abbreviation for a member of the women's liberation movement, and often itself abbreviated further to 'libber'. On the whole it is used by opponents of the movement, although with with somewhat less venom than the canard ➪**bra-burner**, which was particularly widespread in the early 1970s.

women's liberation (movement) *n.* [1966]
the liberation of women from traditional subservient roles; a synonym for the feminist upsurge of the late-1960s and 1970s and as such often cited as the Women's Liberation Movement.

* *'Women's Liberation take note in case you get pissed later when I use the word "chick".'* (A. Hoffman, *Woodstock Nation*, 1969)
* *'This was before the Women's Movement and she had been brought up to know that man was her all.'* (*Sunday Correspondent*, 3 June 1990)

women's movement *n.* [1969]
see **women's liberation.**

women's studies *n.* [1970]
academic courses that centre on the history of women, their role in society, the rise of feminism, and similar topics.

wonga *n.* [1980]
a slang term for money.

* *'We will not, understand, be talking big wonga here.'* (J. Meades, *Peter Knows What Dick Likes*, 1989)

woodentop *n.* [1981]
a slang term for a uniformed police constable.

Woodstock Nation *n.* [1969]
a synonym for the ⇨alternative society or ⇨counterculture, with strong overtones of militant unity; the term stems from the Woodstock Festival of 1970, a supposedly epochal three-day rock concert held in upstate New York, at which the whole ⇨hippie ethos of the era was seen, by such visonaries as Abbie Hoffman, as coming together. Woodstock Nation is the antithesis of ⇨Pig Nation.

* *'I emerged exhausted, broke and bleeding from the Woodstock Nation. It was an awesome experience but one that made me have a clearer picture of myself as a cultural revolutionary.'* (A. Hoffman, *Woodstock Nation*, 1970)

woofter *n.* [1977]
a homosexual, mimicking the better-known (and older) poof or poofter.

Woolmark *n.* [1964]
an international quality symbol for wool created by the International Wool Secretariat.

word *n.* [1964]
in computing: a fixed number of bits, varying as to the the overall capacity of the machine, but always representing the maximum number of bits that a machine can handle at any one time; the majority of current (1991) office ⇨microcomputers operate on a 32-bit word (using the 80386 chip).

word processing *n.* [1970]
the storage, editing, and retrieval (either to disk or to a printer) of written text by electronic means, as formatted by a ⇨dedicated word processing ⇨program. The program is the **word processor**, as are certain machines – typically those produced by Wang – which resemble computers but are in fact advanced electronic typewriters with a ⇨VDU and a restricted memory. – **word process,** *v.*

* *'Examples are games, payroll, word processing, anthing that does what you want your computer to do.'* (D. Jarrett, *The Good Computing Book for Beginners*, 1980)

word-wrap *v., n.* [1977]
in ⇨word processing, for a line of type to break automatically as it reaches the right-hand margin of the screen and for the text to start again on the next line. The term can be used as a noun, e.g. *word-wrap facility.*

workaholic *n., adj.* [1968]
on the pattern of alcoholic, an individual who is addicted to working.

* *'Baker is a classic workaholic who dislikes socialising and often tries to sneak out of state dinners.'* (*Sunday Correspondent,* 3 June 1990)

worker participation *n.* [1973]
the participation of the workforce (or its representatives) in management of the company or industry in which they work.

worker-director *n.* [1968]
a worker who is appointed as a director of his or her firm.

workerist *adj.* [1984]
relating to a view of society that is derived from the attitudes of the employed, rather than the employers.

workfare *n.* [1986]
a welfare system, originated in the US, whereby recipients of welfare payments are forced to perform some type of unpaid work to justify their handouts.

working dinner/lunch *n.* [1970, 1964]
any meal, which would normally be reserved for relaxation and socializing, that is devoted instead to business discussions. The adjective ⇨power is usually applied to a breakfast.

workrate *n.* [1969]
1. *in soccer: a synonym for* running hard and continuously; the antithesis of skill and seen by many as the abiding principle in British football – certainly it was that best loved by Sir Alf Ramsay, manager of the 1966 World Cup-winning team. To critics, who value skills over blind effort, work-rate is seen as the main drawback in the national game.
2. the rate of work.

* *'But somewhere along the line he missed the plot, and thus the book turns out to be a mish-mash . . . and Mr Green must take the blame, mainly for his workrate.'* (*Liverpool Daily Post,* 14 October 1990)

workstation *n.* [1977]
a powerful computer terminal, attached remotely to a mainframe computer, which offers high-quality graphics and extremely fast processing.

* *'IBM's acknowledgement that the word "work-station" means something like a very powerful personal computer.'* (*PC World,* April 1990)

world music *n.* [1988]
also known as **global music**: any music outside the Western mainstream, especially that of Africa.

* *'Rhythm of the Saints (11.40pm C4) is the story of Paul Simon's latest raid on global music.'* (*The Independent,* 20 October 1990)

WORM *n.* [1986]
in computing:
1. *an acronym for* Write Once Read Many Times: a form of mass storage, often in excess of 300 megabytes (*see* **byte**) of data, which can be 'read' by the computer but which cannot be augmented with new data; such WORMs

are ideal storage for large dictionaries, city directories, and other large reference works.

* *'The obvious way was to dedicate a Maximum Storage WORM . . . disk to RJP's files and put them all on that.'* (*Byte*, January 1990)

2. worm, *n.* [1986]
in computing: a form of ➪virus.

* *'A "worm" is a robust kind of distributed program that invades workstations on a network and consists of several processes or segments that keep in touch through the network.'* (*PC World*, July 1990)

worry beads *n.* [1964]
a string of beads, something like an amber rosary – that can be manipulated between the fingers to alleviate stress and tension. The beads have a long history in the Middle East and elsewhere, but the term only emerged in the Britain in the 1960s.

worst-case *adj.* [1964]
often as *worst-case scenario*: the worst feasible situation that occurs to those assessing a range of future possibilities.
See also **nightmare scenario.**

* *'Analysts believe that the Kremlin drew up a worst-case scenario.'* (*The Times*, 18 January 1980)

WP *abbrev.* [1970]
➪word processing.

wrap *n., v.* [1974]
the end of a day's shooting, often announced as 'It's a wrap!'.

wraparound (shades) *n.* [1966]
a style of dark glasses that have lenses that extend around the side of the head and thus 'wrap around' the face.

wrecked *adv., adj.* [1968]
a slang term for very drunk or very debilitated by drugs.
See also **twisted.**

wrecking amendment *n.* [1967]
any form of amendment designed to defeat the purpose of the parliamentary bill to which it has been attached.

wrinkly *n.* [1972]
one of a set of terms – including ➪crumblies (somewhat older) and ➪dusties (very old indeed) – describing the ageing and old, based presumably on skin-tone; a more general term is 'past (one's) ➪sell-by date'.

wristband *n.* [1969]
in sport: a strip of material worn around the wrist to prevent perspiration reaching the hand.

write-in *adj.* [1972]
usually used in combination with candidate and referring to a candidate whose name has not been included on the printed ballot-paper and who has thus to be written into the blank space provided by those voters who wish to offer their support. Other combinations include **write-in vote**: the votes registered by those who wrote in their favoured candidate and eschewed those offered by the main parties; and **write-in campaign** political campaign in which the voters are urged to back a candidate whose name is not on the ballot paper, and to write it in.

write-protect *v.* [1981]
to protect a disk from accidental erasure by making sure that it is impossible (usually by covering the notch on a floppy disk) to write over the material it holds.

WYSIWYG *abbrev.* [1982]
an acronym for What You See Is What You Get: the description of the product matches its capabilities; there are no hidden extras. When the term refers to ➪word processing ➪programs, it means that the copy as typed onto the screen will be the copy that appears on paper; such programs probably include on screen italics, underlining, boldface, etc.

✱ *'WYSIWYG editing shows what each page will look like before it's printed, a feature that's easy on paper. Not to mention your patience.'* (ad for Microsoft Word for Windows in *Byte,* April 1990)

yakuza *n.* [1964]
from the Japanese *ya*, (8), *ku* (9), and *za* (3): a Japanese gangster or racketeer; the term refers to 8-9-3, which is the worst possible hand in a popular gambling game and thus, by extension, means the worst (type of gangster).

yardie *n* [1986]
a member of a gang of organized Jamaican criminals who specialize in purveying drugs and violence on an international level; from 'yard', Jamaican for 'home'.

✱ *'A much publicised raid on a yardie stronghold had first been simulated at Riot City.'* (R. Chesshyre, *The Force*, 1989)

yarg *n.* [1988]
a form of cheese made in Cornwall and launched in 1988, named by reversing the surname of its creators Allan and Jennifer Gray.

yellow card *n.* [1976]
in soccer. a card shown by a soccer referee to a player who persistently infringes the rules. It signifies a caution. Two yellow cards shown in succession to the same player are the equivalent of the more severe ⇨red card, and he must leave the pitch.

yellow rain *n.* [1979]
a form of chemical pollution that has become mixed with the rain and has fallen over several areas of SE Asia, causing severe blistering on human skin, and sometimes death.

yesterday's men *n.* [1966]
in general, faded, waning politicians; originated much earlier, the term was widely popularized as a celebrated slogan used by the Labour Party on posters caricaturing Tory leaders during the election campaign of May 1970. It was subsequently the title of a BBC TV programme about Labour leaders, broadcast on 17 June 1971.

Yippie *n. adj.* [1968]
activist hippies – '⇨hippies who had been hit on the head by a policeman' – led by Abbie Hoffman and Jerry Rubin, who used anarchic theatrical politics – tossing money from the balcony of the New York Stock Exchange, putting up a pig as a candidate in the 1968 presidential election – to promote their attacks on US involvement in Vietnam.

✱ *'I also did a unique Yippie calendar, ten or so street theatre events, wasted time battling SDS, gave about seventy speech-performances.'* (A. Hoffman, *Woodstock Nation*, 1969)

yips *n.* [1963]
a slang term used by golfers to describe the nervous fumbling and twitching that ruin one's concentration and one's swing.

✱ *'If need be, he could run a school on how to succeed with the yips.'* (*The Independent*, 22 March 1990)

yobbish tendency *n.* [1984]
on the pattern of the ⇨Militant tendency, that section of the Labour left which is seen as using the tactics of drunken yobs to attack its rivals, and promote its own allegedly grass-roots ideology.

yomp *v.* [1982]
a Royal Marine term for the marching with weapons and a 120lb pack across appalling terrain in extremely hostile conditions on the premise that once this ultimate in route marches is concluded, the troops will be prepared to fight a battle at the other end; possibly from a Norwegian word used by skiers to describe the crossing of obstacles. The term gained widespread currency during the Falklands War of 1982.

* *'One hears of . . . night patrols under fire, of yomps and tabs, of days in ditches on subsistence rations.'* (J. Meades, *Peter Knows What Dick Likes*, 1989)

yonks *n.* [1968]
a slang term for a long time, often found as *for yonks.* The word originated among the upper-middle classes, but has gradually permeated through society.

yoof *adj., n.* [1989]
an all-purpose adjective to describe a variety of television programmes – high on pop gossip and fashion, low (in critical eyes) on intelligence – that are aimed at the young. Yoof, meaning 'youth', is a deliberate mimickry of the ⇨street-cred London accents of presenters of such programmes.

* *'And will the next contestant step right up for the early Friday evening yoof slot.'* (*Sunday Correspondent*, 19 August 1990)

YOP *abbrev.* [1978]
an acronym for Youth Opportunities Programme: one of a number of programmes devised by the Labour government in 1978 to help train unemployed young people, and, by convenient coincidence, to remove them from the unemployment statistics. It lasted until 1983.

young fogey *n.* [1985]
a young(ish) middle-class man of the 1980s who poses in dress, attitude, and mannerisms as his middle-aged predecessor of the 1950s. Evelyn Waugh at his crustiest is supposedly the supreme avatar, the author A.N. Wilson its most perfect embodiment.

* *'He might even write it himself and suggested that the hero might be a young fogey like himself.'* (N. Garland, *Not Many Dead*, 1990)

young meteor *n.* [1967]
from the title of Jonathan Aitken's overview of the mid-1960s, any of those self-made individuals – models, photographers, advertising men, property developers, clothes designers, rock stars – who were seen as forming the ⇨'new aristocracy' of the ⇨Swinging 1960s in London.

* *'All are thought to have made meteoric rises in their own worlds. Hence the title* The Young Meteors.' (J. Aitken, *The Young Meteors*, 1967)

youthquake *n.* [1967]
the youth revolution, especially as seen in the student revolt of the late 1960s.

* *'A unique feature of today's Youthquake – as Vogue once dubbed it – is its intense, spontaneous internationalism.'* (R. Neville, *Play Power*, 1970)

YTS *abbrev.* [1984]
an acronym for Youth Training Scheme: the successor to the ⇨YOP scheme, introduced in 1983 with a similar rationale by the Conservative government.

yuck *exclamation.* [1966]
unpleasant, distasteful; used either as an exclamation or as an adjective (1972), when it becomes **yucky**. The onomatopoeic term was orignated by young children, or their parents, but has spread into the adult world.

yummy *n.* [1969]
a nubile young girl, probably under the age of consent but nonetheless an object of male lust.

* *'Honeybunch Kaminski, 13, of LA. What a little yummy!'* (R. Crumb, *OZ*, 1971)

yuppie *n.* [1984]
the first and most durable of the sociological acronyms of the 1980s – Young Upwardly-Mobile Professionals. Originally found as 'yumpie', the 'm' was dropped almost at once. The 1880s preferred 'counter-jumper', but now a buzz-word (once favourable, now generally derogatory) for anyone under 40 who prospered in the decade.

Yuppie has spawned many similar terms, among them are: **guppie** (gay upwardly-mobile professionals), **buppie** (black upwardly-mobile professionals). One of the best known was **dink** (dual income, no kids), or ⇨dinky (dual income no kids yet). Perhaps the most amusing of these acronyms lacks the '-ie' suffix: **Lombard**: (loads of money but a right dickhead). In US use is **Yucca**: '*Miami Mensual*, Frank Soler's magazine for the so-called Yuccas – young and up and coming Cuban Americans.' (D. Rieff, *Going to Miami*, 1987)

* *'I dealt to all sorts: women, estate agents, yuppies, and buppies.'* (*Sunday Correspondent*, 8 April 1990)

yuppie flu *n.* [1986]
see **ME.**

zaire *n.* [1967]
the national currency of the Republic of Zaire – the former Democratic Republic of the Congo, which took its new name in 1971.

Zambia *n.* [1964]
the current name of the former country of Northern Rhodesia, renamed on gaining its independence in 1964.

* *'A narrow extension to the north-east, the Caprivi strip, gives [Namibia] a frontier with Zambia and a point of contact with Zimbabwe.'* (P. Brogan, *World Conflicts*, 1989)

ZANU *abbrev.* [1963]
an acronym for Zimbabwean African National Union: one of the rival guerrilla groups fighting to overthrow white minority rule in Southern Rhodesia (now Zimbabwe).
See also **ZAPU**.

* *'The Zimbabwean African National Union (ZANU) based on the Shona tribe in the north and east of the country.'* (P. Brogan, *World Conflicts*, 1989)

zap *v.* [1964]
to kill. The term came to prominence during the Vietnam War, both among the US troops and via a famous piece of journalism by Nicholas Tomalin headlined 'The general goes zapping Charlie Cong' (Sunday Times, 1966). It has since been adopted by British troops, and understood by many civilians.

* *'A gunman complete with Armalite rifle about to zap at a foot patrol.'* (A.F.N. Clarke, *Contact*, 1983)

Zapata moustache *n.* [1968]
a style of moustache, with ends drooping on either side of the mouth, popular in the late 1960s and early 1970s, that was modelled on that worn by the Mexican revolutionary Emilio Zapata (1879–1919).

ZAPU *abbrev.* [1961]
an acronym for Zimbabwean African People's Union: one of the rival guerrilla groups fighting to overthrow white minority rule in Southern Rhodesia (now Zimbabwe).

* *'The Zimbabwean African People's Union, based on the Matabele in the south-west and led by Joshua Nkomo.'* (P. Brogan, *World Conflicts*, 1989)

Z-car *n.* [1961]
a police patrol car; from the code-letter *Z* for Zulu which was allotted to a group of such cars; *Z Cars* was also the name of a highly successful and long-running BBC television series.

zero option *n.* [1981]
the zero option was originated as the *Null-Lösung* (zero solution) to the problem of nuclear weapons on both sides of the Iron Curtain by German Chancellor Helmut Schmidt in 1981. It was briefly espoused by President Reagan as a ⇨bargaining chip during the ⇨INF talks of 1981–83. It stated that if

the USSR would scrap their medium range SS-20 missiles, then the US would not deploy their ⇨cruise missiles. This idea, more a propaganda ploy than a real policy, did not survive the talks. A development was **double zero/zero-zero**: a nuclear weapons moratorium in which neither superpower would incease their nuclear arsenals: a short-lived concept that emerged during the INF talks and did not survive their demise.

* *'In Bonn, [Haig] was asked what the Soviet Union would have to do to make the zero option possible.'* (S. Talbott, *Deadly Gambits*, 1984)
* *'The Europeans were satisfied with the zero-zero proposal as it stood; they would deploy on schedule; there was no need to change. Nitze looked more and more glum.'* (S. Talbott, *Deadly Gambits*, 1984)

zero population growth *n.* [1967]
a situation in which population growth is static, such a situation is seen as the only realistic response to the world's increasing population crisis.

zero-rated *adj.* [1972]
referring to any commodity which is not eligible for ⇨VAT and is rated at 0%. **zero-rate** *v.*

zero-zero *n.* [1986]
see **zero option.**

Zimbabwe *n.* [1980]
the current name for for the former British colony of Southern Rhodesia, adopted when the country attained independence under black majority rule in 1980.

* *'South Africa encouraged a settlement, which was eventually reached in London in 1980, and Rhodesia became Zimbabwe.'* (P. Brogan, *World Conflicts*, 1989)

zimmer (frame) *n.* [1974]
the proprietary name for an orthopaedic metal walking frame designed for use by the aged and infirm.

zinger *n.* [1970]
a wisecrack, a punchline.

zit *n.* [1966]
an acne spot, a pimple; originally in the US, the term is now used by UK teenagers who have no trouble understanding an advertisement that tells them, 'Blitz those zits!'.

* *'Your little sister. Neatly dismissed as the cause of a teenage zit rash.'* (T. Blacker, *Fixx*, 1989)

zonked *adj.* [1967]
intoxicated, either with drugs or (less often) liquor.
See also **twisted; wasted.**

* *'She's zonked out of her nut, but it's all in wild manic Elizabethan couplets.'* (T. Wolfe, *The Electric Kool-Aid Acid Test*, 1969)

zydeco *n.* [1960]
a type of Afro-American dance music, found in Southern Louisiana; the name comes (possibly) from the Creole pronunciation of the French words *les haricots*, (beans), which is found in the dance-tune 'Les haricots ne sont pas sales'.